FORUM PAPERS
FIRST SERIES

FORUM PAPERS

FIRST SERIES

Edited for College use by

BENJAMIN A. HEYDRICK

Essay Index Reprint Series

BOOKS FOR LIBRARIES PRESS

FREEPORT, NEW YORK

First Published 1924
Reprinted 1970

STANDARD BOOK NUMBER:
8369-1465-1

LIBRARY OF CONGRESS CATALOG CARD NUMBER
72-86750

PRINTED IN THE UNITED STATES OF AMERICA

PREFACE

For a number of years the Forum Magazine has been the medium through which many of our leaders of thought have expressed their opinions on various phases of our civilization. Some of the most notable of these papers have been brought together in the present volume, which has been prepared for the use of college students. To place before them examples of clear thinking and effective expression, to show them that a command of English is a tool that will serve many purposes, to suggest topics through which their own powers of thought and expression may be strengthened,—such is the purpose of this book.

CONTENTS

PAGE

THE FIFTEEN FINEST NOVELS
By *William Lyon Phelps* 1

THE ETHICS OF ANCIENT AND MODERN ATH-
LETICS
By *Price Collier* 17

BOOKS THAT HAVE HELPED ME
By *Edward Eggleston* 34

ON PLEASING THE TASTE OF THE PUBLIC
By *Brander Matthews* 48

MY FOUR FAVORITE PARTS
By *Henry Irving* 64

YOUNG RADICALS IN AMERICA
By *George Santayana* 73

THE PARADOX OF OXFORD
By *Robert P. Tristam Coffin* 79

THE ESSAY AS MOOD AND FORM
By *Richard Burton* 87

THE DUTY OF EDUCATED MEN IN A DEMOCRACY
By *Edwin L. Godkin* 103

WHAT IS A NOVEL?
By *F. Marion Crawford* 125

CONTENTS

WHEREIN POPULAR EDUCATION HAS FAILED
  By Charles W. Eliot 140

IMMIGRATION AND DEGRADATION
  By Francis A. Walker 170

MORAL ASPECTS OF COLLEGE LIFE
  By Charles Kendall Adams 187

A DEFINITION OF THE FINE ARTS
  By Charles Eliot Norton 204

CAUSES OF BELIEF IN IMMORTALITY
  By Lester F. Ward 221

FORUM PAPERS

FIRST SERIES

THE FIFTEEN FINEST NOVELS

By William Lyon Phelps

THIS has been another year for the making of lists; we have been handed the ten books one would take to a desert island, the best ten books of the twentieth century, and a comparison of the books in English published from 1900 to 1923 with those that appeared in 1800 to 1823. I declined to enter the desert-island competition, for I do not see how anyone can decide what he will do until the emergency arrives, and this particular crisis seems as remote as the end of the world. However, if I should go to a desert island, the first volume I should take would be a blank book, in order to note new impressions.

One more list can do no harm. It may arouse some opposition; what is known in modern novels as a "cold fury." Nothing pleases me more than to bring readers and critics into a state of violent rage, and nothing is surer to attain that end than to publish a list of best books. The fact that the list-maker can never prove he is right and nobody can prove he is wrong, constitutes an irresistible temptation.

Whatever may be the relative value of the literary production of the early years of the nineteenth as compared with the twentieth century, there can hardly be much doubt that the golden age of the novel

1

came in the thirty years or so that followed 1850. In that period flourished Turgenev, Tolstoi, Dostoevski, Dickens, Thackeray, George Eliot, Meredith, Thomas Hardy, Hawthorne, Mark Twain, Dumas, Flaubert, Victor Hugo, Björnson, and others who would seem big in other epochs.

In the list that follows, England scores six times, France four, Russia three, America two. Every reader will wish to make additions and subtractions, and it is vain for me to attempt to "explain" my list, which speaks for itself. But certain omissions are glaring. Germany, which leads and will probably forever lead the world in music, and has made magnificent contributions to poetry and drama, has almost no place in the history of the novel, so far as the production of masterpieces is concerned Undoubtedly *Wilhelm Meister* has a wider influence than *The Scarlet Letter;* but in a discussion confined to novels, which is a strict art form, some attention must be paid to construction. Goethe, who had perhaps the most spacious mind since Aristotle, enriched the pages of *Wilhelm Meister* as he adorned every subject he touched except mathematics; but the book is a commentary on human nature rather than a novel. Still, I feel qualms in omitting it.

To leave out the name of Walter Scott is curious. If we could take the whole bulk of his work rather than one book, he would certainly be included among the fifteen novelists, and Swift would have to depart; but we are considering single works. Scott is like a mountain range rather than a peak. If I had included any of his books, it would be *The Bride of Lammermoor.* I hate to leave out one of my prime favorites,—Jane Austen's *Pride and Prejudice,* which to my notion is a flawless novel. But looking at the subject from a world standpoint, her masterpiece does not have the standing in foreign countries equal to that of any other book on my list. Perhaps it is too exclusively English. Thus no woman appears in my list.

I ought, of course, to add that my fifteen include only modern works, that is, books that can strictly be called novels, not considering works like Malory's *Morte d' Arthur* or Cervantes' *Don Quixote*. I present by list in chronological order.

1. *Robinson Crusoe* (1719) by DANIEL DEFOE.

This is the first English novel. It is curious that the novel in England began with a masterpiece, but such is the fact. Defoe was fifty-eight years old when he wrote his first story, and indeed most masterpieces of prose fiction have been written in years of maturity. Music and poetry come early; by the mysterious processes of genius, composers and poets are enabled to express in perfect form the profoundest truths of life at a time when they have had hardly any experience of it; but it is not so with the novelists. In the whole range of English fiction, Dickens is the only one who produced masterpieces before he was thirty. In *Robinson Crusoe*, Defoe added to the scant population of immortal personages by creating a character who is more real than fact, and who is known to men, women, and children throughout the world. The verisimilitude of his style is so perfect that the practical curiosity of children is abundantly satisfied.

Defoe's personality is as mysterious as Shakespeare's. Nobody knows what he really thought. No one can tell whether his elaborate moralizings were sincere, or whether he wrote them with his tongue in his cheek.

2. *Gulliver's Travels* (1726) by JONATHAN SWIFT.

Defoe was a germinal writer, and his "grave, imperturbable lying" was adopted by an even greater genius, Swift, whose prose style has never been excelled. Swift was also fifty-eight when he wrote this work, which exhibits the full maturity of his powers as yet untouched by decay. Although he intended it as a satire "on that animal called man," and so completely succeeded that it is probably the most terrible satire ever written, he brought to its composition such art, such imagination, such humor, that for two hundred years it has delighted the object of its scorn.

By a curious irony of fate, it has been a standard book for children. Could Swift, who wrote it with vitriolic passion, have imagined that for all time it would be the particular joy of boys and girls? Like *Robinson Crusoe*, it answers all their definite questions, for the drawings in the first two books are exactly according to scale. In the third book he made an amazing prophecy of the two satellites of Mars, which were not discovered till 1878.

3. *Clarissa* (1747-8) by SAMUEL RICHARDSON.

Alfred de Musset called this *le premier roman du monde*. Like the two preceding books, it was written when its author was fifty-eight, which seems to have been a lucky age for our first novelists. It is one of the longest of English works of fiction, filling eight volumes; but those who have the patience to read it, as I have, will find that it steadily grows in interest, and that its length is essential to its plan. When it was first published, readers were kept in suspense as to the outcome; the women read it sobbing, the men cursing, and all implored Richardson to spare the life of his heroine. He was deaf to their entreaties; heard only the voice of his artistic conscience. To-day probably every one who reads it knows its tragic conclusion; that knowledge does not detract from its intensity. It rather adds to it, for we see the horrible fate approaching, as sure as it is slow. Barrett Wendell once told me that he endeavored to reread *Clarissa*, but could not, for he constantly burst out crying. No novel was ever written with more sincerity or more dignity, and anyone who doubts Richardson's genius has never read the book through. Its influence in foreign countries has been prodigious, and it practically loses nothing in translation.

4. *The History of Tom Jones* (1749) by HENRY FIELDING.

Many believe this to be the greatest of English novels; personally I prefer *David Copperfield*. Fielding is as modern in his temperament as if he were living today, and Tom Jones is the natural man of all time. Fielding's greatness was as immediately recognized as was that of his enemy, and indeed there is not a single man on our list who did not enjoy fame in his lifetime. It is an error to suppose that works of genius are not speedily recognized and appreciated. It is easy to slight contemporary criticism, and point out cases of overvaluation; but as a rule contemporary opinion rates works of genius at their full value, and for the same reasons that are clear to posterity.

Fielding, to whom Richardson's morality in *Pamela*

was abhorrent, began to write a burlesque in *Joseph Andrews;* but the book got away from him and stands on its own merits. Still one ought to be additionally grateful to Richardson for stirring up such hostility, as he gave Fielding a good start. Although the supreme excellence of *Tom Jones* was immediately apparent, the true character of Fielding was not fully understood till the twentieth century, when his biography appeared, written by Wilbur Cross. This admirable work may be regarded as the final judgment on its hero.

5. *Eugénie Grandet* (1833) by HONORE DE BALZAC. This is universally acknowledged to be one of the best by its author, and it is my favorite. I like it better than *Père Goriot,* which was written the year following, because it is free from the exaggeration which mars that powerful book. The absolute simplicity of the style, the smooth course of the narrative, the absence of author's interference, the noble objectivity of the thing, combine to give it that serenity which characterizes so many immortal works of art. The contrast between Eugénie and her father, together with the similarity, make a lasting impression. He is more terrible than an army with banners, more terrifying than the hobgoblins of romance, and as real as life. His dry expression, *"Nous verrons cela,"* is like a death sentence from the bench. Balzac, unlike most English novelists, stands completely outside the circle· of his story, and simply reports what happens.

6. *Les Trois Mousquetaires* (1844), and its sequels: *Vingt Ans Après* (1845), *Le Vicomte de Bragelonne* (1848-1850) by ·ALEXANDRE DUMAS.

I never enjoyed any novel more than this. D'Artagnan and the three musketeers ought to be among the intimate friends of every man, woman, and child in the world who knows how to read. This is the ideal romance, where something happens on every page, where the personages abound in vitality, where the conversations sparkle with vivacity and wit. It is for the latter reason that every one who can should read these volumes in the original. Like everybody else, I read them first in my native tongue, which does not prevent one from enjoying the story and appreciating the people in it; but it was when I read them in French that I saw what I had lost. The conversations have that piquancy which French alone can give. Let me advise those who wish to reread these books in the original to get them in the cheap and attractive Nelson series, nine small volumes printed in clear type and attractively bound. For those who cannot read French, I recommend the new edition in one volume by Appleton, which contains the original pictures. The best appreciation of this romance and the best appraisal of the character of D'Artagnan may be found in Stevenson's essays in *Memories and Portraits,* called *A Gossip on a Novel of Dumas's.* Stevenson shows that while this story amuses, it also inspires.

7. *David Copperfield* (1849-1850) by CHARLES DICKENS.

To my mind Dickens is the greatest English novelist because he made the largest contribution and because he is irreplaceable. Should the works of any other disappear, we could find a substitute, which, while not perhaps "just as good," might serve. But who could take the place of Dickens? He produced an astonishing number of masterworks, and never had a barren period. From *Pickwick Papers*, written in the twenties, to *Edwin Drood*, which he left unfinished, his genius had free and full expression. We have outgrown him in only one respect. Sentimental pathos, which was fashionable in the fifties, was his weak point. Little Paul and Little Nell are overworked.

But his spontaneous humor, his power of characterization, his skill in construction, his glowing style are sufficiently in evidence in everything he wrote. It is absurd to call him a caricaturist, for he has created more living characters than any other novelist, and they live because they are human. On the whole, I put *Copperfield* first among his books, because it has more of him. The best essay on Dickens is to be found in George Santayana's *Soliloquies in England* (1922).

8. *The Scarlet Letter* (1850) by NATHANIEL HAWTHORNE.

If one were lecturing to a class of pupils who had never read a novel, and wished to make it clear to them what particular kind of art is represented by the word, the best illustration that could be found would conceivably be *The Scarlet Letter*. It is impeccable. The evolution of the story is as perfect as a flower; the characters are set before the reader in full completeness; the style is as near perfection as seems possible; the intensity of the tragedy is felt by all readers, young and old. No one can read a dozen pages without coming under the spell, and no one can outgrow the book.

9. *Henry Esmond* (1852) by WILLIAM MAKEPEACE
THACKERAY.

I have never shared the feeling, avowed by so
many, who first read Dickens, and then Thackeray,
that the latter drives the former out of existence. I
wonder if this is as common an experience as apparently it used to be. "My wife," said Carlyle, "says
that Thackeray beats Dickens out of the world."
Professor Beers said that as a young man, when he
began to read Thackeray, the new man drove Dickens
out of his head as one nail drives out another. If I
could have only one of the two, I would choose Dickens; but I am thankful to have both, nor do I see any
reason for placing them in comparison.

Just as I like Dickens' historical romance, *A Tale
of Two Cities,* the least of all his works, so I prefer
Esmond even to *Vanity Fair* and *Pendennis,* and like
it infinitely better than *The Newcomes,* which I do
not like at all. Thackeray produced *Esmond* in one
volume without any serial publication; it is the most
unified of his works, written with the most zest, and
filled with the most impressive scenes. It is a brilliant performance. George Saintsbury said there
were five heroines of nineteenth century fiction he
would have been happy to marry: Elizabeth Ben-
net, of *Pride and Prejudice;* Di Vernon, of *Rob Roy;*
Beatrix Esmond; Argemone Lavington, of *Yeast;*
Barbara Grant, of *David Balfour.* I think Beatrix
would have interfered considerably with his profes-
sorial duties.

10. *Madame Bovary* (1857) by GUSTAVE FLAU-
BERT.

Robert Browning read this when it appeared, and

it was his "favorite novel." It remained so, though he never recovered from his disappointment in reading *Salammbô*, which has all the marks of pseudo-masterpieces, like near-beer. In view of the books now written in America for Americans and by Americans, it seems strange that *Madame Bovary* was suppressed in France. The trial was a *cause celèbre*, if ever there was one. Henry James said it would make an admirable book for American Sunday-schools, and while Mr. James knew more about French fiction than he knows about Sunday-schools, he did justice to the truth, honesty, and sincerity of this story. Here is a book containing not a single character worthy of admiration, not one whom we should like to have as an acquaintance; the environment would make Main Street seem exciting; but the story is unforgettable because we know it is true.

One winter day in Rouen, I thought I would buy a copy as a souvenir of the scenes it describes. I visited the bookshops, and there was not a copy to be found; finally, on returning to the largest, I told the proprietor he must have one somewhere, and he said, No, there was no demand for it; but that he had amongst his treasures a copy of the first edition, which of course I would not care for, as the price was so high. (And yet he must have known I was an American). I asked to see it,—it was genuine. In an awe-struck whisper, he informed me the price was twelve francs. I still have it.

11. *Fathers and Children* (1861) by IVAN S. TURGENEV.

Of all novelists, Turgenev is the foremost artist, for he never wrote a faulty book. George Moore says he is the greatest artist since antiquity, and he ought to know. The outline of his stories is as perfect as Greek sculpture. Through the translations, one can almost hear the style of the original,—almost but not quite. In his prose fictions, Turgenev somehow had the qualities belonging to music and painting. No novelist ever succeeded more admirably in combining truth and beauty.

In this book, which everyone ought to reread just now, when so much is being said about the younger generation, Turgenev brought fathers and children together in a manner that, while intensely contemporary, is also ageless, for the same thing happens in every country and at every period. Here he coined the word "nihilist." The best proof of the honesty and faithfulness of the book is the fact that both old and young attacked it. Bazarof is an immortal figure; but I like best of all the portrait of his parents. The picture of the old couple visiting the tomb is a revelation of the author's heart, and I suppose there never was a more beautiful personality than Turgenev.

12. *Les Misérables* (1862) by VICTOR HUGO.

Although among the French, Hugo ranks highest as a lyric poet, it is by this novel that he conquered the world. Jean Valjean is a character that will live as long as literature; and everybody knows Javert, Fantine, Cosette, Marius, Gavroche, old Gillenormand, Thénardier, and his terrific wife. It seems strange enough that these people had no existence until Victor Hugo put them on paper.

Very few novels have so many "supreme moments." Hugo had vitality enough for ten men, and when he wrote this book he had what the Methodists used to call "liberty." Let me urge those who have not read *Les Misérables* since their youth to read it again. You will recover all the early enthusiasm, plus much.

13. *Anna Karenina* (1873-1876) by LEO N. TOL-STOI.

I know that there are many who prefer *War and Peace,* but I don't. If I had to name the greatest novel ever written, I would name *Anna Karenina.* It is interesting to remember that Tolstoi would have destroyed both this and *War and Peace,* if he could. He professed to be ashamed that he had ever written them, and preferred his later writings on religion, morals, and politics. What an enormous difference there is between the artist Tolstoi and the moralist! As artist he is always right. No passion is too colossal, no caprice too trivial, to be beyond his reach. To read *Anna Karenina* is simply to live, and live abundantly.

But in other spheres Tolstoi became quite plainly mad. His spiritual teaching in his short parables is indeed beautiful, and has had a universal influence; but his practical propositions, such as abolishing law-courts, police, and private property are insane. I have intense sympathy for his wife. He was to be left free to write, and she was to take care of the house-work, the children, and the expenses with no receipts. Read her recently published diary, and judge for yourself.

In *Anna Karenina,* Tolstoi lifted fiction to a higher plane. One is overwhelmed by the truthfulness of the characters, conversations, and scenes. All the younger writers of Russia,—Chekhov, Gorki, Andreev, Artsybashev, Kuprin,—have been his disciples in art, and have done their best to follow his manner. It

is curious that one who was so wholly Russian as
Tolstoi should by his novels have made the whole
world kin.

14. *The Brothers Karamazov* (1879-1880) by
FEDOR M. DOSTOEVSKI.

If Dickens is a horizontal novelist, covering an
enormous surface of men and manners, Dostoevski is
vertical. He plunges into depths below the lowest
yet explored; he rises to heights where no other could
live. He holds the altitude record. Although *Crime
and Punishment* is the most popular, there is no doubt
in my mind that the greatest of his works is *The
Brothers Karamazov*, first completely translated into
English by Constance Garnett, who has given us such
admirable versions of Turgenev, Tolstoi, Gogol, and
Chekhov.

His speciality is the abnormal. He is like a com-
poser who would require a new piano, with all the
bass lower and all the treble higher than that shown
on a Steinway. His work abounds in grotesque de-
fects, in excrescences, in doldrums; there is no steady
illumination as in Turgenev; he reveals truth by
flashes of lightning. The family history of the
Karamazovs will teach us much about the Russians,
much about humanity, and a great deal about ourselves that hitherto we had not even suspected.

15. *Huckleberry Finn* (1884) by MARK TWAIN.

It may be too soon to place this work among the
fifteen, but its steadily growing fame has all the signs
of permanence. Here is America, its authentic voice.
This is an epic of the Mississippi River, and no one
who has ever read *Huck* will see the Mississippi or

read its name without thinking of the raft. Tom Sawyer, Huck Finn, and Jim are representative specimens, true in everything except small-boy coarseness in conversation, which cannot possibly be printed, but which everybody knows. It is full of drama,—tragedy and mirth. The feud, the drunken Boggs and the mob scene. the dead-beats at the funeral,—no one but Mark Twain could have produced such things.

He is unique in American literature as Dickens is in English, and the world has made up its mind that it cannot possibly get along without him.

NOTES AND QUESTIONS

William Lyon Phelps (1865—) professor of English Literature at Yale University, is widely known as a lecturer and author.   He was graduated at Yale in 1887, and later did graduate work at Harvard and at Yale, receiving the degree of Ph. D. from Yale in 1891.   He has taught English at Yale since 1892, and since 1901 has held the Lampson chair of English there.   He has also lectured widely on literary subjects, and writes for *Scribner's Magazine* each month an article on books, under the heading ''As I Like It.''   His wide reading, his personal acquaintance with writers, his keen interest in current literature, and his enthusiasm for his subject are qualities which make his lectures and writings deservedly popular.   He has edited the works of many English authors, including Gray's poems, the novels of Richardson and of Jane Austen, Marlowe's plays and Stevenson's essays.   In addition he has published a series of volumes of literary and dramatic criticism, including *Essays on Modern Novelists*, *Essays on Russian Novelists*, *The Advance of the English Novel*, *The Advance of English Poetry*, *The Twentieth Century Theatre*, *Essays on Modern Dramatists* (2 volumes).

What one ought to get from this article is a wider view of the field of fiction. Most of us have read novels because they happened to be in the house, or because the titles attracted us on the library shelves. In other words, our choice has been rather hap-hazard. In this article a professor of literature at a leading university, a man who has read practically all the worth-while fiction in every language, gives his judgment as to the best of it. The first thing to do is to check off his list and see how many you have read. Then the question comes, which of those not read are you most attracted to by Professor Phelps' account? Which do you think he considers the greatest of all? The most artistic of all? Read one, and write your own impressions of it.

Page 1, paragraph "Whatever may be." What does Professor Phelps call "The golden age of the novel?"

Page 2, paragraph "To leave out." Why does he not include Scott? Do you agree with his choice of the best of Scott's novels? Jane Austen is omitted. What other woman novelist might one expect to find in his list?

Page 3, paragraph "This is the." Discuss the statement that Robinson Crusoe is "a character more real than fact."

Page 4, paragraph "By a curious." *Gulliver's Travels* is made up of four parts, or voyages: few people have read more than the first two. In the third voyage he tells a method of learning mathematics without study.

Page 6, paragraph "This is universal." What is meant by the statement that Balzac stands completely outside the circle of his story and simply reports what happens? Show how this differs from the method of an English novel you have read.

Theme Subjects

Is there a novel which you think should be included in this list? If so, write a brief account, telling why it deserves a place. Title: The Sixteenth Novel.

My impressions of one of the books on Professor Phelps' list.

Should a novelist introduce his own comment into a story?

It would be an interesting thing to make up a list of "The Fifteen Finest Short Stories." If each member of the class would bring in his own list, by comparing these and selecting those most frequently mentioned, a list could be made, that would express the judgment of the class. Then if each student chose a story from this composite list and wrote a short appreciation of it, the resulting article might be published in the college magazine.

The subject, The Ten Finest Plays or The Ten Finest Poems might be handled in the same way.

THE ETHICS OF ANCIENT AND MODERN ATHLETICS

By Price Collier

IN discussing athletic matters it is often forgotten how very recent is the widespread interest in amateur sport. The modern system of athletic sports was practically introduced at the beginning of the last century—about 1812—by the Military College at Sandhurst. It was nearly fifty years later, however, before the English public schools and universities found a place for athletic sports among themselves, and made them, as they now are, both in England and America, almost a part of the curriculum. Advisory committees of graduates, paid "coaches," and the participation by the faculties of colleges and universities in the regulation of athletic sports are all innovations of the last few years.

It is not so much cause for surprise, then, that rules and regulations are still imperfect, and that the ethics of athletic sports are still under discussion—discussion frequently of an irritating kind. Trained athletes became a professional class in Greece as long ago as 350 B.C., and for centuries their rules, their methods, and their manners were practically the only criteria by which such contests might be judged.

There are certain circumstances which may well comfort those who are often disheartened at the apparently slow progress made in ousting both the fact

17

and the spirit of professionalism from our modern athletic sports. At any rate we have arrived at a point where professional methods are frowned upon by all who are sincerely interested in amateur athletics; at a point, too, where unmanly behavior, either in defeat or in victory, is generally considered cause for shame and repentance. It may be doubted, indeed, whether physical contests between young men have ever been conducted on so high a plane as now, or whether sport has ever before been made to minister so directly to the moral and mental, as well as the physical, development of our "young barbarians all at play." The *laudator temporis acti*, however, is as much at home in athletics as in morals and manners. All Harvard men have heard the Greek athlete lauded at the expense of his modern prototype, and the vulgarity of modern athletic contests dwelt upon at length; and doubtless in other classic shades are men of profound learning who deplore our degeneracy as athletes. All this rather superficial commentary on comparative athletics has its effect in inducing many people to believe that we have made little or no progress in our endeavors to make sport contribute, and that notably, to the education of our youth.

No doubt Greek sculpture has had more to do with the sentiment about the superiority of the ancient athlete over the modern than any real knowledge of the subject. The few relics we possess of the Periclean age of Greek art have been used as typical of the physical development of that time. As a matter of fact, they were probably no more typical than Mr. French's Minute-Man is typical of the sculpture of an age which rejoices in such amorphous artistic callosities as are to be found in New York, and even in Boston.

But whether or not the physical development of the ancients was more symmetrical, their ethical standards in such matters we should now consider beneath contempt. Every school-boy in these days is taught, not only by his masters, but by the overwhelming influence of his school-fellows, that he may succeed by fair means only, and that he must not lose heart when he fails. Or, as it has been said by one of our greatest literary athletes: "It is not our business in this life to succeed, but to continue our failures in good spirits." Golden words these are, in days of commercial and social scrambling, when the Ten Commandments are mere rungs on the ladder of financial and social success. At any rate, in our school and college athletics no such cynicism exists, and commercial methods are strictly debarred. But whether this was true of the athletics of two thousand years ago one may well doubt.

We are fortunate in having, for purposes of comparison, a detailed account of certain athletic games from the pen of one of the most distinguished poets of the golden age of Rome. He was writing for his countrymen, and of his countrymen. The epic which contains this account was written primarily to glorify Rome and the Julian house to which the great Augustus belonged. The poet himself was a young man. He died when only fifty-one years old, and his sympathies were, therefore, the sympathies of a comparatively young man. He was writing to please, not to malign; for, as we should phrase it nowadays, he was in receipt of many favors from the Admin-

istration. He was extolling the ancestors of those
who were to buy and read his poem. It is to be supposed, then, that he would dwell only upon the pleasing traits, the daring deeds, the distinguished and
glorious aspects, of the life of that time; that he
would write of the ancestors of Augustus, of the
houses of Memmius, Sergius, Cluentius, and others,
only in the most complimentary terms.

It is important to call attention to this point, and
to emphasize it, because in the games to be described
later the participants conducted themselves, at least
according to modern ethical athletic standards, in a
way that should have made their descendants blush
to own the relationship. Though the description is
not a description of games that actually took place,
it is none the less a fair account; for if the poet erred
in over-elaboration or in exaggeration, he may be
counted upon to have made his heroes not worse, but
better, than they were. We find that tales of the war
of 1860-64, or of the war of 1898, lose nothing of
their complimentary and glorious character in the
telling as the years go by. So our Latin poet, in his
epic, may be trusted to tell of what he thought most
welcome to the vanity and patriotism of those for
whom he was writing. He believed, and his contemporaries believed, that to play games as he writes
of them was the best way to play them. If this, then,
is the kind of sport that Virgil's contemporaries ap-
plauded as a picture, and a flattering one, of the
past, there is no reason why we should not consider
the ethical standards held up by him for approbation
as fairly representative of those of the Augustan Age.

First, there is a boat-race. Four boats enter: the
Pristis, commanded by Mnestheus; the Chimæra, com-

manded by Gyas; the Centaur, commanded by Sergestus; and the Sylla, commanded by Cloanthus. On a rock at some distance from the shore a branch of oak is placed, and this is to be the turning-point for the contestants. The distance out and back is not given, though the rock is said to be "apart in the sea and over against the foaming beach," and where "the swollen waves beat" upon it. The boats start at a signal given by a trumpet. Gyas in the Chimæra gets away first, with Cloanthus in the Scylla a close second; while the Centaur and the Pristis are having it nip and tuck behind them. All goes well until they near the rock which marks the turning-point. Gyas, who still holds a short lead, calls out to his pilot Menoetes not to steer so wide of the rock, but to make a closer turn. The pilot fears, for some reason, that there may be a hidden reef, and as he steers wide to avoid any such danger, Cloanthus, in the Scylla, steers to the left under the stern of the Chimæra, shaves the rock in safety, and turns for home in the lead. As to Gyas, "then indeed grief burned fierce through his strong frame, and tears sprang out on his cheeks." He entirely forgets himself, seizes the old pilot, and flings him bodily into the sea. This feat of infantile fury is apparently looked upon by the other oarsmen as a huge joke; for "the Teucrians laughed out as he fell and as he swam, and laugh to see him spitting the salt water from his chest." The old man is left to take care of himself as best he may, and Gyas takes the steerman's place himself; but he is so incompetent that he is caught and passed by Mnestheus in the Pristis, and only succeeds in finishing in the third place because Sergestus lands his boat, the Centaur, on the rocks, by steering too close to the

turning-point. At the end everybody gets a prize,
even Sergestus, who arrives in his badly battered
boat amid the jeers of this sportsmanlike crowd.

With the literary value of this piece of writing we
are not now dealing; but it is not amiss to refer
parenthetically to the two illustrations wherein the
boat of Mnestheus is compared to a dove scared from
its nest, and the Centaur to a snake bruised by a passing wheel. For our purpose it is enough to call attention to the shouting, the scolding, and the weeping
of the contestants; to the cowardice of Gyas; and to
the equanimity with which Æneas and the crowd of
spectators look upon these childish ebullitions of
temper, as being part of the game. Cloanthus, when
he sees that Mnestheus has left Sergestus fast upon
the rocks, and has even overhauled and passed Gyas,
gets upon the poop of his vessel and delivers an ora-
tion addressed to the gods of the waters, in which he
promises to sacrifice a white bull to them if he comes
in first. The whole picture is of youths of little
self-control and of explosive temper, who have had
no schooling in the laws that should govern contests
between friendly amateurs, who are bent upon winning by fair means or foul, and who at the very
thought of losing give way to hysterical despair.

In the next contest, a foot-race, the judicious
chronicler grieves indeed to find all notions of fair
play thrown to the winds. Those who enter for this
race are: Nisus, Salius, Euryalus, Helymus, Diores,
Patron, Panopes, and others. Nisus gets away first
with a good lead upon upon his opponents, Salius
being second, Euryalus third, and Helymus and
Diores close together behind. Everything goes well,
with the men running in this order, until near the

finishing line, where the ground is slippery with the
blood of some bullocks lately killed upon the spot.
Nisus, still in the lead, slips and falls, but recovers
himself sufficiently to roll over in front of Salius and
bring him also to the ground. This he does, so says
the poet naïvely, because Euryalus, the third man, is
a dear friend of his, and by thus bringing Salius to
grief he enables his friend to come in first. Thus,
instead of Nisus first, Salius second, and Euryalus
third, the race finishes with Euryalus first, Helymus
second, and Diores third; Helymus and Diores getting second and third place respectively, through the
outrageous trickery of Nisus.

There follows a rare row. Salius "fills with loud
clamor the whole concourse of the vast theatre, demanding restoration of his defrauded prize." Euryalus, who only came in first by the grace of this
monstrous blackguardism of Nisus, begins to weep
at the thought of losing the first prize. Diores, who
had been left well behind, and who gets his third
place only through the trickery to Salius, backs up
the tears of Euryalus, and his claim for first place,
in order that his own claim to third place may not be
questioned.

Was ever such a group of athletic mountebanks
written of as men and heroes before? We have made
progress since then in these matters, in all our sports,
whether professional or amateur, except, perhaps, in
professional baseball. But none of the spectators,
not even pious Æneas, seems in the least surprised
by the result of this race. It was no new thing to
them apparently. That must have been the spirit
in which these contests were generally conducted.
Æneas declines to interfere in the matter, and gives

first, second, and third prize to whimpering Euryalus, to Helymus, and to grasping Diores, respectively. To Salius, however, as solace for his misfortune,
he gives the hide of an African lion whose paws are
inlaid with gold.

Then follows a piece of impudence probably un-
paralleled in the history of athletics. Nisus, whose
dishonorable action was the cause of all the trouble,
appears and asks, if so much be given to the vanquished and to the fallen, "what fit recompense will
you give to Nisus?" Various gifts adapted to the
manners and methods of Nisus at once suggest themselves to the modern athlete. Tar, feathers, and a
rail to ride on; the toe of a quickly lifted and well-
directed boot—all or any of these seem appropriate.
But, no; that ineffable prig Æneas laughs and gives
him as compensation for his villany a handsome shield,
calling him at the same time an "excellent youth"!
In some of our military annals there have been traces
of boasting, of jealousy, of bitterness, and of downright self-glorification. But outside of the police-
court records nothing, for lack of chivalry, for contemptible meanness, for impudent self-assertion,
equals this story of the foot-race at the anniversary
of the funeral of Anchises.

Imagine a race with two Harvard men, a Yale man,
and a man each from Columbia and Princeton entered.
The Harvard man, leading, falls; twists himself over;
grabs the Yale man, who is running second, by the
legs; upsets him, and thus enables his Harvard mate,
who is running third, to come in first. Then imagine
all these young gentlemen grouped in front of the
grand-stand. The Harvard man who came in first
is blubbering away, with his fists in his eyes, lest he

be deprived of first prize; the Yale man, who was
bowled over, is shouting his grievance; the Columbia
man, who by the series of accidents gained third place,
is insisting upon his right to profit by the trickery;
and one and all of them, including the Harvard man
who had been the cause of all the trouble, demanding
to be given something. The modern imagination
stumbles at the bare outline of such a predicament.
Our whole standard of conduct, all our notions of fair
play, all our ideas of decency have changed; and we
can no more believe such manners possible to-day than
we can bring ourselves to believe in Neptune and
Hercules.

But all this is poetry, says some one. These games
were not intended to be taken seriously, either by the
poet or by his readers. That phase of the subject was
dealt with at the beginning of this article. The
games were not real, but the spirit of them was.
There are athletic contests described by Shakespere,
by Scott, by Kipling, by Stevenson, and it would be
quite fair to judge, from the imaginative writings
of these authors, of the manners and of the ethics of
the age described. The clothes, the weapons, the surroundings, the writer makes appropriate; but the
spirit and the customs of those he holds up to us as
heroes are the spirit and the customs that he, the
author, regards as the most manly and the most digni-
fied.

Virgil's epic stands in much the same relation to
the men of the Augustan Age as do Shakespere's historical plays to the men of the Elizabethan Age.
Both men were writing imaginative history, and Virgil was as little tempted to hold up his actors to
ridicule and scorn as was Shakespere. Here and there

are despicable characters, to be sure; but it is understood that they are despicable, and Shakespere never
for a moment allows his readers to suspect him of
sympathizing with them. The same is true of Kipling
and of Stevenson. But these figures on the stage at
the games presided over by Æneas are held up to us to
admire, and the great poet is only mirroring the ethics
of his time when he pictures them as heroes. He no
more suspects Gyas and Nisus of being young cads,
even though he himself created them, than do they
themselves, or Æneas and his companions. Virgil
lived in an atmosphere where such conduct was not
unusual on such occasions; in an atmosphere, in short,
where in amateur athletics the trickster, the boaster,
and the baby all had their place, and all might expect to receive a prize.

The next contest is a boxing-match, and here we
seem to hear echoes more familiar to modern ears.
Dares, a famous boxer, who in his day had sparred
with Paris and had beaten Butes, strides into the
ring. He brandishes his arms, shakes his shoulders,
makes passes in the air, and generally behaves as does
the modern circus girl before some particularly hazardous feat. As no one appears, this modest gladi-
ator, imagining that he has things all his own way,
blows his own horn as follows: "Goddess-born, if no
man dare trust himself to battle, to what conclusion
shall I stand? How long is it seemly to keep me?"
Thus, in varying phrases, have many of our modern
prize-fighters halloed in the columns of the yellow
journals. But Dares had scarce finished his modest
speech, and the applause of the crowd had hardly died
away, when Entellus, urged by Acestes, throws into
the ring his huge gauntlets—of oxhide, weighted with

lead and iron—and follows them himself. Then more discussion. How familiar is all this! Dares does not like the gloves. They are too big, and too hard. He declines to fight in them. After some pardonable boasting by Entellus, it is finally agreed to fight in gloves provided by Æneas, and the two boxers take their places and begin.

Young Dares is quicker, but Entellus is the more powerful. The fight favors first one and then the other, until Entellus, in attempting a mighty slog with his right, misses Dares and falls to the ground. Acestes rushes in to help him. Entellus, on his feet again, and furious at this mishap, renews the fight with redoubled energy. He chases Dares all over the ring, confusing him with the number and rapidity of his punches. Dares is practically beaten, when Æneas steps in and stops the fight. Dares is carried off on a litter by his friends, "spitting from his mouth clotted blood mingled with teeth." Entellus then tells the crowd how strong he used to be in his younger days, and shows them from what misfortune Dares had been rescued, by drawing off, and felling the bull, his prize, to the ground with a single blow between the horns. It "rolls over, and quivering and lifeless lies along the ground." As a last taunt to his vanquished enemy, Entellus says, as the bull lies dead at his feet: "This life, Eryx, I give to thee, a better payment than Dares' death." Of course this rhetorical kicking a fellow when he is down marks out Entellus, though old enough to know better, as of much the same type as Gyas, Nisus, Dares, and the rest.

The sparring match seems less absurd to us only because we are somewhat accustomed to our own bullies of the prize-ring of to-day. The combination of pantomimist, peacock, and bully, who poses and talks fifty weeks for every fifteen minutes he fights, is so familar to us, that Dares and Entellus do not so greatly shock us with their boasting, their antics, and their lack of magnanimity. We should be dumfounded, however, if at the games in the gymnasium at Harvard, Yale, Groton, or St. Mark's our young athletes, with the gloves on, should indulge themselves in such posturing, or in such vituperation, as passed unnoticed among the companions in arms of the pious Æneas. Fancy a freshman who thinks well of his powers at sparring, dancing on to the floor of the Harvard gymnasium, brandishing his arms about, making feints at an imaginary opponent, side-stepping, and ducking, to show off his agility before his opponent comes in. It is no exaggeration to say that if such a spectacle were possible nine-tenths of the spectators would believe the boy to be half-witted, or, if not that, to be laboring under some momentary lapse of reason due to over-excitement.

Two centuries of athletics show at least that much change for the better. It would be as impossible today for a young gentleman to behave as did Dares as it was easy, and apparently quite proper, then. Though there are streaks of rowdyism, of trickery, and of unfair play in our college and school games even now, such things have no signification as they are unpopular and unrepresentative. The college mates of a man who should go blubbering to the judge to give him a prize would wrap him hastily in blankets, carry him off to the dressing-rooms, and excuse him on the ground that he was a bit "off his head." Should the stroke oar of a freshman crew jump on the coxswain of the boat and pitch him overboard for faulty steering, the young man, unless proved to be insane, would never sit in a boat again, and would probably be expelled from college. Self-control, good temper, and "continuing our failures in good spirits" are now recognized as being as much a part of the game as feathering the oar, or as running with the mouth shut, or as knowing how to counter. The ethical side of all these exercises dominates all kinds of athletics, and he who breaks the laws of the spirit of sport is as much a felon in spirit as at law is he who breaks into his neighbor's house.

Of the other games celebrated on this same day little need be said, for there is little that serves the purpose of this discussion. A mast is set up, a pigeon is tied to the end of it, and four archers, among them our old friends Mnestheus and Acestes, shoot for the prizes. The first strikes the mast with his arrow; the second cuts the string that holds the bird; the third brings down the bird as it flies; the fourth, Acestes, has nothing left to shoot at. But the poet, ever ready to make the best of his heroes, tells us that Acestes let fly his arrow into the air, where, to the amazement of the whole company, it was seen to catch fire, and to sail like a meteor out of sight among the clouds. There, again, the poet has no mind to discredit the honor of these games. If to us there is in these descriptions much that is silly and treacherous, it is not because the poet has tried to give such an impression. On the contrary, wherever by his art—and a very lofty art it is—he can add solemnity or dignity to the proceedings, he has done so. When he describes what to our notions of manliness are the tricks of the "tough," he does it all unconscious that such manners and such methods are in any way con-

temptible. These were the athletic ideals of his time;
these were the ethical laws by which the athletes of
the century before the Christian era governed their
games.

It would be interesting to trace the development of
manliness in these matters. Whoever has read his
Benvenuto Cellini and dipped into the literature of
the Italian Renascence, and remembers Scott's "Fair
Maid of Perth," "Tom Brown's Schooldays," "Tom
Brown at Oxford," "Verdant Green," Aldrich's
"Story of a Bad Boy," Robert Grant's delightful description of a boat-race, and the various encounters
in Stevenson's stories must see readily enough how
we have made progress, slowly, perhaps, but steadily.
Nowadays we prevent foul play against wild animals
by our game laws, and against our beasts of burden by
the societies for the prevention of cruelty to animals.

It is hardly to be doubted that the lads who have
the good fortune to spend six years at our game-
playing schools, like Exeter, Groton, St. Paul's, St.
Mark's, and then four years more at college, must
enter life with a sense of justice and a repugnance
to foul play that will leave a mark upon our whole
civilization. The game-playing Englishman has been
successful in managing the Hindoos in India, the
negroes in South Africa, the Egyptians in Egypt, and
the aborigines in Australia and New Zealand. Certainly the Englishman is not of the imaginative temperament that sympathizes readily with those who
differ from him socially and religiously. Rather is
he to be described as the school-boy described the
head-master of his school to his father—"a beast, but
a just beast!" This world-wide notion among the
weaker peoples of the earth, that one will get fair play

at the Englishman's hands, has made England the successful colonizer that she is.

We should demand and expect no less from our own "young barbarians." We have our colonies to govern; we have the poison of the fierce lust of money, for which a wholesome antidote should be provided; we have the rude jostling of the self-advertising social strugglers to beware of, we have in our midst the disease of political corruption, for which a remedy is sorely needed; we have a powerful press to tame; we have the fads in religion and in morals, always rampant in secluded communities of active ability and little culture, to meet and vanquish; and, though we are taking matters rather gayly in these days of our youth and prosperity, it needs no prophet to foresee that our Hercules will need some hard training to accomplish all his labors successfully.

In every bit of work, from sawing wood to polishing a poem, it is encouraging to look back and see how much has been done—how many sticks are actually sawn, how many verses are satisfactory in sense and sound. So we may turn back to this literature of our school days, and see that we have gone a long way toward the goal of manliness in our sports and pastimes. Though there is always much to do in turning out a first-rate man, in this particular phase of his development much has already been done. Not only may those who are professionally interested and those who are participants in playing games feel encouraged, but every man who loves his country wisely will welcome any proof that men are more manly than they were. The ideal is a long way off, to be sure, but a little honest praise can do no harm. The critics are always with us! It is something gained

that thousands of our boys are being taught to play
with all their might, to play fair, and to win if they
can. A lad who has had ten years of such training
can scarcely fail to retain something of that same
spirit when he comes to take part in the real contests of life. Living in the richest and the most unkempt country in the world, where standards are
mostly tentative, and where the levelling of a democracy offers huge bribes to wealth, to notoriety, and
to popularity, the man who holds that it is not everything to succeed, but that whatever happens he must
continue his failures in good spirits, is well worth
producing, even at the price, in time and money, of
teaching him how to play his games.

NOTES AND QUESTIONS

Price Collier (1860-1913) was an American clergyman,
editor and author. His early education was received in Swit-
zerland and in Germany; later he came to America and entered
the Divinity School of Harvard University, graduating in
1882.   He spent nine years as a minister in the Unitarian
church; then entered literary work.   He was European editor
of *The Forum* for a time, and later editor of *Outing*. During
the Spanish American War he was an officer in the United
States Navy.   A keen observer, familiar with foreign affairs,
and a student of social problems, he wrote several books dealing with the characteristics of various nations: one of these,
Germany and the Germans, was widely read during the World
War. His other books include: *A Parish of Two; England
and the English; The West in the East, America and the
Americans.*

Page 17, Sandhurst. The Royal Military College at Sandhurst, England is an institution somewhat like our West Point.
Cadets are trained here for officers in the cavalry and infantry
regiments of the British army.

Page 17, paragraph "It is not." What reason is given
for the criticisms directed against college athletics?

Page 18, *laudator temporis acti*, (Lat.) one who praises
the doings of the past.

Page 19, "The poet himself." Virgil is the writer referred to, and the poem is the *Æneid*.

Page 20, paragraph "First there is." What is there in
this event which we would consider unsportsmanlike?

Page 22, paragraph "In the next." What bad sportsmanship here?

Page 25, paragraph "But all this." What is the author's
reply to the objection that these contests were not real?

Page 26, paragraph "The next contest." In what one of
our modern sports does Mr. Collier imply we have made least
advance over the ancients? Does your own observation bear
this out? Can you suggest a reason why standards here are
different?

Page 30, paragraph "It is hardly." What theory does the
author advance here?

Page 31, paragraph "In every bit." Select what seems
to you the most important sentence in this paragraph.

THEME SUBJECTS

Professionalism in College Athletics.

Standards of sport in boxing compared to those in other
sports.

Sportsmanship as seen at a recent athletic meet.

Athletic contests in literature. (Read one of the books
mentioned on page 30, paragraph "It would be.")

BOOKS THAT HAVE HELPED ME

By Edward Eggleston

BOOKS that have helped me may not help you. Specific direction in reading will hardly be found in such a series of articles as the present, unless incidently. He who wishes specific advice may rather be commended to those who find amusement in the intellectual pharisaism of choosing a "best hundred books" for other folks to study. The helpfulness of a book is largely relative. Not only is it quite possible that the books which have helped one may not be of assistance to another, but it is certain that books helpful at one period of life are quite useless at another. It follows, therefore, that in order to give an account of the helpful books one has encountered, it is necessary to relate the circumstances in which they were of use, and the mental states which made their aid of importance. This makes a certain amount of autobiography inevitable, and I am embarrassed at the outset by a sense that autobiography is presumptuous in any but an old man or a great one.

To what humble friends are we indebted at the outset? I will not insist on "Webster's Elementary," with its fables, and its frontispiece of a boy gazing upon a shabby little "Temple of Fame" far above him, at the summit of a hill, drawn with so little perspective that it seemed a sheer precipice. But there lay tossing about the house, when I was a little lad, a copy of Lindley Murray's "Introduction to the

34

English Reader'' and the latter half of a copy of ''The English Reader'' itself. These were relics of the school-days of my mother, who once pointed out to me in one of them a poem that she had committed to memory under distressing circumstances. Sent to the dunce block for some childish mischief, she had suffered such mortification that she had not ventured to raise her eyes or even to turn a leaf. The piece before her was the address to two swallows who had entered a church in service time, beginning, ''What seek ye here, ye winged worshipers?'' This my mother knew by heart when school was ''let out'' for the day, and for her spontaneous diligence in committing it she was highly commended at home, where the occasion for her poetic studies was unknown. These two books made not even the slightest concessions to the immaturity of a child's mind; they were merely a collection of pieces from English authors of established fame, classified with scientific rigidity into ''Narrative Pieces,'' ''Didactic Pieces,'' and heaven knows what beside. But in turning those musty pages I first made the acquaintance of literature. That is a great day in which one learns to distinguish and like works of genius. In this day of the deluge, many and many a boy is described by his friends as a ''great reader,'' who never in his life has perceived any difference between a real work of literary art and mere rubbish. I think it was in Lindley Murray's collections that I first read ''The Hermit'' of Beattie and the ''Elegy'' of Gray, two favorites of my childhood.

In this world of ours, where a great part of most lives is spent in grinning and bearing it, the first letter in the alphabet of life is fortitude. I remember with gratitude a little book called ''Robert Dawson; or, the Brave Spirit.'' It was published as a Sunday-school book, I believe, but it had much more gristle to it than the ordinary Sunday-school book of that or our time. In many a season of difficulty afterward, when ever-recurring sickness seemed destined to defeat all my boyish ambitions, I have been heartened by remembering Robert Dawson facing a rain-storm with the words, ''Only a few drops at a time.'' It was the first story that I ever read which had a New England background. The minister's wife from New England, who lent me ''Robert Dawson,'' kept a little collection of books to lend about the village with missionary intent, and I, for one, was her debtor. But I do not think she did me any good by putting Dr. Todd's ''Hints to Young Men'' into my hands. Dr. Todd was a good deal of a prig; the advocate and exemplification of much that is least admirable in the New England spirit. In his eyes life was meant for hum-drum; the value of a day consisted solely in its devotional exercises and the visible amount of work achieved. He did not recognize the use of enjoyment for its own sake, and its bearing on the education of the spirit; and he confirmed me in the two worst habits I ever fell into, those of early rising and overwork.

It was the evil of the religious prejudices in which I was bred that all novels, except those with a ticketed moral, were put into the index. I read nearly all of Miss Edgeworth's tales, but I do not remember one beneficial lesson derived from her commonplace minor moralities. To this day, however, I cannot cut the string in unwrapping a parcel without compunction, so strong was the impression made by her ''Waste not, Want not.'' I have saved a few feet of twine,

and wasted time much more valuable in picking out
knots. Nothing is more to be dreaded than a moralist or an economist destitute of the sense of proportion. But to the gentle Jacob Abbott I owe a considerable debt. The "Rollo" books early taught me
to observe nature thoughtfully, to try experiments
for myself, and to reason on questions of duty.
Rollo's maxim, that "responsibility devolves," still
recurs to me as a safe guide in certain circumstances.
In carrying out the provisions of my father's will,
my mother exchanged my father's law library for
books likely to prove of advantage to her children.
Her selection was mostly of serious works of history,
quite beyond a boy's taste. The only juvenile books
in the lot were Abbott's "red-backed histories," as
we called them. These were my introduction to historical study. I think they might be excelled by
books prepared in these later times, but as yet I
know of none of their kind that are better.

It was my lot at fifteen to resume my studies, much
belated by ill-health, under the instruction of Mrs.
Julia L. Dumont, a writer of some distinction in the
days when the country west of the Alleghanies had
a provincial literature all its own. She was a woman of exceptional acquirements in that time, and
I got more from her, perhaps, than from any other
teacher. Something led her to believe that I would
be a writer and she took especial pains with my school
compositions. I once presented a rambling essay on
"The Human Mind," based chiefly on Combe's
"Phrenology," which had fallen by chance into my
hands. Nor was Combe wholly useless to me; from
him I got the notion of the compositeness of what
seem to be single traits in character, and this recogni-

tion of what may be called "the resolution of force" in the formation of character has been of the greatest service in the writing of fiction. But my composition on "The Human Mind," which got its psychology from Combe, and its adornments from certain swinging passages quoted from Pope's "Essay on Man," was bad enough, and Mrs. Dumont made short and severe work with it, in a conference with me after school. Better than that, she took from her own shelves a volume of the "Encyclopedia Britannica," which contained Priestley's exposition of the Hartleian system of mental philosophy. This widened my horizon at once, and to this day certain facts of mental action which Priestley there insists on stand out in relief in my conceptions of mind. Mrs. Dumont followed up her prescription of Priestley by lending me Locke "On the Conduct of the Human Understanding," which I sat up late to read, but which did not leave upon my mind any such impression as Priestley's paper. Yet, however I might accept the Hartleian notion of the importance of association of ideas, I was not prepared to receive it when pushed into the region of æsthetics. I soon after this read Jeffrey's review of Alison's "Nature and Principles of Taste;" perhaps, also, Alison's original. This traced all beauty to association of ideas, and I, grown quite a philosopher, fell out with the theory and sought an opportunity to discuss the question with somebody; but I could not find anybody in the whole village who cared a button about the origin of our perceptions of beauty, so that my intellectual ferment cooled down after a while, with no other result than that of bringing on again my old physical prostration, and driving me from school.

It was during the next summer that I made almost
my first acquaintance with Washington Irving. Before this I knew him only by certain little pieces in
the school readers. I was, at sixteen, sent to Virginia to spend a year among my father's relatives,
and while there I was put into a boarding-school
known as the "Amelia Academy." It was for over
forty years conducted by one man, Mr. W. H. Harrison, a lovable master and a genuine scholar, whose
familarity with the classic tongues was so great that
he often unconsciously said his prayers in Greek. In
the parlor of Mr. Harrison's dwelling was a small
library behind glass doors. I had longed for access to
this, but in my eagerness to make up lost time I had
taken up studies enough to engross thirteen hours of
every day. The principal was suddenly called away
one day, and we had an unexpected rest. The boys
fell to their favorite pastimes of "town ball" and
high jumping with poles. It would have been wise
for me to join them, but I went to the house and
begged for the key to the library. Alas! it had gone to
Richmond in Mr. Harrison's pocket. I had no recourse
but to go into the parlor and read the tantalizing titles
through the glass. One pane of glass high up was
broken; I climbed to this, and thrusting my hand
through, managed to draw out the "Sketch Book."
It was a lovely spring day, and the fertilizing impression made upon my susceptible mind by this first
dash into Irving was most wholesome. The head-
less horseman, Rip Van Winkle, Little Britain, and
all the rest are yet associated in my memory with the
brightness of a Virginia sky and the resinous smell
of old field pines. All my old impulses to a literary
life were awakened by the reading of Irving. I hard-

ly dare look into the "Sketch Book" nowadays, for fear of disturbing that first impression.

The value of a book like the "Sketch Book," breathing an atmosphere of artistic playfulness, was very great to a nature like mine, pushed both by hereditary traits and religious influences to take life over-scrupulously. Under very different circumstances I became acquainted with another more original, if less imaginative, writer than Irving, who exerted a similar influence on me. After my return from Virginia to Indiana my physical ailments, aggravated by over-application to study, threatened to foreclose upon me once for all. I was, therefore, at eighteen, sent to Minnesota, the great sanitary resort of that time. Fortunately, I had a relish for rough life; my persistent illness and the consequent disappointment in my education had made me desperate. Refusing money from home, I undertook some gentle farm-work; then I took a humble place as chain-carrier in a surveying party, and at length hired myself out to drive three yoke of oxen in a breaking plow. My diseases got sick of such treatment, and I was soon eating and sleeping as robustly as my oxen. What I felt most keenly was the intellectual starvation I suffered in the strenuous pioneer life of Minnesota in 1856. About this time there came along a man who conducted the book business on a plan I have never heard of since. He carried the priced catalogue of Derby & Jackson, and took orders for any book on the list. I bought in this way a copy of Charles Lamb's Works. It was my only book in a land where books were not, and it was no end of advantage to me. I was, just at this period of my life, deeply interested in settling the six days of creation; for in that time, when Darwin and evolution were yet below the horizon, our chief bother was to get the stratified rocks correctly created according to Moses. I had read Hugh Miller with eagerness, and had even followed the wiredrawn speculations in Hitchcock's "Religion of Geology." To a youth who has assumed such cosmical tasks Lamb could not but be wholesome. His delicious and whimsical humor is a great prophylactic against priggery. I cleave still to my stout one-volume copy of Lamb. There are many better editions, but none so good for me as this, with its margins covered by pencil notes, humiliating enough now, for they reveal the crudities, prejudices, immaturities of the young man who wrote them.

I have got little good out of long poems. What I read of the "Æneid" in school made no sort of impression on my imagination, except in a single description. When I was driven by invalidism to carry on my studies alone, I gave up the "Æneid" and read the "Eclogues" with genuine pleasure. I count them among the vitalizing influences of my education. In an old Virginia house I read the "Paradise Lost" with great attention when I was sixteen, and I plumed myself, boy like, on my discrimination in selecting the great passages. But I am not aware that the great epic exercised any permanent influence upon my education. Half a dozen years later I passed a night at the house of the chief inhabitant of a little hamlet on the Minnesota bank of the St. Croix River. Finding myself unable to sleep, I rose at four o'clock and made my way to the parlor. Upon the center table was Brydges's edition of Milton, and, opening that, I fell upon "L'Allegro" for the first time. I read it in the freshness of the early morning, and in

the freshness of early manhood, sitting at a window
embowered in honeysuckles dropping with dew, and
overlooking the deep trap-rock dalles through which
the dark, pine-stained waters of the St. Croix run
swiftly. Just abreast of the little village the river
opened for a space, and there were islands; and a
raft, manned by two or three red-shirted men, was
emerging from the gorge into the open water. Alter-
nately reading "L'Allegro" and looking off at the
poetic landscape, I was lifted out of the sordid world
into the region of imagination and creation. When,
two or three hours later, I galloped along the road,
here and there overlooking the dalles and the river,
the glory of a nature above penetrated my being, and
Milton's song of joy reverberated still in my thoughts.
I count such an experience as that of high value.

But there is an influence other than that on character and intellectual development, and this I suppose
every author of experience can recognize. Sometimes the genesis of a work can be traced to the reading of a book of a very different sort. The starting-
point of novel-writing with me was the accidental
production of a little newspaper story, dashed off in
ten weeks, amid pressing editorial duties, and with no
thought of making a book. The "Hoosier Schoolmaster," faulty and unfinished as it is, first won
public attention for me, and now, after sixteen years,
the exasperating public still buys thousands of copies
of it annually, preferring it to the most careful work
I can do. I am often asked in regard to the immediate impetus to the writing of this story, and the
answer seems paradoxical enough. I had just finished
reading Taine's "Art in the Netherlands." Apply-
ing his maxim, that an artist ought to paint what he

has seen, I tried my hand on the dialect and other traits of the more illiterate people of Southern Indiana.

The long and painful struggle for emancipation from theological dogma can hardly be treated in such a paper as this without liability to misunderstanding. Strange as it may seem, the starting-point of the change with me was the reading of the works of Dr. Thomas Chalmers, whose writings were great favorites with me in the early years of my life as a minister. Some of his books I read on horseback, riding from one preaching place to another. I recall particularly the "Astronomical Discourses," the Bridgewater treatise, and certain portions of the "Institutes of Theology." Dr. Chalmers believed himself to be a sound Calvinist, but there were certain things, rather in his method than in his conclusions, that changed my way of thinking on these things. Dr. Bascom, in a preceding paper, mentions his obligation to Bushnell and Robertson, who were also influential with me. I ought to add also George Macdonald's novel of "Robert Falconer" to this list, as well as Stanley's "Jewish Church," and the writings of the broad churchmen generally. Stanley himself, by implication, compares such men to Samuel the Prophet, in that they serve their generation by reconciling the past with the inevitable future. They release the mind from a sentimental bondage to dead dogmas by substituting a higher kind of sentiment. But with me the movement could not arrest itself at this point. There came a time, later in life than crises usually come, when my intellectual conscience insisted that sentiment of every sort ought to be put aside in the search for truth. Doubtless there were numberless

influences back of this break-up of opinion and intellectual habits.   Such a revolution is the ultimate
result of all the forces of one's nature and education.
But I remember three words of Sainte-Beuve—to
whose writings I owe a hundred debts—three words
that stung me like a goad when this change was approaching.   It is in one of the "Nouveaux Lundis"
that he describes the mental state of Lammenais, I
think, by saying that there were certain doctrines
which that ex-priest had *mis en reserve*.   These words
recurred to me over and over as a rebuke to my lack
of intellectual courage.   I also had put many things
in reserve; if I discussed them at all it was always
under shelter of certain sentiments.   Were sentiments
proper media for the discovery of truth?   I will not
dwell on the painfulness of the decision to which I
was forced.   There are few driven to this dilemma,
I believe; it is for that few that I write.   From the
time that I resolved that nothing should be any more
"put in reserve" by me, but that all my opinions,
even the most sacred and venerable, should go into
the crucible, I date what I deem a truer and freer intellectual life than I had known before.   Such a life
has its serious risks of many sorts, its pains, its depri-
vations, its partial isolation.   It is not to be chosen
by him who is not willing to pay at a dear rate for
the disentanglement of his intellectual powers.   What
conclusions the detached mind reaches on grave questions is a matter of secondary import.   Such conclusions may well be inconstant quantities, for the sphere
of the universe is large and that of a human brain
very small.   But the resolute refusal to have reserves
under shelter is the important and wholesome fact in

the history of a man who has a vocation for the intellectual life.

I was moved by the allusion of my good friend Mr. Hale to his growing love for Thomas à Kempis. There is a little copy of à Kempis that I used to carry on journeys with the purpose of quickening my spirit, and perhaps, also, with a notion, only half confessed, of keeping my Latin from entirely disappearing. I am sure it did me good. But reading à Kempis is like saying one's prayers in a crypt. There are people who are the better, no doubt, for resorting to an underground chapel. Nowadays such things are a little out of date, and it is hard for a real nineteenth-century man to go down stairs to pray. My little Thomas à Kempis has long been pushed to a top shelf near the ceiling, and it seems more trouble than it is worth to mount the step-ladder. Besides, Mr. Hale himself, in an excellent little story, taught me and many others that the true way is to "look upward and not downward, outward and not inward, forward and not backward." À Kempis may rest where he is; I would rather walk in wide fields with Charles Darwin; and, above all, I would rather, if it were possible, get one peep into the epoch-making book of the next century, whatever it may be, than to go back to the best of the crypt-worshipers. Perhaps it is but a reaction from the subjective training of my youth, but the objective life seems the better. I doubt whether one can be greatly benefited by a too constant dia-monologue with his own soul, such as à Kempis is given to.

NOTES AND QUESTIONS

Edward Eggleston (1837-1902), a well-known novelist of the nineteenth century, is an example of a man who achieved success in literature with very little school training.   He was born at Vevay, Indiana.   His early education, scattered as it was, is told by himself in the article here given.   At an early age he became a circuit rider, the name given to ministers of the Methodist church who rode horseback from one small settlement to another, preaching to scattered congregations of the frontier.   Later he went to Chicago as editor of *The Sunday School Teacher*, and in 1870 removed to New York to become editor of *The Independent*, a well-known weekly journal.   He held other editorial positions, and served as pastor of a church in Brooklyn.   In later years he retired to his country place at Joshua's Rock, Lake George, New York, to devote himself to literary work.   His first novel, *The Hoosier Schoolmaster* (1871) was one of the most popular books of its time.   As a picture of life in the frontier settlements of Indiana it is still unrivalled.   His experiences as a circuit rider had given him an intimate knowledge of pioneer life, with its crudities, its humor, its resourcefulness, its elemental virtues: all are told in picturesque and lively fashion in this book.   He wrote other novels, including *The Hoosier School Boy* and *The Circuit Rider*, but none equalled his first book.   He was much interested in early American history, and published a series of books for young people dealing with the lives of American Indians, including *Tecumseh, Pocahontas and Powhatan, Brant and Red Jacket*.   His latest works were two careful historical studies dealing with the early colonial period of our history, *The Beginnings of a Nation*, and *The Transit of Civilization*.

Page 37, paragraph "It was my."
How did Eggleston learn to write?   It is interesting to learn how authors developed their powers.   Benjamin Franklin tells in his *Autobiography* that he learned to write by imitating, or rather rewriting articles in Addison's Spectator. R. L. Stevenson, in the essay "A College Magazine," in *Memories and Portraits*, tells how he learned to write.

Page 39, paragraph "It was during."
Under what circumstances did Eggleston first read Irving's *Sketch Book?*

Page 41, paragraph "I have got."
Under what circumstances did he read Milton's *L'Allegro?*

What conclusion do you draw from this circumstance? What is Eggleston's opinion about long poems? Do you agree? Edgar Allan Poe held that there is no such thing as a long poem: what appears to be such is really a succession of short poems.

Page 42, paragraph "But there is."
What led to the writing of *The Hoosier Schoolmaster?*

Page 43, paragraph "The long and."
What influence did Sainte Beuve, a noted French critic, have upon Eggleston?

THEME SUBJECTS

How authors learned to write.
Eggleston's struggle for intellectual freedom.
My own list of "books that have helped me."

ON PLEASING THE TASTE OF THE PUBLIC*

By Brander Matthews

TWO lines of the prologue for the opening of
Drury Lane Theatre which Dr. Johnson wrote
to be spoken by his former pupil, David Garrick, still
linger on our lips as a familiar quotation:—

"The drama's laws the drama's patrons give,
And we that live to please must please to live."

This pair of rhymes is characterized by the robust
common sense which at once limits Johnson's criticism
and gives it its chief value. Common sense kept the
man who could thus compact a simple truth into a
striking couplet from giving to his assertion an extension not warranted by his own long continued observation of the methods and the motives of men of
letters. An absence of this caution has led later
writers to ascribe the broad success of this or that
author to the skill with which this or that author has
gauged the popular taste at the moment of publication, artfully preparing his literary wares to meet a
widespread demand which he has shrewdly foreseen.

This is a most unsatisfactory and a most un-
scientific attempt to explain away what seems often
inexplicable,—the interest sometimes shown by the

*From *Aspects of Fiction*, copyright 1902 by Brander
Matthews; published by Charles Scribners Sons. By permission of the publishers.

book-buying public in the writings of an author whose
works are not esteemed by his fellow-craftsmen. As
it is hard to prove a negative I will not maintain that
no author has ever been clear-sighted enough to guess
at the probable duration of the next swing of the
pendulum; but I am certain that the lucky hits of
this sort must be very far between, and that any
author who should rely mainly on his ability to guess
at the kind of book the public was going to thirst
after six months or a year later, would be very likely
to go hungry himself.

And I venture to believe also that there is a fallacy
concealed in the phrase which speaks of "the taste
of the public," for it assumes that there is a public,—
one public, having a taste in common with all its members. I am inclined to think that, so far from there
being only one public, the number of publics having
widely divergent likes and dislikes is indefinite, not
to say infinite. These smaller publics are no two of
them of the same size; and no doubt the membership
of some of them is too limited for an author to hope
to make his living by pleasing it. There are in fact
as many different publics as there are separate
authors; and there must be, since no two writers ever
made precisely the same appeal to their readers. No
two leaders in literature ever had exactly the same
set of followers. The admirers of Byron when he
burst forth first had been many of them the admirers
of Scott; but the two circles had not the same radius;
and they were intersecting and not concentric.

The broad reading public to which a popular author
is supposed to address himself, is really rent in twain
by the differences of its disputes over literary principles. Just as a man must take either the Hebraic

view of life or the Hellenic, to use the distinction that
Matthew Arnold borrowed from Heine, just as he
must be either an Aristotelian or a Platonist, whether
he knows it or not, so he is also (perhaps from inquiry and conviction but more probably from native
temperament) either an Ancient or a Modern, either
a Classicist or a Romanticist, either an Idealist or a
Realist. The standards are opposed and the conflict
is irrepressible. Whoever enlists under one of these
banners is ready with the torch to torture those who
volunteer to uphold the other. The very acrimony
of these discussions is all the evidence anyone can
demand before being assured that the public is not
one, single, and indivisible.

The public is really but a congeries of warring
factions; and sometimes these factions are representative of the degree of development to which those who
compose it have attained. Each, as it rises a step
higher in the scale of civilization, naturally despises
that which remains below on the plane it has just
abandoned, and it is in turn detested by that over
which it boasts its new superiority. Probably a similar state of affairs is visible wherever there is progress; those who are going to the front looking back
with contempt on those who linger in the rear,—a
contempt which is repaid with frank and justifiable
hatred. Perhaps as apt an illustration of this as any
now available may be found in the present state of
affairs existing among the vast body of men and
women who are fond of the game of whist.

In Dr. Pole's calm and scientific discussion of the
"Evolution of Whist, a Study of the Progressive
Changes which the Game has passed through from its
Origin to the Present Time," we are told that the

development of whist has had four periods. In the first of these the player relied chiefly on his master-cards and his trumps, following suit with any one of his low cards; and this Dr. Pole calls the Primitive Game. In the second stage the game was raised into a really intellectual pastime by Hoyle and his followers, and long whist gave way before short whist. The Game of Hoyle was the basis of the development taking place during the third period, during which there was evolved the Philosophical Game, indissolubly connected with the names of Clay and "Cavendish." The fourth period is that of the Latter-day Improvements, in which the American Leads have been adopted with other concomitant devices of like delicacy and subtlety.

As it happens there is a department of literature in which the development is singularly similar to the evolution of whist, and in which we can also declare four chronological periods, the one following the other and flowing from it. This is the art of Fiction. In the beginning Fiction dealt with the Impossible,—with wonders, with mysteries, with the supernatural; and these are the staple of the "Arabian Nights," of Greek romances like the "Golden Ass," and of the tales of chivalry like "Amadis of Gaul." In the second stage the merely Improbable was substituted for the frankly Impossible; and the hero went through adventures in kind such as might befall anybody, but in quantity far more than are likely to happen to any single man, unless his name were *Gil Blas* or *Quentin Durward, Natty Bumppo,* or *d'Artagnan.* Then, in the course of years, the Improbable was superseded by the Probable; and it is by their adroit presentation of the Probable that Balzac and

Thackeray hold their high places in the history of
the art. But the craft of the novelist did not come
to its climax with the masterpieces of Balzac and of
Thackeray; its development continued perforce; and
there arose story-tellers who preferred to deal rather
with the Inevitable than with the Probable only; of
this fourth stage of the evolution of fiction perhaps
the most salient examples are the "Scarlet Letter"
of Hawthorne and the "Romola" of George Eliot,
the "Smoke" of Turgeneff and the "Anna Karénina"
of Tolstoi.

"We have noticed four steps or stages marking the
progress, and producing four varieties of game, all
really Whist, but Whist in different stages of development," says Dr. Pole, and his words can be applied
absolutely to the four varieties of Fiction also. "The
later forms have, indeed, grown out of the earlier
ones, but have not necessarily extinguished or abolished them,"—and this is true of fiction too. "The
admirers of any late step are perfectly justified in
showing its superiority to the one before it, but there
is room enough in the world for both to continue to
exist side by side"; and it is from this lofty attitude
of broad toleration thus recommended by Dr. Pole,
that the late Professor Boyesen departed when he
commented on the amazing predilection Mr. Andrew
Lang had declared for the more primitive forms of
Fiction. The novel-readers who prefer tales of the
Impossible or of the Improbable resemble the whist-
players who prefer the Primitive Game, which, so
Dr. Pole informs us, is still—

"—played by enormous numbers of domestic players, who find
incidents enough in it to amuse them for hours together. And
though many of them would doubtless be able to learn and

to enjoy a more intellectual form, there is no reason why
it should be thrust upon them, or why they should be calumni-
ated for adhering to their innocent form of entertainment.
It is probable that they follow fairly the general mode of play
in the infancy of the game.''

We all see that it was in the infancy of Fiction that
it dealt with the Impossible and in its boyhood that it
began to attempt the Improbable. Although the
liking for the Impossible still survives among children
and it is likely to survive among them always, I am
inclined to think that it is almost dead among men
and women who have attained their majority. The
bulk of the novel-readers of this last decade of the
nineteenth century are either in the second stage of
development or in the third; they have been wearied
by the exploiting of the Impossible, but they are not
yet ready to enjoy the discussion of the Inevitable;
and they do not care much whether the incidents of
the stories they lounge through negligently are doubt-
fully improbable or actually probable. But there is
a certain portion of the public which takes its fiction
seriously, which respects the art of narrative, which
sees the possibilities now open before the novelist, and
which holds the story-teller up to the highest standard.
This portion of the public—welcoming warmly the
fiction which gives the most truthful interpretation of
life—is steadily gaining in numbers and in influence.

I fear that its swifter increase is not a little re-
tarded by its own intolerance toward the novel-
readers who yet delight in the Primitive Game. This
attitude is easy to understand but none the less is it
unfortunate. ''We may take it for granted that,
whatever may be the exclusive notions of the select
Whist aristocracy, there will always be a large dem-

ocratic body who will please themselves as to what
sort of game they will play,'' says Dr. Pole very
pertinently. ''The amiable lady who begins by
playing out her aces, or the pleasant club-member who
leads his lowest card from five, ought not be to up-
braided for bad play. All that should be said is that
they play varieties of the game differing from that
recommended in 'Cavendish's' latest edition.'' In
like manner Prof. Boyesen should not have berated
Mr. Lang for preferring Mr. Haggard's gory
romances to Tolstoi's more serious discussions of human experience. The American critic should have
contented himself with pointing out that his British
colleague liked the Primitive Game better than the
Latter-day Improvements. And really it was unreasonable in Prof. Boyesen to expect that Mr. Lang
should appreciate the New American Leads, either in
literature or in life.

Any movement forward by the more intelligent is
like the sending ahead of skirmishers, and we have no
right to expect to find the main body of the army
close at the heels of the advance guard. The most we
can hope is that the ground taken by the few pioneers
yesterday shall be held in force to-day. Generally
any improvement in taste makes its way slowly, and
the bulk of the public must always lag along behind
the keener intellects that delight to spy out a new
land for themselves. In New York city, for instance,
the last thirty years have seen a most extraordinary
increase in the popular appreciation of music.

Toward the end of the 'sixties Mr. Theodore Thomas
and his orchestra played every summer night in the
old Central Park Garden and the programme was
made up largely of medleys from Offenbach's operet-

tas and of dance-music. Owing to Mr. Thomas's increasing efforts to give better and better music as he educated the New York concert-goer, and owing also to the labors of Dr. Damrosch and Mr. Seidl, there is now perhaps no city in the world where more music of the highest class is heard in the course of the year than in New York, and none where it is more delicately enjoyed. The finest of Wagner's music-dramas are not now too solid fare for the subscribers of the Metropolitan Opera House, who no longer find any satisfaction even in the most expensive performance of sugary trifles like the "Lucia" of Donizetti.

But though the subscribers of the Metropolitan Opera House have lost their liking for "Traviata" and for "Trovatore," the occasional experiments of other opera-companies in other New York theatres and in opera-houses in other cities of the Union seem to show that there are perhaps as many music-lovers as ever who have advanced just far enough to understand and enjoy these simple favorites of former days. The opera-goers of this class are like the whist-players who stick to the Primitive Game, or the novel-readers who revel in romances of the Improbable. And I have no doubt that if a young conductor possessing such shrewdness and force as Mr. Thomas revealed, should give summer night concerts in New York, placing on its programme dance-tunes and medleys from operettas, he would have now quite as large a following as Mr. Thomas had thirty years ago; and in time he could slowly lead on this portion of the public to the acceptance of music demanding a more careful appreciation.

There is ready at hand yet another example of the

ease with which a portion of the public can be educated to have a relish for the finer forms of art. It
was in the 'sixties that Mr. Thomas began his ele-
vating work here in New York; and it was in the
'seventies that the American magazines began to seek
for a fresher and a richer pictorial embellishment, a
search which slowly brought into existence the illustrated monthly due to the loving co-operation of the
editor, the artist, the engraver, and the printer. The
best of these sumptuous publications, having gradually created the taste by which they were estimated,
attained to an enormous circulation,—a fact which
might seem to prove them to be precisely "the kind
of periodical that the public wants."

Yet early in the 'nineties we saw the appearance of
a swarm of cheaper monthlies, filled with process-
blocks from photographs; and some of these slight
magazines also attained to an enormous circulation.
But as the success of these new periodicals affected
only a little (if at all) the sale of the older and solider
magazines, it is obvious that "the kind of periodical
that the public wants" is a question to which there
are now two answers. In other words, while one segment of the reading circle has been led to develop a
liking for the more substantial merits of the established magazines, another segment is attracted by the
cheap tawdriness of the more flimsy novelties. And
it is quite within bounds of possibility that an inven-
tive editor might now devise a third form of periodical which should also attain to an enormous circulation without interfering with the profits of either
class of monthly now most in favor; he would be
proving only the existence of a third segment of the
reading circle.

So I return to the assertion made in an early paragraph of this paper; there is really no such entity as *the* public. There is *a* public ready to welcome everything which is good in its kind; and there are as many publics as there are different kinds of good things. Few of us are so limited in our likings as to belong to one public only. The extreme Wagnerite is often warmest in praise of a captivating waltz by Strauss; and the extreme veritist can acknowledge the charm of a romantic fantasy of Stevenson's. Perhaps a reader of extraordinary catholicity might belong almost to all the different publics.

Some of these publics are very large indeed and some of them are very small. "Hamlet," for example, appeals to almost every type of play-goer, while the performance of Ibsen's "Ghosts" pleases only a chosen few. In general, of course, the higher up the pyramid is cut, the smaller will be the area of the cross-section,—"Hamlet" being one of the rare works which are so nearly universal as rather to bisect the pyramid than to cut across it. When one has once grasped firmly the idea that the people at large are massed in a pyramid, one layer above the other, with the most intelligent at the apex, one cannot but see the futility of all assertions that "the public wants to be amused," and "the public wants sensation and excitement," and "the public does not want analysis and disquisition." There is a public that wants to be amused; and perhaps the larger portion of this public wants sensation and excitement and does not want analysis and disquisition. But there is a public also which does want analysis and disquisition and does not want sensation and excitement. There is a segment of the reading circle with the keenest relish for airy fantasy and for delicate humor. There is another segment hungry for the naked truth. There is yet another which has no real liking for knowledge of itself and which therefore likes to hear over and over again the old outworn tales and to listen again and again to old outworn rhymes of *love* and *dove,* of *heart* and *part.*

This diversity of public taste has always existed—except perhaps in the compact community of Athens. In the prologue he wrote for the third performance of one of his comedies, Terence denounced the foolish spectators because at the first performance they were all excitement over an exhibition on the tight-rope which was to follow, and because at the second performance the theatre emptied itself suddenly in the middle of the play, when a rumor ran around the house that there were going to be gladiators elsewhere in the neighborhood. (If I may open a parenthesis here, I should like to drop the query as to whether Gresham's Law may not be as potent in art as it is in finance, the inferior product driving out the superior, as the bloody shows of the arena in Rome finally extinguished the Latin literary drama.) In England under Elizabeth the wooden theatres in which Shakespeare's sublimest tragedies were acted, served on other days of the week as a ring for the sport of bear-baiting. In the early part of the nineteenth century in London, when Sarah Siddons and John Philip Kemble were in the plenitude of their powers, they played often to the bare benches of Drury Lane, while the same night Covent Garden would be packed with people eager to behold a real elephant take part in a spectacular pantomime. The elephant and the bear-baiting and the gladiators, each in their turn, pleased that part of the public which was still playing the Primitive Game—to use Dr. Pole's phrase—and which therefore was wholly incapable of understanding the Philosophical Game, so to speak, of Mrs. Siddons, of Shakespeare, and of Terence.

And yet that portion of the public which clings to the Primitive Game has at least one fine quality; it is perfectly sincere. It is not a humbug, or a sham. It knows what it likes and it is not ashamed of its prejudices. It makes no pretence of regard for the more advanced art it is unable to appreciate. It is frank and outspoken in its conviction that Hawthorne is slow and Turgeneff dull; and it makes no effort whatever to conceal its opinion that Ibsen is tiresome and that Mr. Howells is colorless. It is wholly without the snobbishness which induces not a few of those readers who really most enjoy the romances of Mr. Haggard to pretend that they prefer the novels of Mr. Meredith merely because there was once a Meredith cult among the cultured.

I am inclined to believe that the position of that portion of the public which retains its primitive taste in literature, is often misrepresented and even more often misunderstood. For one thing this portion of the public is composed of plain people who are not only sincere themselves in their literary likes and dislikes, but are also swift to detect insincerity in the authors who seek to interest them. They revolt at the slightest hint of condescension. They insist on being taken seriously;—and this is why Mr. Andrew Lang's ingenious sensational story "The Mark of Cain" fell flat, while hundreds of thousands were sold of the sensational stories of "Hugh Conway" who had not a tithe of Mr. Lang's cleverness.

Here we find a possible explanation of a problem which has puzzled more than one generation of literary critics;—why do the writings of certain authors have an immense vogue when these authors are seen to be without the really great qualities? Is success in literature only a lottery? Is the general public a fool then, easily to be led by the nose? As there is no effect without a cause, there must be a reason for the popularity which sometimes seems to us unaccountable. The real explanation of the welcome which was bestowed on the "Proverbial Philosophy" of the late Martin Farquhar Tupper, for example, or on the novels of the late E. P. Roe, is to be sought in the sincerity of these two writers. Neither was in any way a charlatan. Both of them gave the public the best they had in them; and, as it happened, they thus voiced the unformulated feelings of the segment of the reading circle to which they themselves belonged. So far from writing *down* to the public taste, as they were accused of doing, they were, in fact, writing *up* to the taste of the portion of the public that welcomed their works. By their own birth and bringing up, both Mr. Tupper and Mr. Roe were in a measure representative of the "plain people," as Lincoln phrased it; and they could not help taking the plain people's point of view. This the plain people recognized promptly; and the writers had their reward on the spot. Their writings lacked the permanent qualities of literature, no doubt, and that is why their vogue was temporary only.

More accomplished men of letters than either Mr. Tupper or Mr. Roe have not taken this point of view

naturally and thus they have failed to voice the feelings of the very segment of the reading circle they
hoped to please. Indeed, I doubt if any author, who
has tried to guess at the taste of the public that he
might flatter it, has ever made a hit satisfactory to
himself; and I am certain that no author who really
despised his audience, as more than one author may
have pretended to despise it, has ever really pleased
those to whom he made his appeal thus cynically. It
happens that I have met at one time or another many
of the novelists and dramatists of France, of England,
and of America, those whom the critics delight to
honor and those also at whom the criticasters joy to
gird; and the quality which the latter class seemed to
me to have most abundantly was earnestness. They
believed in their own work and they were doing it as
well as in them lay. Their success was due to the fact
that their best corresponded absolutely with the ideal
of a certain segment of the reading circle or of a certain proportion of the play-goers. In other words,
and to use another of Lincoln's always keen phrases,
these popular novelists and dramatists were producing
"just the kind of thing that a man would like who
liked that kind of thing." And that is why they met
with a far wider success than the far cleverer and far
more accomplished men of letters whose merits might
be vaunted by all who had so far progressed themselves in literature as to appreciate the Latter-day
Developments, as Dr. Pole calls them. It is only now
and again that there comes a rare writer able to delight at once his brethren of the craft and the plain
people also; and he does this not by trying to please
the public but rather by expressing himself and by
doing always the best he knows how. His segment of

the reading circle subtends a very wide angle because his art is as firm as his outlook on our common humanity is broad.

NOTES AND QUESTIONS

Brander Matthews (1852—) is one of the best-known American men of letters of the present day.   He was born in New Orleans, and educated at Columbia University—then Columbia College, New York.   He studied law after completing his college course, but the profession of letters had too strong an attraction for him, and his life has been devoted to this.   He was always greatly interested in the drama; he was one of the founders of the Players' Club (New York), and one of his earliest books was on *French Dramatists of the Nineteenth Century*.   In 1892 he was made professor of literature at Columbia University, and in 1900, professor of dramatic literature, a position which he still holds.   He has published more than fifty books, including essays, short stories, plays, dramatic history and criticism.   He is recognized as an authority upon the drama.   His books on this subject include: *Studies of the Stage, The Theatres of Paris, Moliere, Shakespere as a Playwright, On Acting, The Development of the Drama, and A Book about the Theatre*.   *Vignettes of Manhattan* is a book of short stories.   In the field of literary criticism he has published *Aspects of Fiction, The Historical Novel and Other Essays, The Philosophy of the Short Story, Americanisms and Briticisms, Essays in English, The Tocsin of Revolt*.   In addition he has edited many books, and written numerous book reviews.

Page 48, paragraph "Two lines."
In this and the following paragraph the author discusses the theory that a popular book owes its success to the fact that the writer has shrewdly planned to hit the taste of the public.   What is Professor Matthews opinion of this theory?   His reason?

Page 49, paragraph "And I venture."
What is the leading idea in this paragraph?   Is it familiar or new to you?   Would it apply to the play-going public as well as to the reading public?

Page 51, paragraph "As it happens."

Into what periods does he divide the history of fiction?
This classification is a valuable one.   Think of some novels
you have read recently, and see in which group they belong?

Page 53, paragraph "We all see."

Which type of fiction does Professor Matthews seem to
rate highest?

Page 54, "Mr. Haggard's gory romances."

H. Rider Haggard's *She* and *King Solomon's Mines* are
stories of the impossible type which had a wide popularity.

Page 54, paragraph "Any movement forward."

Note how Professor Matthews' knowledge in various fields
helps to make clear his discussion of a topic in literature.

Page 54, paragraph "Toward the end."

In this and the following paragraph, what conclusion is
drawn about the development of taste in music?   Does this
discussion belong under his title?

Page 55, paragraph "There is ready."

Summarize in a sentence the thought of this and the next
paragraph.

Page 57, paragraph "Some of these."

Note how in this paragraph the author gathers up the
thought of all that has gone before and expresses it in an apt
figure of speech.

Page 60, paragraph "Here we find."

What literary problem is discussed here?   What answer
is suggested?   Whose novels today have a tremendous sale.
but are ridiculed by the critics?

Page 60, paragraph "More accomplished men."

What quality does the author ascribe to the popular writers?
To what does he say their success is due?

THEME SUBJECTS

The Four Kinds of Fiction.
The Pyramid of Popular Taste.
Why Certain Novels are Popular.
Public Taste in the Drama.
Public Taste in Music.
Public Taste in Motion Pictures.

MY FOUR FAVORITE PARTS

By Henry Irving

EVERY actor goes through the experience of being constantly pressed to name his favorite impersonations. It is an embarrassing request, for two reasons. First, the actor who has in his time played many parts, extending over a very wide range, finds it difficult to make a choice, to say he feels happiest in this or that character. Secondly, the choice itself seems to suggest that he is passing a final judgment on his own achievements, that he says to the world, "This is my best; on this my reputation rests." As many people will not in the least agree with him, his personal opinion may wear the aspect of a challenge, and of an egoistic display.

I am risking this misapprehension, simply to put on record a few impressions of four parts in Shakespeare which I chiefly love—Hamlet, Richard III., Iago, and King Lear. Perhaps I may preface what I have to say of them by remarking the curious perversity which has prompted some distinguished artists to decry the art of acting. We all know Macready's story of his performance of "Virginius" a few hours after he had buried his daughter. He never played the part so well; his personal grief made more poignant the pathos of the Roman father, and when it was over he felt that his art was degrading. I read, the other day, in a charming paper by Mrs. Ritchie, how Fanny

Kemble told her that acting was repulsive because
it quenched the springs of natural emotion. Why
this should be the misfortune of the actor and not of
the novelist—why Dickens, for example, who lived in
the joys and sorrows of the creatures of his brain,
and walked the streets all night in the deepest dejec-
tion after describing the imaginary woes of an imaginary death, ought not to have given up novel writing
to preserve his sensitiveness to real bereavements—I
have never been able to understand. What is the
degradation of representing parental tenderness on
the stage when your heart is bleeding for the loss of
a child, if there is no degradation in passing from a
death-bed to your desk to tell in a story what has
wrung your heart-strings in your own home? The
idea is as crude as that the actor who plays the villain
of the piece with convincing iniquity must himself
be dead to every virtue. An extraordinary prejudice
has been excited in many simple minds by Fanny
Kemble's renunciation of the art which made her
family illustrious. I believe they picture the actor
as a human phonograph, which, having delivered its
message of unreal woe to a weeping audience, remains absolutely callous to every moving scene and
sentiment in the everyday world till the curtain rises
on the next performance. Incredible as it may appear, the actor may take an acute interest in the common affairs of mankind and have no less than his fair
share of humanity. He fashions his impersonations
by a mental process which is not entirely humiliating.
which is capable, indeed, of some exalted moments,
and of association of ideas which have the charm of
psychological mystery. Every character has its own
atmosphere, and as he divests himself of one person-

ality, and possesses himself of the spirit as well as the suits and trappings of another, he is conscious of an intellectual transmigration not wholly contemptible. When I am about to resume a part which I have not played for some time, I often sit in my dressing-room, while recaptured sensations and images steal gradually into my mind; and, sad to relate, I find the operation exhilarating and not degrading.

For Hamlet I have that affection which springs naturally in the actor towards the most intensely human of Shakespeare's creations. If Hazlitt could have had his way, and if "Hamlet" had been forbidden to the stage as "hardly capable of being acted," some of the purest pleasures actors have ever known would have been denied to them. All the striving, all the most lovable weaknesses of humanity, the groping after thoughts beyond the confines of our souls, the tenderest attributes of our common nature, fate and free-will, love and death, passions and problems, are interwoven in the character of Hamlet, till he touches us at every point of our strange compound of clay and spirit. To achieve so complete a command over all these elements as to place the impersonation beyond cavil has been given to none of us. But to represent in Hamlet the type of filial love, to suggest that sense of the supernatural which holds the genius of romance like a veil, and that haunted look of one who is constantly with the spirit which has "revisited the glimpses of the moon," to disentangle the character from traditions which are apt to overlay with artifice one of the most vividly real of all the conceptions in art, to leave upon your generation the impression of Hamlet as a man, not as a piece of acting—this is, perhaps, the highest aim

which the English-speaking actor can cherish. This
is why one or two Hamlets—Edwin Booth's for instance—have an enduring hold upon the memories of
playgoers. Something of the chivalry, the high-
strung ecstasy, the melancholy grace of the man clings
to the mind when the sterner grandeur of other creations of the poet may have lost its spell.

In playing Richard III. I undertook a duty which
the stage had long owed to Shakespeare's reputation.
This was the restoration of the play in the form so
long displaced by Colley Cibber. It is true that Macready made a determined effort to dethrone Cibber,
and that the same example was followed by the late
Charles Calvert in his revival of the play at Man-
chester, but in both cases the acting edition contained
portions of "King Henry VI.," whereas the Lyceum
version had no single line which was not in the
original. Some famous actors have made great
names as Cibber's Richard, and the part was played
with a pictorial villany, of which the best idea is given
by the portraits of George Frederick Cooke. They
are monuments of crime—lowering, truculent, robusti-
ous, extremely effective in the blood and bombast
vein, and, in the last act, more like a pugilist at bay
than the prince who has a fateful premonition of his
end. Edmund Kean, however, who was very great in
this part, played it with an original power which gave
a Shakespearian quality even to Cibber. Shakespeare's Richard is a Plantagenet with the imperious
pride of his race, a subtle intellect, a mocking, not a
trumpeting duplicity, a superb daring which needs
no roar and stamp, no cheap and noisy exultation.
Moreover, the true Richard has a youthful audacity
very different from the ponderous airs of the heavy

villain. In this character, as in Iago, the great element is an intrepid calculation. The wooing of Lady Anne, sufficiently startling as an experiment in amorous subjugation, is not carried off by the formidable graces with which tradition invested the part.

The mingled subtlety and simplicity of Iago have never, perhaps, been better indicated than in Macaulay's description of the Italian statesman of Machiavelli's time :—

"We see a man whose thoughts and words have no connection with each other, who never hesitates at an oath when he wishes to seduce, who never wants a pretext when he is inclined to betray. His cruelties spring, not from the heat of blood or the insanity of uncontrolled power, but from deep and cool meditation. His passions, like well-trained troops, are impetuous by rule, and in their most headstrong fury never forget the discipline to which they have been accustomed. His whole soul is occupied with vast and complicated schemes of ambition; yet his aspect and language exhibit nothing but philosophical moderation. Hatred and revenge eat into his heart; yet every look is a cordial smile, every gesture a familiar caress. He never excites the suspicion of his adversaries by petty provocations. His purpose is disclosed only when it is accomplished. His face is unruffled, his speech is courteous till vigilance is laid asleep, till a vital point is exposed, till a sure aim is taken; and then he strikes for the first and last time. To do an injury openly is, in his estimation, as wicked as to do it secretly, and far less profitable. With him the most honorable means are the surest, the speediest, and the darkest. He cannot comprehend how a man should scruple to deceive those whom he does not scruple to destroy. He would think it madness to declare open hostilities against rivals whom he might stab in a friendly embrace, or poison in a consecrated wafer."

Although Iago was a simple soldier and no politician, he reproduces all the traits of the mediæval Italian adventurer delineated by Macaulay. Manifestly, such a character should be played with a devilry not writ large in every look and action.   The quality of youth, moreover, is all-important.   Iago I take to be a young man about eight and twenty ("I have looked upon the world for four times seven years") not embittered by disappointments which have come in middle age, but instinct in all his manhood with the duplicity which belongs to his temperament and his generation. To me he has also a slight dash of the bull-fighter, and during the brawl between Cassio and Montano, I used to enjoy a mischievous sense of mastery by flicking at them with a red cloak, as though they were bulls in the arena.   To impersonate the veritable spirit of a creation so foreign to our native thought and atmosphere demands an abstinence from some obvious devices of the stage which enhance a moral monstrosity at the expense of the intellectual *vraisemblance*.   Iago is no monster, but perfectly human and consistent, though there is probably no character in Shakespeare which needs to be represented with more delicacy of suggestion and less rhetorical artifice, if we are to saturate the imagination with a cold and constant purpose.

Of Lear, I may candidly say that I doubt whether a complete embodiment is within any actor's resources. For myself the part has two singular associations. It broke down my physical strength after sixty consecutive nights, and when I resumed the part after a brief rest I was forced reluctantly to the conclusion that there is one character in Shakespeare which cannot be played six times a week with impunity.   On the first night I had a curious experience.   As I stood at the wings before Lear makes his entrance I had a sudden idea which revolutionized the impersonation and launched me into an experiment unattempted at rehearsal. I tried to combine the weakness of senility with the tempest of passion, and the growing conviction before the play had proceeded far that this was a perfectly impossible task, is one of my most vivid memories of that night. Lear cannot be played except with the plenitude of the actor's physical powers, and the idea of representing extreme old age is futile.

There will always be a controversy as to the precise point where Lear's mind is manifestly unhinged. The old argument is that he is sane enough till the conduct of his daughters drives him mad, and the earlier scenes have generally been played as though an aged man of perfectly sound faculties, but imperious temper, would probably divide his kingdom among his daughters, one of whom is likely to carry her share to a foreign prince. Moreover, though the division is in equal parts, Cordelia is tempted with a third "more opulent than the others." Kent, the king's stanchest friend and most faithful counsellor, is banished in a fit of frenzy. It seems to me that Lear's action throughout this episode is inconsistent with absolute sanity, that the decay of his intellect has begun before the opening of the play, and that the actor has to represent the struggles of an enfeebled mind with violent self-will, a mind eventually reduced to the pathetic helplessness of a ruin in which some of the original grandeur can still be traced. This is without doubt the most difficult undertaking in the whole range of the drama. If a complete mastery of such tremendous elements is not within the compass of histrionic art, there remains the not inconsiderable satisfaction of suggesting the colossal proportions of the greatest of tragedies. To impress

upon an audience a conception appealing so strongly
to that pity for human frailty which is the most
universal of social bonds, is an achievement which
will always engage the actor's highest ambition. In
Lear, more than in any other conception of the poet,
he is overshadowed by the supreme majesty of
Shakespeare's genius, but to interpret that, however
imperfectly, must always be a cherished hope and a
most gratifying reward.

NOTES AND QUESTIONS

Sir Henry Irving (1838-1905) was one of the most famous
actors of the nineteenth century. His real name was John
Brodribb, but on his first public appearance as an actor, in
Lytton's *Richelieu*, he was billed as Henry Irving, and continued to use the name. His early dramatic training was obtained by a ten years' experience in stock companies, in
which time he played more than five hundred parts. His first
London appearance was in 1866, at the St. James Theatre;
he played later at the Haymarket, the Gayety, Drury Lane and
the Lyceum. In 1874 his production of Hamlet had a run
of two hundred nights, an unprecedented record for the play.
In 1878 he became manager of the Lyceum Theatre in London.
Here, in association with Miss Ellen Terry, he put on a
series of classic and modern plays, staged with great beauty,
and acted with such art and power that they set a new
standard for the English stage. Among the plays produced
at the Lyceum were *The Merchant of Venice, Othello, Romeo
and Juliet, Macbeth, King Lear, Much Ado About Nothing,
Twelfth Night, Henry VIII*, and of modern plays Tennyson's
Becket, Lewis' *The Bells*, Sardou's *Madame Sans-Gene* and
Dante, and Conan Doyle's *Waterloo*. He made repeated visits
to the United States, where his productions drew crowded
houses. His services to the stage were recognized by the
honor of knighthood, conferred upon him in 1895: the first
time that an English actor had ever received a title of nobility.
Both as an actor and as manager he was governed by the
highest ideals of his art. Commercial success was not his

aim; he did not gain great wealth, but he rests in Westminister Abbey. His published works include a volume of addresses on the drama, and the *Henry Irving Shakespere*, an edition showing what cuts were made in his production of various plays, and with notes describing the costumes, etc.

Page 64, paragraph "I am risking."

Why did Macready think his art degrading? What is Irving's opinion? Note the irony in the latter part of the paragraph.

Page 66, paragraph "For Hamlet I have."

What is meant by the remark that Hamlet "touches us at every point of our strange compound of clay and spirit"?

Page 67, paragraph "In playing Richard III."

Irving's analysis of the interpretation of Hamlet by various actors shows us how closely he studied his art, determining exactly the traits of character which his impersonation was to reveal. In Ellen Terry's *Reminiscences* many incidents are told illustrating the infinite pains Irving took, not only with his own part, but with the work of every member of his company, to secure the right interpretation of the lines.

Page 68, paragraph "The mingled subtlety."

Note Irving's mention of the use of a red cloak in playing the part of Iago in Othello. It is a fine example of the use of suggestion. Observe also, in the closing sentence of the paragraph, that Irving knows how to use words exactly and effectively.

Page 69, paragraph "Of Lear."

What was the effect upon Irving of playing this part? To what was this due?

Page 70, paragraph "There will always."

What is Irving's view of the sanity of Lear?

THEME SUBJECTS

The art of the actor.

Lear as a part for an actor.

An actor I have seen as Hamlet.

What the motion picture cannot give.

Hamlet touches us at every point of our nature.

Irving as a manager. (See Ellen Terry's *Reminiscences*, or the *Life* by Bram Stoker.)

YOUNG RADICALS IN AMERICA

By GEORGE SANTAYANA

WHEN I was a college professor, I sometimes wondered why there was no socialism among the sophomores. Now that I am not there to welcome it, the thing seems to have come.

I say to *welcome it,* because although I am a high Tory in my sympathies, I recognize that different hearts must be set on different things, and I like young people who have hearts, and who set them on something. It is a great pity if, for lack of self-knowledge or a congenial environment, they set them on the wrong thing, and miss their possible happiness, or miss even the noble martyrdom of knowing why they are unhappy. But they will not have set their hearts on the wrong thing simply because that thing may be indifferent or disagreeable to *me.* My personal feelings have nothing to do with the genuineness of their ideals, or with the worth of their happiness, if they are able to attain it. At most, my experience may make me suspect that these ideals may be unattainable, or that in choosing them these young men, in some cases, may have misunderstood their own nature, and may be pursuing something which, if they got it, would make them very sick. When that is so, a word of warning from an outsider may not be entirely useless.

The reason why it is easy to mistake the demands of one's own nature is that human instincts are very complex and confused, and that they mature at different times, or are suppressed or disguised altogether; whereas the fancy is peopled only by the shallow images of such things as we happen to have come upon in our experience. We cannot love, nor warmly imagine, what we have never seen; even when we hate things as we find them (as every fresh soul must in a great measure) our capacity to conceive better things is limited to such hints as actual things have vouchsafed us. We may therefore have no idea at all of what would really satisfy us; even if it were described to us in words, we should not recognize it as our ideal of happiness. It would seem cold, exotic, irrelevant, because nothing of that sort had as yet entered our experience, or lay in the path immediately open before us.

I was accordingly not at all surprisd that the life of the ancients, although alone truly human and addressed to a possible happiness, should not appeal to young America. It is too remote, too simple; it presupposes the absence of this vast modern mechanical momentum, this rushing tide of instrumentalities on which young America is borne along so merrily. What surprised me a little was that everybody seemed content to go on swimming and swimming: for even when a man grumbled and worried about his difficulties or mishaps—athletic training, college clubs, family friction, dubious prospects, unrequited love— he yet seemed to be entirely at peace with the general plan of existence as he found it; not at all oppressed by the sense of any surrounding ugliness, vulgarity, vanity, servitude, or emptiness. Was there

in these youths, I used to ask myself, so engaging
often in their personal ardor, no human soul at all,
but rather the soul of some working ant or unques-
tioning bee, eager to run on its predetermined errands,
store its traditional honey, and build its geometrical
cell, for the queen of the hive, the future Mrs. Ant or
Mrs. Bee, to lay her eggs in? I am far from regarding romantic man as necessarily the best of animals,
or a success at all, so far; and I am quite willing he
should be superseded, if nature, in America or elsewhere, can evolve a superior species to take his place;
but this sudden extinction of human passion seemed
a little strange, and I doubted whether perfect happiness in mechanism was as yet possible even for the
healthiest, busiest, most athletic, most domestic, and
most conventional American. Might not the great
American panacea for human wretchedness, Work,
be not so much a cure as an anaesthetic?

And now, apparently, the awakening has come,
at least to a few, and the sophomores (who are many
of them out of college) have discovered the necessity
of socialism. I call it socialism for short, although
they are not all advocates of socialism in a technical
sense, but style themselves liberals, radicals, or (mod-
estly) the *Intelligentsia*. The point is that they all
proclaim their disgust at the present state of things
in America, they denounce the Constitution of the
United States, the churches, the government, the colleges, the press, the theatres, and above all they denounce the spirit that vivifies and unifies all these
things, the spirit of Business. Here is disaffection
breaking out in that which seemed the most unani-
mous, the most satisfied of nations: here are Americans
impatient with America.

Is it simply impatience? Is it the measles, and by
the time these sophomores are reverend seniors will it
have passed away? Or is it a tragic atavism in individuals, such as must appear sporadically in all ages
and nations, an inopportune sport of nature, hatching
a bird of paradise in the arctic regions? Even in this
case, pathetic as it is, nothing can be done except to
wait for the unhappy creatures to come to a fluttering
end, for lack of sunshine and appropriate worms.
Untoward genius must die in a corner. I am ready
to believe that these young radicals are geniuses and
birds of paradise, as they evidently feel themselves to
be; if so, their plaints ought to make a beautiful elegy;
but it would still be a dying song. Or is it possible,
on the contrary, that they are prophets of something
attainable, boy-scouts with a real army behind them,
and a definite future?

I have made a severe effort to discover, as well as
I may from a distance, what these rebels want. I
see what they are *against*—they are against everything
—but what are they *for?* I have not been able to
discover it. This may be due to my lack of understanding or to their incapacity to express themselves
clearly, for their style is something appalling. But
perhaps their scandalous failure in expression, when
expression is what they yearn for and demand at all
costs, may be a symptom of something deeper: of a
radical mistake they have made in the direction of
their efforts and aspirations. They think they need
more freedom, more room, a chance to be more spontaneous: I suspect that they have had too much
freedom, too much empty space, too much practice in
being spontaneous when there was nothing in them
to bubble out. Their style is a sign of this: it is not

merely that they have no mastery of the English language as hitherto spoken, no clear sense of the value of words, and no simplicity; that they are without the vocabulary or the idiom of cultivated people.

That might all be healthy evolution, even if a little disconcerting to us old fogies, who can't keep up with the progress of slang. America has a right to a language of its own, and to the largest share in forming that pigeon-English which is to be the "world-language" of the future. But it is not comparatively only that the style of the young radicals is bad, nor in view of traditional standards: it is bad intrinsically; it is muddy, abstract, cumbrous, contorted, joyless, obscure. If their thoughts were clear, if the images in their minds were definite and fondly cherished, if their principles and allegiances were firm, we should soon learn to read their language and feel it to be pure and limpid, however novel its forms. Dante wrote in a new dialect, provincial and popular; yet how all his words shine like dew on a sunny morning! But Dante had looked long and intently; he had loved silently; he knew what he felt and what he believed. No: it is not more freedom that young America needs in order to be happy: it needs more discipline.

NOTES AND QUESTIONS

George A. Santayana (1863—) is known as a poet, professor and philosopher. He was born in Madrid, of Spanish parentage, and came to the United States in 1872. He attended Harvard, graduating in the class of 1886, and taking the degree of doctor of philosophy in 1889. He also studied at the University of Berlin. He taught philosophy at Harvard University from 1899 to 1911, and lectured at the Sorbonne, Paris in 1905-6.   His lectures were noted for their finished style as well as for their content.   He is known as a poet as well as a philosopher, having published several books of poems, including *Sonnets and Other Verses, Lucifer, A Theological Tragedy*, and *The Hermit of Carmel*.   His writings in philosophy and aesthetics include *The Sense of Beauty, Interpretations of Poetry and Religion.   The Life of Reason* (five volumes), *Winds of Doctrine*.   A recent book, well worth reading, is his *Soliloquies in England*.

Page 73, paragraph "When I was."   This paragraph seems to say that the writer is in sympathy with socialism. Does the next paragraph bear this out?   Read the last two sentences of the second paragraph carefully.

Page 74, paragraph "I was accordingly."   What was it in the attitude of college students that surprised Professor Santayana?   What does he mean by his comparison of a college student to an ant or a bee?

Page 75, paragraph "And now apparently."   What tendencies does he group under the name of Socialism?   Have any of these things come under your observation in college life?

Page 76, paragraph "Is it simply."   What two theories are suggested as to this new spirit in the colleges?

Page 76, paragraph "I have made."   What is Professor Santayana's criticism upon the young radicals?

Page 77, paragraph "That might all."   What statement is made about the relation of style to thought?   How is it applied to the subject of this paper?

Does this article end effectively?

THEME SUBJECTS

Radical theorists in our college.
Clear thinking and clear writing.
Can a foreigner judge American life'
Why radical ideas are spreading.
Professor Santayana's opinion of young radicals.

THE PARADOX OF OXFORD

By Robert P. Tristram Coffin

MANY people have written about the riddle of Oxford. To many serious academic minds it has been a mystery that this odd collection of separate colleges, without alumni organizations and without advertising, with antiquated prejudices and mediaeval buildings, should continue to be a power in the world of learning. To an outsider, and especially to an American, Oxford is a mess of paradoxes stirred together by a spoon. It is something as if one had a whole group of our small colleges in one town, each competing with all the others in scholarship and athletics, in general prestige. There *must* be a secret to this University.

Great scholarliness in a place of no plumbing to speak of: "Why should we install bathrooms?" a college head asked indignantly not so many years ago, "The young gentlemen are here only eight weeks at a time!" I remember my first college bath; the years turned back, and I saw again the look of injured dignity in the haughty eyes of a pet gander when the saucer he had chosen for his bath vanished under his feathers.

Dr. Johnson's college still uses candles. And Oxford flourishes on an endowment that would hardly keep the wolf from the door of a small American college. There are no campaigns launched to make "the

79

sunset years'' of the faculty secure. Yet men with
fame in their names teach there while their hairs
grow white and their names grow golden, and their
books go around the world. Many a don on a salary
of an American high school principal fills shelves of
our university libraries with sound learning.

And there are more paradoxes than this of lean
purses and rich scholarship. Some of these dons
write books that children love, that men who come
home with grime on their hands enjoy. Others give
their names to the world on a new kind of pun. Some
of them, authorities on the morphology of Homeric
verbs, catch astounding fish or climb all manner of
Alps. They put off gowns and play Homeric tennis.
Bearded like the major prophets, book-laden and
gowned, they pedal ahead of captains of crew and
rugby. They do things well, the dons: they drink
ale, they crawl under hedges, wear old clothes, eat
strawberry jam and cheese with ditches and diggers
in village inns, and take nobody's backwash in talk
of ferretting and poaching; they know how to play;
they set down their learning so that it is pleasant to
read; they know how to live.

Oxford is the home of such paradoxes. There are
no ''drives'' for new equipment. Yet the old place
grows, is full of the youth and the promise of the
best of England and the Colonies. No great alumni
bodies with secretaries and reunions assist in keeping
alive an Oxonian tradition. But the tradition is
there, and the old men come swarming back to college
cups and college boats from the underside of the earth,
from India and Manitoba, from veldt and pampas.
Poets write verses about Oxford; all her sons bring
their renown home to her towers and green gardens.

There is no great cult of athletics, no great Diana of the muscles before whom graduates prostrate themselves and gouge their purses. There are no professional coaches to say that games shall be work and not play, no gladiatorial schools hardening a handful of men for shows for the many. Yet teams of the dark blue set up world records and do glorious things in lands overseas.

The University is one without classrooms, without quizzes, without lectures if you wish; each college has its own tutors in subjects offered elsewhere; there is no close co-operation of departments as we have it; dons overlap and contradict one another; it is their glory. There is no real central office of information; the *Excerpta e Statutis*, written partly in the learned tongue of Chaucer's day, is like an essay in mediæval metaphysics or astrology. No advertising! I know an American professor who spent five years in getting the *Excerpta*, and another five in attempting to decipher it.

There is a library, the Bodleian, the best university library in the world; but you cannot take books out of it, you must spend days in getting admitted to it, it takes hours to have books found and fetched by irresponsible shavers who play marbles on the way; you must read by such light as filters through old glass covered with Virginia creeper. The home of priceless manuscripts, the "jewels of the learned," is unlighted, unheated, and it closes at four in the afternoon.

It is no wonder that the newly matriculated man from overseas goes about with a smile on his face the first week. And yet that smile changes, grows into the smile of the believer, stays on his face for better or for worse to the end of his Oxford days, stays to sweeten all the days and the ways of his life. This unique and refreshing Oxonian pleasure, incredulous at first, becomes a creed for living, for finding the humor in all things, for the gospel and glory of old age.

There is a riddle to Oxford. But it is simple of solution. It is nothing more mysterious than this: here is a university that teaches life, the life each undergraduate is going to live. Other universities give one setting-up drills, preparation for life; others teach departments of life, athletics, teaching, business, religion; but all as *specialities*. Say what one may, there is a Puritanic intensity to all that most American undergraduates do. Hence most American colleges are treadmills; in them one goes through the steps that will give training in the one set of interests of one's choosing, be they athletic or intellectual. We go in for football or Greek poetry. In rare instances for both; but always *separately*. We do not combine the two. One has the Puritan's feeling of the sanctity and aloofness of the affair at hand from all that is easy and pleasant and comfortable and decorative. And so we often miss the liberal and the magic of proportion and vitality; and, missing these, miss life. For life seems to be a mixed matter: geraniums and gerunds, pancakes and talk of friends. We scrimmage or we scan; and with our whole souls. A sense of the artistic or the historical is as much out of place on the football field as a joviality such as only a rare sense of the physical can give is out of place among dead participles. Either way we strain and contort and narrow ourselves, go into a sort of

mediæval absorption in the thing contemplated; the
green beauty of trees and blue loveliness of sky or
the red pulse of life we lose from our beings along
this *Via Negativa*. On the playing fields our books
are sealed to us; among our books the kingliness of
bodily well-being is an unbidden guest.

Now obviously people must exercise, even though
they are business magnates or professors; and people
must read and think after the hours of bricklaying.
Every man must be able to get the fullest pleasure
possible out of all he does. Colleges ought to teach
him so to do. Oxford does teach a man this.
Whatever else the University might teach, she schools
him in the way best to enjoy himself, here and now,
while the bloom of his prime is still upon him. If a
boy cannot feel the pulses of a book beat when his
own are all April and morning, his books will always
be mummies. If a young oarsman cannot feel the
rhythm that all the poets have found singing in their
hearts and the glory that all kingly minds have worn,
then his exercise in age will be a cheating of the grave
and not a daily poetry.

Youthful impressions go deepest; if the young can
rub elbows with all sorts of pleasant things, academic
and unacademic, if they can learn to live just as they
would like to live right up to the sunset, as they will
live if they are wise, then the race is won at the start.
The young Oxonian tastes the pleasant, varied things
in store for him beyond the University. On matri-
culation he is put squarely upon the two feet that are
to bear him to the end. He can work or play, or find
the golden mean.

So much, in theory at least, the liberty of the Oxford system allows him, this system without classroom

exercises, periodic examinations, or close scrutiny of his academic progress. Actually, however, he is guided on every side by the example of older students and dons, men who have caught the magic of Oxford and who are making life seem a thing of great ease and gracefulness. There is about Oxford, as about so many of the older English things, something Chaucerian, something of the grace of the Cavalier. Perhaps our fathers left our racial aptitude for lightness and joviality behind them with the easier life and surroundings when they spread out their Puritan canvas to the West. Certainly, we take our genealogies, our sports, our wars, and our learning much more seriously than the English take theirs.

The very setting of Oxford is a paradox, the paradox of life. Pigs would be out of place on most American campuses; they are always about your feet in Oxford; they gather especially about the steps of the Bodleian. Lean cows and sheep, too, are always under your windows. The whole soils of Berkshire and rich Oxfordshire move into the City of Towers once a week on market days. You can read Homer with Homer's men and Homer's beasts beside you; a sheep drover may turn out another Nestor when you get him into conversation.

The simplicities of life, the holy miracle of daily bread, the stark kingliness of poverty, the wealth of simple faith and belief,—these you can learn from unspoiled children of field and furrow right in the shadow of St. Mary's. The cabmen alone are as good as Rabelais for your education. You can look up from living books and see living men of all picturesque sorts around you. Besides, outside the City are a hundred villages where rich courses in uncommercial-

ized human nature can be had for the walking.
Great men of the cottages, "village Hampdens," can
join the great men of the colleges in teaching you that
life is a breathless beauty, that the commonest things
and the simplest are the brass and bronze that time
cannot move.

The scholars of the University can instruct one in
the Greek tenet of the golden mean, too. They go
out every afternoon, all of them, to row or hunt or
play cricket, just as they will do all their lives, not
because they are being loyal to their college or
because they wish to win from Cambridge, but simply
because they like to play games, and simply because
the games they play are, not prayerful exercises in
Spartan discipline or grimly weeded-out drills for the
very expert, but pleasant and sociable affairs for even
the inexpert into which tea can and does intrude always at the stroke of five,—tea for which the British
Tommy was wellnigh ready to stop the late War,—
tea that nearly disrupted one disgruntled American
regiment I know of, newly arrived into the paradox
of English life at old Winchester. All boys like to
play; they are boys for good and all, even when their
beards will be gray; so they play their games. So
runs the paradox of the scholars.

The athletes offer their paradox in turn. They
are men who can usually write astonishingly well and
who like books so well that their minds are full of the
figures of speech and rhetorical and humane orna-
mentation of great ideas even when they chase a football. I once heard a prince of rugby players recite
quite apropos a line of Virgil after a hard tackle had
smeared him with mud. No one ridiculed him. I

think some one went him one better and quoted Homer.

I am confident that there is not one such college in our country. The "blue" and the "first" at Oxford are absolutely as great in the undergraduate estimation. In fact, it is hard to tell them apart; for the "blue" is usually a scholarly man, and the "first" is probably an excellent man with an oar or bat. They mix the good things of life well.

But, best of all, there are the dons. It would be a strange sight in America to see a graybeard in running shorts pursuing a college boat and pushing people into the river as he ran, shouting and shooting a revolver likely; it would be doubly strange if that venerable runner were a professor of Latin. It is no uncommon sight at Oxford. Or a college dean, perhaps, pouring out port for one. What is there wrong about it? Why is it wrong to mix two zestful matters? I know a vice-chancellor of Oxford who, in a tall and respectable hat which one had to rescue from under the very wheels of a 'bus, led one through ploughland and thorn to show one a mediæval carving in a village church, a carving in which a bagpipe player piped and a listener held hands to his ears in self defense. Double symbolism. . . And to crown it all the august man led his undergraduate, on a short cut, straight into a barnyard.

Why should a vice-chancellor keep his pedestal always? It is not fair to his university to have him so. Oxford tutors like the picturesque in quaint and simple ways and men. November wheatfields are golden things, so are young men, likewise the learned. It is impossible to disentangle the threads of gold that make up the fabric of Oxford. The old are so young and the young so venerable in the wisdom of doing things wholeheartedly that age or station in life ceases to matter.

Why should one make education a matter of a hermit's cell, a bitter, a hard exercise, or even a compartment of life? There is no reason why aristocracy, good clothes, and good living are not best for right thinking. Oxford, since the day of Laud the most aristocratic of universities, has proved it. There is no reason why the glory of the mind should not go hand in hand with the glory of the body. So the Oxonian man of books plays games. There is no reason why learning should be uncomfortable, or should make a hedgehog of a man, or a pedant, or a dry statistician. Again Oxford proves it.

There is no justification for getting shut off by one's education from one's fellows, from one's sympathy with the lusty, grimy book of human nature that is a mender of roads. At Oxford one reads him, with other books. There is no call for learning to shut one away from other beauties in field flowers, in trees, in animals, from dawn and stars. There is no reason why learning should not make of you a richer man, a better father of a family, a playmate of boys, a lover of games, a greater lover of the old hills and the new babies, of talking and smoking, of wine and books and walks, of all things good and sweet and fair.

NOTES AND QUESTIONS

Robert P. Tristram Coffin is assistant professor of English at Wells College, Aurora, N. Y. He is a graduate of Bowdoin, 1915, where he was editor in chief of the college literary monthly and a member of Phi Beta Kappa. He spent a year as a graduate student at Princeton, where he took the degree of A. M. In 1916 he was elected Rhodes Scholar from Maine, and entered Trinity College, Oxford. When the United States entered the World War, he joined the Oxford University Officers Training Corps, and was later transferred to the United States Army, serving for two years as lieutenant in the Heavy Artillery. After the war he returned to Oxford, where he took the degree of Bachelor of Letters in 1921. He has written a volume of poems, *Christchurch*, and essays for various magazines.

In this article, one who knows college life, both in England and America, brings out some marked differences. It is the sort of article to set one thinking. We are all apt to take for granted that the thing to which we are accustomed—especially if it is agreeable to us—is the natural thing and probably the most desirable thing. And it takes a real intellectual effort to comprehend a thing widely different. Nearly all students in American colleges would agree in saying that college life is almost an ideal existence; indeed many of them consider it more important than the studies. Here comes a man to challenge our complacent belief.

The first thing to do is to find out exactly what he means. Re-read the paragraphs beginning ''There is a riddle to Oxford,'' to the end of the article. Then answer these questions:

Exactly what is the difference between the training given by Oxford and that given in our colleges?

What is the result, in later years, of this different training in youth? Look at a copy of the English ''Who's Who,'' and note that every person gives his recreation.

In what ways might our college life be modified to attain some of these results?

The outcome of your thinking might be expressed in a theme, devoting a paragraph to answering each of these questions.

Compare this article with Mr. Collier's paper on ''The Ethics of Ancient and Modern Athletics.'' In what points do the two articles agree?

THE ESSAY AS MOOD AND FORM*

By Richard Burton

IT is odd that while the essay as a distinctive form in modern literature is so well cherished and enjoyable, it has received so little expert attention. Books upon the drama, upon poetry in its many phases, upon the novel even, a thing comparatively of but yesterday, are as leaves in Vallombrosa for number; but books on the essay—where are they? It is high time the natural history of the essay was written; for here is a fascinating literary development which has had a vigorous, distinguished life of more than three hundred years in English, and which counts among its cultivators some of the abiding names in our native literature. Here is a form, too, interesting because of its relations to such other forms as fiction, which is connected with it by the bridge of the character-sketch; the drama, whose dialogue the essay not seldom uses; and such later practical off-shoots as the newspaper editorial and the book review.

This neglect of the essay is not altogether inexplicable. Scholars have been shy of it, I fancy, in part at least, because on the side of form—the natural and proper side to consider in studying the historical evolution of a literary *genre*—it has been thus fluent and expansive, a somewhat subtle, elusive thing. We

---

*From *Forces in Fiction and other Essays*. Bobbs Merrill Co. Reprinted by permission.

can say, obviously, that an essay is a prose composition. But can we be more explicit than this rather gross mark of identification? The answer is not so easy. Moreover, the question has become further confused by a change in the use and meaning of the word within a century. A cursory glance at the history of the English essay will make this plain.

Lord Bacon was, by his own statement, fond of that passed master of the essay in French, Montaigne. It is small wonder, then, that when, at the end of the sixteenth century, he put a name to his "dispersed meditations," he called them essays, after the Frenchman, using the word for the first time in our tongue. Not the name only but the thing was new. The form was slight, the expression pregnant and epigrammatic: there was no attempt at completeness. The aim of this early prince of essayists was to be suggestive rather than exhaustive—the latter a term too often synonymous with exhausting. Bacon's essays imply expanded note-book jottings. Indeed, he so regarded them. In the matter of style, one has but to read contemporaries like Sidney, Lyly, and Hooker, to see to what an extent Lord Bacon modernized the cumbersome, though often cloudily splendid, Elizbethan manner. He clarified and simplified the prevailing diction, using shorter words and crisper sentences, with the result of closer-knit, more sententious effect. In a word, style became more idiomatic, and the relation of author and reader more intimate, in the hands of this Elizabethan essay-maker. The point is full of significance for the history of this alluring form. Its development ever since has been from this initiative. Slight, casual, rambling, confidential in tone, the manner much, the theme unimportant in itself, a mood to be vented rather than a thought to add to the sum of human knowledge, the frank revelation of a personality—such have been and are the head-marks of the essay down to the present day. This fact is somewhat obscured by our careless use of the word at present to denote the formal paper, the treatise. The current definition of the essay admits this extension, and of course we bandy the word about in such meaning. But it is well to remember that the central idea of this form is what removes it forever from the treatise, from any piece of writing that is formal, impersonal, and communicative of information.

Little was done for the development of the essay, after Bacon, during the seventeenth century. But with Addison, Steele, and the "Spectator" in the early eighteenth, the idea is reinforced, and some of the essential features of this form are brought out the more clearly. The social, chatty quality of the true essayist is emphasized; the writer enters into more confidential relations with his reader than were ever sustained with the stately Verulam; and the style approaches more nearly to the careless, easy elegance of the talk of good, but not stiff, society. The "Spectator" papers unquestionably did more than any other influence to shape the mould of essay writing in English. At the same time, to speak, as some critics do, as if Mr. Bickerstaff originated the form, is to overlook its origin with Bacon. The essay idea—this colloquial, dramatic, esoteric, altogether charming sort of screed—was cultivated quite steadily through the eighteenth century. It became, as a rule, more ponderous in the hands of Johnson, and was in danger of taking on a didactic, hortatory tone foreign to its nature; yet occasionally in the "Rambler" papers Johnson exhibits a lightness of touch and tone that is surprising, and that suggests that we have perhaps regarded the dictator as too exclusively a wielder of sesquipedalian words. That this God of the Coffee House had a clear and correct idea of the essay is shown by his own description of it: "A loose sally of the mind," he says, "an irregular, indigested piece, not a regular and orderly performance."

Goldsmith, a light-horse soldier in contrast with Johnson, full panoplied and armed cap-à-pie, broadened the essay for literary and social discussion, although Grub Street necessity led him at times to become encyclopedic; and he was never happier than when, as in the "Reverie at The Boar's Head Tavern, Eastcheap," he played upon some whimsical theme, pizzicato, surcharging it with his genial personality. Minor writers, too, in the late eighteenth century had a hand in the development, none more so, to my mind, than the letter and fiction makers, Chesterfield and Walpole, Lady Mary Wortley Montagu and Fanny Burney—these and that inimitable fuss and chronicler, Boswell. If one would know how society talked in the second half of that Tea-Cup century, one must read not the dialogue of the novelists, where the art is too new to have caught quite the accent of life, but these off-hand epistles dashed off without a thought of print—to print were half-way vulgar then—and hence possessing all the freshness and naturalness of life itself, the ideal essay note. We may be thankful that as yet the habit of publishing everything, from one's thrills to one's table tastes, had not gained popularity: those ladies and gentlemen could afford to be charmingly unreserved in their private correspondence. To-day, in the very act of penning a note, intrudes the horrid thought that it may be incorporated as an integral part of one's "works."

The letter, as a literary form, offers an interesting line of side inquiry in connection with the essay. It has influenced that form beyond doubt, and is in a sense contributory to it. In the same way, dialogue—a modern instance like Landor comes to mind—has had its share in shaping so protean a form.

But it was reserved for the nineteenth century to contribute, in the person of Charles Lamb, the most brilliant exemplar of the essay, the prince of this especial literary mood—not primarily a thinker, a knowledge-bringer, a critic; but just a unique personality expressing his ego in his own fascinating way, making the past pay rich toll, yet always himself; and finding the essay accommodative of his whimsical vagaries, his delicious inconsistencies, his deep-toned, lovable nature. And that incomparable manner of his! 'Tis at once richly complex and tremulously simple, an instrument of wide range from out whose keys a soul vibrant to the full meaning of humanity might call spirits of earth and heaven in exquisite evocations and cadences at times almost too piercing sweet. Turn to the Elia papers and see how perfectly this magic of Lamb's illustrates and supports the qualities of mood and form I am naming as typical of the essay as an historic growth. The themes, how desultory, audacious, trivial, even grotesque! The only possible justification for a Dissertation on Roast Pig is the paper itself. Note, too, how brief some of the choicest essays are—half a dozen small pages, even less—and with what seeming carelessness they vary, stretching themselves at will to four times their normal

length. Study the construction of any famous essay
to see if it can be called close-knit, organic, and you
will find a lovely disregard of any such intention.

The immortal "Mrs. Battle's Opinions on Whist"
gives a capital example. If you turn to the end of
that inimitable deliverance you will find it to contain
one of the most charming digressions in all literature.
Lamb leaves that delicious old gentlewoman for a moment, to speak of Cousin Bridget, Bridget Elia, the
tragic sister Mary of his house; and playfully, tender-
ly, picturing their game at cards, he forgets all else
and never returns to Mrs. Battle. But who cares?
Is not lack of organic connection (to call it by so
harsh a name) more than justified by that homely-
heartful picture of Charles and Mary Lamb, bent over
their "mere shade of play," a game not for shillings
but for fun—nay, for love. "Bridget and I should
be ever playing," says he, and the reader is charmed
and stirred clean out of all thought of Mrs. Battle.
It is ever so with your essayist to the manner born!
To wander and digress is with him a natural right.
He is never happier than when he is playing mad
pranks with logic, respectability, and the mother-
tongue. Yet should his temperament be sensitive, his
nature broad, deep, and noble. The querulous-gentle
Elia was surely of this race.

To turn from Lamb to any contemporary is an
effect of anticlimax. None other was like to him for
quality. Yet Hazlitt and Hunt were his helpers, doing good work in extending the gamut of this esoteric
mood in literature. De Quincey, too, though losing
the essay touch again and again because of didacticism
and a sort of formal, stately eloquence, wrote papers
in the true tradition of the essayist. Passages in the

"Opium Eater" are of this peculiar tone; and that great writer's intense subjectivity is always in his favor—since the genuine essay-maker must be frankly an egoist. Hunt is at times so charming, so light of touch, so atmospheric in quality that he deserves to be set high among essayists of the early century. A man who could produce such delicately graceful vignette work as his sketches of the Old Lady and the old Gentleman was a true commensal of Lamb. In such bits of writing the mood and manner are everything, the theme is naught; the man back of the theme is as important in the production of the essay as is the man back of the gun in warfare. Herein lies Hunt's chief claim on our grateful remembrance—here, and in certain of his verses, rather than in the more elaborate papers to be found in such a volume as "Imagination and Fancy."

But already we must begin to recognize in writers like Hunt, Hazlitt, and De Quincey, and still more in later men, a tendency distinctly modern and on the whole antagonistic to the peculiar virtues of the esoteric essay, the *causerie* of literature: it is moving fast toward the objective, rounded out, formally arranged treatise. It becomes argumentative-critical, acquisitive-logical, expository, laden with thought. Hence, when we reach masters like Ruskin, Carlyle, Arnold, we see what is natural to them as essayists in one sense deflected into other, and no doubt quite as welcome, forms: one and all they have messages, and missions. Now, your *bona fide* essayist has nothing of the kind. He would simply buttonhole you for a half-hour while he talks garrulously, without a thought of purpose, about the world, and himself, especially the latter. Splendid blooms grow from out the soil which gives us our Ruskins and Carlyles; but when we are considering this sensitive plant of the literary garden, it were well to agree that it is another thing, and to save for its designation the word essay. Nor is this to deny essay touches, essay moments, essay qualities to Ruskin or Carlyle: it is only to make the point that their strenuous aim and habitual manner, so far as they went, were against the production of a very different kind of literature.

Earlier American writings have at least supplied one real essayist to the general body of English literature, the genial Irving, who was nurtured on the best eighteenth-century models and carried on the tradition of the "Spectator" and Goldsmith in papers which have just the desired tone of genteel talk, the air of good society. There are hints in Benjamin Franklin that, had politics not engulfed him, as they afterward did Lowell, he might have shown himself to the essay born. Irving is sometimes spoken of as a fictionist, but all his stories have the essay mood and manner; and he had the good sense practically never to abandon that gentle *genre*. His work always possesses the essay touch both in description and the hitting-off of character; thus offering an illustration of the fact that the essay, by way of the character sketch, debouches upon the broad and beaten highway of the novel, the main road of our modern literature. There are plenty of Irving's papers which it is rather puzzling to name as either essay or fiction— "The Fat Gentleman," for example. A later and very true American essayist, Dr. Holmes, furnishes the same puzzle in the "Autocrat" series. They have dialogue, dramatic characterization, even some slight story interest. Why not fiction then? Because the trail of the genuine essayist is everywhere; the characters, the dramatic setting, are but devices for the freer expression of Dr. Holmes's own delightful personality, which, as Mr. Howells testifies, Holmes liked to objectify. It is our intimate relation with him that we care about in converse with the essayist born: we sit down to enjoy his views. The fictionist's purpose, contrariwise, is to show life in a representative section of it, and with dramatic interplay of personalities moving to a certain crescendo of interest called the climax.

And so Dr. Holmes remains one of our most distinctive and acceptable essayists of the social sort; possessing, I mean, that gift, perhaps best seen with the French, of making vivid one's sense of one's relation to other men and women in the social organism. It is the triumph of this kind of essay to be at once individualistic and social, without eccentricity, on the one hand, or vulgarity, on the other. Vulgarity, by the way, is a quality impossible to the heaven-called essayist: it can be better tolerated in poetry even. For the intimacy between the essayist and his reader—I say "reader" rather than "audience," with a feeling that the relation is a sort of solitude *à deux* —is greater than in the case of any other form of literary expression. Hence, when one enters, as it were, the inner rooms of a friend's house, any hint of the *borné* is more quickly detected, the more surely insufferable.

The voice of a natural essayist like Thoreau is somewhat muffled by being forced now and then into the public pulpit manner. Yet an essay-writer by instinct he certainly is, particularly in his journal, but often in the more formal chroniclings of his

unique contact with nature. In Emerson, too, we encounter a writer with a vocation for the essay, but
having other fish to fry—doubtless a loftier but a
different aim. No man, English or American, has a
literary manner which makes the essay an inspired
chat more than the Concord Sage-Singer; and the inspired chat comes close to being the beau-ideal of
your true-blue essayist. With less strenuousness of
purpose and just a bit more of human frailty—or,
at least, of sympathy with the frail—here were indeed
a prince in this kind!

How much of the allurement of the essay style did
Lowell keep, however scholarlike his quest, in papers
literary, historical, even philological! In a veritable
essay-subject like "On a Certain Condescension in
Foreigners," he displays himself as of the right line
of descent from Montaigne. There is in him then all
that unforced, winsome, intimate, yet ever restrained,
revelation of self which is the essayist's model, and
despair. In the love-letters of the Brownings may
be found some strictures by both Robert and Elizabeth
upon an early book of this great American's, which
must pain the admirer of the Brownings as well as
of Lowell. It displays a curious insensitiveness to
just this power of the Cambridge man's which made
him of so much more value to the world than if he had
been scholar and nothing more. One can hardly rise
from anything like a complete examination of Lowell's
prose without the regret that his fate did not lead
him to cultivate more assiduously and single-eyed this
rare and precious gift for essay—a gift shared with
very few fellow-Americans.

A glance among later Victorian prose writers must
convince the thoughtful that the essay in our special

sense is gradually written less; that as information comes in at the door, the happy giving-forth of personality flies out of the window. It is in shy men like Alexander Smith or Richard Jeffries that we come on what we are looking for—in such as they, rather than the more noisily famed. Plenty of charming prose writers in these latter days have been deflected by utility or emolument away from the essay into criticism, like Lang, Gosse, Dobson, and Pater; into preaching and play-making, like Bernard Shaw; into journalism, like Barry Pain and Quiller-Couch; into a sort of forced union of poetry and fiction, as with Richard Le Gallienne. All these and others still have been touched by fiction for better or worse.

The younger Americans with potential essay ability are also for the most part swallowed up in more "useful" ways of composition. Her old-fashioned devotion to the older idea of the essay makes a writer like Miss Repplier stand out with a good deal of distinction: so few of her generation are willing or able to do likewise. Mr. Howells has reached a position of such authority in American letters that what he produces in the essay manner is welcome—not because it is essay, but because it is he. His undeniable gift for the form is, therefore, all the better. Often he strikes a gait happily remindful of what the essay in its traditions really is: the delightfully frank egoism of his manner covering genuine simplicity and modesty of nature. Since "Venetian Days" he has never ceased to be an essayist.

The twin dangers with the younger essayists both of the United States and England are didacticism and preciosity. The former, I believe, is most prevalent in this country; and it is of course the death-blow

of the true essay. The danger of being too precious
may be overcome with years. We should not despair
of the essayist: no type of writer is rarer. The
planets must conspire to make him. He must not be
overwhelmed by life and drawn into other modes of
expression.

Our generation has been lucky to possess one English essayist who has maintained and handed on the
great tradition: I mean Stevenson. Although, in
view of the extent and vogue of his novels and tales,
Stevenson's essay work may seem almost an aside, it
really is most significant. He is in the line of Charles
Lamb. Where a man like Pater writes with elegance
and suggestion after the manner of the suave and
thoroughly equipped critic, Stevenson does a vastly
higher thing: he talks ruddily, with infinite grace,
humor, pathos, and happiness, about the largest of
all themes—human nature. From "Ordered South"
to "Pulvis et Umbra," through many a gay mood of
smile and sunshine to the very depths of life's welter-
ing sea, Stevenson runs the gamut of fancy and emotion, the fantasticality of his themes being in itself the
sign manual of a true essayist. In the "Letters" no
man using English speech has chatted more unreserv-
edly, and with more essential charm: it is the undress
of literature always instinctively stopping the right
side of etiquette, of decency. The Stevenson epistles
drive us on a still-hunt outside of the mother-tongue
for their equal, with little prospect of quarry save
within French borders.

The essay is thus a literary creature to the making
of which go mood and form; and the former would
seem by far the paramount thing. Great and special
gifts does it demand. 'Tis an Ariel among literary

kinds, shy, airy, tricksy, elusive, vanishing in the
garish light that beats down upon the arena where
the big prizes of fiction are competed for amidst noise,
confusion, and *éclat*. But ever in its own slight, winsome way does it compel attention, and gain hearts
for its very own. 'Tis an aristocrat of letters: nowhere is it so hard to hide obvious antecedents. Many
try, but few triumph in it. Therefore, when a real
essayist arrives, let him be received with due acclaim
and thanks special, since through him is handed on so
ancient and honorable a form.

NOTES AND QUESTIONS

Richard Burton (1861—), professor of English Literature
at the University of Minnesota, is one of a group of college
men, such as William Lyon Phelps of Yale, Brander Matthews
of Columbia and Bliss Perry of Harvard, who not only teach
literature but write it themselves.   Professor Burton was
born at Hartford, Conn., and attended Trinity College there.
later taking his doctor's degree at Johns Hopkins. He
taught English for a time at Johns Hopkins and at the University of Chicago before going to his present position as head
of the English department at Minnesota. He has done
much editorial work, serving as assistant editor of the Warner
Librarz of the World's Best Literature, and as editor of the
Living Literature Series.   His published works number more
than twenty titles, including poetry, essays, fiction, biography
and dramatic criticism.   Among them are: *Dumb in June,*
a volume of poems, *Forces in Fiction,* (essays), *Masters of
the English Novel,* (criticism) and *How To See a Play.*

Page 90, paragraph "Lord Bacon was."
Who was the earliest English essayist? In what sense did
he use the word essay? Where did he get the word?

Page 91, "the stately Verulam," A reference to Francis
Bacon, who held the title of Lord Verulam.

Page 92, paragraph "Goldsmith, a light-horse."
What other forms of writing influenced the essay? How
are these forms related to the essay?

Page 93, paragraph "But it was."

What place is given to Lamb as an essayist?   Do you notice that the author's style in this paragraph is different from that of the preceding paragraphs? What is the difference?   What is it due to?

Page 94, paragraph "The immortal Mrs. Battle."

What characteristic of the essay is brought out in this paragraph?

Page 97, paragraph "The voice of."

Explain the statement that an essay is "an inspired chat."

Page 99, Alexander Smith was the author of *Dreamthorp;* Richard Jefferies of *The Story of My Heart.*   Both are fine examples of the essay which reveals the personality of the author.

Could this paper itself be called an essay, as the author uses the word?   Why so, or why not?

THEME SUBJECTS

This paper gives, in a brief way, the development of the essay in English literature.   It naturally means most to one who is familiar with the authors discussed.   How many of them have you read?   Which one does Professor Burton's account tempt you to read?   Try an essay by this author, and then write out your impressions.

What is an essay?

The essay as "an inspired chat."

My favorite essayist.

THE DUTY OF EDUCATED MEN
IN A DEMOCRACY*

By Edwin L. Godkin

PERHAPS I ought not to say it, but college
graduates are not, as a rule, remarkable for the
amount of knowledge, properly so called, which they
bring away from the universities. Everything they
learn there in the way of languages or of science
makes a comparatively small impression on the great
mass of them. The great use of the college course is
the formation of the habit of attention and study at
the age when mental and other habits are most easily
formed. But a college education has a perceptible
general effect on the intellectual outlook. Its most
marked effect on men in relation to their duties to the
community at large is in raising their standards.
Their notions of how things ought to be done are
changed. They expect a good deal more in the character and attainments of public men, and in the order
of public business. The municipal government, for
instance, which the educated men would set up, if
they had their way, would be something considerably
different from any municipal government now in
existence. Congress and the State legislatures, too,
would be, if the suffrage were confined to college grad-

---

*From *Problems of Modern Democracy*, copyright, 1896 by
Charles Scribners Sons. By permission of the publishers.

uates, composed of another class of men from that
which now fills them. A very large portion of our
present legislation would never be enacted, and the
probabilities are that the ceremonial side of the government would be much enlarged. I remember that
two or three years ago President Eliot wrote in the
Forum pointing out that our municipal government
would never be what it ought to be until all our city
officials had received a special training for their work,
and he mentioned the various kinds of training which
they needed. Now this was distinctly the college
graduate's view of the matter. The popular mind was
not then occupied with the need or the difficulty of getting trained men for such work. It would have been
satisfied with men of ordinary honesty. The notion
that trained men were a possibility probably never
occured to the bulk of the citizens.

We should probably, in a college-graduate government, witness the disappearance from legislation of
nearly all acts and resolutions which are passed for
what is called "politics"; that is, for the purpose of
pleasing certain bodies of voters, without any reference to their real value as contributions to the work
of government. This would of course effect a very
great reduction in the size of the annual statute-book.
For, to the mind of the ordinary legislator of to-day,
the duty of pleasing the voters is even more obligatory
than the duty of furnishing him with good government. In this duty of pleasing the voters there is no
question that a college education as a rule unfits a
man. He cannot discharge it without a fight with his
ideals formed at a susceptible age. James Russell
Lowell furnishes an illustration of my meaning. He
was unquestionably as patriotic an American as ever

lived, and a thorough democrat. Democracy has
never received so fine a tribute as he paid to it in
Birmingham. But somehow, as an educated man, he
was out of tune with the multitude. The West never
quite took to him. The *New York Tribune* denied
him the right to be considered "a good American."
Senator Sherman and other Republicans wrote "Ichabod" on him when he supported Mr. Cleveland. The
cause of all this really was that his political standards
differed from theirs. He lived in an earlier republic of the mind, in which the legislation was done by
first-class men, whom the people elected and followed.
In a republic in which the multitude told the legislators what to do, he never really was at home. This
brings me to the question, what is really the attitude
of educated men toward universal suffrage today?
As a general rule I think they really mistrust or regret it, but accept it as the inevitable. Probably no
system of government was ever so easy to attack and
ridicule, but no government has ever come upon the
world, from which there seemed so little prospect of
escape. It has, in spite of its imperfections and oddi-
ties, something of the majesty of doom, and nobody
now pretends that any people can avoid it. There
has been, however, a notable change within forty
years, in the opinion of the educated class, as to
its value, owing to its numerous mistakes; but,
curiously enough, these mistakes seem often to be
due to the difficulty experienced in finding out
what its mind is. Its mass in countries in which
it exists is so large, that the process of interrogat-
ing it is one of extraordinary difficulty even for
the most expert. Politicians, of all varieties, think
they know what the people think upon any given

question of the day, but most of them are always
wrong. There could not be a better illustration
of this than the mistake made by Senator Hill,
Governor Flower, and other politicians in this State
about Maynard's nomination. They had the deepest
interest in knowing what the popular judgment on
this nomination would be, but fell into an immense
error about it. This difficulty is not likely to decrease, and is likely to produce a great many legislative follies; because, unhappily, it seems to be the
way of most politicians in all countries, when puzzled
or uncertain about the drift of public sentiment, to
choose the course which seems the least wise or most
childish,—meaning, by that, the course which seems to
promise most immediate gratification, or to display
most indifference to remoter results. One consequence
of this is that universal suffrage has taken the blame of
a great many mistakes for which it is not responsible,
and which have come to pass simply owing to want
of skill in questioning it on the part of law-makers.
But after all allowances and excuses have been made,
its errors are sure to be frequent and on a considerable scale. We may expect, for instance, such mistakes as our silver policy, with increasing frequency,
because the politics of the world are becoming more
and more a controversy between rich and poor. The
influential and the rich man are taking the place of
the feudal baron and the absolute monarch as objects
of popular attack, and moderate physical comforts for
all, or a "living wage," have taken the place of political liberty. But the rich man cannot and will not be
openly robbed. He runs no risk of having his head
cut off, or his property confiscated. He will probably be got at through experiments in taxation, or in

currency, which unfortunately rarely reach the precise objects at which they are aimed, and sooner or later, like the silver purchases, involve the whole community in great distress.

The idea that *distribution* must be, in some manner, reformed is taking greater and greater hold of the world, and the popular mind is so much impressed with what seems to be the injustice of the present system, that hardly any attention is paid to the size of the earth's dividend. And yet, to divide among the people of every country all the accumulated wealth there is in it, or to divide among them the annual yield of its land and labor, is one of the simplest of arithmetical problems. In no case would any such dividend make any material change in the condition of the great bulk of the population. There is no deduction from the operation of nature more certain than that the earth is not meant to afford much more than a fair subsistence to the dwellers on it. The mass of mankind have been poor from the earliest ages, simply because they multiply close up to the provision which the earth normally makes for them. They have always done so, and probably will always do so, in every country. It is true that their condition has improved since the introduction of steam into the work of production; but their content has not increased, and the contrast between their mode of life and that of the very rich remains about the same. There is no wider interval now between the house of the modern rich man, and the laborer's cottage, than there was between the castle and the hut of the Middle Ages. If all that needed to be done to make everybody comfortable and contented was to pull down the rich man's palace, and decree that no more should be built, the problem of modern politics would be easy. But the truth is that there is no cure for the evils of our present condition but a great increase in the produce of the earth, without any corresponding increase in population, and without any abatement in the industry, enterprise, and energy of the existing workers. When we think of the enormous resources of the globe which are still untouched, we are apt to forget that, in order to get at them, we have to go on breeding an increased number of men and women, who will keep alive, generation after generation, the old story of unequal and unjust distribution.

But to divide the earth's products equally, or anywhere near equally, among the people, would be to ignore the claims of superior talent, industry, or frugality upon the larger share, or, in other words, to ignore differences of character. I think most educated men will agree that in the long run our civilization could not stand this. All progress has been made hitherto on the competitive principle, which means giving the prize to the best man; and we can hardly conceive of it being made in any other way. To prescribe that no one shall do better than any one else is to reproduce China.

Now, in the presence of all this, the rôle of the educated man is really a very difficult one. No intelligent man can or ought to ignore the part which hope of better things plays in our present social system. It has largely, among the working classes, taken the place of religious belief. They have brought their heaven down to earth; and are literally looking forward to a sort of New Jerusalem, in which all the comforts and many luxuries of life will be within easy reach of all. The great success of Utopian works like

Bellamy's shows the hold which these ideas have taken of the popular mind. The world has to have a religion of some kind, and the hope of better food and clothing, more leisure and a greater variety of amusements, has become the religion of the working classes. Hope makes them peaceful, industrious, and resigned under present suffering. A Frenchman saw a ragged pauper spend his last few cents on a lottery ticket, and asked him how he could commit such a folly. "In order to have something to hope for," he said. And from this point of view the outlay was undoubtedly excusable. It is literally hope which makes the world go round, and one of the hardest things an educated man who opens his mouth about public affairs has to do, is to say one word or anything to dampen or destroy it. Yet his highest duty is to speak the truth.

Luckily there is one truth which can always be spoken without offence, and that is that on the whole the race advances through the increase of intelligence and the improvement of character, and has not advanced in any other way. The great amelioration in the condition of the working classes in Europe within this century, including the increasing power of the trades-unions, is the result not of any increase of benevolence in the upper classes, but of the growth of knowledge and self-reliance and foresight among the working classes themselves. The changes in legislation which have improved their condition are changes which they have demanded. When a workingman becomes a capitalist, and raises himself in any way above his early condition, it is rarely the result of miracle or accident. It is due to his superior intelligence and thrift. Nothing, on the whole, can be more delusive than official and other inquiries into the labor problem, through commissions and legislative committees. They all assume that there is some secret in the relations of labor and capital which can be found out by taking testimony. But they never find anything out. Their reports during the last fifty years would make a small library, but they never tell us anything new. They are meant to pacify and amuse the laborer,—and they do so; but to their constant failure to do anything more we owe some of the Socialist movement. The Socialists believe this failure due to want of will, and that Karl Marx has discovered the great truth of the situation, which is, that labor is entitled to the whole product. The great law which nature seems to have prescribed for the government of the world, and the only law of human society which we are able to extract from history, is that the more intelligent and thoughtful of the race shall inherit the earth and have the best time, and that all others shall find life on the whole dull and unprofitable. Socialism is an attempt to contravene this law, and ensure a good time to everybody independently of character and talents; but Nature will see that she is not frustrated or brought to nought, and I do not think educated men should ever cease to call attention to this fact,—that is, ever cease to preach hopefulness, not to everybody, but to good people. This is no bar to benevolence to bad people or any people, but our first duty is loyalty to the great qualities of our kind, to the great human virtues, which raise the civilized man above the savage.

There is probably no government in the world to-day as stable as that of the United States. The chief advantage of democratic government is, in a country like this, the enormous force it can command on an emergency. By "emergency" I mean the suppression of an insurrection or the conduct of a foreign war. But it is not equally strong in the ordinary work of administration. A good many governments, by far inferior to it in strength, fill the offices, collect the taxes, administer justice, and do the work of legislation with much greater efficiency. One cause of this inefficiency is that the popular standard in such matters is low, and that it resents dissatisfaction as an assumption of superiority. When a man says these and those things ought not to be, his neighbors, who find no fault with them, naturally accuse him of giving himself airs. It seems as if he thought he knew more than they did, and was trying to impose his plans on them. The consequence is, that, in a land of pure equality, as this is, critics are always an unpopular class, and criticism is, in some sense, an odious work. The only condemnation passed on the governmental acts or systems is apt to come from the opposite party in the form of what is called "arraignment," which generally consists in wholesale abuse of the party in power, treating all their acts, small or great, as due to folly or depravity, and all their public men as either fools or knaves. Of course this makes but small impression on the public mind. It is taken to indicate not so much a desire to injure the public service as to get hold of the offices, and has as a general rule but little effect. Parties lose their hold on power through some conspicuously obnoxious acts or failures; never, or very rarely, through the judgments passed on them by hostile writers or orators. And yet nothing is more necessary to successful government than abundant criticism from sources not open to the suspicion of particular interest. There is nothing which bad governments so much dislike and resent as criticism, and have in past ages taken so much pains to put down. In fact, a history of the civil liberty would consist, largely, of an account of the resistance to criticism on the part of rulers. One of the first acts of a successful tyranny or despotism is always the silencing of the press or the establishment of a censorship.

Popular objection to criticism is, however, senseless, because it is through criticism—that is, through discrimination between two things, customs, or courses—that the race has managed to come out of the woods and lead a civilized life. The first man who objected to the general nakedness, and advised his fellows to put on clothes, was the first critic. All genuine criticism consists in comparison between two ways of doing something, and it is by such comparison that the world has advanced. Criticism of a high tariff recommends a low tariff; criticism of monarchy recommends a republic; criticism of vice recommends virtue. In fact almost every act of life in the practice of a profession or the conduct of a business condemns one course and suggests another. The word means *judging,* and judgment is the highest of the human faculties,—the one which most distinguishes us from the animals.

There is probably nothing from which the public service of the country suffers more to-day, than the silence of its educated class; that is, the small amount of criticism which comes from disinterested and competent sources. It is a very rare thing for an educated man to say anything publicly about the questions of the day. He is absorbed in science, or art, or literature, in the practice of his profession, or in the conduct of his business; and if he has any interest at all in public affairs, it is a languid one. He is silent because he has not much care, or because he does not wish to embarrass the administration or "hurt the party," or because he does not feel that anything he could say would make much difference. So that on the whole it is very rarely that the instructed opinion of the country is ever heard on any subject. The report of the Bar Association on the nomination of Maynard in New York was a remarkable exception to this rule. Some improvement in this direction has been made by the appearance of the set of people known as the "Mugwumps," who are in the main men of cultivation. They have been defined in various ways. They are known to the masses mainly as "kickers"; that is, dissatisfied, querulous people, who complain of everybody and cannot submit to party discipline. But they are the only critics who do not criticise in the interest of party, but simply in that of good government. They are a kind of personage whom the bulk of the voters know nothing about, and find it difficult to understand, and consequently load with ridicule and abuse. But their movement, though its visible recognizable effects on elections may be small, has done inestimable service in slackening the bonds of party discipline, in making the expression of open dissent from party programmes respectable and common, and in increasing the unreliable vote in large States like New York. It is of the last importance that this unreliable vote— that is, the vote which party leaders cannot count on with certainty—should be large in such States. The mere fear of it prevents a great many excesses.

But in criticism one always has hard work in steering a straight course between optimism and pessimism. These are the Scylla and Charybdis of the critic's career. Almost every man who thinks or speaks about public affairs is either an optimist or a pessimist: which he is, depends a good deal on temperament, but often on character. The political jobber or corruptionist is almost always an optimist. So is the prosperous business man. So is nearly every politician, because the optimist is nearly always the more popular of the two. As a general rule people like cheerful men and the promise of good times. The kill-joy and the bearer of bad news has always been an odious character. But for the cultivated man there is no virtue in either optimism or pessimism. Some people think it a duty to be optimistic, and for some people it may; but one of the great uses of education is to teach us to be neither one nor the other. In the management of our personal affairs, we try to be neither one nor the other. In business, a persistent and uproarious optimist would certainly have poor credit. And why? Because in business the trust-worthy man, as everybody knows, is the man who sees things as they are; and to see things as they are, without glamour or illusion, is the first condition of worldly success. It is absolutely essential in war, in finance, in law, in every field of human activity in which the future has to be thought of and provided for. It is just as essential in politics. The only reason why it is not thought as essential in politics is, the punishment for failure or neglect comes in politics more slowly.

The pessimist has generally a bad name, but there is a good deal to be said for him. To take a recent illustration, the man who took pessimistic views of the silver movement was for nearly twenty years under a cloud. This gloomy anticipation of 1873 was not realized until 1893. For a thousand years after Marcus Aurelius, the pessimist, if I may use the expression, was "cock of the walk." He certainly has no reason to be ashamed of his rôle in the eastern world for a thousand years after the Mohammedan Hegira. In Italy and Spain he has not needed to hang his head since the Renaissance. In fact, if we take various nations and long reaches of time, we shall find that the gloomy man has been nearly as often justified by the course of events as the cheerful one. Neither of them has any special claim to a hearing on public affairs. A persistent optimist, although he may be a most agreeable man in family life, is likely in business or politics to be just as foolish and unbearable as a persistent pessimist. He is as much out of harmony with the order of nature. The universe is not governed on optimistic any more than on pessimistic principles. The best and wisest of men make their mistakes and have their share of sorrow and sickness and losses. So also the most happily situated nations must suffer from internal discord, the blunders of statesmen, and the madness of the people. What Cato said in the Senate of the conditions of success, *"vigilando, agendo, bene consulendo, prosperé omnia cedunt,"* is as true to-day as it was two thousand years ago. We must remember that though the optimist may be the pleasantest man to have about us, he is the least likely to take precautions; that is, the least likely to watch and work for success. We owe a great deal of our slovenly legislation to his presence in large numbers in Congress and the legislatures. The great suffering through which we are now passing, in consequence of the persistence in our silver purchases, is the direct result of unreasoning optimism. Its promoters disregarded the warnings of economists and financiers because they believed that—somehow, they did not know how —the thing would come out right in the end. This silver collapse, together with the Civil War over slavery, are striking illustrations to occur in one century, of the fact that, if things come out right in the end, it is often after periods of great suffering and disaster. Could people have foreseen how the slavery controversy would end, what frantic efforts would have been made for peaceful abolition! Could people have foreseen the panic of last year, with its widespread disaster, what haste would have been made to stop the silver purchases! And yet the experience of mankind afforded abundant reason for anticipating both results.

This leads me to say that the reason why educated men should try and keep a fair mental balance between both pessimism and optimism is that there has come over the world in the last twenty-five or thirty years a very great change of opinion touching the relations of the government to the community. When Europe settled down to peaceful work after the great wars of the French Revolution, it was possessed with the idea that the freedom of the individual was all that was needed for public prosperity and private happiness. The old government interference with people's movements and doings was supposed to be the reason why nations had not been happy in the past. This became the creed, in this country, of the Democratic party which came into existence after the foundation of the Federal government. At the same time there grew up here the popular idea of the American character, in which individualism was the most marked trait. If you are not familiar with it in your own time, you may remember it in the literature of the earlier half of the century. The typical American was always the architect of his own fortunes. He sailed the seas and penetrated the forest, and built cities and lynched the horse-thieves, and fought the Indians and dug the mines, without anybody's help or support. He had even an ill-concealed contempt for regular troops, as men under control and discipline. He scorned government for any other purposes than security and the administration of justice. This was the kind of American that Tocqueville found here in 1833. He says:[1]

"The European often sees in the public functionaries simply force; the American sees nothing but law. One may then say that in America a man never obeys a man, or anything but justice and law. Consequently he has formed of himself an opinion which is often exaggerated, but is always salutary. He trusts without fear to his own strength, which appears to him equal to anything. A private individual conceives some sort of enterprise. Even if this enterprise have some sort of connection with the public welfare, it never occurs to him to address himself to the government in order to obtain its aid. He makes his plan known, offers to carry it out, calls other individuals to his aid, and struggles with all his might against any obstacles there may be in his way. Often, without doubt, he succeeds less well than the State would in his place; but in the long run the general result of individual enterprises far surpasses anything the government could do."

Now there is no doubt that if this type of character has not passed away, it has been greatly modified;

---

[1] "Democracy in America," Vol. I., p. 157.

and it has been modified by two agencies,—the "labor problem," as it is called, and legislative protection to native industry. I am not going to make an argument about the value of this protection in promoting native industry, or about its value from the industrial point of view. We may or we may not owe to it the individual progress and prosperity of the United States. About that I do not propose to say anything. What I want to say is that the doctrine that it is a function of government, not simply to foster industry in general, but to consider the case of every particular industry, and give it the protection that it needs, could not be preached and practised for thirty years in a community like this, without modifying the old American conception of the relation of the government to the individual. It makes the government in a certain sense a partner in every industrial enterprise, and makes every election an affair of the pocket to every miner and manufacturer and to his men; for the men have for fully thirty years been told that the amount of their wages would depend, to a certain extent at least, on the way the election went. The notion that the government owes assistance to individuals in carrying on business and making a livelihood has in fact, largely through the tariff discussions, permeated a very large class of the community, and has materially changed what I may call the American outlook. It has greatly reinforced among the foreign-born population the socialistic idea which many bring here with them, of the powers and duties of the State toward labor, for it is preached vehemently by the employing class.

What makes this look the more serious is that our political and social manners are not adapted to it.

In Europe, the State is possessed of an administrative machine which has a finish, efficacy, and permanence unknown here, and on the absence of which Tocqueville comments and explains, and which it is, as all the advocates of civil-service reform know, very difficult to supply. All the agencies of the government suffer from the imposition on them of what I may call non-American duties. For instance, a custom-house organized as a political machine was never intended to collect the enormous sum of duties which must pass through its hands under our tariff. A post-office whose master has to be changed every four years to "placate" Tammany, or the anti-Snappers, or any other body of politicians, was never intended to handle the huge mass which American mails have now become. One of the greatest objections to the income tax is the prying into people's affairs which it involves. No man likes to tell what his income is to every stranger, much less to a politician, which our collectors are sure to be. Secrecy on the part of the collector is, in fact, essential to reconcile people to it in England or Germany, where it is firmly established; but our collectors sell their lists to the newspapers in order to make the contributors pay up.

In all these things we are trying to meet the burden and responsibilities of much older societies with the machinery of a much earlier and simpler state of things. It is high time to halt in this progress until our administrative system has been brought up to the level even of our present requirements. It is quite true that, with our system of State and Federal Constitutions laying prohibitions on the Legislature and Congress, any great extension of the sphere of government in our time seems very unlikely. Yet the assumption by Congress, with the support of the Supreme Court, of the power to issue paper money in time of peace, the power to make prolonged purchases of a commodity like silver, the power to impose an income tax, to execute great public works, and to protect native industry, are powers large enough to effect a great change in the constitution of society and in the distribution of wealth, such as, it is safe to say, in the present state of human culture, no government ought to have and exercise.

One hears every day from educated people some addition to the number of things which "governments" ought to do, but for which any government we have at present is totally unfit. One listens to them with amazement, when looking at the material of which our government, for the matter of that, all governments are composed, for I suppose there is no question that all legislative bodies in the world have in twenty years run down in quality. The parliamentary system is apparently failing to meet the demands of modern democratic society, and is falling into some disrepute; but it would seem as if there was at present just as little chance of a substitute of any kind as of the dethronement of universal suffrage. It will probably last indefinitely, and be as good or as bad as its constituents make it. But this probable extension of the powers and functions of government make more necessary than ever a free expression of opinion, and especially of educated opinion. We may rail at "mere talk" as much as we please, but the probability is that the affairs of nations and of men will be more and more regulated by talk. The amount of talk which is now expended on all subjects of human interest—and in "talk" I include contri-

butions to periodical literature—is something of which
a previous age has had the smallest conception. Of
course it varies infinitely in quality. A very large
proportion of it does no good beyond relieving the
feelings of the talker. Political philosophers maintain, and with good reason, that one of its greatest uses
is keeping down discontent under popular government. It is undoubtedly true that it is an immense
relief to a man with a grievance, to express his feelings
about it in words, even if he knows that his words will
have no immediate effect. Self-love is apt to prevent
most men from thinking that anything they say with
passion or earnestness will utterly and finally fail.
But still it is safe to suppose that one-half of the talk
of the world on subjects of general interest is waste.
But the other half certainly tells. We know this from
the change in ideas from generation to generation.
We see that opinions which at one time everybody
held became absurd in the course of half a century—
opinions about religion and morals and manners and
government. Nearly every man of my age can recall
old opinions of his own, on subjects of general interest, which he once thought highly respectable, and
which he is now almost ashamed of having ever held.
He does not remember when he changed them, or why,
but somehow they have passed away from him. In
communities these changes are often very striking.
The transformation, for instance, of the England of
Cromwell into the England of Queen Anne, or of the
New England of Cotton Mather into the New England
of Theodore Parker and Emerson, was very extraordinary, but it would be very difficult to say in detail
what brought it about, or when it began. Lecky has
some curious observations, in his *History of Ration-*

alism, on these silent changes in new beliefs *apropos* of the disappearance of the belief in witchcraft. Nobody could say what had swept it away, but it appeared that in a certain year people were ready to burn old women as witches, and a few years later were ready to laugh at or pity any one who thought old women could be witches. "At one period," says he, "we find every one disposed to believe in witches; at a later period we find this predisposition has silently passed away." The belief in witchcraft may perhaps be considered a somewhat violent illustration, like the change in public opinion about slavery in this country. But there can be no doubt that it is talk,—somebody's, anybody's, everybody's talk,—by which these changes are wrought, by which each generation comes to feel and think differently from its predecessor. No one ever talks intimately about anything without contributing something, let it be ever so little, to the unseen forces which carry the race on to its final destiny. Even if he does not make a positive impression, he counteracts or modifies some other impression, or sets in motion some train of ideas in some one else, which helps to change the face of the world. So I shall, in disregard of the great laudation of silence which filled the world in the days of Carlyle, say that one of the functions of an educated man is to talk,—and of course he should try to talk wisely.

NOTES AND QUESTIONS

Edwin Lawrence Godkin (1831-1902) is one of the important names in the history of American journalism. Born in Ireland, and educated at Queens College, Belfast, he entered journalism as a war correspondent, representing the London Daily News during the Crimean War. He came to the United States in 1856, studied law, and later became an editorial

writer for the *New York Times*.   In 1861 he established a
weekly journal called *The Nation*, intended for the thoughtful
discussion of current affairs.   In 1881 *The Nation* was merged
with the New York *Evening Post*, and Mr. Godkin acted as
editor of both.   His strength as a journalist was not in the
field of getting more news than his rivals, but as a great
editorial writer.   His direct style, his clear-cut convictions,
his courage in asserting them, his vigor in attacking his
opponents, made the editorial page of his paper a great influence among thoughtful people.   His spirited opposition of
the "Spoils System" in politics, and his telling attacks
upon Tammany Hall are examples of his attitude in public
affairs.   In addition to his work for *The Nation* he wrote
frequently for the leading magazines.   These articles have
been reprinted in book form, with the following titles:
*Reflection and Comment; Problems of Modern Democracy;
Unforeseen Tendencies of Democracy.*

Page 103, paragraph "Perhaps I ought."
What does Mr. Godkin consider is the great use of a college
education?

Page 105, "Ichabod."   A reference to a passage in the
Bible, I. Samuel, IV, 23: "And she named the child Ichabod,
saying, The glory is departed from Israel."

Page 104, paragraph "We should probably."
In the closing sentences of this paragraph, what contrast
is drawn between our government today and in earlier times?

Page 105, "This brings me."
What does he say is the attitude of educated men towards
democracy?   Test this statement by asking several educated
men.   This might be made a class project, each member
submitting the statement made in the first two sentences of
the paragraph to several educated persons, and then getting
a consensus of opinion.

Page 106, "our silver policy."   A reference to the attempt
to keep up the price of silver by passing a law requiring the
government to purchase it at a fixed price.   It led to a
financial panic, followed by hard times.

Page 107, paragraph "The idea that."
What statement is made here about the total wealth of

the world? What general statement about the cause of poverty?

Page 109, "Utopion works like Bellamy's." A reference to Edward Bellamy's novel *Looking Backward*, a glowing picture of a state of society in which all people were happy and prosperous, under socialism.

Page 109, paragraph "Luckily there is."

What statement is made about inquiries into the labor problem?

Page 110, paragraph "There is probably."

What does he say is the chief strength of democracy? Its great weakness? Can you give instances of the former? of the latter?

Page 112, paragraph "There is probably nothing."

What statement is made about educated men in this country? Can you name any exceptions to the rule?

Page 115, "*Vigilando, agendo, bene consulendo, prospere omnia cedunt*," (Lat.) By being watchful, by being active, by deliberating wisely, all things turn out prosperously.

Page 116, paragraph "This leads me."

What change does he say has come about in the relations of the government to individuals? Can you give recent instances which show this new attitude?

Page 120, paragraph "One hears every day."

Does Mr. Godkin believe in further extension of the power of the government? What is his reason? Do you consider it a sufficient reason?

On the whole, is Mr. Godkin an optimist or a pessimist?

What does he consider to be the duty of educated men in a democracy?

Did he follow his own advice?

THEME SUBJECTS

The chief value of a college course.

Politics as a controversy between rich and poor.

Is democracy the right theory of government?

Discuss this statement: "There is no cure for the evils of our present condition but a great increase in the produce of the earth without any corresponding increase in population and without any abatement in the industry, enterprise and energy of the existing workers."

WHAT IS A NOVEL?*

By F. Marion Crawford

MY answer can only be a statement of opinion, which I make with much deference to the prejudices of my brethern. Whether it will be of interest to general readers I do not know; but the question I propose is in itself more or less vital as regards novel-writing. No one will deny that truism. Before going to work it is important to know what one means to do. I pretend, however, to no special gift for solving problems in general or this one in particular. To give "the result of one's experience," as the common phrase puts it, is by no means so easy as it sounds. An intelligent man mostly knows what he means by his own words, but it does not follow that he can convey that meaning to others. Almost all discussion and much misunderstanding may fairly be said to be based upon the difference between the definitions of common terms as understood by the two parties. In the exact sciences there is no such thing as discussion; there is the theorem and its demonstration, there is the problem and its solution, from which solution and demonstration there is no appeal. That is because, in mathematics, every word is defined before it is used and is almost meaningless until it has been defined.

---

*This essay was later printed under the title *The Novel: What it is.*

It has been remarked by a very great authority concerning the affairs of men that "there is no end of the making of books," and to judge from appearances the statement is even more true to-day than when it was first made. Especially of the making of novels there is no end, in these times of latter-day literature. No doubt many wise and good persons and many excellent critics devoutly wish that there might be; but they are not at present strong enough to stand against us, the army of fiction-makers, because we are many, and most of us do not know how to do anything else, and have grown gray in doing this particular kind of work, and are dependent upon it for bread as well as butter; and lastly and chiefly, because we are heavily backed, as a body, by the capital of the publisher, of which we desire to obtain for ourselves as much as possible. Therefore novels will continue to be written, perhaps for a long time to come. There is a demand for them and there is profit in producing them. Who shall prevent us, authors and publishers, from continuing the production and supplying the demand?

This brings with it a first answer to the question, "What is a novel?" A novel is a marketable commodity, of the class collectively termed "luxuries," as not contributing directly to the support of life or the maintenance of health. It is of the class "artistic luxuries" because it does not appeal to any of the three material senses—touch, taste, smell; and it is of the class "intellectual artistic luxuries," because it is not judged by the superior senses—sight and hearing. The novel, therefore, is an intellectual artistic luxury—a definition which can be made to include a good deal, but which is, in reality, a closer one than it appears to be at first sight. No one, I think, will deny that it covers the three principal essentials of the novel as it should be, of a story or romance, which in itself and in the manner of telling it shall appeal to the intellect, shall satisfy the requirements of art, and shall be a luxury, in that it can be of no use to a man when he is at work, but may conduce to peace of mind and delectation during his hours of idleness. The point upon which people differ is the artistic one, and the fact that such differences of opinion exist makes it possible that two writers as widely separated as Mr. Henry James and Mr. Rider Haggard, for instance, find appreciative readers in the same year of the same century—a fact which the literary history of the future will find it hard to explain.

Probably no one denies that the first object of the novel is to amuse and interest the reader. But it is often said that the novel should instruct as well as afford amusement, and the "novel-with-a-purpose" is the realization of this idea. We might invent a better expression than that clumsy translation of the neat German *"Tendenz-Roman."* Why not compound the words and call the odious thing a "purpose-novel"? The purpose-novel, then, proposes to serve two masters, besides procuring a reasonable amount of bread and butter for its writer and publisher. It proposes to escape from any definition of the novel in general and make itself an "intellectual moral lesson" instead of an "intellectual artistic luxury." It constitutes a violation of the unwritten contract tacitly existing between writer and reader. So far as supply and demand are concerned, books in general and works of fiction in particular are commodities and subject to the same laws, statutory and traditional, as other articles of manufacture. A toy-dealer would not venture to sell real pistols to little boys as pop-guns, and a gun-maker who should try to sell the latter for Colt's revolvers would get into trouble, even though he were able to prove that the toy was as expensive to manufacture as the real article, or more so, silver-mounted, chiselled, and lying in a Russia-leather case. I am not sure that the law might not support the purchaser in an action for damages if he discovered at a critical moment that his revolver was a plaything. It seems to me that there is a similar case in the matter of novels. A man buys what purports to be a work of fiction, a romance, a novel, a story of adventure, pays his money, takes his book home, prepares to enjoy it at his ease, and discovers that he has paid a dollar for somebody's views on socialism, religion, or the divorce laws.

Such books are generally carefully suited with an attractive title. The binding is as frivolous as can be desired. The bookseller says it is "a work of great power," and there is probably a sentimental dedication on the fly-leaf to a number of initials to which a romantic appearance is given by the introduction of a stray "St." and a few hyphens. The buyer is possibly a conservative person, of lukewarm religious convictions, whose life is made barren by "marriage, or death, or division"—and who takes no sort of interest in the laws relating to divorce, in the invention of a new religion, or the position of the labor question. He has simply paid money, on the ordinary tacit contract between furnisher and purchaser, and he has been swindled, to use a very plain term for which a substitute does not occur to me. Or say that a man buys a seat in one of the regular theatres. He enters, takes his place, preparing to be amused, and the curtain goes up. The stage is set as a church, there is a pulpit before the prompter's box, and the Right Reverend, the Bishop of the Diocese, is on the point of delivering a sermon. The man would be legally justified in demanding his money at the door, I fancy, and would probably do so, though he might admit that the Bishop was the most learned and edifying of preachers. There are indeed certain names and prefixes to names which suggest serious reading, independently of the words printed on the title-page of the book. If the Archbishop of Canterbury, or General Booth, or the Emperor William published a novel, for instance, the work might reasonably be expected to contain an exposition of personal views on some question of the day. But in ordinary cases the purpose-novel is a simple fraud, besides being a failure in nine hundred and ninety-nine cases out of a thousand.

What we call a novel may educate the taste and cultivate the intelligence; under the hand of genius it may purify the heart and fortify the mind; it should never under any circumstances be suffered to deprave the one or to weaken the other; it may stand for scores of years—and a score of years is a long time in our day—as the exposition of all that is noble, heroic, honest, and true in the life of woman or man; but it has no right to tell us what its writer thinks about the relations of labor and capital, nor to set up what the author conceives to be a nice, original, easy scheme of salvation, any more than it has a right to take for its theme the relative merits of the "broomstick-car" and the "storage system," temperance, vivisection, or the "Ideal Man" of Confucius. Lessons, lectures, discussions, sermons, and didactics generally belong to institutions set apart for especial purposes and carefully avoided, after a certain age, by the majority of those who wish to be amused. The purpose-novel is an odious attempt to lecture people who hate lectures, to preach at people who prefer their own church, and to teach people who think they know enough already. It is an ambush, a lying-in-wait for the unsuspecting public, a violation of the social contract—and as such it ought to be either mercilessly crushed or forced by law to bind itself in black and label itself "Purpose" in very big letters.

In art of all kinds the moral lesson is a mistake. It is one thing to exhibit an ideal worthy to be imitated, though inimitable in all its perfection, but so clearly noble as to appeal directly to the sympathetic string that hangs untuned in the dullest human heart; to make man brave without arrogance, woman pure without prudishness, love enduring yet earthly, not angelic, friendship sincere but not ridiculous. It is quite another matter to write a "guide to morality" or a "hand-book for practical sinners" and call either one a novel, no matter how much fiction it may contain. Wordsworth tried the moral lesson and spoiled some of his best work with botany and the Bible. A good many smaller men than he have tried the same thing since, and have failed. Perhaps "Cain" and "Manfred" have taught the human heart more wisdom than "Matthew" or the unfortunate "Idiot Boy" over whom Byron was so mercilessly merry. And yet Byron probably never meant to teach any one anything in particular, and Wordsworth meant to teach everybody, including and beginning with himself.

I do not wish to be accused of what is called smart writing. It is much easier to attack than to defend and much more blessed to give hard knocks than to receive them. A professed novelist is perhaps not a competent judge of novels from the point of view which interests the reader, and which is of course the reader's own. We know the "*technique*" of the trick better than the effect it produces, just as it is hard for a conjuror to realize the sensations of the old gentleman in the audience who finds a bowl of goldfish in his waistcoat pocket. We do not all know one another's tricks, but we have a fair idea of the general principle on which they are done, and a very definite opinion about our own business as compared with that of the parson or the professor. We know our books from the inside and we see the strings of the puppets, while the public only guesses at the mechanism as it sits before the stage, watching the marionettes and listening to the voice from behind the scenes. A novel is, after all, a play, and perhaps it is nothing but a substitute for the real play with live characters, scene-shifting, and footlights. But miracle-plays have gone out of fashion in modern times, except at Ober-Ammergau. The purpose-novel is a miracle-play—and if it be true that any really good novel can be dramatized, nothing short of a miracle could put a purpose-novel on the boards.

Most people have a very clear conception of what a good play ought to be, and of the precise extent to which realism can be effective without being offensive. But it is strange, and it is a bad sign of the times, that persons who would not tolerate a coarse play read novels little, if at all, short of indecent. An answer suggests itself which may be comprehensive as an explantation, but is insufficient as an excuse. In our Anglo-Saxon social system the young girl is everywhere, and, if the shade of Sterne will allow me to say so, we temper the wind of our realism to the sensitive innocence of the ubiquitous lamb. Once admit that the young girl is to have the freedom of our theatre, and it follows, and ought to follow and very generally does follow, that our plays must be suited to maiden ears and eyes. It is a good thing that this should be so, but the effect is rather strange. The men who hear plays in English are not, perhaps, much more moral than their contemporaries of Paris, Vienna, and Berlin. We like to believe that our women are better than those of foreign nations. We owe it to them to put more faith in them because they are our own, dear mothers and wives and sisters and daughters, for whom, if we be men, we mean to do all that men can do. But we are all men and women nevertheless, and human, and we have the thoughts and the understanding of men and women and not of school-girls. Yet the school-girl practically decides what we are to hear at the theatre and, so far as our own language is concerned, determines to a great extent what we are to read.

Yet the taste for "realism" is abroad and in opposition to all this. Out of the conflict arises that very curious production, the realistic novel in English—than which no effort of human genius has sailed nearer to the wind, so to say, since Goethe wrote his *Elective Affinities,* which an Anglo-Saxon young girl pronounced to be "a dull book all about gardening." That our prevailing moral literary purity is to some extent assumed—not fictitious—is shown by the undeniable fact that women who blush scarlet and men who feel an odd sensation of repulsion in reading some pages of *Tom Jones* or *Peregrine Pickle,* are not conscious of any particular shock when their sensibilities are attacked in French. Some of them call Zola a "pig" with great directness, but read all his books industriously and very often admit the fact. When they call him names they forget that he writes for a great public of men and women—not young girls —and when they read him he makes them remember that he is a great man—mistaken perhaps, possibly bad, mightily coarse to no purpose, but great never- theless—a Nero of fiction. But Zola's shadow, seen through the veil of the English realistic novel, is a monstrosity not to be tolerated. We see the apparent contradiction in our own taste between our theory and our practice in reading, but we feel instinctively that there is a foundation of justice to account for the seeming discrepancy. Both are coarse, but the one is great and bold and the other is damned by its own smallness and meanness. The result of the desire for realism in men who try to write realistic novels for the clean-minded American and English girl is un- satisfactory. It is generally a photograph, not a picture—a catalogue, not a description.

A community of vices is a closer and more direct bond between human beings than a community of virtues. This may be because vice needs solidarity among those who yield to it in order to be tolerated at all, whereas virtue is its own reward, as the pro- verb says, and is happily very often its own protection —far more often than not in our day. This seems to be the reason why the realistic method is better suited to the exposition of what is bad than of what is good. Wordsworth and Swinburne are two realistic poets.

Most people do not hesitate to call Wordsworth the greater man. I need not express an opinion which few would care to hear, but so far as the relative effect of their works is concerned it can hardly be denied that, of the two, Swinburne appeals far more strongly and directly to sinful humanity as it is. Wordsworth speaks to the higher and more spiritual part of us, indeed, but too often in language which rouses no response in the more human side of man's nature which is most generally uppermost. These are but illustrations of my meaning, not examples, which latter should be taken among novelists—a task, however, which may be left to the discriminating reader.

It has always seemed to me that the perfect novel, as it ought to be, exists somewhere in the state of the Platonic idea, waiting to be set down on paper by the first man of genius who receives a direct literary inspiration. It must deal chiefly with love. For in that passion all men and women are most generally interested, either for its present reality or for the memories that soften the coldly vivid recollection of an active past and shed a tender light in the dark places of by-gone struggles, or because the hope of it brightens and gladdens the path of future dreams. The perfect novel must be clean and sweet, for it must tell its tale to all mankind, to saint and sinner, pure and defiled, just and unjust. It must have the magic to fascinate and the power to hold its reader from first to last. Its realism must be real, of three dimensions, not flat and photographic; its romance must be of the human heart and truly human, that is, of the earth as we all have found it; its idealism must be transcendent, not measured to man's mind but

proportioned to man's soul. Its religion must be of
such grand and universal span as to hold all worthy
religions in itself. Conceive, if possible, such a story,
told in a language that can be now simple, now keen,
now passionate, and now sublime; or rather, pray,
do not conceive it, for the modern novelist's occupation would suddenly be gone, and that one book would
stand alone of its kind, making all others worse than
useless—ridiculous, if not sacrilegious, by comparison.

Why must a novel-writer be either a "realist" or a
"romantist"? And, if the latter, why "romanticist"
any more than "realisticist"? Why should a good
novel not combine romance and reality in just proportions? Is there any reason to suppose that the
one element must necessarily shut out the other?
Both are included in every-day life, which would be
a very dull affair without something of the one, and
would be decidedly incoherent without the other.
Art, if it is "to create and foster agreeable illusions,"
as Napoleon is believed to have said of it, should represent the real, but in such a way as to make it seem
more agreeable and interesting than it actually is.
That is the only way to create "an agreeable illusion," and by no other means can a novel do good
while remaining a legitimate novel and not becoming
a sermon, a treatise, or a polemic.

It may reasonably be inquired whether the prevailing and still growing taste for fiction expresses a
new and enduring want of educated men and women.
The novel, as we understand the word, is after all a
very recent invention. Considering that we do not
find it in existence until late in the last century, its
appearance must be admitted to have been very sudden, its growth fabulously rapid, and its develop-

ment enormous. The ancients had nothing more like
it than a few collections of humorous and pathetic
stories. The Orientals, who might be supposed to feel
the need of it even more than we do, had nothing but
their series of fantastic tales strung rather loosely together without general plan. Men and women seem to
have survived the dullness of the dark age with the
help of the itinerant story-teller. The novel is a distinctly modern invention, satisfying a modern want.
In the ideal state described with so much accuracy by
Mr. Bellamy, I believe the novel would not sell. It
would be incomprehensible or it would not be a novel
at all, according to our understanding. Do away practically with the struggle for life, eliminate all the unfit
and make the surviving fittest perfectly comfortable—
men and women might still take a curious interest in
our present civilization, but it would be of a purely
historical nature. To gratuitously invent a tale of
a poor man fighting for success would seem to them a
piece of monstrously bad taste and ridiculously useless. Are we tending to such a state as that? There
are those who believe that we are—but a faith able
to remove mountains at "cut rates" will not be more
than enough to realize their hopes.

It may fairly be claimed that humanity has, within
the past hundred years, found a way of carrying a
theatre in its pocket, and so long as humanity remains what it is it will delight in taking out its
pocket-stage and watching the antics of the actors,
who are so like itself and yet so much more interesting. Perhaps that is, after all, the best answer to
the question, "What is a novel?" It is, or ought to
be, a pocket-stage. Scenery, light, shade, the actors
themselves, are made of words and nothing but words,

more or less cleverly put together. A play is good in proportion as it represents the more dramatic, passionate, romantic, or humorous sides of real life. A novel is excellent according to the degree in which it produces the illusions of a good play—but it must not be forgotten that the play is the thing, and that illusion is eminently necessary to success.

Every writer who has succeeded has his own methods of creating such illusion. Some of us are found out and some of us are not, but we all do the same thing in one way or another, consciously or unconsciously. The tricks of the art are without number, simple or elaborate, easily learned or hard to imitate, and many of us consider that we have a monopoly of certain tricks we call our own and are unreasonably angry when a competitor makes use of them.

But this is not the place for a study of methods. So far as I have been able, I have answered the question I asked, and which stands at the head of this article. But I have answered it in my own way. What am I, a novel-writer, trying to do? I am trying, with such limited means as I have at my disposal, to make little pocket-theatres out of words. I am trying to be architect, scene-painter, upholsterer, dramatist, and stage manager, all at once. Is it any wonder if we novelists do not succeed as well as we could wish, when we try to be masters of so many trades?

NOTES AND QUESTIONS

F. Marion Crawford (1854-1909) was one of the most popular novelists of the late nineteenth century. He was born in Italy, the son of Thomas Crawford, a noted American sculptor, and the nephew of Julia Ward Howe. His education was cosmopolitan: he was a student at St. Paul's school, Concord, N. H., at Cambridge University, England, at Heidel-

berg and at Rome.   In 1879 he went to India, where he
edited a daily paper and studied Sanskrit.   Returning to
America, he continued his studies at Harvard, and wrote for
various magazines.   His first novel was *Mr. Isaacs* (1882) a
tale of life in India.   It proved that he was a born story-
teller, and was the first of a series of novels, such as *Zoroaster*,
in which a story of today has its interest heightened by a
touch of oriental mysticism.   For the rest of his life his
residence was in Rome, where a year by year he wrote novels
which were welcomed by a great reading public both in
England and America.   Henry James speaks of him as a
man as "a splendid figure, romantic in all his gestures, so
handsome and vigorous, driving his boats fearlessly into the
most dangerous seas, building his palaces on the Mediterranean shores, travelling over every queer corner of the globe,
fearless and challenging and heroic."   His most successful
books were *Zoroaster, Saracinesca, A Roman Singer, Sant
'Ilario* (three stories dealing with Rome), *In the Palace of
the King, Via Crucis*, and *The Children of the King*.   As a
writer of fiction he belonged to the romantic school.   There
is in his novels no subtle analysis of character, in the manner
of George Eliot; no attempt to present the repulsive side of
life, in the manner of the realists, but a good plot, a picturesque background, and a lively interest that holds us to the end
of the tale.

Page 126, paragraph "It has been."

More novels are published each year than all other kinds
of books put together.   What reason for this is given in this
paragraph?

Page 127, paragraph "Probably no one."

What definition of a novel is set forth here?

What is Mr. Crawford's opinion of the purpose-novel?
None of his stories are of this type, but such novels as
Dickens' *Nicholas Nickleby*, Mrs. Humphrey Ward's *Marcella*,
Upton Sinclair's *The Jungle*, Winston Churchill's *The Inside
of the Cup*, Jack London's *Valley of the Moon*, and most
of the novels of H. G. Wells are examples of stories
in which the author has used fiction as a means to set forth
his views on social or religious subjects.   Think of the books
of this type you have read, and ask yourself whether you
"felt swindled" after reading them.

Page 130, "In art of all kinds the moral lesson is a mistake." This is a sweeping statement. Having begun with the declaration that the novel should not attempt to teach a lesson, Mr. Crawford now says that the poet, the dramatist, the sculptor, have no business to make their work the means of conveying a moral. Think this over, and see whether you agree.

Page 134, paragraph "It has always."

Here is an interesting description of "the perfect novel." What novel that you have read comes nearest to this? In what respects does it fall short?

Page 136, "Mr. Bellamy." The reference is to Edward Bellamy, author of *Looking Backward*, a novel which pictured an ideal state of society, attained by adopting socialism.

Page 136, paragraph "It may fairly."

Here is a new definition of the novel. Think it over, and tell whether you find it accurate.

THEME SUBJECTS

Mr. Crawford's two definitions of the novel.
Is the purpose-novel "a simple fraud"?
Is the novel a pocket stage?
The perfect novel.

WHEREIN POPULAR EDUCATION HAS FAILED

By Charles W. Eliot

IT cannot be denied that there is serious and general disappointment at the results of popular education up to this date. Elementary instruction for all children and more advanced instruction for some children have been systematically provided in many countries for more than two generations at great cost and with a good deal of enthusiasm, though not always on wise plans. Many of the inventions of the same rich period of seventy years have greatly promoted the diffusion of education by cheapening the means of communicating knowledge. Cheap books, newspapers, and magazines, cheap postage, cheap means of transportation, and free libraries have all contributed to the general cultivation of intelligence, or at least to the wide use of reading matter and the spread of information. In spite, however, of all these efforts to make education universal, all classes complain more than ever before of the general conditions of society.

Now, if general education does not promote general contentment, it does not promote public happiness; for a rational contentment is an essential element in happiness, private or public. To this extent universal

education must be admitted to have failed at the end
of two generations of sincere and strenuous, if sometimes misdirected, effort. Perhaps it is too soon to
expect from public education any visible increase of
public contentment and happiness. It may be that
general discontent is a necessary antecedent of social
improvement and a preliminary manifestation of increased knowledge and wisdom in all classes of the
community. Yet after two whole generations it seems
as if some increase of genuine reasonableness of
thought and action in all classes of the population
ought to be discernible. Many persons, however, fail
to see in the actual conduct of the various classes of
society the evidence of increasing rationality. These
skeptical observers complain that people in general,
taken in masses with proper exclusion of exceptional
individuals, are hardly more reasonable in the conduct
of life than they were before free schools, popular colleges, and the cheap printing-press existed. They
point out that when the vulgar learn to read they want
to read trivial or degrading literature, such as the common newspapers and periodicals which are mainly devoted to accidents, crimes, criminal trials, scandals,
gossip, sports, prize-fights, and low politics. Is it not
the common school and the arts of cheap illustration,
they say, that have made obscene books, photographs,
and pictures, low novels, and all the literature which
incites to vice and crime, profitable, and therefore
abundant and dangerous to society? They complain
that in spite of every effort to enlighten the whole
body of the people, all sorts of quacks and impostors
thrive, and that one popular delusion or sophism succeeds another, the best-educated classes contributing
their full proportion of the deluded. Thus the astrol-

oger in the Middle Ages was a rare personage and
usually a dependent of princes; but now he advertises
in the popular newspapers and flourishes as never before. Men and women of all classes, no matter what
their education, seek advice on grave matters from
clairvoyants, seers, Christian scientists, mind-cure
practitioners, bone-setters, Indian doctors, and for-
tune-tellers. The ship of state barely escapes from
one cyclone of popular folly, like the fiat-money delusion or the granger legislation of the seventies, when
another blast of ill-informed opinion comes down on
it, like the actual legislation which compels the buying and storing of silver by Government, or the pro-
jected legislation which would compel Government to
buy cotton, wheat, or corn and issue paper money
against the stock.

The educated critics of the practical results of public education further complain that lawless violence
continues to break out just as it did before common
schools were thought of, that lynch law is familar in
the United States, riots common from Berlin to
Seattle, and assassination an avowed means of social
and industrial regeneration. Even religious persecution, these critics say, is rife. The Jews are ostracized
in educated Germany and metropolitan New York,
and in Russia are robbed and driven into exile by
thousands. Furthermore, in spite of the constant in-
culcation of the principles of civil and religious liberty, new tyrannies are constantly arising. The tyrant,
to be sure, is no longer an emperor, a king, or a feudal
lord, but a contagious public opinion, a majority of
voters inclined to despotism, or an oppressive combination of owners, contractors, or workmen. From
time to time the walking delegate seems to be a formi-

dable kind of tyrant, all the more formidable because
his authority is but brief and his responsibility elusive. Popular elections and political conventions and
caucuses provide another set of arguments for the
skeptics about the results of universal education.
Have these not been carried on with combined shout-
ings, competitive, prolonged howlings, banners,
torches, uniforms, parades, misrepresentations, sup-
pressions of truth, slanders and vituperation, rather
than with arguments and appeals to enlightened self-
interest, benevolence, patriotism, and the sense of public duty? Are votes less purchasable now than they
were before the urban graded school and the State
university were known? How irrational is the preparation made by the average voter for the exercise of
the function of voting! He reads steadily one intensely partisan newspaper, closes his mind to all information and argument which proceed from political opponents, distrusts independent newspapers and
independent men, and is afraid of joint debates. Such
are some of the allegations and doubts of the educated critics with regard to the results of popular education.

On the other hand, the least-educated and most
laborious classes complain that in spite of universal
elementary education, society does not tend toward a
greater equality of condition; that the distinctions
between rich and poor are not diminished, but intensified; and that elementary education does not
necessarily procure for the wage-earner any exemption
from incessant and exhausting toil. They recognize
indeed that machine labor has in many cases been substituted for hand labor; but they insist that the direction of machines is more exacting than old-fashioned

hand work, and that the extreme division of labor in modern industries is apt to make the life of the operative or mechanic monotonous and narrowing. They complain that the rich, though elaborately instructed in school and church, accept no responsibilities with their wealth, but insist on being free to break up their domestic or industrial establishments at their pleasure, or in other words, to give or withhold employment as they find it most convenient or profitable. They allege that the rich man in modern society does not bear, either in peace or in war, the grave responsibilities which the rich man of former centuries, who was a great land-owner, a soldier, and a magistrate, was compelled to bear; and that education, whether simple or elaborate, has not made the modern rich man less selfish and luxurious than his predecessor in earlier centuries who could barely sign his name. They admit that the progress of science has made mankind safer from famine and pestilence than it used to be, but they point out that wars are more destructive than ever, this century being the bloodiest of all the centuries; that European armies are larger and more expensively equipped than ever before, and hence are more burdensome to the laboring populations which support them; while in the American Republic the annual burden of paying the military and naval pensions which result from a single great war is heavier, twenty-seven years after the war ended, than the annual burden of maintaining the largest standing army in Europe. Clearly, the spread of education has not enabled the nations to avoid war or to diminish its cost either in blood or treasure. If universal education cannot abolish, or even abate, in seventy years, the horrible waste and cruelty of war, can anything great be hoped from it for the laboring classes?

They complain also that the education of the employer and the employed has not made the conditions of employment more humane and comfortable; that almost all services and industries—agricultural, domestic, and manufacturing—are organized on the brutal principle of dismissal on the instant or with briefest notice, and that assured employment during good behavior and efficiency, which is almost a prerequisite of happiness for a reasonable and provident person, remains the privilege of an insignificant minority of well-to-do people, like judges, professors, and officers of financial and industrial corporations. How much has all this boasted education increased the intelligence and insight of even the best-educated and most capable people, if they still cannot devise just and satisfying conditions of employment in their own households, shops, ships, and factories? It is much more important that fidelity, constancy, loyalty, and mutual respect and affection between employer and employed should be fostered by the prevailing terms of employment than that more yards of cotton cloth or more tons of steel should be produced, more miles of railroad maintained, or more bushels of wheat raised. Those fine human qualities are the ultimate product to be desired. Have they been developed and fostered during the two generations of popular education? Or have dishonesty in labor, disloyalty, mutual jealousy and distrust between employer and employed, and general discontent increased?

These indictments against universal education as a cure for ancient wrongs and evils are certainly formidable; but they exaggerate existing evils and leave out of sight great improvements in social condition which the last two generations have seen. It is only necessary for us to call to mind a few of the beneficent changes which the past seventy years have wrought, to assure ourselves that some powerful influences for good have been at work in the best-educated nations. Consider, for example, the mitigation of human miseries which the reformation of penal codes and of prisons, the institution of reformatories, the building of hospitals, asylums, and infirmaries, and the abolition of piracy and slavery have brought about. Consider the positive influence toward the formation of habits of industry and frugality exerted by such institutions as savings-banks, mutual-benefit societies, and life-insurance corporations. Unanswerable statistics show that during the past seventy years there has been a steady improvement in the condition of the most laborious classes in modern society, the wage-earners, and this improvement touches their earnings, their hours of labor, their lodgings, their food and clothing, and the means of education for their children. Consider how step by step terrors have been disarmed, superstitions abolished, the average duration of human life lengthened, and civil order extended over regions once desolate or dangerous. Think how family and school discipline have been mitigated within two generations, and how all sorts of abuses and cruelties are checked and prevented by the publicity of modern life, a publicity which depends on the universal capacity to read.

Let us remember that almost all business is nowadays conducted on trust, trust that the seller will deliver his goods according to sample and promise, and trust that the buyer will pay at the time appointed.

Now, this general trustworthiness is of course based on moral qualities which inhere in the race, but these qualities are effectively reinforced and protected by the publicity which general education has made possible. Consider how freedom of intercourse between man and man, tribe and tribe, nation and nation has been developed even within a single generation; how the United States have spread across the continent, how Italy has been made one nation, and Germany one, and the Austrian Empire confederated from three distinct nationalities. Every one of these great expansions or consolidations has resulted in greater freedom of intercourse and in the removal of barriers and of causes of strife and ill-will. Moreover, on taking a broad view of the changes in civilized society since 1830, do we not see that there has been great progress toward unity,—not indeed toward uniformity, but toward a genuine unity? The different classes of society and the different nations are still far from realizing the literal truth of the New Testament saying, "We are members one of another," but they have lately made some approach to realizing that truth. Now, unity of spirit with diversity of gifts is the real end to be attained in social organization. It would not be just to contend that popular education has brought to pass all these improvements and ameliorations; but it has undoubtedly contributed to them all. Moreover, we find on every hand evidences of increased intelligence in large masses of people. If war has not ceased, soldiers are certainly more intelligent than they used to be, else they could not use the arms of precision with which armies are now supplied. The same is true of all industry and trade—they require more intelligence than formerly in all the work-peo-

ple. While, therefore, we must admit that education
has not accomplished all that might fairly have been
expected of it, we may believe that it has had some
share in bringing about many of the ameliorations of
the social state in the past two generations.

It is somewhat comforting to recall, as we confess to
disappointment with the results of universal education, that modern society has had several disappointments before of a nature similar to that it now experiences. There was a time when it was held that a true
and universally accepted religious belief would bring
with it an ideal state of society; but this conviction
resulted in sanguinary persecutions and desolating
wars, for to attain the ideal state of society through
one true religion was an end so lofty as to justify
punishing and even exterminating all who did not accept the religion. Again, when modern representative institutions were first put into practice it seemed
as if the millennium were near—popular government
seemed of infinite promise for the happiness of mankind. Were not all despotisms to be done away with?
Were not all men to enjoy liberty, equality, and
fraternity? It was a painful surprise to discover that
under a *régime* of general liberty a few could so use
their freedom as to gain undue advantages over the
many. It was a disappointment to find that superior
shrewdness and alertness could secure, under public
freedom and public law, a lordship such as superior
force could hardly win when there was little freedom
and little law. How high were the expectations based
on universal suffrage, that exaltation of man without
regard to his social condition, that strong expression
of the equality of all men in political power! Yet
all these successive hopes have proved in a measure

delusive. On the whole, the most precious and stable result of the civilized world's experience during the past three hundred years is the doctrine of universal toleration, or liberty for all religious opinions under the protection of the state, there being as yet no such thing in Christian society as one true and universal religion. We have all had to learn that representative institutions do not at present necessarily produce good government—in many American cities they coexist with bad government—and that universal suffrage is not a panacea for social ills, but simply the most expedient way to enlist the interest and support of us all in the government of us all. Never yet has society succeeded in embodying in actual institutions a just liberty, a real equality, or a true fraternity.

It was reasonable, however, to expect more from universal education than from any of the other inventions to which I have alluded. Public education should mean the systematic training of all children for the duties of life; and it seems as if this systematic training could work almost a revolution in human society in two or three generations, if wisely and faithfully conducted. Why has it not? It seems to provide directly for a general increase of power to reason and, therefore, of actual reasonableness in the conduct of life. Why is it possible to doubt whether any appreciable gain has thus far been made in these respects? I think I perceive in popular education, as generally conducted until recently, an inadequacy and a misdirection which supply a partial answer to these disquieting questions.

The right method of developing in the mass of the population the reasoning power and general ration-

ality which are needed for the wise conduct of life
must closely resemble the method by which the intelligence and reasoning power of an individual are developed. Let me next, therefore, present here in some
detail the main processes or operations of the mind
which systematic education should develop and improve in an individual in order to increase his general intelligence and train his reasoning power. The
first of these processes or operations is observation;
that is to say, the alert, intent, and accurate use of
all the senses. Whoever wishes to ascertain a present
fact must do it through the exercise of this power of
observation, whether the fact lie in the animal, vegetable, or mineral kingdom; whether it be a fact of
physics, physiology, sociology, or politics. Facts, dili-
gently sought for and firmly established, are the only
foundations of sound reasoning. The savage has
abundant practice in observation; for he gets his daily
food only by the keenest exercise of this power. The
civilized man, whose food is brought to him on a railroad, is not forced by these elementary necessities to
keep his observational powers keen and quick, and
many of his occupations call for only a limited use
of the observing organs; so that systematic education
must provide in his case against the atrophy of these
faculties. For the training of this power of observation it does not matter what subject the child studies,
so that he study something thoroughly in an observational method. If the method be right, it does not
matter, among the numerous subjects well fitted to
develop this important faculty, which he choose, or
which be chosen for him. The study of any branch of
natural history, chemistry, or physics, any well-con-
ducted work with tools or machines, and many of the

sports of children and adults, such as sailing, fishing, and hunting, will develop this power, provided thorough exercise of the observational powers be secured. For the purpose we have now in view, it is vastly better that he study one subject thoroughly than several superficially. The field within which the power is exercised may be narrow or special; but these words do not apply to the power. During this training in accurate observation, the youth should learn how hard it is to determine with certainty even an apparently simple fact. He should learn to distrust the evidence of his own senses, to repeat, corroborate, and verify his observations, and to mark the profound distinction between the fact and any inference, however obvious, from the fact.

The next function, process, or operation which education should develop in the individual is the function of making a correct record of things observed. The record may be either mental only, that is, stamped on the memory, or it may be reduced to writing or print. The savage transmits orally to his children or his tribe such records as his brain contains of nature's lore and of his experience in war and the chase; but civilized man makes continuous and cumulative records of sifted, sorted, and grouped facts of observation and experience, and on these records the progress of the race depends. Hence the supreme importance that every child be instructed and drilled at every stage of his education in the art of making an accurate and vivid record of things seen, heard, felt, done, or suffered. This power of accurate description or recording is identical in all fields of inquiry. The child may describe what it sees in a columbine, or in the constellation of Orion, or on the wharves, or in the market, or in the Children's Hospital, and its power of description may be exercised in speech or in writing; but for the benefit of the community, as distinguished from the satisfaction of the individual and the benefit of his family or associates, the faculty should be abundantly exercised in writing as well as speech. In this constant drill the conscience cannot fail to be refined and instructed; for to make a scrupulously accurate statement of a fact observed, with all needed qualifications and limitations, is as good a training of the conscience as secular education can furnish.

The next mental function which education should develop, if it is to increase reasoning power and general intelligence, is the faculty of drawing correct inferences from recorded observations, a faculty which is almost identical with the faculty of grouping or coördinating kindred facts, comparing one group with another or with all the others, and then drawing an inference which is sure in proportion to the number of cases, instances, or experiences on which it is based. This power is developed by practice in induction. It is often a long way from the patent fact to the just inference. For centuries the Phœnician and Roman navigators had seen the hulls of vessels disappearing below the blue horizon of the Mediterranean while their sails were visible; but they never drew the inference that the earth was round. On any particular topic or subject it may take generations or centuries to accumulate facts enough to establish a just inference or generalization—the earlier accumulations may be insufficient, the first grouping wrong, or the first samplings deceptive—and so the first general inference may be incorrect; but the method, rightly

understood and practised, leads straight to truth.   It
is the patient, candid, impartial, universal method of
modern science.

Fourthly, education should cultivate the power of
expressing one's thoughts clearly, concisely, and
cogently. This power is to be procured only by much
practice in the mother tongue, and this practice
should make part of every child's education from beginning to end.   So far as a good style can be said to
be formed or created at all, it is ordinarily formed
by constant practice under judicious criticism.   If
this practice and criticism are supplied, it is unimportant whether the student write an historical narrative, or a translation from Xenophon, or a laboratory
note-book, or an account of a case of hypnotism or
typhoid fever, or a law-brief, or a thesis on comparative religion; the subject-matter is comparatively indifferent, so far as the cultivation of accurate and
forcible speech or writing is concerned.   In cultivating any field of knowledge this power of expression
can be won if the right means be used, and if these
means be neglected it will not be won in any field.
For cultivating the habit of reasoning justly, however, there is one kind of practice in expressing one's
thoughts which has special importance, namely,
practice in argumentative composition—in the logical
and persuasive development of an argument, starting
from well-selected premises and brought to a just conclusion.

Let no one imagine that I am omitting poetry from
systematic education.   In that highest of all arts of
expression, the art of poetry, the four mental functions or operations we have now considered—observing, recording, comparing and inferring, and express-

ing—may be seen in combination, each often exhibited
to high degree. The poet's power of observation
often supplies him with his most charming verses.
Tennyson noticed that the ash put out its leaves in
spring much later than the other trees, and this is the
exquisite use he made of that botanical observation:

> "Why lingereth she to clothe her heart with love,
>   Delaying, as the tender ash delays
>   To clothe herself, when all the woods are green?"

The poet's power of describing, and of stirring and
inspiring by his descriptions, depends on the combination in him of keen observation, rare susceptibility
to beauty and grandeur, spiritual insight, and faculty
of inferential suggestion.   In four lines Emerson puts
before us the natural and spiritual scene at the Concord River on the 19th of April, 1775:

> "By the rude bridge that arched the flood,
>   Their flag to April's breeze unfurled,
>   Here once the embattl'd farmers stood,
>   And fired the shot heard round the world."

In twenty-eight words here are the whole scene and
all the essential circumstances—the place and season,
the stout actors, their rustic social state, the heroic
deed and its infinite reverberation. What an accurate, moving, immortal description is this! Even
for logical and convincing argument poetry is often
the finest vehicle. If anybody doubts this let him
read again the twenty-third Psalm from its opening
premise, "The Lord is my shepherd," to its happy
conclusion, "Surely goodness and mercy shall follow
me all the days of my life"; or let him follow the
reasoning of God with Job from the inquiry, "Where
wast thou when I laid the foundations of the earth?"

to Job's conclusion, "Wherefore I abhor myself and repent in dust and ashes."

These, then, are the four things in which the individual youth should be thoroughly trained, if his judgment and reasoning power are to be systematically developed: observing accurately; recording correctly; comparing, grouping, and inferring justly, and expressing cogently the results of these mental operations. These are the things in which the population as a mass must be trained in youth, if its judgment and reasoning power are to be systematically developed.

Let us now consider whether the bulk of the work done in free public schools for the mass of the children contributes materially to the development of the mental capacities just described. More than ninety per cent of the school-children do not get beyond the "grades," or the grammar school, as we say in New England. Now, what are the staples of instruction in the "grades," or in the primary and grammar schools of New England? They are reading, spelling, writing, geography, and arithmetic. In very recent years there has been added to these subjects some practice in observation through drawing, manual training, kindergarten work in general, and lessons in elementary science; but these additions to the staple subjects are all recent, and have not taken full effect on any generation now at work in the world. Moreover, it is but a small proportion of the total school-time which is even now devoted to these observational subjects. The acquisition of the art of reading is mostly a matter of memory. It is of course not without effect on the development of the intelligence; but it does not answer well any one of the four fundamental objects in an education directed to the development of reasoning power. The same must be said of writing, which is in the main a manual exercise and one by no means so well adapted to cultivate the powers of observation, the sense of form, and the habit of accuracy as many other sorts of manual work, such as carpentering, turning, forging, and modelling. As to English spelling, it is altogether a matter of memory. We have heretofore put much confidence in the mere acquisition of the arts of reading and writing. After these arts are acquired there is much to be done to make them effective for the development of the child's intelligence. If his reasoning power is to be developed through reading, he must be guided to the right sort of reading. The school must teach not only how to read, but what to read, and it must develop a taste for wholesome reading. Geography, as commonly taught, means committing to memory a mass of curiously uninteresting and unimportant facts.

There remains arithmetic, the school subject most relied on to train the reasoning faculty. From one-sixth to one-fourth or even one-third of the whole school-time of American children is given to the subject of arithmetic—a subject which does not train a single one of the four faculties to develop which should be the fundamental object of education. It has nothing to do with observing correctly, or with recording accurately the results of observation, or with collating facts and drawing just inferences therefrom, or with expressing clearly and forcibly logical thought. Its reasoning has little application in the great sphere of the moral sciences, because it is necessary and not probable reasoning. In spite of the common impression that arithmetic is a practical subject, it is of very limited application in common life, except in its simplest elements—the addition, subtraction, multiplication, and division of small numbers. It indeed demands of the pupil mental effort; but all subjects that deserve any place in education do that. On the whole, therefore, it is the least remunerative subject in elementary education as now conducted.

But let us look somewhat higher in the hierarchy of educational institutions. It has been roughly computed that about five per cent of the school-children in the United States go on to the secondary schools. In these schools is attention chiefly devoted to the development and training of the reasoning faculty? By no means. In most secondary schools of a high class a large part of the whole time is given to the study of languages. Thus in the Cambridge Public Latin School twenty-eight hundred and twenty lessons are devoted in the course of six years to the languages; to all other subjects ten hundred and seventy. At the Ann Arbor High School, in the seven distinct courses all taken together, there are twenty-seven hundred and forty-six lessons in languages, against forty-one hundred and eighty-four in all other subjects,—and this although many options are allowed to the pupils of the school, and the variety of subjects not linguistic is large. In the Lawrenceville School, a well-endowed preparatory school in New Jersey, twenty hundred and thirty-three lessons are devoted to languages, against nineteen hundred and seventeen devoted to all other subjects. Now, the teaching of a language may be made the vehicle of admirable discipline in discriminating thinking; but it is a rare language-teacher who makes it the vehicle of such thinking. The ordinary teaching of a foreign language, living or dead, cultivates in the pupil little besides memory and a curious faculty of assigning the formation of a word or the construction of a phrase to the right rule in the grammar—a rule which the pupil may or may not understand. The preponderance of language lessons in many secondary schools presents, therefore, great dangers. Moreover, in most secondary schools, among the subjects other than languages, there will generally be found several which seem to be taught for the purpose of giving information rather than of imparting power. Such are the common high-school and academy topics in history, natural history, psychology, astronomy, political economy, civil government, mechanics, constitutional law, and commercial law. These subjects, as they are now taught, seldom train any power but that of memory. As a rule, the feebler a high school or academy is, the more these information subjects figure in its programme; and when a strong school offers several distinct courses, the shorter and weaker courses are sure to exhibit an undue number of these subjects. I need not say that these subjects are in themselves grand fields of knowledge and that any one of them might furnish the solidest mental training. It is the way they are used that condemns them. The pupil is practically required to commit to memory a primer or a small elementary manual for the sake of the information it contains. There can be no training of the reason in such a process.

If now we rise to the course which succeeds that of the high school or academy, the college course, we find essentially the same condition of things in most American institutions.   The cultivation of the memory predominates; that of the observing, inferring, and reasoning faculties is subordinated. Strangest of all, from bottom to top of the educational system, the art of expressing one's thought clearly and vigorously in the mother tongue receives comparatively little attention.

When one reviews the course of instruction in schools and colleges with the intention of discovering how much of it contributes directly to the development of reasoning power, one cannot but be struck with the very small portion of time expressly devoted to this all-important object. No amount of *memoriter* study of languages or of the natural sciences and no attainments in arithmetic will protect a man or woman—except imperfectly through a certain indirect cultivation of general intelligence—from succumbing to the first plausible delusion or sophism he or she may encounter. No amount of such studies will protect one from believing in astrology, or theosophy, or free silver, or strikes, or boycotts, or in the persecution of Jews or of Mormons, or in the violent exclusion of non-union men from employment. One is fortified against the acceptance of unreasonable propositions only by skill in determining facts through observation and experience, by practice in comparing facts or groups of facts, and by the unvarying habit of questioning and verifying allegations, and of distinguishing between facts and inferences from facts, and between a true cause and an antecedent event. One must have direct training and practice in logical speech and writing before he can be quite safe against specious rhetoric and imaginative oratory. Many popular delusions are founded on the commonest of

fallacies—this preceded that, therefore this caused
that; or in shorter phrase, what preceded, caused.
For example: I was sick; I took such and such a medicine and became well; therefore the medicine cured
me. During the Civil War the Government issued
many millions of paper money, and some men became
very rich; therefore the way to make all men richer
must be to issue from the Government presses an indefinite amount of paper money. The wages of
American workingmen are higher than those of English in the same trades; protection has been the policy
of the United States and approximate free trade the
policy of England; therefore high tariffs cause high
wages. Bessemer steel is much cheaper now than it
was twenty years ago; there has been a tariff tax on
Bessemer steel in the United States for the past twenty
years; therefore the tax cheapened the steel. England, France, and Germany are civilized and prosperous nations; they have enormous public debts;
therefore a public debt is a public blessing. He must
carry Ithuriel's spear and wear stout armor who can
always expose and resist this fallacy. It is not only
the uneducated or the little educated who are vanquished by it. There are many educated people who
have little better protection against delusions and
sophisms than the uneducated; for the simple reason
that their education, though prolonged and elaborate,
was still not of a kind to train their judgment and
reasoning powers.

Again, very few persons scrutinize with sufficient
care the premises on which a well-formed argument
is constructed. Hence a plausible argument may have
strong influence for many years with great bodies of
people, when the facts on which alone the argument

could be securely based have never been thoroughly
and accurately determined. The great public discussion now going on throughout the country affords
a convenient illustration. For generations it has
been alleged that high tariffs are necessary in this
country in order to protect American workmen from
the competition of European workmen, whose scales
of living and of wages are lower than those of the
American; but until within four years no serious attempt has been made to ascertain precisely what the
difference really is between the cost of English labor
and of American labor on a given unit of manufac-
tured product in the several protected industries.
Such inquiries are complicated and difficult, and demand extensive and painstaking research with all the
advantages governmental authority can give.

The publication made in 1891 by the Commissioner
of Labor at Washington concerning the cost of producing iron and steel is the first real attempt to
determine the facts upon which the theory of a single
group of important items in our tariff might have
been based. This admirable publication is a volume
of fourteen hundred pages—mostly statistical tables.
One of Mr. Wright's carefully-stated conclusions is
that the difference between the direct labor-cost of
one ton of steel in the United States and in England is three dollars and seventy-eight cents. If we
allow the large margin of fifty per cent each way for
possible error in these figures, we arrive at the conclusion that the excess of the direct labor-cost of producing from the assembled materials one ton of steel
rails in this country lies somewhere between one dollar
and eighty-nine cents and five dollars and sixty-seven
cents, with the probability in favor of three dollars

and seventy-eight cents. Now, the duty on one ton of steel rails is thirteen dollars and forty-four cents; so that it is obvious that the amount of this tax stands in no close relation to the difference between the cost of the American and the English labor, and that some other motive than the protection of American *labor* determined the amount of the tax. Yet the argument that the high-tariff taxes exist for the protection of American wage-earners has long had great weight in the minds of millions of Americans who can read, write, and cipher. For my present purpose it is a matter of indifference whether the assumption which underlies this argument, namely, that workmen are not productive and valuable in proportion to their scale of wages and standard of living, be true or false. What I want to point out is that the argument has no right to much influence in determining the amount of taxes which burden the entire population, inasmuch as the facts on which alone it can be securely based are as yet wanting for a great majority of the pro- tected industries. Is it not quite clear that the people, as a whole, have not been taught to scrutinize severely the premises of an argument to which they are in- clined to give weight, and that popular education has never afforded and does not now afford any adequate defence against this kind of unreason?

Let me further observe that throughout all edu- cation, both public and private, both in the school and in the family, there has been too much reliance on the principle of authority, too little on the progressive and persistent appeal to reason. By commands, or by the authoritative imposition of opinions, it is possible for a time to protect a child, or a generation or nation of childish men, from some dangers and errors; but the habit of obedience to authority and of the passive reception of imposed opinions is almost inconsistent with an effective development of reasoning power and of independence of thought.

What, then, are the changes in the course of popular education which we must strive after if we would develop for the future more successfully than in the past the rationality of the population? In the first place, we must make practice in thinking, or in other words the strengthening of reasoning power, the constant object of all teaching, from infancy to adult age, no matter what may be the subject of instruction. After the most necessary manual and mental arts have been acquired, those subjects should be taught most which each individual teacher is best fitted to utilize for making his pupils think, or which develop best in the individual pupil his own power to reason. For this purpose the same subject will not be equally good for all teachers or for all pupils. One teacher can make her pupils think most eagerly and consecutively in the subject of geography, another in zoölogy, and another in Latin. One pupil can be induced most easily to exercise strenuously his powers of observation and discrimination on the facts of a language new to him, another on the phenomena of plant life, and another on the events of some historical period. If only this training could be everywhere recognized in daily practice as the supreme and ultimate object in all teaching, a great improvement would soon be wrought in the results of public instruction.

Besides recognizing in practice this prime object of all education, we can make certain specific changes in the common subjects or methods of instruction which will greatly further this object, and we can promote such useful changes as have already been introduced. Thus we can give wise extension to the true observation studies already introduced into the earlier years of the school system. Again, we can give much more time than is now given to the practice of accurate description and argumentative composition in writing. This practice should begin in the kindergarten and be pursued through the university. We expect to teach children to write English with a very small part of the practice they get in speaking English. With all the practice and criticism of their speech that school-children get every day, correct speech is by no means common. Should we expect to get correct writing with much less attention than we give to speech?

We must also teach elaborately in schools those subjects which give practice in classification and induction. The natural sciences all lend themselves to this branch of school work; but they must be taught in such a way as to extract from them the peculiar discipline they are fitted to yield. It is of no use to commit to memory books on science. A little information may be gained in this way, but no power. They must be taught by the laboratory method, with constant use of the laboratory note-book, and with careful study of trains of experimentation and reasoning which in times past actually led to great discoveries. Yet to study the natural sciences is not a sure way to develop reasoning power. It is just ,as easy to teach natural science, even by laboratory methods, without ever making the pupils reason closely about their work, as to teach Latin or German without cultivating the pupils' powers of comparison and discrimination. Effective training of the reasoning powers

cannot be secured simply by choosing this subject or
that for study. The method of study and the aim in
studying are the all-important things.

For the older pupils, the time devoted to historical
studies ought to be much increased; not that they may
learn the story of dynasties or of wars, but that they
may learn how, as a matter of fact, arts came into
being, commerce was developed by one city or nation
after another, great literatures originated and grew
up, new industries arose, fresh discoveries were made,
and social conditions were ameliorated. They should
discover through what imagining, desiring, contriving, and planning, whether of individual leaders or of
masses of men, these great steps in human progress
came to be taken. They should study the thinking
and feeling of past generations for guidance to right
thoughts and sentiments in the present and future.
It is a disgrace to organized education that any nation should refuse, as our own people are so apt to do,
to learn from the experience of other nations; the
schools must have failed to teach history as they should
have done. As Benjamin Franklin said, ''Experience keeps a dear school; but fools will learn in no
other, and scarce in that.''

In the higher part of the system of public instruction two difficult subjects deserve to receive a much
larger share of attention than they now obtain,—
political economy and sociology. They should be
studied, however, not as information subjects, but as
training or disciplinary subjects; for during the past
thirty years the means of using them as disciplinary
subjects have been accumulated in liberal measure.
They can now be studied in their elements on broad
foundations of fact, the results of scientific research;

and many of their fundamental principles can be placed within the reach of minds not yet adult.

Finally, argumentation needs to be taught systematically in schools; not in the form of a theoretical logic, but in concrete form through the study of arguments which have had weight in determining the course of trade, industries, or public affairs, or have made epochs in discovery, invention, or the progress of science. The actual arguments used by the participants in great debates should be studied, and not the arguments attributed to or invented for the actors long after the event. Books preserve many such epoch-making arguments; and during the present century many which were only spoken have been preserved by stenography and the daily press. For these uses, arguments which can be compared with the ultimate event, and proved true or false by the issue, have great advantages. The issue actually establishes, or disproves, the conclusion the argument sought to establish. As examples of instructive arguments I may cite Burke's argument on conciliation with the American colonies, and Webster's on the nature and value of the Federal Union; the debate between Lincoln and Douglas on the extension of slavery into the Territories; the demonstration by Sir Charles Lyell that the ancient and the present system of terrestrial changes are identical; the proofs contrived and set forth by Sir John Lubbock that the ant exhibits memory, affection, morality, and cooperative power; the prophetic argument of Mill that industries conducted on a great scale will ultimately make liberty of competition illusory, and will form extensive combinations to maintain or advance prices; and that well-reasoned prophecy of disturbance and disaster in the trade of the United States written by Cairnes in September, 1873, and so dramatically fulfilled in the commercial crises of that month. Such arguments are treasuries of instruction for the rising generation, for they furnish safe materials for thorough instruction in sound reasoning. We have expected to teach sound reasoning incidentally and indirectly, just as we have expected to teach young people to write good English by teaching them foreign languages. It is high time that we taught the young by direct practice and high examples to reason justly and effectively.

Such are some of the measures which we may reasonably hope will make popular education in the future more successful than it has been in the past in developing universal reasonableness.

NOTES AND QUESTIONS

Charles William Eliot (1834—) is one of the leading educators in America. He was born in Boston, his father having served as mayor of that city. He attended the Boston Latin School and Harvard College, graduating in 1853 with high honors. He began his teaching as a tutor in mathematics at Harvard, later becoming assistant professor of chemistry. The years 1863-65 were spent in Europe, where he studied the educational systems of France, Germany and England. In 1865 he was appointed professor of analytical chemistry in the Massachusetts Institute of Technology, and in 1868 he was chosen president of Harvard. This position he held for forty years, during which time he exerted more influence upon American education than any other man of his time. The elective system, as known in American colleges, was devised by him, and first put into practice at Harvard. He also served as chairman of a committee of ten on the reorganization of secondary education. The report of this committee had a marked influence upon the high school course of study. In 1909 he resigned the presidency of Harvard to devote himself to the cause of international peace. His achievements have been recognized by his appointment as a member of the

Legion of Honor of France, and a Grand officer of the Crown of Italy, besides other honors bestowed by Germany, Belgium and Japan. His chief published works are: *Manual of Qualitative Chemical Analysis; American Contributions to Civilization; Educational Reform; Four American Leaders; The Durable Satisfactions of Life; The Road Toward Peace.*

Page 140, paragraph ''Now if general.''

In what respects does Dr. Eliot say general education has failed?   What does he mention as evidences that people are not reasonable in the conduct of life?

Pages 142-4.   What further evidences are cited on these pages?   These statements are rather unpleasant truths: not many public speakers or writers have the courage to say them. Oliver Wendell Holmes remarked that ''when truth tastes like medicine, it is a pretty sure sign we are sick.''   Do these statements taste like medicine?

Page 145.   In the paragraph ''These indictments,'' and the following one, Dr. Eliot gives the other side of the picture. What are the chief ways in which he says that society has improved?   Are these improvements all due to education? Does he say they are?

Page 148, paragraph ''It is somewhat.''

What other disappointments of human hopes does he name? Note how broad a view he takes: he is writing about education, but he illuminates his subject by his knowledge of history, of politics, of industry, of the labor problem,—in a word, of our present civilization.

Page 149, paragraph ''The right method.''

What does Dr. Eliot name, in this and the following paragraphs, as the processes of the mind which education should develop?   Think over your last year's education, in various subjects, and see whether all these four qualities have been systematically trained.   Have they been equally trained?

Page 155, paragraph ''Let us now.''

In this and the next paragraph, what criticism is made upon elementary education?

Page 157, paragraph ''But let us.''

What criticism is here made upon our high school education?   From your observation, do these statements still hold true?

Page 159, paragraph "When one reviews."

What is the chief criticism upon our educational system as a whole? Do his instances bear out this statement?

Page 163, paragraph "What then are."

Note how, in most paragraphs, the first sentence shows clearly the line of thought to be developed in the paragraph. From this and the following paragraphs, summarize the changes named as necessary to make our education more effective.

THEME SUBJECTS

How far does my own education satisfy Dr. Eliot's four requirements?

How far do school activities train in these four requirements?

Present day instances of failure to reason correctly in common life.

What I have learned from this article.

IMMIGRATION AND DEGRADATION

By Francis A. Walker

TO me, as a student of the American census, the statistics of the foreign elements of our population have had a peculiar interest. To note the first appearance, in the web of our national life, of these many-colored threads; to watch the patterns which they formed as they grew in numbers during the successive stages of our development, was always a fascinating study. But, curious and even instructive as are inquiries into the varying aptitudes, as to residence and occupation, manifested by the several foreign nationalities represented among us, or into their varying liabilities to different forms of disease, of physical infirmity, or of criminal impulse, I shall confine myself in this paper to speaking of the influence exerted by our foreign arrivals upon the native population in the past, and to considerations arising upon the contemplation of the overwhelming immigration of the present time.

False and absurd as are many of the views prevalent in the old world regarding things American, there is no other particular in which European opinion has

170

been so grotesquely in the wrong, as in respect to the continuous immigration from abroad. Conclusions have been announced and unhesitatingly accepted in Europe, and, indeed, copied and repeated long without contradiction here, which are of the most astonishing character, in the highest degree derogatory to the vitality of our native American stock, and to the sanitary influences of our climate. Thus, Mr. Clibborne, in a paper entitled "The Tendency of the European Races to Become Extinct in the United States," read before the British Association for the Advancement of Science, in 1856, stated the following stupendous result of his investigation:

"From the general unfitness of the climate to the European constitution, coupled with occasional pestilential visitations which occur in the healthier localities, on the whole in an average of three or four generations, extinction of the European races in North America would be almost certain, if the communication with Europe were entirely cut off."

In speaking of entirely cutting off communication with Europe Mr. Clibborne did not, could not, mean such a painful severance of relations as would deny the American people the privilege of studying their own character and manners in the discriminating, dispassionate, yet genial narratives and essays of a Mrs. Trollope or a Lepel Griffin; but only such restriction of intercourse as would put a stop to Europeans coming hither, as seals resort to the Alaskan islands, to deposit their young, the proper fruit of more benignant climes. Were this constantly renewed supply of fresh blood from other lands cut off, Mr. Clibborne declared, the white race on this continent would soon become extinct.

With the readiness so characteristic of Europeans to swallow any opinion or statement of fact regarding Americans, provided only it be sufficiently disparaging, it is not to be wondered at that an Englishman should have been found to announce such a result; and that millions of Englishmen, Frenchmen, and Germans should have been found to believe and to repeat it; but unfortunately similar conclusions were at about the same time promulgated by two persons resident in the United States, assuming the air, at least, of careful sociological investigators. In the same year that Mr. Clibborne's paper was read, Mr. Louis Schade, of Washington, put forward some elaborate statistical computations to establish the proposition that the rate of natural increase in the descendants of the original population of the United States, in 1790, had, by that time, been reduced to 1.38 per cent. per annum. Vastly the greater part of the mighty increase which had raised the four millions of 1790 to the twenty-eight millions of 1856, Mr. Schade attributed to the fecundity of the immigrants into the country subsequent to 1790. I trust that it is not below the dignity of this magazine to allow me to say that Mr. Schade's elaborate demonstration of the decay of reproductive vigor among the elder population of the United States was simply bosh. Blunder had been piled upon blunder to reach this Olympian height of absurdity. Yet so lacking was this country in trained statisticians competent to deal with such a piece of charlatanry, that Mr. Schade's conclusions remained unchallenged at home, and were widely circulated abroad, to the confusion of all good Americans.

In 1870 Mr. Frederic Kapp, a scholar and a man of some pretensions to statesmanship, read a paper before the American Social Science Association, in which he warmly supported Mr. Schade's views, giving that person much credit for his original and penetrating methods of statistical analysis. Original they certainly were. Mr. Kapp proceeded, by methods entitled to equal praise on the same account, to complete the work in this field, reaching the conclusion that, of the population' of 1850, but 36 per cent., and of the population of 1860, but 29 per cent. were American, in the sense of being derived from the inhabitants of 1790, all the vast remainder consisting of the survivors or the descendants of immigrants since that date.

By this time it was not so easy or safe an exploit to pluck the feathers of the American eagle. Statistics had begun to be cultivated in a small way here; and Kapp's performance called forth a reply from the late Dr. Edward Jarvis, the first president of the American Statistical Association. Dr. Jarvis's paper will be found in the "Atlantic Monthly" for 1872. In it he completely demolished the flimsy structures which Schade and Kapp had reared. Time will not serve to follow Dr. Jarvis's exposure of the successive statistical blunders which had allowed conclusions so disparaging to the vitality of our people. Two instances will suffice. Mr. Schade had confounded the number of children surviving at the end of a year with the number of children born during the year; the fact being that from 109 to 115 or more children (according to conditions of infant life prevailing in the community) must be born during a year, in order that 100 shall survive at the end of it. Mr. Kapp, on his part, had to his own satisfaction established a natural increase of the foreigners supposed, in the absence of exact data, to have arrived in the country between 1790 and 1800, which would have required every female among them to bear 18.07 children each year, to satisfy the requirements of the assumption. Dr. Jarvis reached the conclusion that of the population of 1850, more than 80 per cent., and of the population of 1860, more than 71 per cent., were American in the sense given to that word by Mr. Kapp, instead of only 36 and 29 per cent. respectively, according to the deductions of that writer.

Now, it is to be freely admitted that between 1850 and 1870 the rate of increase in the pre-existing population of this country fell sharply off; and that between 1870 and 1890 that decline has gone on at an accelerated ratio. From the first appearance of foreigners in large numbers in the United States the rate of increase among them has been greater than among those whom they found here; and this disproportion has tended continually, ever since, to increase. But has this result been due to a decline in physical vitality and reproductive vigor in that part of the population which we call, by comparison, American, or has it been due to other causes, *perhaps to the appearance of the foreigners themselves?* This is a question which requires us to go back to the beginning of the nation. The population of 1790 may be considered to have been, in a high sense, American. It is true that (leaving the Africans out of account) it was all of European stock; but immigration had practically ceased on the outbreak of the Revolution, in 1775, and had not been renewed, to any important extent, at the occurrence of the first census; so that the population of that date was an acclimated, and almost wholly a native population. Now, from 1790 to 1800, the population of the United States increased 35.10 per cent., or at a rate which would have enabled population to be doubled in twenty-three years; a rate transcending that maintained, so far as is known, over any extensive region for any considerable period of human history. And during this time the foreign arrivals were insignificant, being estimated at only 50,000 for the decade. Again, from 1800 to 1810, population increased by 36.38 per cent. Still the foreign arrivals were few, being estimated at only 70,000 for the ten years. Again, between 1810 and 1820 the rate of increase was 33.07 per cent. and still immigration remained at a minimum, the arrivals during the decade being estimated at 114,000. Meanwhile the population had increased from 3,929,214 to 9,633,822.

I have thus far spoken of the foreign arrivals at our ports, as estimated. Beginning with 1820, however, we have custom house statistics of the numbers of persons annually landing upon our shores. Some of these, indeed, did not remain here; yet rudely speaking we may call them all immigrants. Between 1820 and 1830, population grew to 12,866,020. The number of foreigners arriving in the ten years was 151,000. Here, then, we have for forty years an increase, substantially all out of the loins of the four millions of our own people living in 1790, amounting to almost nine millions, or 227 per cent. Such a rate of increase was never known before or since, among any considerable population, over any extensive region.

About this time, however, we reach a turning point in the history of our population. In the decade 1830-40 the number of foreign arrivals greatly increased. Immigration had not, indeed, reached the enormous dimensions of these later days. Yet, during the decade in question, the foreigners coming to the United States were almost exactly fourfold those coming in the decade preceding, or 599,000. The question now of vital importance is this: Was the population of the country correspondingly increased? I answer, No! The population of 1840 was almost exactly what by computation it would have been had no increase in foreign arrivals taken place. Again, between 1840 and 1850, a still further access of foreigners occurred, this time of enormous dimensions, the arrivals of the decade amounting to not less than 1,713,000. Of this gigantic total, 1,048,000 were from the British Isles, the Irish famine of 1846-47 having driven hundreds of thousands of miserable peasants to seek food upon our shores. Again we ask, Did this excess constitute a net gain to the population of the country? Again the answer is, No! Population showed no increase over the proportions established before immigration set in like a flood. In other words, as the foreigners began to come in large numbers, the native population more and more withheld their own increase.

Now, this correspondence might be accounted for in three different ways: (1) It might be said that it was a mere coincidence, no relation of cause and effect existing between the two phenomena. (2) It might be said that the foreigners came because the native population was relatively declining, that is, failing to keep up its pristine rate of increase. (3) It might be said that the growth of the native population was checked by the incoming of the foreign elements in such large numbers.

The view that the correspondence referred to was a mere coincidence, purely accidental in origin, is perhaps that most commonly taken. If this be the true explanation, the coincidence is a most remarkable one.

In a recent number of the Forum, I cited the predictions as to the future population of the country, made by Elkanah Watson, on the basis of the censuses of 1790, 1800, and 1810, while immigration still remained at a minimum. Now let us place together the actual census figures for 1840 and 1850, Watson's estimates for those years, and the foreign arrivals during the preceding decade:

	1840.	1850.
The census,	17,069,453	23,191,876
Watson's estimates,	17,116,526	23,185,368
The difference,	—47,073	+6,508
Foreign arrivals during preceding decade,	599,000	1,713,000

Here we see that, in spite of the arrival of 599,000 foreigners during the period 1830-40, four times as many as had arrived during any preceding decade, the figures of the census coincided closely with the estimate of Watson, based on the growth of population in the pre-immigration era, falling short of it by only 47,073 in a total of 17,000,000; while in 1850 the actual population, in spite of the arrival of 1,713,000 more immigrants, exceeded Watson's estimates by only 6,508 in a total of 23,000,000. Surely, if this correspondence between the increase of the foreign element and the relative decline of the native element is a mere coincidence, it is one of the most astonishing in human history. The actuarial degree of improbability as to a coincidence so close, over a range so vast, I will not undertake to compute.

If, on the other hand, it be alleged that the relation of cause and effect existed between the two phenomena, this might be put in two widely different ways: either

that the foreigners came in increasing numbers because the native element was relatively declining, or
that the native element failed to maintain its previous
rate of increase because the foreigners came in such
swarms. What shall we say of the former of these
explanations? Does anything more need to be said
than that it is too fine to be the real explanation of a
big human fact like this we are considering? To assume that at such a distance in space, in the then state
of news-communication and ocean-transportation, and
in spite of the ignorance and extreme poverty of the
peasantries of Europe from which the immigrants
were then generally drawn, there was so exact a degree
of knowledge, not only of the fact that the native element here was not keeping up its rate of increase, but
also of the precise ratio of that decline, as to enable
those peasantries, with or without a mutual understanding, to supply just the numbers necessary to
bring our population up to its due proportions, would
be little less than laughable. To-day, with quick
passages, cheap freights, and ocean cables, there is
not a single wholesale trade in the world carried on
with this degree of knowledge, or attaining anything
like this point of precision in results.

The true explanation of the remarkable fact we
are considering I believe to be the last of the three
suggested. The access of foreigners, at the time and
under the circumstances, constituted a shock to the
principle of population among the native element.
That principle is always acutely sensitive alike to
sentimental and to economic conditions. And it is
to be noted, in passing, that not only did the decline
in the native element, as a whole, take place in singular correspondence with the excess of foreign ar-

rivals, but it occurred chiefly in just those regions to which the new-comers most freely resorted.

But what possible reason can be suggested why the incoming of the foreigner should have checked the disposition of the native toward the increase of population at the traditional rate? I answer that the best of good reasons can be assigned. Throughout the north-eastern and northern middle States, into which, during the period under consideration, the new-comers poured in such numbers, the standard of material living, of general intelligence, of social decency, had been singularly high. Life, even at its hardest, had always had its luxuries; the babe had been a thing of beauty, to be delicately nurtured and proudly exhibited; the growing child had been decently dressed, at least for school and church; the house had been kept in order, at whatever cost, the gate hung, the shutters in place, while the front yard had been made to bloom with simple flowers; the village church, the public school-house, had been the best which the community, with great exertions and sacrifices, could erect and maintain. Then came the foreigner, making his way into the little village, bringing—small blame to him!—not only a vastly lower standard of living, but too often an actual present incapacity even to understand the refinements of life and thought in the community in which he sought a home. Our people had to look upon houses that were mere shells for human habitations, the gate unhung, the shutters flapping or falling, green pools in the yard, babes and young children rolling about half naked or worse, neglected, dirty, unkempt. Was there not in this, sentimental reason strong enough to give a shock to the principle of population? But there was, besides, an economic reason for a check to the native increase. The American shrank from the industrial competition thus thrust upon him. He was unwilling himself to engage in the lowest kind of day labor with these new elements of the population; he was even more unwilling to bring sons and daughters into the world to enter into that competition. For the first time in our history the people of the free States became divided into classes. Those classes were natives and foreigners. Politically the distinction had only a certain force, which yielded more or less readily under partisan pressure, but socially and industrially that distinction has been a tremendous power, and its chief effects have been wrought upon population. Neither the social companionship nor the industrial competition of the foreigner has, broadly speaking, been welcome to the native.

It hardly needs to be said that the foregoing descriptions are not intended to apply to all of the vast body of immigrants during this period. Thousands came over from good homes; many had had all the advantages of education and culture; some possessed the highest qualities of manhood and citizenship.

But let us proceed with the census. By 1860 the causes operating to reduce the growth of the native element, to which had then manifestly been added the force of important changes in the manner of living, the introduction of more luxurious habits, the influence of city life, and the custom of ''boarding,'' had reached such a height as, in spite of a still-increasing immigration, to bring the population of the country 310,503 below the estimate. The fearful losses of the civil war and the rapid extension of

habits unfavorable to increase of numbers, make any
further use of Watson's computations uninstructive,
yet still the great fact protrudes through all the subsequent history of our population that the more rapidly foreigners came into the United States, the smaller
was the rate of increase, not merely among the native
population separately, but throughout the population
of the country, as a whole, including the foreigners.
The climax of this movement was reached when, during the decade 1880-90, the foreign arrivals rose to
the monstrous total of five and a quarter millions
(twice what had ever before been known); while yet
population, even including this enormous re-enforc-
ment, increased more slowly than in any other period
of our history, except, possibly, that of the great
civil war.

If the foregoing views are true, or contain any considerable degree of truth, foreign immigration into
this country has, from the time it first assumed large
proportions, amounted not to a re-enforcement of our
population, but to a replacement of native by foreign
stock.   That if the foreigners had not come, the native element would long have filled the places the
foreigners usurped, I entertain not a doubt.   The
competency of the American stock to do this it would
be absurd to question in the face of such a record
as that for 1790 to 1830.   During the period from
1830 to 1860 the material conditions of existence in
this country were continually becoming more and
more favorable to the increase of population from
domestic sources.   The old man-slaughtering medicine
was being driven out of civilized communities; houses
were becoming larger; the food and clothing of the
people were becoming ampler and better.   Nor was

the cause which, about 1840 or 1850, began to retard
the growth of population here, to be found in the
climate which Mr. Clibborne stigmatizes so severely.
The climate of the United States has been benign
enough to enable us to take the English short-horn
and greatly improve it, as the re-exportation of that
animal to England at monstrous prices abundantly
proves; to take the English race-horse and to improve
him to a degree of which the startling victories of Pa-
role, Iroquois, and Foxhall afford but a suggestion; to
take the English man and to improve him too, adding
agility to his strength, making his eye keener and his
hand steadier, so that in rowing, in riding, in shooting, and in boxing, the American of pure English
stock is to-day the better animal. No! Whatever
were the causes which checked the growth of the native
population, they were neither physiological nor cli-
matic. They were mainly social and economic; and
chief among them was the access of vast hordes of
foreign immigrants, bringing with them a standard of
living at which our own people revolted.

Opinions may differ widely on the question whether
the United States have, as a whole, gained or lost by
so extensive a replacement of the native by foreign
elements in our population. But whatever view may
be taken of the past, no one surely can be enough of
an optimist to contemplate without dread the fast
rising flood of immigration now setting in upon our
shores. During the years 1880-90, five and a quarter
millions of foreigners entered the ports of the United
States. We have no assurance that this number may
not be doubled in the current decade. Only a small
part of these new-comers can read, while the general
intelligence of the mass is even below what might be

assumed from such a statement. By far the greater part of them are wholly ignorant of our institutions, and, too often, having been brought up in an atmosphere of pure force, they have no sympathy with the political ideas and sentiments which underlie our social organization; often not even the capability of understanding them.

What has just now been said would, of course, have been true in some degree of the body of immigrants in any preceding period. But the immigration of the present time differs unfortunately from that of the past in two important respects. The first is, that the organization of the European railway and the ocean steamship service is now such as to reduce almost to a minimum the energy, courage, intelligence, and pecuniary means required for immigration; a result which is tending to bring to us no longer the more alert and enterprising members of their respective communities, but rather the unlucky, the thriftless, the worthless. The second characteristic of the immigration of the present, as contrasted with that of the past, is that it is increasingly drawn from the nations of southern and eastern Europe—peoples which have got no great good for themselves out of the race wars of centuries, and out of the unceasing struggle with the hard conditions of nature; peoples that have the least possible adaptation to our political institutions and social life, and that have thus far remained hopelessly upon the lowest plane of industrial life. So broad and straight now is the channel by which this immigration is being conducted to our shores, that there is no reason why every stagnant pool of European population, representing the utterest failures of civilization, the worst defeats in the struggle for existence, the lowest degradation of human nature, should not be completely drained off into the United States. So long as any difference of economic conditions remains in our favor, so long as the least reason appears for the miserable, the broken, the corrupt, the abject, to think that they might be better off here than there, if not in the workshop, then in the workhouse, these Huns, and Poles, and Bohemians, and Russian Jews, and South Italians will continue to come, and to come by millions.

Has not the full time arrived when the people of the United States should set themselves seriously to consider whether the indiscriminate hospitality which has thus far cheerfully been exercised, should not be, at least for a while, withheld, to give the nation opportunity to digest and to assimilate what it has already received; whether justice, if not to ourselves, then to our posterity, does not require that the nation's birthright shall no longer be recklessly squandered, whether we are not under obligations, as the inheritors of a noble political system, to "see to it that the Republic sustains no harm" from an invasion in comparison with which the invasions under which Rome fell were no more than a series of excursion parties? For one, I believe that the United States have, by a whole century of unrestricted hospitality, and especially by taking in five and a quarter millions of foreigners during the past ten years, fully earned the right to say to all the world, "Give us a rest."

NOTES AND QUESTIONS

Francis A. Walker, (1840-1897) soldier, statistician, economist, and editor, was a distinguished American. Born in

Boston, he attended Amherst College, and after graduation in 1860, began the study of law. The Civil War put an end to his studies: he served with distinction in the Federal Army, attaining the rank of lieutenant-colonel. Then came a period of teaching and journalism, after which he entered the employ of the government. He was advanced until he was in charge of the Bureau of Statistics of the United States Treasury. Later he was Superintendent of the Census for the ninth (1870) and tenth (1880) census of the United States. From 1873 to 1881 he was professor of political economy and history in the Sheffield Scientific School of Yale University. In 1881 he was appointed president of the Massachusetts Institute of Technology, holding this position until his death in 1897. The Walker Memorial Building, a students' club house at the Institute, was erected in his memory in 1916. In the field of economics he is regarded as one of America's leading scholars. His text book on *Political Economy* is used in many colleges. Other works of his include: *The Wages Question, The Making of the Nation* and *International Bimetallism.*

Note that the first six paragraphs are introductory: What is the general topic of these paragraphs?

Page 175, paragraph "I have thus."
Select from this paragraph a sentence that summarizes the thought of this and the preceding paragraph.

Page 175, paragraph "About this time."
What thought is developed in this paragraph? What explanation of this is given in the paragraph "But what possible reason" (page 179)?

Page 180, "For the first time in our history the people of the free states became divided into classes."
Does your own observation confirm this statement?
Note the vigor of expression in the two concluding paragraphs.

Page 183, paragraph "What has just."
What prophecy is made in this paragraph? Have events since then justified the prophecy?

THEME TOPICS

Native vs. immigrant standards of living.
The occupations of native vs. immigrant Americans.
The benefits of our past immigration policy.
Should immigration be still further restricted?

MORAL ASPECTS OF COLLEGE LIFE

By Charles Kendall Adams

I FANCY that there is a somewhat widespread impression that life in American colleges and universities is less favorable to the development of individual morality than is life in society at large or in the business world. We often hear it intimated, and sometimes even boldly asserted, that nothing but the restraining power of stringent requirements will keep college and university students from falling into habits and methods that are injurious, if not, indeed, fatal, to the building up of a true and noble character. All this is founded on the belief that college and university students are too young to be left alone, and therefore that they must be kept under constant watch and ward. Those who entertain this belief are also apt to suppose that the personal habits of the student in a large institution are less commendable than are the habits of students in an institution of the paternal, or monastic, type. There are, probably, not a few who suppose that upon student life in itself moral obligations sit rather loosely, and that, if this life is compared with the life of young men in other occupations, it will be found that the general habits of university students leave much to be desired.

The reasons for these impressions are not difficult to

understand or to set forth. It must be admitted that, aside from all selfish and interested considerations, facts sometimes seem to favor such a supposition. In a collection of students, especially if the collection be large, it would be strange indeed if there were not to be found occasionally one or two evil-doers. The manner of the time, moreover, gives publicity to every offense. Sobriety and industry attract no attention, while profligacy and idleness have a marvelous knack of getting themselves reported. If the great business of a university is not industrious and steady work of a profitable kind, then, of course, the doors of the institution might as well be closed. But this kind of work attracts no attention. It blows no horns and rings no bells. Like all great forces, it is apt to move on quietly and silently. But if at any moment a single indiscretion occurs, not only the community, but, perhaps, even the country at large, is filled with noise.

Colleges and universities in this respect are not very unlike society as a whole. A city or a village may attend to its own business peacefully and profitably for generations, and attract no outside attention whatever; but let a scandalous event take place, and the reporters of all the newspapers are immediately on the spot. Every college and university now has its purveyors of what is called news, and these purveyors get more or less of pocket money by sending to their newspapers what their newspapers will pay for. So far as I know, these are worthy young men, who would not willingly do harm to the institutions with which they are connected. But they are under the constant pressure of a strong pecuniary temptation; and I fear they are sometimes too fully impregnated with the sentiment of that editor who, not long since, was reported as declaring that he was not ashamed to describe anything that Providence had permitted to happen. Such a spirit is contagious, and if it is the spirit of the managing editor, the reporter, of course, is likely to catch the disease. Not many years ago, the manager of a metropolitan journal was said to have telegraphed to one of his reporters to send a "rank" account of what was a very proper, though unusual, event in a woman's college. The result answered to what was doubtless desired. With such a spirit abroad, it may safely be assumed that whatever evil "Providence permits to happen" in a large college or university will get itself reported.

It is not my purpose here to denounce, or even to characterize, this spirit. It is enough to point it out, and to indicate the impression it is likely to leave on the public mind.

It can hardly escape observation that this impression in one of its phases is akin to that which is somewhat prevalent in regard to the present moral condition of society at large. Not a few persons suppose that immorality and crime are increasing, although there are many reasons for thinking that the contrary is the fact. However this may be, it is certain that, if we are to judge from the reports of crime in the newspapers of the day, as compared with the reports two or three generations ago, we shall be left in no doubt as to the moral degeneracy of the age. But this is not a safe criterion. The only fact that seems to be certain is that crime and immorality are much more generally reported and described than they were a hundred years ago. But if we look a little more closely into the subject, a very different judgment is formed. When one examines the literature of the seventeenth or the eighteenth century, especially the literature of the drama, one cannot fail to be convinced that gross immorality was by no means so uncommon as it is at the present day. We are not, therefore, to be too hasty in our inferences. A newspaper may tell nothing but the truth, but by telling only one side of the truth it may say what has all the effect of the most dangerous kind of falsehood. It is the partial truths that are the worst lies; and this may be said of life in college, as well as of life elsewhere. In regard to the conduct of students, it is these partial truths, often reported in exaggerated and distorted form, that go to make up too many of the popular impressions concerning college life.

It is also to be said that a college or a university is a corporation that is constantly before the public eye. Vast numbers are interested in it, and consequently it attracts general attention. Its membership ordinarily comes from a wide area. Any striking event occurring in a college is therefore likely to be much more generally noticed than would be the same event occurring in society elsewhere. These and other considerations that might be adduced make it certain that the worst things of college life will always be kept very prominently before the public. It is equally certain that the best things, that is to say, the hard, honest, conscientious, silent work, which is more than nine tenths of all the work of the college, will attract no attention whatever, and consequently will be in danger of being entirely overlooked.

Now, making due allowance for these considerations, what are we to infer from the influence of life in college upon the moral impulses and habits of students? In the first place, it may as well be said that what has been called the "intellectual life" may be influenced by two distinct, and perhaps even contradictory, forces. On the one hand, it is evident that the successful training of the mind increases the power of perceiving the force and the benefits of moral obligations. But, on the other hand, it is doubtful if such training does anything whatever to increase the power of resisting impulses of an immoral kind. It has to be admitted, therefore, that in an intellectual education, pure and simple, there is very little moral power. It is for this reason that the average intelligence in our reformatories and penitentiaries falls so little below, if indeed it falls at all below, the average intelligence of the community at large. Something more than a knowledge of evil is necessary to prevent evil. Evidently, then, the only way to improve morality is either to strengthen the moral impulses, or to weaken the forces tending to immorality. Does college life accomplish these ends? If it is wisely conducted, I should say, unquestionably, yes.

But it must not be forgotten that moral impulses are in no sense a product of pure intelligence. It may be quite possible to have the most perfect understanding of the significance of evil, and yet not avoid evil; and this is equivalent to saying that intellectual instruction alone, even in ethics, or morality, affords no guarantee that the one instructed will not lead an immoral life. Men do not do evil because they do not know the nature of evil, or that evil is wrong, but because the impulses to evil are stronger than the impulses to resist evil. It is the impulses, therefore, that need to be educated. Those leading upward are to be strengthened, in order that those leading downward may be controlled.

This process, no doubt, may be accomplished in one

or all of several ways. The right impulses may become infallibly dominant from an all-controlling obligation of a religious nature. In other cases they may be fortified to the degree requisite for respectability by a generally-prevalent wholesomeness of public opinion. In the absence of fear of God or man, a like result may come from obedience to that philosophic dogma which holds that the largest good is attained by an invariable subordination of the lower impulses to the higher. Or, finally, this education of the impulses may come from the impelling and encouraging power of good example. But, whatever in a given case is likely to be the motive, it is evident that morality, in the largest sense, will best be subserved where all of these forces have the freest play for the exercise of their influence. Morality, in a single person, may need nothing more than either religion, philosophy, public opinion, or example; but in a community it unquestionably needs them all. This brings us to the inquiry as to the opportunities for the play of these forces in college life. Let us briefly consider each one of them.

I confess that I have very little faith in a religion that is promulgated by force. If there is anything that is infallibly true, it is that an act to be either essentially good, or essentially bad, must be an act of free will. It seems to me, therefore, that as soon as the process of educating the child has gone so far as to bring him into a friendly attitude toward any truth, an attempt to enforce that truth against the will of the child is likely to arouse opposition and revulsion. Of course there is a debatable question as to when that period comes in the process of education. There are differences of opinion among the governing bodies of colleges as to whether it comes to a student before entering college or after. Those who hold that obligatory religious instruction should be made a part of a college course, act upon their belief and give the instruction they recommend. Those who, on the other hand, are of the opinion that all religious instruction at this age should be optional with the student, give at least as great opportunities for such instruction as are afforded in society at large. It would probably be quite within the truth to say that they give far more. Not only have students in the class of institutions holding these views all the opportunities afforded by the churches, but they almost without exception have additional advantages of no small importance.

The greatest of these opportunities and advantages is afforded by the college Christian Association. There is some difference of opinion as to whether the first association of this character was founded at the University of Virginia, or at the University of Michigan; but it is interesting to know that the first one came into existence at a state institution. At Cornell University where attendance at religious exercises is absolutely voluntary, the Christian Association, housed in an elegant and commodious building, counts a membership of more than 500, thus falling but a little short of one half of the entire body of students. My point is, that even in those institutions that make no claim of having about them any denominational odor of sanctity, there are the best of opportunities for religious life and religious encouragement. And this would be true even if a predominant portion of the faculty were not distinctively and actively religious men. Of the moral influences of those colleges that are under denominational control, of course I have no need to speak; but within those institutions where all religious exercises are purely optional, I am unhesitatingly of the opinion that those "forces which make for righteousness" are much more active and more potent than they are in the community at large.

Then, if we turn to the influence of public opinion, we shall find that here, likewise, a comparison will reveal college life at no disadvantage. It is no doubt true that the ethical ideas of students are somewhat peculiar to students themselves. One of these peculiarities shows itself in the firmness with which a student will often support his class in the wrong, as against himself in the right. The persistent refusal of students to testify one against another, has often provoked unfavorable comment, and sometimes has even been vigorously denounced. But, whatever opinion is entertained as to the propriety of this general attitude, there can be no denial of the fact that it shows great firmness of public opinion. Whoever has had much to do with college life knows that such opinion among students is quick and intolerant. It has strong dislikes, and, in its best moods, it perhaps has strong likes as well. But it is worthy of note that its dislikes are apt to be stronger than its likes. It denounces with more energy than it approves. It is in far more danger of excess in underestimating than of excess in overestimating. If the *nil admirari* spirit is not uncommon, what may be called the *nil condemnare* spirit does not go to college at all.

It is by reason of this quickness of college opinion to detect what it deems wrong and to denounce it, that many colleges have recently found it safe and wise to intrust matters of conduct largely to the students themselves. The judgment of students may sometimes be faulty; but their impulses, their desires, their purposes, their moral tone, will almost always be found correct. I do not hesitate a moment to avow my belief that, as an almost invariable rule, what may be called public opinion among American students is not only strong, but is also clean and wholesome. It approves and it denounces with more discrimination and with more energy than does public opinion in society at large.

So, too, in the colleges and universities, philosophy has a better chance. By philosophy is here meant simply that course of reasoning which sometimes brings men to believe that in the long run morality "pays" better than vice. There are doubtless to be found here and there men whose lives are kept free from reproach by considerations of this kind. They are probably very few; but still we teach ethics, not simply for the purpose of defining moral obligation, but also for the purpose of pointing out the consequences of moral obliquity. Whatever advantage, great or small, comes from this process, is likely to be more strongly felt where philosophy is taught than where it is not.

In the matter of example, also, the student has the advantage over his brother in the street or in the shop. It is the pick of the youth that come to college. Let outsiders say what they will, every college man knows that the great mass of students are earnestly devoted to the work of preparing themselves for the duties of life. There may be colleges where this is not the rule, but I believe they are exceedingly few, and I know of none. Students generally have a strong and manly purpose, and it would be a slander to intimate that as a rule they are not straight-forward, downright, and truthful.

For reasons that have already been given, the lad who devotes ten, twelve, or sixteen hours a day to the business for which he came to the university, attracts no attention. But in spite of this fact he goes steadily on with what, after all, is the great work of his life in college; and the number in this class is not so small as is often supposed. Although the outside world hears nothing of them, the student world knows perfectly well what they are about. They influence the tone of the whole college. They lift it to a higher plane of moral as well as of intellectual life. It is now strong and now weak, but it never fails completely to make its power felt. As I said above, the mass of our students go the somewhat monotonous round of their daily duties without attracting either comment or attention; but it must never be forgotten that it is work of this kind that makes up the main business of college life.

In the early part of this paper it was assumed that the only way to improve morality was to strengthen the moral impulses, or to weaken the forces tending to immorality. Having looked at the former, let us now glance for a moment at the latter.

It cannot be denied that what may be called the subjective forces tending to immorality in our colleges are strong and in need of constant restraint. So far as these forces are amenable to moral and spiritual influences, they have already been considered. But they are largely physical in their nature; they are therefore influenced by physical as well as by moral considerations. Here, for example, is a young man of overflowing physical vitality. Following either his own desire or the desire of his parents, he finds himself in college. He may be a strong scholar, or a weak one; but the time comes when his pent-up physical energies demand scope. Twenty-five years ago this exuberant vitality had a vile habit of spending its energies in the unhanging of gates, in the tearing up of sidewalks, in those multitudinous escapades with accounts of which the alumni of '50 or '60, with more or less of shame, are now apt to regale one another. It is certain that a great change has taken place. Nothing is more true than that there is vastly less of riotous disorder in our colleges than there was a generation ago. What has been the cause of this? The answer, I have no doubt, is to be found very largely, if not chiefly, in the moral power of regularly-prescribed gymnastic exercise and athletic sports.

The nature of this influence needs only to be stated to be fully understood. It has sometimes been said that the college gymnasium is chiefly used by those who need it least; that those who are already strong are the ones that resort to it most frequently and most willingly. It is inferred that because the well need not a physician, therefore the strong need not a gymnasium. But this assumption is based on nothing better than a very incomplete view of the truth. Those who take this view must suppose that the only function of physical exercise is the invigorating of the body. But, important as this purpose is, there is another advantage in careful and vigorous physical training that must not be overlooked. I believe there has been far too little understanding of the moral import of college athletics.

And here perhaps I may be permitted to declare

my belief that the best results of gymnastic training
will never be secured, unless regularly-prescribed exercise be rigorously made a part of the work required
of all students during the first two years of the course.
Such required exercise should perhaps not be carried
beyond the first two years. Juniors and seniors, having experienced the advantages of the training, may
safely be left to take their exercise in their own way;
but I am firm in the belief that it is better during the
first two years to require regular physical exercise of
every student. It is unnecessary in this connection to
say anything of the advantages of a purely physical
nature that come from such a requirement, or of its
influence upon scholarship. The sermon I would here
preach, if there were time and space, would be devoted simply to the moral uses of the gymnasium and
of the athletic field.

Everybody knows that the time when college boys,
as well as others, incline to mischief, is the evening
and the night. The work of the day is done, and, if
there is no anxious fear of coming examinations, the
temptation to physical exuberance is just in proportion to the degree of healthy physical vitality. Now,
if those hours can be tided over, if the exuberant
impulses can be turned to other uses, if the physical energies can be cared for and satisfied in some
well-regulated way, a great moral end will have
been subserved. And this is just what the gymnasium is admirably adapted to do. At four or
five o'clock in the afternoon, an hour, or hour
and a half, under the direction of a skillful
teacher of gymnastics, does the work completely. The
moral use of the gymnasium, therefore, is in the fact
that it breaks the force of temptation by furnishing

an outlet for all superabounding physical energy.
The boy that has had to keep his arms and legs a-fly-
ing for an hour is in no mood to do what used to be
called "making night hideous." He yields himself
to the proprieties of life with the utmost docility, and
prepares himself by a fair amount of study, and a
large amount of sleep, for the duties of the next day.
While the physically weak, therefore, are developed,
the physically strong are kept in moral, as well as in
physical, tone.

A similar consideration may be urged in behalf of
athletic sports, and even, though to a less extent, in
behalf of intercollegiate games. It has often been asserted that as a rule the great college athletes are poor
scholars. There has been gross exaggeration in the
statement, though at times there may have been truth
enough in it to give it color. But even if it were absolutely true, what would it signify? Is it probable
that the great athletes would have been great scholars
if they had not been athletes? Nay, is it not more
than probable that, if their superabounding vitality
had not been turned in the direction of athletics, it
would have found more questionable expression?
One thing is certain, and that is the impossibility of
training successfully for a great athletic contest without strict adherence to moral, as well as physical, requirements. The motto of such training invariably
is, Regular work, and no excess of any kind; and it
is strictly true that nobody can go through a training
of this sort without something of an uplift of a moral
as well as of a physical, character. More than that,
the amount of moral benefit will be in proportion to
the rigor of the training. It would be curious to
know just how much the improved order in our col-

leges in the last twenty-five years is due to athletic
sports. That they have had not a little influence in
this direction, there is no reason whatever to doubt.

The game in itself, moreover, is an exercise of moral
and mental, as well as of physical, powers. This is
especially the fact in football, the sport that has received the most active popular criticism. Everybody
knows that as a game it exacts the prolonged and vigorous use of all the physical powers. But what is
obvious only to close inspection, is the fact that it
calls into active effort the mental and moral, no less
than the bodily, faculties of the players. No greater
mistake could be made than to suppose that it is a
game of mere physical skill. On the contrary, it is
difficult to see how anybody can watch a game, and
understand it, without perceiving that it is in a large
sense essentially also a game of mind and *morale*. It
not only calls for the most active, the most instan-
taneous, exercise of intellectual discrimination, but it
also demands the most complete subordination of the
individual will to the good of the whole. There is
probably no other of the popular games that is so full
of vicissitudes. More than all others, it calls, no
doubt, for the reiterated mental determination of
what to do and how to do it. To an appreciative observer, the strategy and the tactics of the game must
be far more interesting and striking than what may
be called the play of physical forces. Still further,
the necessity of self-restraint is as imperative as the
necessity of prompt action. As there is no higher
exercise of the mind than that of determining in an
emergency precisely the line between too much and
too little, so there is no greater moral test than that
which calls for self-restraint at the moment of over-

whelming temptation. That such temptation often comes to the foot-ball player with tremendous force, there can be no doubt. But it comes under circumstances that help him to resist. He is waging battle, not in silence and alone, but in the presence of spectators and an umpire that demand fair play. If he allows his opponents to ruffle his temper, he is subject to disgrace. If he yields, he knows that he may be sent off the field by the umpire. In a recent game it was said that when a prominent player was disqualified for losing his temper, he cried like a child. To hold one's self with perfect self-restraint under severe temptation and provocation, is one of the greatest of moral achievements; and any game which tends unmistakably to develop such an ability cannot be regarded as destitute of moral power.

So much, I think, may be said with confidence. As to how many counterbalancing evils there may be in the system of inter-collegiate games, as at present conducted, there is here no space to consider. That those evils are neither few nor small, ought, I think, to be freely conceded. But whether they ought to be met with a policy of temperance or with a policy of total abstinence, is a question about which even wise men may honestly and earnestly differ.

NOTES AND QUESTIONS

Charles Kendall Adams (1835-1902) holds a distinguished place in the history of higher education in America. He graduated at the University of Michigan in 1861, and two years later joined the faculty as instructor in Latin and history. In 1865 he became assistant professor of history, and in 1867 was appointed full professor, succeeding Andrew D. White. He had spent a year in study at the universities of France and Germany, and was one of the first to introduce

into America the German seminar method for advanced classes.
In 1885 he was made president of Cornell University, and in
1892 became president of the University of Wisconsin, holding
this position until his death.   He was a scholar of wide
interests.   He was editor-in-chief of Johnson's *Universal
Cyclopedia*, and served as president of the American Historical Association.   His writings include: *Democracy and
Monarchy in France, Higher Education in Germany*, and a
Manual of Historical Literature.

Note how in the opening paragraph the general topic is
first stated, then amplified, then restated at the end.

Page 187, paragraph "The reasons for."
What point is brought out in this paragraph?

Page 188, paragraph "Colleges and Universities."
What is said about newspapers here?   How far is this
statement still true?

Page 189, paragraph "It can hardly."
What new idea is developed in this paragraph?   Note how
gradually the author approaches the main topic.   Burke was
described as "winding into his subject like a serpent";
somewhat the same skill is shown in this article.

Page 190, paragraph "Now, making due."
What does Dr. Adams say is the relation between mental
power and moral standards?   What is given as proof of this
statement?   Does your own observation bear this out?

Page 192, paragraph "I confess that."
Draw your inference from this paragraph as to whether
or not President Adams believed in compulsory attendance at
college chapel.

Page 194, paragraph "Then if we."
What is said here about public opinion in college life?
What is your own observation on this point?

Page 196, paragraph "It cannot be."
What is said here of the influence of athletics in college
life?

Page 199, paragraph "A similar consideration."
What further points in relation to athletics are developed
here?

Page 200, paragraph "The game in."

What does he say about the effects of football in particular?

How does the view of athletics given in this article compare with that of Price Collier in his article, "The Ethics of Ancient and Modern Athletics"?   How does it compare with that of Professor Coffin in "The Paradox of Oxford"?   In what points do the three writers agree?

THEME SUBJECTS

Athletics and Morals.

College morality vs. the morality of the outside world.

College life as portrayed in the newspapers.

Some points that President Adams overlooked.

College athletics, as seen by Price Collier and Charles Kendall Adams.

A DEFINITION OF THE
FINE ARTS

By Charles Eliot Norton

WHEN the editor of the Forum proposed to me to contribute to that journal the opening paper of a series by different writers on subjects relating to the fine arts, it occurred to me that it was not unlikely that there might be little harmony in the tone of the essays, owing to want of agreement as to the nature and function of these arts, and to the various points of view from which they might be regarded. And this reflection led me to consider whether it might not be of interest to make an attempt to reach some definition of the term which should help to clear thought in regard to the fine arts, and should meet the need of intelligent persons bewildered by the variety of statements and the vague assertions made concerning them. So much, indeed, has been said and written about them during this century, and in the main to so little purpose, that sensible men have grown tired of the subject and turn from a discussion of it as from a strife of words likely to end in no satisfactory conclusion. And yet, doubtless, there are many people who are seeking for clear and correct ideas in regard to the matter, and who find themselves in the same condition as Carlyle when he wrote in his journal, ''What is art?'' and could find no satisfactory answer to his question.

It is, indeed, generally taken for granted that everybody must know what the fine arts are, as well as that
everybody must have an opinion concerning them. I
open a recent sketch of the history of art by an accomplished French writer, and read the first sentence
of the introduction as follows:

"We shall not undertake to define art; this difficult task
belongs to æsthetics. Besides, whatever formula may be
adopted, the word awakens in the mind sufficiently precise general ideas to allow us to employ it without fear."

But these general ideas to which M. Bayet trusts
are likely to be vague, are likely to be incorrect.
Moreover, the definition of art, or of the fine arts, difficult as it may be, does not properly belong to æsthetics.
Æsthetics treats of the nature and sources of the
pleasure derived from the fine arts, and of the emotions aroused by them, but it presupposes a knowledge
of what these arts actually are.

The difficulty of defining the term is increased by
the ambiguity occasioned by the common use of
the word "art," and of the words "fine arts," as if
they were synonymous. Thus, in the opening sentences of his incomparable book on the "Archæology
of Art," that great scholar and man of genius, Karl
Otfried Müller, says with a Delphic utterance:

"Art is a representation, that is, an activity, by means of
which something internal or spiritual is revealed to sense. Its
only object is to represent, and, by its being satisfied there-
with, it is distinguished from practical activities which
are directed to some particular purpose of external life."

It is plain that Müller here uses the word "art"
for the fine arts alone. Indeed, this use is so common
as to excite no attention; and by such a title as that

of Müller's book everyone would understand that the archæology of the fine arts only was intended.

In truth, this term of "fine arts" is of comparatively late introduction. The Italians seem to have been the first to feel the need of such a term, but even their phrase "*le belle arti*" is not of very long date. It was not, I believe, in use in the sixteenth century, and is not to be found with its modern acceptation in the works of Vasari or his contemporaries. Near the beginning of the pleasant book, whose contents justify its title, "*Il Riposo,*" of Raffaello Borghini, first published in 1584, the author, speaking of "the most beautiful and noble arts of painting and sculpture," refers to the students of these *belle arti,* without intending to designate the two arts as belonging to a class. It was apparently during the seventeenth century that the conception gradually took form of a class of arts possessed of common characteristics which admitted of their being grouped under the specific term of *le belle arti.* At any rate, not long after the beginning of the eighteenth century the term was in use with its modern significance, and in the course of the century it became familiar.

The term was so useful that a translation of it was soon adopted into the other European languages, but in English, at least, it was long in coming into general use. When, in 1769, Sir Joshua Reynolds delivered his "Discourse at the Opening of the Royal Academy," he spoke of the "polite arts"; and when, in 1778, he dedicated his "Discourses" to the King, he said, "to found an academy for the arts of elegance was reserved for your majesty." In his famous "Essay on the Sublime and Beautiful," which was published in 1773, Burke never employs the term, as he would have been likely to do had it been in common use; and it is not to be found, I believe, in the lectures of Barry or Opie, or even of Fuseli, the last of which was delivered in 1825. The earliest instance of its use given in the new "Historical Dictionary" is dated 1767, and is from Fordyce's "Sermons to Young Women." The phrase cited is as follows: "They wanted instruction in the fine arts." This might seem to imply that young women felt the same need a hundred and twenty years ago that many of them experience to-day; but without the context there remains some uncertainty whether the reverend author meant by the fine arts what is meant by the words to-day.

Since 1825 the term has become altogether common, but there is room for reasonable doubt if its meaning be clearly understood by most of those who use it. The risks of attempting a definition of a term, the meaning of which everybody supposes himself to know, are proverbial. "I am warned," says Emerson in his essay on "Beauty," "by the ill fate of many philosophers not to attempt a definition." But it is on definitions that soundness of thought depends. The excellence of our arts themselves depends greatly on the clearness of our thought concerning them.

"If I were to define art," says Mill, "I should be inclined to call it the endeavor after perfection in execution." This is good, but it does not differentiate the fine arts. How then are they specially distinguished from the arts in general? Plainly their first distinction is that they are arts of expression. There is no fine art that is not primarily an art of expression. Every method of expression belongs to them, and their domain is consequently as wide as the compass of thought, sentiment, and emotion—of everything within the spirit of man that seeks for conscious and controlled utterance. But the word "fine" involves further the conception that the expression should be not mere utterance, but expression in its most perfect attainable form. And this suggests as a definition of the fine arts—the arts of expression in its most adequate or beautiful form. If we accept this definition as partially correct, a large conclusion follows. To conceive worthily of life, we must recognize that speech, manners, conduct, are all subjects of the fine arts; and that our systems of education are imperfect so long as they fail to inspire a youth with the desire, and to help him to the method of expression of himself in the noblest form which he may be capable of attaining. But the perception of beauty of form in any mode of expression is rare, and is the outcome of a peculiar felicity of constitution. The possession of this perception, combined with the power of justly expressing the impressions received through it, is the distinction of the artist.

But our definition of the fine arts is not yet complete, for in their highest exercise they depend on the activity of the imagination, through which their work becomes a work of creation, not of mere imitation or reproduction.

In that exquisite little dialogue, the "Ion," in which Plato discourses of poetry, he represents Socrates as saying:

" 'Tynnichus, the Chalcidian, wrote nothing that any one would care to remember but the famous pæan which is in every one's mouth, one of the finest poems ever written, and truly an invention of the Muses, as he himself says. For in this way the God would seem to indicate to us that these beautiful poems are not the work of man, but divine and the work of God; and that the poets are only the interpreters of the Gods by whom they are severally possessed. Was not this the lesson which the God intended to teach when by the mouth of the worst of poets he sang the best of songs? Am I not right, Ion?' 'Yes, indeed, Socrates, I feel that you are; for your words touch my soul, and I am persuaded somehow that good poets are the inspired interpreters of the Gods.' "

The modern Ion, accepting this question and answer metaphorically, finds this "divine possession" to be the action of the imagination, when, roused to fullest energy, it displays power beyond what "cool reason can ever apprehend." It is the imagination that quickens the other faculties to their highest exercise. By it perception is intensified so as to discern behind the external image and the changeable show of things, their permanent and typical characteristics, and to see the universal traits revealed through the particular, individual aspect. It is by means of the imagination that memory is helped to order its contents in their true relations and mutual bearings, and that the understanding is vivified to genuine intelligence. Thus acting upon all the faculties which combine in the arts of expression, the creative imagination enables them to attain to the forms of beauty, and makes their productions works of the fine arts, so that we may complete our definition of these arts, as the arts of expression in forms of beauty created by the imagination, or, in briefer form, as the arts of expression transfused with imagination.

It is the function of imagination to conceive that which nature and experience suggest but never completely attain or afford—the ideal, which is the essential truth and reality that lie concealed within the husk of the actual, and of which the test and warrant are its correspondence with the desires of the mind

for those forms in which beauty is more or less completely revealed. But the soul's imaginary sight, as
Shakespeare calls it, is often dim. No less than the
outward eye it needs a clear atmosphere and favoring
conditions. Special endowments of temperament and
of character, special attainments of culture, special
outward circumstances are required for its happiest
exercise. The imaginative perception of beauty is
not a common faculty, and even when it exists, the
conditions on which its expression, its creation, depends are not to be summoned at will. For the most
essential of these conditions is passion—"passion, or
the sympathy of all the senses in an ecstasy of contemplation in which self is utterly renounced, yet so
as to find itself expressed and completed in the object
contemplated." This is the meaning of "possession"
or "inspiration." It is in the moments of passionate
emotion that the artist's mind is transfigured, and
that he becomes capable of creating shapes of beauty
that rouse a corresponding emotion in the duller souls
of his fellows, that serve as types of the ideal to which
they would conform the image of their own natures,
and that teach them to think nobly of themselves.

The works of art which belong to this highest order
are not many. Even the Greeks have bequeathed to
us few in which, to use Plato's phrase, "the artist
seems the inspired interpreter of the gods." It is to
lay down a too exclusive dictum to assert, with Blake,
the most imaginative of English painters, that "he
who does not imagine in stronger and better lineaments, and in stronger and better light, than his
perishing mortal eye can see, does not imagine at all."
But of the great host of artists very few catch distinct sight even of the hem of the garment of beauty,

and the works of a vast majority have, consequently, only a relative and imitative value of small permanent and intrinsic worth. Yet in every generation there will be some who will succeed more or less completely in embodying the ideals which they have seen through and not with the eye, and in producing true works of the poetic faculty.

The fine arts are, indeed, all of them arts of poetry; for though, in common use, the word poetry is confined to expression in verse, the highest form of every mode of expression is the poetic. Titian and Turner are poets no less than Ariosto and Wordsworth; Phidias no less than Sophocles; and among the living, Burne-Jones no less than William Morris. But language is so imperfect in its discriminations that the name of poet or artist is readily given to all who compose verse or practice art, whether they possess the poetic faculty, the creative power of the imagination, or not. *Cucullus non facit monachum.* In Chalmers's vast collection of the British poets so-called, what an intolerable deal of sack to every half-penny-worth of bread! And yet the number of poets and artists by courtesy is always on the increase. So far as the real interest of society is concerned, this increase is rather to be deprecated than encouraged; but it is not surprising, for the profession is attractive, and the popular demand for certain classes of works of art is great and not highly discriminating. The artistic temperament is not a national trait of the English race. Our complex and exciting civilization has, indeed, developed, especially in America, a sensitiveness of nervous organization which often wears the semblance of the artistic temperament, and shows itself in manual dexterity and refined technical skill. And this tends to make mere workmanship, mere excellence of execution, the common test of merit in a work of the fine arts. Such excellence is readily appreciated, it can be valued in money's worth, it gives a certain legitimate pleasure, and it is with productions of art of this sort that we are in great measure obliged to content ourselves so well as we may.

The imagination of our time has for the most part taken a different direction from the fine arts in their high sense. It has been dazzled by the magnificent achievements of science and by the splendid promises of the spirit of this world; it has been allured from the pursuit of the lofty ideals of the mind by the material charms of the practical ends embodied in wealth and luxury. Especially here in America the success of our experiment has been so unexampled in the mastery of nature, in the rapidity of the physical growth of the nation, and in the diffusion of material comfort, as to engender a spirit of self-satisfaction that deadens the imagination and takes little heed of what may be deficient in our national life of true elegance, dignity, and elevation. Of all civilized nations we are the most deficient in the higher culture of the mind, and not in the culture only but also in the conditions on which this culture mainly depends. We are both ignorant and largely indifferent to our ignorance. There is among us little of the spirit of noble discontent that stimulates to emulation of greatness, quickens generous ambitions, and is the source of steadfast effort to attain to better things. These, doubtless, may seem hard words; and it were indeed to be desired that their truth was as questionable as it is unacceptable. Of course the individual exceptions to such broad statements are so numerous that,

if only these exceptions be regarded, the statements
may appear to need modification. But if they be considered with a clear view of the whole field, free from
the illusions of national conceit, it must, I fear, be
admitted that they rest on a solid basis of fact. Platitudes in regard to the general diffusion of intelligence
and morality have no place here. Everything that
can be justly claimed in regard to the wide diffusion
of intelligence in the community, and to the vast
mental activity implied by its material progress, may
be admitted, without weakening the force of the conclusion that the nobler elements of the life of the
imagination do not abound in it.

And so far as this conclusion is correct, it compels
us further to admit, however unwillingly, that the conditions are unfavorable for the development of some
of the chief of the fine arts.

In one of these arts, and the one of widest diffusion
and influence, it has indeed been the happiness of
America during the last generation to find expression
of her highest moral ideals. For fifty years her poets
in verse have rendered her the best service; and when
the achievements of the century come to be recorded
and its permanent acquisitions reckoned up, the works
of these poets will be found to be among the most important and the most lasting of all. There will be
little to show of the works of the other fine arts, for
though the product has been abundant, it has lacked
vitality.

The conditions requisite for the nurture and expression of the poetic imagination in the arts of design have indeed been deficient in America from the
beginning. Allston was perhaps the first American
to give proof of a poetic imagination striving to ex-

press itself in the fine arts. His story is pathetic, for it is that of an exquisitely-endowed nature struggling to exist in an atmosphere that was wholly uncongenial. He was like a plant needing a rich soil that had struck its roots in the sand. He never succeeded in expressing himself. The fire that burnt within him needed more oxygen than the air about him supplied. Cambridgeport was not the fitting place for the home of a poet whose sensibility to beauty was acute, whose perceptions were delicate, whose sense of color was Venetian. But nowhere else in America in the first half of this century could he have found himself much better off. The conditions in which he was forced to live made the greater part of his work ineffectual.

But the barrenness of a hundred, or even of fifty years ago, has given place to such culture as wealth can provide, and the poet or artist to-day need not dwindle or starve. The risk to which he is exposed is of a different sort, and has been vividly exhibited in the life and work of Richardson, who died before he had done justice to his own great powers. With the enormous rapidity of growth of our cities in all parts of the country during the past twenty years, the demands made upon a popular architect, especially upon one who like Richardson impressed his own large and vigorous character upon his designs, is so great as to become exhausting, and, unless resisted, as to deprive him of leisure for the meditation, the study, and the tranquillity of mind requisite for the conception and production of original architectural designs, at once beautiful and appropriate. Justly confident in himself, Richardson tasked his powers too much. His work often gives evidence of his want

of time to think it out. The marks of genius in it are
associated with feeble strokes, with marked man-
nerisms, with inappropriateness of ornament, and de-
fects of arrangement. In his preference for the
round-arched style, he not infrequently adopted from
the Romanesque builders whose powerful style had
impressed his imagination, forms and modes of building natural to the times of war and violence for which
they had originally been devised, but wholly foreign
and unsuited to our modern needs and peaceful conditions. He did not leave himself leisure enough for
the reflection which the thorough and consistent execution of every important architectural design requires. And yet so little thought is given by the
public to the essential qualities of this superb art,
which more than any other of the fine arts appeals to
practical good sense as well as to the imagination,
that the manifest incongruities between the style and
detail of some of Richardson's most striking works
and the uses for which they are intended, has excited little intelligent attention. To judge correctly
of a great architectural design demands indeed no less
special training than to judge of any other great work
of art; but simple common sense is all that is needed
to determine whether it satisfactorily and appropri-
ately fulfills the object for which it is intended. The
effect of such an example as Richardson's is likely to
be harmful. The style made fashionable by his vigorous, picturesque treatment of it, is adopted by
weaker hands, and the elements in it that have impressed the popular fancy are exaggerated and vul-
garized.

Wealth, judiciously used, can do much to conceal
for a time the want of the products of the imagination.

It can employ the ready talents and cunning hands
of artificers in works of display and outward splendor.
Rome, in the time of the empire, made herself magnificent with the treasures that she stole or purchased
from Greece, and with the labors of Greek craftsmen
who had inherited the methods but not the genius of
their ancestors. But the arts never took root and
flourished in Rome. The Roman imagination was
not creative, and among all the superb monuments of
her greatness there is not a single one that appeals
to the deepest poetic sympathies, or that belongs to
the highest order of the creations of the imagination.
It is very striking that Virgil, the poet who most truly
represents the Roman genius in all its greatness and
with all its limitations, even thinks to exalt the Roman
fame by depreciating the very arts by which the living image of Rome might be perpetuated when she
herself was in the dust.

Vulgarity, exhibited in the preference of what is
showy, sentimental, sensational, and fantastic, to what
is simple, refined, and unpretending, is the stamp of
much of the popular art everywhere to-day. *"Die
Schönheit ist für jetzt ein Schimpfwort,"* said a well-
informed German, speaking of the taste of his com-
patriots. The harsh saying would hardly be true in
America, for as yet as a people we have cared too little
for beauty in our work and lives either to prize it or
definitely to scorn it. We still for the most part regard the fine arts as pleasant and becoming ap-
pendages and adornments of life, not understanding
that they are the only real test of the spiritual qualities of a race, and the standard by which ultimately
its share in the progress of humanity must be
measured. For they are the permanent expression

of its soul; of the desires and aspirations by which it has been inspired. If its desires reach no further than the satisfactions which wealth can afford, the fine arts will reveal the fact. They are unconscious, incorruptible witnesses. Their testimony admits of no contradiction. The best that a people has to express will be expressed in its fine arts, and there is no other source of noble works of the fine arts than noble character. To-day in America we have much of such art as wealth can buy; we have what we call "decorative art" and "household art" in abundance. They exhibit a vague and generally ineffectual striving after what may rather be called prettiness than beauty; they are not original, not imaginative, not creative arts. But they are worthy of respect, provided they do not simulate the better things and pretend to be other than they are. The highest manifestation of this sort of art is that afforded by the school of American engravers on wood, who have carried their special craft to a degree of perfection in handiwork and skill in reproduction which exhibits an exquisiteness of imitation and a fineness of touch that can hardly be surpassed, or, within their limits, overpraised. But great as the excellence of their work is, it is only in a secondary and inferior sense poetic. For creative originality and lasting charm one rude vignette of Bewick, one block of Holbein, is worth all that our marvellously skillful craftsmen have engraved.

We are not likely to have anything much better in any of the fine arts of design than this work, so long as the present conditions of our national life continue; except as from time to time some genius may rise with power to control unfavoring circumstance, with imaginative vision to see the ideal that lies latent in our common lives, and with passion to embody it in works that shall lift us above our common selves. But until such genius come to justify our better hopes, let us not think too highly of the decorative, household, profitable, professional art in which the national disposition finds expression; let us not mistake pseudo-Blakes for poets, or ambitious builders for Brunelleschis or Palladios. Let us remember what the fine arts have been at their best when they have justified the definition of them as the arts of expression so transfused by the imagination that their works are creations of immortal beauty.

NOTES AND QUESTIONS

Charles Eliot Norton (1827-1908), for many years professor of art at Harvard University, was one of a group of men, including Lowell, Longfellow, Holmes, and Emerson, who for a quarter of a century made Cambridge the literary center of our country. He was born in Cambridge, graduated at Harvard in 1846, and after a few years spent in business, occupied the rest of his life with the interests nearest his heart, literature and art. From 1864 to 1868 he, with James Russell Lowell, edited the North American Review. In 1875 he was appointed professor of the history of art at Harvard, and held this position for more than twenty years. His lectures dealt not merely with art but with the social conditions which influence the production of great art. They were in fact an interpretation of history, past and present, viewed from the standpoint of the fine arts. To these lectures the students came in such numbers that the largest lecture room in Harvard was required to hold his classes. He was greatly interested in the study of Dante, and with Lowell, Longfellow and others, founded the Dante Society, as well as publishing a translation in prose of Dante's *Divine Comedy* and of his *New Life*. He was the friend of many noted men across the sea, such as Carlyle, Ruskin, and Edward Fitzgerald, the translator of the *Rubiayat*. His correspondence with John Ruskin has been published in book form. He edited the correspondence of Carlyle and Emerson, and the letters of James Russell Lowell. His writings on art include *Historical Study of Church Building during the Middle Ages* and *A History of Ancient Art*. His position in America was somewhat like that of Ruskin in England: a great art critic, and fearless in the expression of his opinions, he exerted a marked influence upon his time.

This essay is the work of a noted scholar, familiar with European literature, and trained in historical research: it is in a sense the fruit of a lifetime of study. Such work is not easy reading: to read it understandingly is a test of your mental power.

Page 207, paragraph "If I were."
What definition of the fine arts is suggested in this paragraph? According to this, is speech a fine art? is conduct? are manners? Do we usually think of them as fine arts?

Page 209, paragraph "The modern Ion."
What definition of the fine arts is given here?

Page 211, *Cucullus non facit monachum*. The hood does not make the monk; *i.e.* outward appearances may be deceptive.

Page 211, paragraph "The fine arts are."
What does Professor Norton say about the English as an artistic race? About Americans?

Page 212, paragraph "The imagination of."
What direction does he say the imagination has taken in America? What is the result of this?

Page 213, paragraph "In one of these."
In which of the fine arts does he say we have made most progress? Do you agree with this statement?

Page 214, paragraph "But the barrenness."
What theory about architecture is advanced in this paragraph?

Page 216, "Die Schonheit ist fur jetzt ein Schimpfwort." Beauty is now a word of scorn.

Page 216, paragraph "Vulgarity, exhibited in."
Here Professor Norton pronounces his verdict upon much in our modern life. Read this slowly, pausing to weigh each

sentence, and see how far your own observation confirms
what he says.

What is the title of this article?   What other subjects
are discussed?   Why are they brought in?   Does the author
write as one well informed upon his subject?   As one who
felt deeply about it?   Have you received any new ideas?

THEME SUBJECTS

The fine arts in American life.
Imagination turned to business
Are we an artistic nation?
Speech as a fine art.

CAUSES OF BELIEF IN IMMORTALITY

By Lester F. Ward

Vere scire est per causas scire.—Bacon.

THERE has been an immense amount of discussion of the doctrine of a future life, but the attempts to explain on natural principles the causes of almost universal acceptance of that doctrine are confined to a class of works that are comparatively little read, and which when read are apt to be regarded merely as accounts of the curious superstitions of primitive peoples having no connection with the conceptions of civilized men.

Most believers in immortality, when asked the reason for the faith that is in them, are content to admit that it is based on revelation; but there are some who are ready to give other reasons. Nothing is more common than to hear it said that it is inconceivable than an organization so highly developed as is that of an enlightened human being should perish utterly at the end of the brief span of a lifetime. Although this is no longer recognized as legitimate reasoning, the same cannot be said of the claim which some make that they actually feel an inner sentiment which tells them that they will survive death. But such a reason satisfies only the particular individual who enjoys the experience. There is, too, no end of objective proofs, inductive and deductive, to the same purpose; but the impartial student of it all usually concludes that these are not the true reasons for this belief, and feels compelled to admit that the chief cause after all is that it has been taught to us, and that each one believes what is believed by others with whom he is associated. But this is very far from saying that there is no good reason for the belief in immortality, and the purpose of this article is not only to show that this belief has its legitimate causes in the nature of things, but also to point out briefly what those causes are.

Science seeks to explain phenomena. It assumes primarily that all phenomena must have natural causes, and it aims to find the several links in the chain of causation leading up to them. Even a belief may become the subject of strictly scientific study, and the belief in immortality has been so studied, as many think, successfully.

The sense in which it is here maintained that the idea of immortality is a natural one, is that it is a product of man's reason. It is proposed to show that the conclusions drawn from the data at hand to reason from, were legitimate products of the rational faculty in normal action.

But it is not among the more advanced races of men that we must look for the explanation of this belief. Among these it occurs in two quite distinct forms. As understood in what are called civilized countries, namely, as the indefinite persistence of the immaterial part, or soul, of man, which comes into existence with the body, it is accepted by two religious sects, Christians and Mohammedans. In the wider and far more logical form of the continuous existence of the spiritual part of man, not only in the indefinite future but from the indefinite past, it is accepted by the immense populations of southern and eastern Asia. In one or the other of these forms, therefore, the doctrine prevails throughout nearly the entire civilized and half-civilized world. But the study of either of these developed forms of the belief does not furnish an explanation of their natural origin. To find this we must go back to the rudest peoples that can be found. It is not, however, a belief in immortality, in the more refined modern sense, that we here find. It is something far simpler, less definite, and more difficult of comprehension. Travelers among savages have sometimes reported tribes so low, as they state, that they have no idea of a future life; but this has been because, in their ignorance of the savage mind, detecting nothing that corresponded to their own advanced conceptions of the immortal soul, they failed to recognize the true homologue, and indeed the germ itself of these conceptions.

At first glance the ideas of the primitive man belonging to this class present a congeries of varying and apparently conflicting beliefs, so unlike the modern doctrine in question as not to be recognizable, except by the trained ethnographer, as related to the differentiated conceptions of civilized races. But a careful study of all this mass of primitive thought enables the competent investigator to reduce it to simpler terms, and ultimately to a single principle common to all such peoples, which is a universal conception underlying not only the doctrine of immortality, but all mythology and all religion. This resi-

dual principle, stripped of all its changing concomit-
ants, may be defined as simply the notion of spirit.

The real problem, then, is not to account for the
wide-spread belief in immortality, but for the universal belief in spirit. How has all mankind come
into possession of this belief? Why do we find it, in
one form or another, in tribes separated most widely
from one another, and in those most completely
isolated from the rest of the world? Two answers
have been given to these questions. One, that the
belief is innate, and belongs to the mind of man the
same as his mental faculties; the other, that the conditions which surround a rational being living anywhere on the globe are such as to cause him irresisti-
bly to infer the existence of spirit. The latter answer
science accepts.

The primary causes of the belief in a spiritual
existence and spiritual beings are twofold, or belong
to two somewhat diverse groups. One of these groups
of causes may be distinguished as subjective, in the
sense of affecting each individual personally in such
a manner as to lead him to the conclusion that he
possesses an invisible or intangible double or spiritual
part, which, for a portion of the time, at least, is detached and separated from his original corporeal self.
The other group of causes may be called objective, being calculated to lead the primitive man to the conclusion that there are intelligent agencies which are
devoid of any material attributes, existing independent of himself and of human beings in general.

To the subjective group belong shadows, reflections,
echoes, dreams, delirium, insanity, epilepsy, swoon-
ing, trance, and death. It is difficult for the well-
informed reader to conceive how utterly devoid the

savage mind is of all knowledge of the true nature of any of these phenomena. There is no greater mistake than to suppose that well-developed mental faculties are any help in understanding such things. There is no degree of intellectual power conceivable which, unaided by science, would be capable of furnishing a correct interpretation of any of them. The enlightened world understands them simply and solely because it has been taught what science, in the face of appearances to the contrary, has laboriously investigated and explained.

In contemplating his shadow the savage has no conception of the nature and effect of light. He simply sees his own form, more or less distorted by perspective, without substance, thickness, or tangibility, moving as he moves, and changing its shape with the altitude of the sun or the angle of the object against which it is cast. He readily perceives that he is the cause of it, that it is in some way a product of himself. He can only conclude that there is something in him, or belonging to him, which can go out and occupy another part of space from that occupied by his real original self—another self, a double, but devoid of flesh and blood, a spiritual nature. And thus we find throughout all mythology, even that of the cultured Greeks and Romans, the terms shadow and spirit inextricably confounded.

When the savage looks into a pool of still water he sees this other self there, only far more distinctly. Instead of being a mere form it now possesses color and recognizable features. Others who see it inform him that all the lineaments are his own. He sees the images of others which agree in all respects with the originals. But when he plunges his hand into the pool there is nothing there. What he sees must be *immaterial,* and this conception does not differ in any essential respect from that of spirit. It is true that animals and inanimate objects also cast their shadows and reflect their images; but every one knows that these, as well as human beings, are endowed by savages with a double existence and a spiritual part. The reasoning is rigidly logical from the premises, far more so than much of the reasoning of the higher races.

The lessons derived from sight are confirmed by those of sound. A chieftain shouts in a mountain gorge and his whoop is repeated from the surrounding hills. It is not an answer; it is his own voice uttering his own words, but from a distant point. He knows that he is not himself far up on the rocky cliff whence the sound proceeds, and yet he cannot doubt that he is its author. It must be his other self through whom he has the power of speaking.

The warrior sleeps, and while sleeping he wanders far away, meets other men and other scenes, performs feats of prowess, or enjoys pleasures never before tasted. He awakes, and every circumstance tells him that he has all this time lain quietly in one place. Yet he recollects all these exploits, and he knows that he has himself experienced them. He is unacquainted with the science of psychology, knows nothing about mind or brain action, and has absolutely no alternative to concluding that the immaterial, but yet feeling, thinking, and remembering part of himself has actually been absent, has seen the objects, performed the deeds, felt the pleasures, and witnessed the events enacted in his dream.

Suppose disease lays him low, fever racks his brain,

and he becomes delirious. Again he wanders, experiences, suffers, but he is usually incapable of recalling these scenes and states. He performs strange actions. which are subsequently described to him. Both he and his friends know that he would not himself have acted thus, and the conclusion is natural that the spirit of another must have entered into and possessed him. Hence we find that everywhere efforts are made in such cases to drive out the evil spirit. Catalepsy, insanity, and all pathologic states fall under this general class, and receive this explanation. And thus it happens, as every one knows, that exorcism is the beginning and the end of the healing art among primitive tribes.

In trance the spirit assumes another state, which by practice and fasting may sometimes be voluntarily superinduced, and all the wild forms of ecstasy brought on. This, which does not essentially differ from modern mediumship, is usually explained as the intentional replacing of the proper spirit by another and superior one. But the trance in the medical sense, and in so far as they differ, the swoon or syncope, imply the complete temporary abandonment of the body by the soul. The latter is supposed to go away, and there is usually nothing to indicate where it has gone or what it is doing. The inference is common that it has gone to take possession for the time being of some other body.

But swoons, and especially cataleptic trance, may have considerable duration, and the transition from this to death is, to the savage mind, very easy and natural. Death is simply a permanent swoon. The double has gone, this time never to return. Where has it gone? This question is variously answered,

but in most triɔes of low rank the idea of any distant
abode for these departed spirits is entirely wanting.
They are usually supposed to remain near the ꞷpot
where they left the body or where the body is finally
placed, and an immense number and variety of mort-
uary and burial customs attest the universality of this
general belief.   These all point to one notion common
to all races, namely, that of the continued existence
after death of the incorporeal part of man.

Here we have a complete genesis of the universal
belief in a spiritual existence and a satisfactory explanation of its universality.   It ends the controversy
between those, on the one hand, who claim that belief
in a future life is universal and must therefore be innate, and those, on the other, who deny such universality.   The premises of the former are practically sustained, but in such a manner as to disprove their
conclusion, while the claim of the latter is shown to
be opposed to the facts.   The simple truth comes forth
that the universal belief in a life after death is a
necessary conclusion which the primitive man must
draw, as soon as he can reason at all, from the phenomena which nature always ᵽresents.   The universal belief in an after-life is due to the simple fact that from
identical phenomena the reasoning faculty, which is
everywhere the same, will uniformly deduce the same
conclusion.

The idea of the survival of individuals that die
could not fail to exert a profound influence upon the
living.   Conceiving, as savages usually do, that the
spirit remains near the scene of its career during life,
they could not stop short of peopling every spot
with innumerable spirits.   With few exceptions these
spirits are regarded as evil-disposed, and to them are

attributed most of the misfortunes that befall the living. All space thus becomes filled with myriads of spiritual beings, the *manes* of departed men, and these have been feared, worshiped, implored, and propitiated under a variety of names.

This, too, furnishes an explanation, satisfactory to the savage's mind, of many of the mysterious phenomena of nature. Unacquainted with the operation of natural forces, he had, as we shall see later on, accounted for all movements in the inanimate world on the principle of an indwelling consciousness, and now, with the vast accumulating hosts of liberated human doubles, there is no lack of material for animating every object in nature. We thus have a rational basis for fetichism as well as for animal-worship.

A still more important consequence of this belief is that which follows on the death of any great chieftain or mighty ruler. The souls of such men also persist. They, too, linger round the places of their glorious achievements, and are the invisible spectators of the doings of their former subjects. What must be the effect of such a belief? For a while elaborate ceremonies are performed over the tomb of the dead hero. His weapons are usually buried with him to arm him in the next life. His possessions are frequently placed in his grave to be used again; too often slaves and even wives are sacrificed to accompany him and minister to his wants. As time goes by his earthly exploits are more and more exaggerated, until they all become marvels and miracles. Complete apotheosis is the ultimate result. This takes the form of ancestor-worship, from which it is not a long step to the worship of beings not conceived as of human origin.

The above are fair samples of the subjective influ-

ences which have led the primitive man to a belief in
the existence of spirit, of a spiritual part in man,
and of spiritual beings in general. They might in
themselves seem adequate to account for such a belief
and for its universality; but to them we have now to
add the causes which I have distinguished as objective, strengthening and confirming the subjective
causes, and swelling the stream of evidence poured
into the receptive mind of untutored man.

Early ideas are necessarily anthropomorphic. They
are based on the individual's experience of his own
powers. The most fundamental of all such experiences are those connected with the power of spontaneous movement. The savage's idea of life is ability
to move, and whatever moves without known external
force is supposed to be alive. Hence, one of the first
results of human reasoning is to attribute life to certain inanimate objects. The activities of inanimate
things are, moreover, generally conceived as conscious
and intentional—as manifestations of intelligent will.
Akin to this conception is that of the presumed power
of metamorphosis which a certain class of phenomena
early led primitive man to ascribe to almost every object in nature. Not only can material objects move,
but they can also change, become other things, vanish,
and dissolve entirely, ceasing longer to exist, or they
can reappear at will in the same or some altered form
and guise.

When we say that early man reasons logically, it
must not be inferred that this has anything to do
with the recognition of the laws of causation as understood by scientific men. He indeed requires and
insists upon a cause, but it is rarely a true cause or
causa efficiens. It is usually a final cause, and the

causa finalis is amply adequate for his purpose. He always demands a reason, but it is rarely or never what is technically called a sufficient reason, the *ratio sufficiens* of the schoolmen or *zureichender Grund* of Kant and Schopenhauer. Yet the efficient cause is the only cause, and sufficient reason is the only reason that modern science recognizes; and this is coming to be so well understood that it has become customary to call that a logical mind which insists upon a strictly mechanical antecedent for the explanation of every phenomenon. This is not the primitive sense of either the term logical or rational, and it is not the sense in which it can be applied to the aboriginal mind of man. The recognition of a will to move or a will to change is all that most minds, even among somewhat advanced races, require; and the great weft of mythology and folk-lore of such races—the "Arabian Nights Entertainments," the Ossianic poems, and the mass of mythic lore and legend that makes up the early literature of every cultured nation, with its diluted and degenerate remains that are taught to our children in the nursery, and the ease and interest with which it is all absorbed by the latter—amply attest the adequacy of what may be distinguished as the logic of magic for all minds not thoroughly trained by prolonged familiarity with science in the logic of law.

The power of natural objects to change their form at will is constantly forced upon the mind of early man. The formation and dissipation of clouds; the succession of daylight, darkness, and the seasons; the changes of the moon; the wanderings of the planets; the apparent revolutions of the sun, moon, and stars; the phenomena presented by comets, meteors, auroras,

rainbows, lightning, halos; the slower processes of
vegetable and animal growth and decay; the emerging of birds from eggs, of moths from chrysalids; indeed, the phenomena of reproduction in general, as
well as of life and death—all these must have rendered
the conception of indefinite transmutability at will
throughout all nature a familiar one to the savage
mind.

The manifestations of apparently inherent power in
nature through earthquakes, tornadoes, and thunder-
bolts, forced these ideas home with a terrible sanction.
The most typical of all these influences is that of wind.
It is the embodiment of power without visible cause.
The savage never thinks of air as a material substance.
To him it is simply a manifestation of will—the ex-
pression of a purpose or wish by a spiritual agency.
Hence the frequent identification of the terms wind
and spirit (*nevua*).

The savage knows nothing of causes except as they
are exemplified in his own muscular actions. With
this narrow induction he can only reason that all effects are produced by such causes. His reasoning is
in all cases teleological. Not a leaf trembles in the
breeze, not a wave washes the shore, but that in his
mind it is the result of will. Eolus and Neptune are
but the refined embodiments, in a more civilized people, of these crude primitive conceptions. All the
imaginary beings conceived as exerting this will-power
are highly anthropomorphic in their character, and
differ from the spiritual part of man only in being
detached from the animal body.

The reader will not, of course, expect, in a short
article like this, that the multitudinous facts upon
which each several proposition is based will be stated.

For these he must go to the great stores of such knowledge that have been accumulated by Tylor, Lubbock, and Spencer, in England, and by Schoolcraft, Morgan, and Powell, in the United States, not to mention the French and German ethnographers.

It would seem, then, that overwhelming evidence, both of the subjective and the objective kind, exists to show that a rational being placed in a world like this must necessarily conclude that there is such a thing as spirit—an invisible, intangible, conscious power, not occupying space, and wholly independent of the conditions that restrict the actions of embodied beings. Not less irresistible are the proofs that the intelligent, conscious motive power of bodily action in each individual is in fact such a spirit, and is capable, under certain circumstances, of quitting the body for a longer or shorter period, of entering another body temporarily or permanently, or of abandoning the body altogether.

As already remarked, this is the chief point to be established. The passage from such a belief to a belief in immortality is exceedingly simple and natural. From the notion of a temporary continuance of the spiritual life to that of its permanent continuance, is but a step; and, in fact, as soon as thought about, it becomes a necessary step, since the spiritual part is naturally conceived as indestructible. The ideas that grow up with regard to metamorphosis in nature, coupled with the belief that animals, too, have spirits, account in a satisfactory manner for the origin of the doctrine of transmigration of souls; while the lopping off of that highly rational accompaniment merely shows that, upon such questions, even the most advanced peoples of the modern world are not yet troubled by the absence of a *ratio sufficiens*.

Finally, the probable absence of the notion of a continued personal existence among the Hebrews, Greeks, and Romans, must be explained on the theory that in gradually sloughing off the adjuncts of savagery, those nations discarded this idea as essentially barbaric. This, however, did not carry with it the rejection of the fundamental conception of spiritual existence which persisted in the form of gods, anthropomorphic, it is true, but wholly incorporeal—a pantheon of great and powerful spirits.

NOTES AND QUESTIONS

Lester F. Ward (1841-1913) was a scientist who attained distinction in the fields of botany and paleontology, as well as in sociology and philosophy. His unusual learning was largely the result of his own efforts. Having served with the Federal armies during the Civil War, at its close he went to Washington and secured a clerical position in the Treasury department. While working here he studied at Columbian University (now George Washington University) completing the college course and the law course. He then took up the study of botany, and published several books on this subject; he was also editor of botanical terms for the Century Dictionary. He later became interested in geology, and for a number of years was geologist for the United States Geological Survey. Later in life his interests turned to sociology; he published several books upon that subject, of which *Dynamic Sociology* is the most important. The total number of his writings, including books and magazine articles, is over six hundred titles.

Page 221. *Vere scire est per causas scire,* To know truly is to know through causes.

Page 222, paragraph "But it is."

In what two forms does he say the belief in immortality exists? Compare Wordsworth's "Ode on Immortality," especially the lines:

Our birth is but a sleep and a forgetting:
The soul that rises with us, our life's star,
  Hath elsewhere had its setting,
  And cometh from afar.

Page 225, paragraph "In contemplating his."

What is the effect upon a savage of seeing his shadow?
of seeing his image in a mirror? of hearing an echo? of
recalling dreams or delirium? Does all this reasoning seem
probable?

Page 228, paragraph "Here we have."

What is the author's conclusion as to the belief in an after
life? Do you think he has established his point?

Page 233, paragraph "As already remarked."

Show the relation between the belief in spirit and the belief in immortality.

If you are interested to read further about the beliefs
of primitive man, try one of these books: *Primitive Culture*,
by E. B. Tylor, *Principles of Sociology*, by Herbert Spencer;
The Golden Bough, (abridged edition) J. G. Frazer.

TOPICS FOR DISCUSSION

What is the most interesting part of this article?
What new ideas have you gained from it?

Studies in American Society: II

Studies in
American Society: II

Edited by DEREK L. PHILLIPS

New York University

THOMAS Y. CROWELL COMPANY

New York, Established 1834

✍Contents

INTRODUCTION *1*

PARTY AND SOCIETY *5*
  by Robert R. Alford

MEN WHO MANAGE *42*
  by Melville Dalton

STRANGERS NEXT DOOR: ETHNIC RELATIONS
IN AMERICAN COMMUNITIES *102*
  by Robin M. Williams, Jr.

GROUP PROCESS AND GANG DELINQUENCY *141*
  by James F. Short, Jr., and Fred L. Strodtbeck

THE URBAN VILLAGERS *180*
  by Herbert J. Gans

BLUE-COLLAR MARRIAGE *222*
  by Mirra Komarovsky

THE AUTHORS *247*

ҽ*Introduction*

This is the second of two volumes concerned with introducing the student of social science to a selected offering of some major sociological studies of American society.[1] These two volumes attempt not only to assist the student in acquiring systematic knowledge about the society in which he lives but also, equally important, to acquaint him with the kinds of problems that concern social scientists doing empirical research. In addition, it is hoped that the student will begin to obtain what Conant calls a " 'feel' for the Tactics and Strategy of Science."[2] Admittedly, it is not possible within a few pages to familiarize the student with more than a portion of the research tactics and strategies employed by professional social scientists. But it is intended that he will at least become aware of the fact that there is no one research "method" systematically employed by all social scientists.

For the social sciences, the fundamental theme of methodological consideration is the existence of a social world, the fact that there is social reality. Methods or techniques for obtaining information or "data" about this social world have changed considerably in the last decade. No longer do most social scientists rely on intuition, speculation, or casual observation. Although it is difficult to compose a list of the essentials of the "scientific method" that all its practitioners would agree upon, there is consensus that science is an organized method for the discovery of knowledge.

The studies in this book use a variety of research methods and

[1] Derek L. Phillips (ed.), *Studies in American Society* (New York: Thomas Y. Crowell, 1965).

[2] James B. Conant, *On Understanding Science* (New Haven, Conn.: Yale University Press, 1947).

techniques in attempting to acquire knowledge about various aspects of American society. While differing from one another according to the particular problems or questions being investigated, the six studies are similar in two respects: (1) they share a conviction that there exists an order of things in nature and, more specifically, that the behavior of human beings, like other natural phenomena, shows regular and recurrent patterns; and (2) they emphasize the appropriateness of employing scientific procedures in discovering and accounting for these patterns.

These six studies appeared originally as volumes averaging almost four hundred pages in length. Clearly, works of such magnitude cannot be condensed adequately within a book of this size. Therefore, the intent of this book is to present, for each of the studies, a representative or central portion of the full-length book. As with the first volume, the selections retain the wording of their authors and differ from the parent studies only in the following respects: (1) A few passages and footnotes of secondary importance are omitted when such omission does not seriously affect the general substance of the selection. (2) A simple phrase or sentence is occasionally inserted to effect a suitable transition when material has been omitted. (3) Footnotes, tables, and graphs are renumbered, and the original graphs redrawn, to conform to the style of this volume.

All of these studies are preceded by short introductions that attempt to provide the reader with an overview of the various studies and the research designs employed. These introductory statements can, of course, do little more than familiarize students with the research focus and data-gathering techniques of the various studies. Hopefully, these introductions, taken together with the selections presented, will whet the appetite of the serious student, so that he will undertake a full reading of the original works.

In order to alert the reader as to what lies ahead, we now turn to a brief discussion of the subject matter of each of the six studies. The first reading, *Party and Society,* is concerned with the relationship between social class position and voting preference. Alford attempts to determine whether workers are coming to resemble middle-class persons in their party loyalties. In the second essay, *Men Who Manage,* Dalton is concerned with behavior in bureaucratic organizations. His particular focus is on problems related to advancement through the organizational hierarchy of one large manufacturing plant. Next, in *Strangers Next Door,* Robin Williams and his associates present an analysis of data pertaining to patterns of segregation, discrimination, and conflict. The fourth reading, *Group Process and Gang Delinquency,* by Short and Strodtbeck, explores various aspects of the behavior of lower-class gang boys in Chicago. In *The Urban Villagers,* Herbert Gans reports on life in the West End of Boston, an area often characterized as a slum. Finally, in *Blue-Collar Marriage,* Mirra Komarovsky presents an account of marriage among manual or "blue-collar" workers and their wives.

Using empirical methods, these six studies add considerably to our knowledge of human behavior and social processes in American society. But in addition to the acquisition of knowledge about our society, it is hoped that some students may "recognize" themselves in these studies. For it is through the process of self-recognition and self-discovery that individuals acquire a new way of seeing. They are enabled to view themselves and their society from a vastly different vantage point; and they may achieve what Peter Berger has called "the precarious vision." [3]

[3] Peter L. Berger, *The Precarious Vision: A Sociologist Looks at Social Fictions and Christian Faith* (New York: Doubleday, 1961).

ᦔ*Party and Society**

ROBERT R. ALFORD

A number of research studies have sought to establish the relationship between a person's behavior and his social class position. Modes of sexual behavior,[1] techniques of child-rearing,[2] rates of mental illness,[3] and politico-economic behavior[4] have each been found to relate to the position of individuals in the status hierarchy. In his Party and Society, Robert Alford examines the relationship between social class and voting preference. His primary research focus is on the effects of social class position upon party loyalties in four Anglo-American Democracies.

Alford's study is a noteworthy example of the method of "secondary analysis." His procedure is to analyze data from more than fifty public opinion surveys previously conducted by others in four Western democracies: the United States, Great Britain, Canada,

[1] Alfred C. Kinsey, Wardell B. Pomeroy, and Clyde E. Martin, Sexual Behavior in the Human Male (Philadelphia: Saunders, 1958).
[2] Daniel R. Miller and Guy E. Swanson, Inner Conflict and Defense (New York: Holt, Rinehart, & Winston, 1960).
[3] Leo Srole, Thomas S. Langner, Stanley T. Michael, Marvin K. Opler, and Thomas A. C. Rennie, Mental Health in the Metropolis (New York: McGraw, 1962).
[4] Angus Campbell, Philip E. Converse, Warren E. Miller, and Donald E. Stokes, The American Voter (New York: Wiley, 1960).

5

and Australia. The surveys had sought answers to a great number of questions about occupational, religious, and political affiliations in the nations studied. The appropriateness of such a body of data to Alford's purpose is clearly indicated by Charles Glock in his foreword to Party and Society: *"It is a characteristic of these [public opinion] surveys that they collect far more information than the investigators are concerned with or are able to use. Often, in fact, only the data having commercial or news value are culled, while great amounts of more fundamental, more interesting, and more complex information remain untouched and unheralded. . . . Often, the same or similar questions have been asked repeatedly in surveys taken at different times or in different countries, making parallel data available not only over time but across cultures. These materials comprise a unique and rich body of knowledge on contemporary societies throughout the world. At relatively small cost, they can be subjected to secondary analysis for a wide variety of scholarly purposes. . . . So far, however, they have been largely untapped."*

In examining the data, Alford's main line of inquiry is to determine whether the sources of "political cleavage"—of differing political loyalties—vary among the four nations, and whether the sources of cleavage change with time. The principal source of cleavage is social class position, which Alford measures by occupational status. He employs as an index of class voting the difference between the proportion of their total vote manual workers gave and the proportion of their total vote non-manual workers gave to the "left" party during the years 1952-1962. Great Britain exhibited the most class voting, followed by Australia, the United States, and Canada. Differences in the degree of class voting among the four countries were maintained when class voting in each country was examined within different age groups, among Protestants and Catholics, in large cities, and within the regions highest and lowest in amount of class voting.

Forces other than class division did, however, play an important part in voting differences. Regionalism was found to be an independent source of political cleavage in the United States and

6

Canada, and religious differences proved significant in the United States, Canada, and Australia. Although these other factors influenced voting preferences, social class exercised a greater effect than either regionalism or religion. Alford concludes that class position is the principal source of political cleavage, and that class voting in the four Anglo-American Democracies is not declining.

The section of Alford's work presented here is concerned with class voting in the United States. In a careful analysis, he examines trends in class voting since the depression years of the 1930's, and the effects on class voting of regionalism, religion, and subjective class identification (respondents had characterized themselves as either "working" or "middle" class). He discusses the findings in light of the work of previous investigators and, in considering the influences of region and religion, comments upon the seemingly inconsistent trends of class voting in the United States.

Party and Society is an outstanding example of the harvest an imaginative scholar can reap from what others might have thought fallow data. Although results of public opinion studies have been accumulating in many different countries, and although there is increased access to such survey materials, relatively few secondary analyses have been made. Alford's work, a pioneer effort of this approach, should serve as a model for future explorations.

The United States: The Politics of Diversity

Social class and political behavior are not as closely associated in the United States as they are in Australia and Great Britain. In several surveys of the national electorate taken from 1952 to 1960, the average level of class voting (the difference in Democratic voting between manual and non-manual occupational strata) was 16 percentage points. This contrasts with average figures of 40 percentage points for Great Britain, 33 for Australia, and 8 for Canada. The national political parties in the United States are not as clearly distinguished by their class support as are the parties in Great Britain and Australia.

7

Diversity in the United States

... The parties in the United States are not explicitly linked to class organizations and do not appeal for support on the basis of class. However, voters do see the parties as linked to specific class interests, and probably many people vote in accordance with an image of the parties as representing their economic interests. These are perhaps the most important reasons why class voting is relatively low and yet still exists.

A number of characteristics of American society and its political system undoubtedly reduce the level of class voting further. The enormous size of the country, its division into fifty states with real degrees of sovereignty, tremendous ethnic and religious diversity, and a decentralized party structure, all reduce the salience of *national* class divisions as the main bases for party cleavages. The decentralized, undisciplined character of American parties makes them difficult to distinguish from pressure groups or from combinations of interest groups. The party system thus reflects the federal, plural character of both American society and the governmental system. As the author of a recent study of American federalism put it, "a powerful 'pressure group' at the national level may be very closely identified with a State or local party in one or more States, yet prefer to remain aloof from the national party battle in order to maintain freedom to exert pressure upon both parties when tactics require it." [1] That national class divisions exist and divide the parties even as distinctly as they do, is a measure of the degree of economic and political integration the United States has achieved.

The diversity of support for the political parties has been shown by a series of studies of voting—more studies than for any of the other countries considered—and this chapter will not reiterate their findings in detail. The initial study, which set a pattern for subsequent research in both the United States and Great Britain, was *The People's Choice;* this was a survey of voting behavior in Erie

[1] M. J. C. Vile, *The Structure of American Federalism* (London: Oxford University Press, 1961), p. 92.

County, Ohio, in the 1940 presidential election.[2] Since it embraced only one northern city and its environs, the regional economic and political diversity of the United States presumably did not affect voting behavior. Still, social class, religion, and rural-urban differences were found crucially to affect the political loyalties of voters. Having a low income, being a Catholic, or living in an urban environment, all predisposed voters toward the Democrats; having a high income, being a Protestant, or living in a rural environment predisposed voters toward the Republicans. The study focused on the consequences of "contradictory" social characteristics that presumably pushed people in opposite political directions—the now classic notion of "cross-pressures." A relatively high proportion of persons in Erie County was under cross-pressures, indicating that the diversity of sources of political loyalties is great in the United States.[3]

The main problem [here] will be not to explain the class or religious or regional bases for party support in the United States but to determine whether class voting has declined since the 1930's, and in which religious or regional groups.

Despite their diversity of support and their ambiguous class base (compared to the British and Australian parties), American political parties are both perceived as supported by, and actually are supported by, persons at different occupational, educational, and income levels, although, as in the other countries, a sizable minority votes for the "other" party. Since voting studies have also made

[2] P. Lazarsfeld, B. Berelson, and H. Gaudet, *The People's Choice* (New York: Columbia University Press, 1948).
[3] Other such voting studies are: B. Berelson, P. Lazarsfeld, and W. McPhee, *Voting* (Chicago: University of Chicago Press, 1954), and a series of studies done by the Survey Research Center at the University of Michigan beginning with the presidential election of 1948. These are reported in A. Campbell, G. Gurin, and W. E. Miller, *The Voter Decides* (Evanston: Row, Peterson, 1954); Angus Campbell and Homer C. Cooper, *Group Differences in Attitudes and Votes* (Ann Arbor: Survey Research Center, The University of Michigan, 1956), and A. Campbell *et al., The American Voter* (New York: Wiley, 1960). For a summary of the findings of many voting studies, see S. M. Lipset, *Political Man* (New York: Doubleday, 1960), chaps. vii, viii, ix.

9

this point clearly, there is no need to go into details. The authors of a study of the 1954 congressional election summarized their results as follows:

Our data make it evident that a number of the major population categories have a persistent inclination toward one or the other of the two parties. The major theme of this group orientation in voting is social class. The prestige groups—educational, economic—are the most dependable sources of Republican support while the laborers, Negroes, unemployed, and other low-income and low-education groups are the strongest sources of the Democratic vote.[4]

And the parties can be distinguished as representing Left and Right positions. According to Max Beloff:

If we take the simple view that there is, other things being equal, likely to be one party of the rich and one party of the poor, the Republicans fill the bill for the former, and outside the South the Democrats fill it for the latter. The former accept roughly the justice of the present distribution of worldly goods between classes and regions; the latter by and large welcome government intervention to alter it.[5]

The phrases "by and large" and "other things being equal" hide a multitude of contradictions in the policies and voting patterns of Democratic and Republican legislators, but if that statement is accepted as substantially correct, the class bases of the major American parties are understandable. Another compilation of poll data from seven national polls conducted from 1944 to 1952 found that two-and-one-half times as many business and professional people thought the Republicans best served their interests as thought the Democrats did, and that seven times as many unskilled workers and four times as many skilled workers thought the Democrats best served their interests as thought the Republicans did. Whether or not the parties actually served their interests better is, of course, not proved by these images of the parties, but this evidence at least

[4] Campbell and Cooper, *op. cit.,* p. 35.
[5] Max Beloff, *The American Federal Government* (New York: Oxford University Press, 1959), pp. 157–58.

shows that American voting behavior is roughly in line with voters' conceptions of their own interests.[6]

Ideologically, party leaders in the United States are even more divided than voters. A recent study of Democratic and Republican leaders (delegates to national conventions) and followers (a national sample of voters) compared opinions on a number of issues. Republican and Democratic leaders were much farther apart than their followers on issues related to class. The ideology of Republican leaders reflected their managerial, proprietary, and high-status connections; the ideology of Democratic leaders, their labor, minority, low-status, and intellectual connections.[7]

But, regardless of the current situations, has the association of class and vote declined since the 1930's? It is by now a commonplace notion that the salience of class for voting was less in the prosperous 1950's than it was in the depressed 1930's.[8] A recent study found a decline of class voting in the period 1948 to 1956, which appears to document the decreasing importance of social class for voting behavior. The authors of *The American Voter* computed an index of "status polarization" which showed that the correlation between the occupational status of respondents and their partisan vote in three separate national surveys in 1948, 1952, and 1956 dropped from 0.44 to 0.26 to 0.12.[9] According to the authors:

The most striking feature of the polarization trend in the recent past has been the steady and rapid depolarization between 1948 and 1956. This decline occurred in a post-war period when the nation was enjoying a

[6] Harold Orlans, "Opinion Polls on National Leaders," Series 1953, Report No. 6 (Philadelphia and Washington: Institute for Research in Human Relations), pp. 71–73. The author points out that almost exactly as many white-collar workers pick the Democrats as pick the Republicans, and that this corresponds to their "middle" position.

[7] H. McClosky, P. J. Hoffman, and R. O'Hara, "Issue Conflict and Consensus among Party Leaders and Followers," *American Political Science Review*, LIV (June, 1960), 406–27. The finding holds when various demographic factors are controlled.

[8] See, for example, V. O. Key, Jr., *Politics, Parties and Pressure Groups* (4th ed.; New York: Crowell, 1958), p. 274.

[9] Campbell *et al., The American Voter, op. cit.*, p. 347.

striking ascent to prosperity and a consequent release from the pressing economic concerns that had characterized the Depression.[10]

The way that this decline of "status polarization" is explained is also relevant here, because the authors infer that changes have taken place since the 1930's, although they have no specific evidence of such changes. A substitute for this is evidence on the status polarization (or class voting, the term which will be used henceforth to avoid confusion) among different age-groups. In their 1948 and 1952 surveys, a marked "depression-effect" was found. Persons in their twenties and thirties during the depression of the 1930's (presumably those most affected by it) exhibited the highest level of class voting. In 1956, this was not evident, and the authors conclude that this illustrates the "fading effects of the Depression." [11]

This finding of highest class voting among the depression generation does not contradict the usual inference that persons in such a generation should be more similar in their political attitudes and behavior than persons not sharing this common experience. Another study of American voting behavior which specifically focused upon the problem of generational differences found that the depression generation (those who were born in the period 1913-1922) was likely to be more Democratic—regardless of sex, occupation, income, or other social differences.[12] In spite of the Michigan finding that manual and non-manual strata in the depression generation are farther apart in their voting patterns than any other age groups, political consensus is still present. Both strata were affected similarly by the Democratic political currents. These two findings reflect the relative independence of the absolute level of vote for a party from the level of class cleavage.

But the Michigan results may not reflect the actual voting patterns in the 1930's. Their results are for persons interviewed in the

[10] *Ibid.,* p. 357.
[11] *Ibid.,* p. 359.
[12] Jane O'Grady, "Political Generations: An Empirical Analysis" (Master's thesis, Department of Sociology, University of California, 1960).

1940's and 1950's, divided by age. That age differences at one point in time truly reflect past behavior and the differential impact of a historical crisis is an inference which may or may not be justified. Data to be presented may clarify the real patterns of class voting and the change in those patterns since the 1930's.

The decline of class voting between 1948 and 1956 is linked by the authors of *The American Voter* to "increasing prosperity and fading memories of the Great Depression of the 1930's." These two factors should imply a continuing decrease of class voting since the 1930's. But the authors must account for another of their own empirical findings—that class-voting was lower in 1944 than in 1948, after which it dropped almost linearly. They suggest that variations in the importance of domestic economic versus foreign policy issues account for this change: When economic issues are important, class voting tends to rise; when non-economic issues, such as foreign policy, are important, class voting tends to drop. ". . . war is a basic public concern that may eclipse those problems of domestic economics leading to cleavage among status interest groups." [13] The authors thus infer what the patterns of class voting *might* have been during the 1930's. Presumably class voting should have been high in the elections of 1932 and 1936, when class issues were dominant. With World War II, "national" issues superseded class ones, and class voting should have been lower in 1940 and 1944. As Campbell *et al.* put it, "Polarization tendencies carrying over from the Great Depression may have been dampened as a result of the national crisis posed by the Second World War, rebounding upward after that conflict was concluded." Domestic economic issues again became important, resulting in the rise of class voting in 1948. After this peak, "the renewal of the threat of global war and the outbreak of hostilities in Korea may have acted, in concert with increasing prosperity, to depress the level of status polarization [class voting] once again." [14]

These inferences are logical ones from the standpoint of the

[13] Campbell *et al.*, *The American Voter, op. cit.*, pp. 360–61.
[14] *Ibid.*, p. 361.

data available to the authors of that study and are relevant to [our] main problem: whether class voting has declined since the 1930's. . . . This particular problem is not of primary concern to these authors, since they are focusing upon "short-term" fluctuations. These inferences as to declining class voting certainly imply that a long-term decline of the importance of social class in the support of the American parties has taken place. But has it?

Trends in Class Voting Since the 1930's

Although fluctuations in the level of class voting have occurred in the period 1936 to 1960, there is some evidence that no consistent decline has taken place. Before the evidence for this conclusion is presented, a brief recapitulation of the assumptions upon which the measure of class voting is based is in order.

In estimating the importance of the class bases of politics, shifts to the Right or to the Left should be minimized because they blur the differences between social strata. In such political systems as the Anglo-American ones, shifts usually occur in the same direction in all politically relevant social groups. A shift to the Right such as the Eisenhower victories in 1952 and 1956 could conceivably be regarded as a decline in the importance of social class as a determinant of political behavior. It is probably true that a large vote for Eisenhower among workers meant that class identifications were less important in those elections than in that of 1948, for example. But it is contended here that only if the *gap* between manual and non-manual support of a party has lessened can one speak meaningfully of a decline of class voting. The data presented in *The American Voter* show without question that not only did all social groups vote more Republican in 1952 and 1956 than they did in 1948, but that *in addition* social classes moved closer together. But, was this part of a long-term decline of the importance of the class bases of politics? Or was this only a fluctuation within the "normal range" of change of the class bases of American politics, given the social and political structure of American society in this historical period?

Figure 1 shows the level of Democratic voting among manual and non-manual occupational groups from 1936 to 1960. Considerable shifting in the Democratic vote is evident, although class voting was not sharply different in the 1950's from the 1930's. About two-thirds of the manual workers voted Democratic in the three elections between 1936 and 1944; their Democratic vote rose sharply in 1948, dropped just as sharply in 1952 and 1956, then rose back to about 60 per cent in 1960. Among the middle class, the Democratic vote stayed between 40 and 50 per cent between 1936 and 1944, dropped below 40 per cent in the following three elections, and rose again to 46 per cent in 1960. The only election in which both strata moved in sharply opposite directions was 1948, which might be termed a "non-consensual election." If that election had been chosen as the beginning of a time-series, the end of class voting might have been predicted, but data for the longer period indicate that 1948 was exceptional.

No pattern of consistent decline of class voting is thus evident, and its level reached that of Britain and Australia only in the 1948 election. Nor has the level of class voting dropped to the average Canadian level in any election. It may be concluded from the evidence presented in Figure 1 that there has been no substantial shift in the class bases of American politics since the 1930's despite the prosperity since World War II and despite the shifts to the Right in the Eisenhower era.[15]

[15] The figures for middle-class and working-class voting patterns given in Heinz Eulau, *Class and Party in the Eisenhower Years* (New York: Free Press of Glencoe, 1962), p. 2, are not comparable to those presented here because Eulau utilized a measure of class based upon a combination of the occupation, income, and education of the respondent. The percentage-point difference in Democratic preferences of the middle class and working class, defined in this way, was 24 in 1952 and only 4 in 1956. Eulau's study was a secondary analysis of the two Michigan election surveys. Actually, for 1956, he dropped income as a component of the class index with the rather curious justification that "it proved so variable as an indicator that it seriously undermined the stability of the index and interfered with the comparability of results" (p. 45). One might ask how results can be comparable if different procedures are used to compute a major index. The variability of the effect of income may reflect the varying effect upon political behavior from election to election of different *components* of stratification.

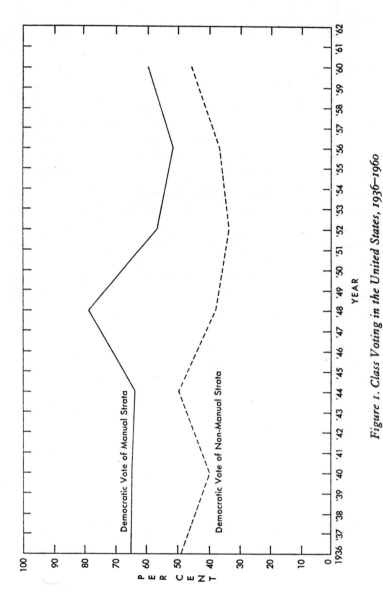

Figure 1. Class Voting in the United States, 1936–1960

The level of class voting found in the various community studies is fairly consistent with the national figures. The 1940 study of Erie County, Ohio, found that class voting was 17. The county at that time had a small and stable population of about 43,000, slightly more than half of which lived in the industrial town of Sandusky. Almost all of the population was native-born white, and the authors described it as largely working-class, with a "cultural and social life . . . perhaps not atypical of the middle western small-town and rural section . . . a 'church town.' " [16]

A later study of the 1948 election in Elmira, New York, found that "the business, professional and white-collar groups supported the Republicans fully 75 per cent; the workers split their vote almost fifty-fifty." [17] Assuming that this description corresponds to a manual-non-manual division, this is a level of class voting of about 24–26, considerably lower than the national level of 41 discovered by a Michigan study. Elmira in 1948 was a Republican community of slightly over 50,000, and class voting might be expected to be lower there than in the larger cities. Detroit in 1957–58 had a level of class voting of 32, much higher than the national level.[18]

The national data also permit some evaluation of the thesis of the authors of *The American Voter* concerning the causes of more short-term fluctuation of class voting. Class voting was not high in 1936, quite the contrary. Two separate national Gallup samples in 1936 show that class voting was as low in that year as in any subsequent year.[19] Figure 1 shows that this low level was due to heavy Democratic voting by persons in non-manual occupations.

[16] Lazarsfeld *et al., The People's Choice, op. cit.,* pp. 10–11. The level of class voting was computed from a table on page 19, which shows that when socio-economic status (as judged by an interviewer) was held constant, occupation made little additional difference in voting patterns.

[17] Berelson *et al., Voting, op. cit.,* p. 57.

[18] Gerhard Lenski, *The Religious Factor* (New York: Doubleday, 1961). The figure was recomputed from a table on page 125. Of course, it is impossible to know whether class voting dropped in either city from 1952 to 1958.

[19] Note that a percentage point difference of at least 8 may be due to errors of calculation, rounding, and other minor errors, so that no stress is laid on individual surveys, elections, or percentages.

All social strata felt a "need for a change" and voted Democratic accordingly. Social classes were not polarized by the class issues of the 1930's, but were attracted to the party that promised change.

Why the "depression-generation" in the later surveys conducted by the Michigan Survey Research Center exhibited more class voting is an interesting question which cannot be fully explored here. Possibly during such periods of crisis a consensus on the proper political path emerges. But after the crisis is over, the *memory* of the crisis assumes a different meaning for different social strata. In this case, for workers, the memory of the crisis reinforced their Democratic allegiances; for the middle class, it reinforced their Republican attachments, since the actual legislation carried out in the crisis period furthered the centralization of government which many see as furthered by Democratic office-holders.

Thus, the inference by the authors of *The American Voter* that class voting is likely to be higher in elections in which domestic economic issues are salient is weakened by some data from 1936. Their inference is also weakened by the rise of class voting in 1940, an election in which presumably the issues of foreign policy rather than issues of class were dominant. The drop in 1944 is also not consistent, since by that time the issues of national interest were abating, and domestic economic conflicts were again assuming importance. But, the purpose here is not to debate the salience of different issues in different elections. The main point is that no inference that class voting is declining can be made from evidence from great numbers of surveys ranging from 1936 to 1960.

Somewhat unreliable data from 1928 and 1932 reinforce, if anything, the conclusion that class voting has not declined since the 1930's. The League of Women Voters gathered 8,419 interviews in twenty-seven states two weeks prior to the 1932 presidential elections. The difference between the Democratic presidential vote of factory workers, on the one hand, and managers or semi-professionals, on the other, was 10 percentage points in 1928 and 22 points in 1932, as Table 1 shows. The Democratic vote went up in all occupational groups from 1928 to 1932 (again showing the consensus that a change was needed), but it increased much more among factory workers, and their greater swing accounts for the increase in class voting.

If any credence at all can be placed in these data, they are further evidence that no decline of class voting has taken place—only a fluctuation around a fairly stable class base for the political parties —since the early 1930's. The League survey is not reported . . . because of the unreliability and lack of comparability of the data. Its sampling accuracy may be judged from its finding that Roosevelt

Table 1. Democratic Preference, by Occupation, United States, 1928–1932

| | PER CENT VOTING DEMOCRATIC | |
OCCUPATION	1928	1932
Professional	25 (2227)*	30 (2215)
Semi-Professional and Managerial	21 (1701)	28 (1790)
Clerical and Skilled	24 (2130)	35 (2468)
Factory Worker	31 (334)	50 (427)
Difference between Highest and Lowest Percentages	+10	+22

Source: Recomputed from estimates in Samuel P. Hayes, Jr., "The Interrelations of Political Attitudes: IV: Political Attitudes and Party Regularity," *Journal of Social Psychology*, X (1939), 504–5. Since clerical workers and skilled tradesmen are combined in his tables, it is impossible to compute a comparable index of class voting. Class voting has been exaggerated, if anything, by using the manual and non-manual occupational groups which were farthest apart in their Democratic voting. The respondents were asked how they voted in 1928 and how they intended to vote in 1932. If the 1932 Thomas vote in each occupation is added to the 1932 Roosevelt vote, the parallel percentage-point difference is +20.
* Total number of respondents in parentheses.

received 30 per cent of the 1932 voting preferences in the survey. Nevertheless, differences between occupational groups are, as stated previously, less subject to sampling error than the actual marginal totals or proportions.

This conclusion holds for congressional as well as presidential elections. Surveys asking about congressional voting in 1946 and 1954, and party identification (whether a person considers himself a "Democrat" or a "Republican," regardless of his actual voting intention) in 1954 and 1958 were also available (the data are not given here in detail), and the index of class voting ranged from 16 to 21. Thus, since several surveys were available for different elections, there can be little doubt that the association of social class and voting behavior has not permanently changed.

Before we can accept the conclusion that class voting has not declined, it is important to consider where it may have declined or where it may have actually increased. Trends in various regions of the United States, as well as among various religious groups, may offer a clue as to the future role of social class in American politics. It is not at all clear, for example, that class voting will remain as low as it is. The disappearance of the loyalties of middle-class southerners to the Democratic party, when and if it occurs, may mean a rise of class voting and therefore a realignment of the social bases of the parties more upon class lines. And the possible dwindling of special religious and ethnic loyalties to the parties may have similar consequences. American political scientist Clinton Rossiter has suggested that in the future:

the influence of class on political behavior and allegiance may become even more visible than it is today, especially as the influences of ethnology and religion fade ever so slowly but steadily from view. . . . we are still a long way from the class struggle in American politics, but that does not mean that class consciousness is a negligible factor. To the contrary, it must inevitably become a more important factor as Americans become ever more alert to the rewards and symbols of status.[20]

The specific questions which can be answered from the survey data include the following: Has class voting declined or increased in any United States region? and Does this change seem to be related to any pervasive social changes taking place—such as urbani-

[20] Clinton Rossiter, *Parties and Politics in America* (Ithaca: Cornell University Press, 1960), p. 166.

zation or industrialization? We might expect that if any trend toward the political re-integration of the South is evident, class voting might have increased in that region since the early 1940's. On the other hand, in the most urbanized and older regions, such as New England or the Middle Atlantic states, class voting might have declined from a formerly high level, somewhat like the pattern in the London metropolitan area of Great Britain. These two trends—in the South and East—might cancel each other out to produce the over-all lack of change of class voting. Or we might find that class voting is higher in the urban South than in the rest of the South and infer that this is a sign of impending change of the social bases of southern politics and an omen of a future national realignment more along class lines.

Similarly, trends in the class voting patterns of Protestants and Catholics may foreshadow the future. It is possible that class voting has dropped among Protestants but increased among Catholics to cancel each other out as far as an over-all index is concerned. The diversity of politics in the United States implies that a single measure of the importance of a single factor for voting behavior is almost meaningless unless the relationship is examined in various other subgroups of the population.

Regionalism and Class Voting

The sectional character of American politics is a commonplace and needs no documentation. Many states, not ony in the South, have had a traditional alignment with one of the major parties. This has meant that each of the parties has long cherished a sectional stronghold within which the other party had little chance of winning legislative representation.

. . . in 1904 less than one-seventh of the population of the United States lived in states in which the parties contested the election on relatively equal terms, while in 1920 only about 12 million out of 105 million Americans lived in states in which they had a choice between two major parties both of which had some prospect of winning.[21]

And, as V. O. Key puts it:

Sectionalism . . . contributes to the multiclass composition of each of the major parties, a characteristic bewildering to those who regard only a class politics as "natural." A politics that arrays the people of one section against those of another pulls into one party men of all social strata. A common interest bound the southern banker, merchant, cotton farmer, and wage earner together against the northern combination of finance, manufacturing, and segments of industrial labor.[22]

One major question which can be answered by survey data, but which is not as readily answerable from ecological studies of the voting patterns of social areas, is whether class voting is actually substantially lower in areas such as the South. The second major question of concern here is, of course, whether class voting has declined in any major regions or whether it has increased, particularly in the South. Since the South is the chief example of political regionalism, and since its special role in the Congress has important political consequences for the nation, the voting patterns of the South will be of primary interest in the discussion of regionalism.

Southern politics is a one-party politics dominated by extremely conservative elements which distort the national party pattern by introducing a Right bias within the Democratic party, the major Left party of the nation. A few examples of the voting patterns of southern Democrats will show this internal contradiction within the Democratic party. On many clearly Left-Right issues in the 1960 Congress, the southern Democrats lined up with the Republicans. In a vote on a housing bill, thirty-five of the forty House Democrats who voted against the bill were southerners. (Only thirteen Republicans voted for the bill.)[23] In a vote on a bill pro-

---

[21] E. E. Schattschneider, "United States: The Functional Approach to Party Government," in Sigmund Neumann, ed., *Modern Political Parties* (Chicago: University of Chicago Press, 1956), pp. 203–4.

[22] Key, *op. cit.,* p. 267.

[23] *New York Times,* April 28, 1960, p. 12.

viding relief for areas suffering chronic unemployment, only one of the eleven Democrats voting against it was not a southerner.[24] In the 1962 session, the coalition of southern Democrats and Republicans appeared repeatedly. Typical are examples from House action on two bills on September 20. The House defeated a Republican-led drive to send the foreign aid bill back to committee. Of the sixty-five Democrats who were for referral (against the bill), sixty were southerners.[25] The farm bill, brought up the same day, was passed in spite of twenty-six southerners who were among the thirty-seven Democrats who opposed it.[26] These particular bills indicate again that the southerners are a conservative block on every type of issue, even on those presumably favoring their agricultural constituents.

Add to these voting patterns the dominance of southerners on key committees that determine which legislation shall come before the whole House of Representatives—a dominance due to their long seniority and lack of opposition—and some measure of the strength of the role of the South in American national politics is evident.[27] It is therefore of both practical and theoretical importance if the regional loyalties of southerners are being replaced by political cleavages similar to those exhibited by other regions.

Table 2 and Figure 2 show the trends and levels of class voting in different United States regions from 1944 to 1960. Table 3 summarizes results.

As with previous findings concerning the over-all level of class voting, there is no consistent pattern of change affecting all regions similarly. The political diversity of America remains great in this respect—that the degree of variation of class voting over time within and between the major regions of the country is considerable. The Eisenhower elections marked not a dwindling of this difference, but an intensification of it. If the single survey available for 1948 is

[24] *Ibid.,* May 7, 1960, p. 8.
[25] *Ibid.,* September 21, 1962, p. 5. Of the thirty-four Republicans against referral, nineteen were from heavily urbanized states.
[26] *Ibid.,* September 21, 1962, p. 4. Only two Republicans favored the farm bill.
[27] See V. O. Key, Jr., *Southern Politics in State and Nation* (New York: Knopf, 1949), Part 2.

Table 2. Democratic Preference, by Occupation Type and Region, United States, 1944–1960

OCCUPATION TYPE	NEW ENGLAND	MIDDLE ATLANTIC	EAST CENTRAL	WEST CENTRAL	SOUTH	MOUNTAIN	PACIFIC	TOTAL
1944								
Manual	77 (109)*	62 (330)	62 (257)	68 (139)	75 (103)	62 (71)	71 (110)	66 (1,119)
Non-Manual	48 (93)	50 (268)	38 (231)	38 (118)	64 (108)	33 (57)	45 (85)	46 (960)
Index of Class Voting	+29	+12	+24	+30	+11	+29	+26	+20
1948								
Manual	54 (94)	47 (319)	51 (243)	55 (117)	69 (81)	54 (69)	50 (114)	52 (1,037)
Non-Manual	29 (88)	31 (249)	27 (255)	30 (113)	53 (86)	47 (38)	32 (112)	32 (941)
Index of Class Voting	+25	+16	+24	+25	+16	+7	+18	+20
1952 (Sample No. 1)								
Manual	55 (56)	53 (137)	55 (156)	59 (73)	57 (189)	62 (21)	60 (65)	56 (697)
Non-Manual	29 (34)	30 (97)	30 (128)	33 (54)	47 (122)	27 (11)	27 (56)	34 (502)
Index of Class Voting	+26	+23	+25	+26	+10	+35	+33	+22
1952 (Sample No. 2)								
Manual	46 (140)	43 (488)	44 (460)	51 (178)	47 (665)	45 (69)	54 (224)	47 (2,224)
Non-Manual	23 (110)	31 (386)	28 (336)	20 (136)	36 (429)	20 (75)	36 (208)	30 (1,681)
Index of Class Voting	+23	+12	+16	+31	+11	+25	+18	+17

Manual	38 (42)	47 (104)	46 (65)	61 (46)	53 (105)	62 (16)	65 (49)	52 (427)
Non-Manual	14 (22)	30 (70)	39 (46)	30 (33)	50 (44)	37 (8)	46 (39)	36 (262)
Index of Class Voting	+24	+17	+ 7	+31	+ 3	+25	+19	+16
1960 (Sample No. 1)								
Manual	67 (67)	64 (370)	57 (302)	54 (120)	60 (317)	62 (37)	53 (137)	60 (1,350)
Non-Manual	68 (97)	57 (295)	30 (228)	36 (121)	42 (173)	48 (60)	42 (154)	45 (1,128)
Index of Class Voting	– 1	+ 7	**+27**	+18	+18	+14	+11	+15
1960 (Sample No. 2)								
Manual	60 (43)	61 (147)	64 (179)	60 (53)	56 (190)	72 (29)	57 (70)	60 (711)
Non-Manual	50 (52)	52 (198)	43 (167)	34 (76)	47 (258)	52 (44)	44 (141)	46 (936)
Index of Class Voting	+10	+ 9	+21	+26	+ 9	+20	+13	+14

Sources: 1944: AIPO Survey No. 323. 1948: AIPO Survey No. 423; Sample No. 1—Michigan 1952 Survey, otherwise reported in A. Campbell, G. Gurin, and W. Miller, *The Voter Decides* (Evanston: Row, Peterson, 1954), Sample No. 2—tabulated from the IBM cards available for the survey reported in Samuel Stouffer, *Communism, Conformity and Civil Liberties* (New York: Doubleday; 1955); 1956: AIPO Survey No. 573; 1960: AIPO Survey No. 636K and Roper Survey No. 75. With one exception, the regions correspond to the census classification.
* Total number of respondents is in parentheses.

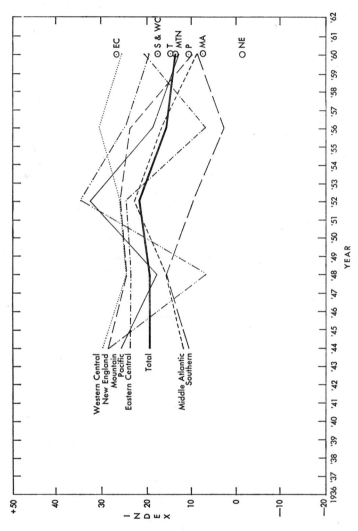

Figure 2. Class Voting in United States Regions, 1944–1960

representative of the electoral shifts in that year, the major regions
—save for the "Mountain" region—drew closer together in that
year—a "class" election—than in any other between 1944 and 1960.[28]

In these surveys, the over-all level of class voting varied between
14 and 22, while the highest level reached achieved in any region
was 35, and the lowest was —1. Unfortunately, sampling error is
so great for particular regional figures that trends within regions
cannot be regarded as reliable, and the few generalizations to be
offered must be regarded as speculative. An attempt to discern some
regular difference between regions in the average level of class
voting is presented in Table 3.

Table 3 lists the number of times each region was found in a
certain rank when the level of class voting was computed for each

Table 3. Rank Order of Class Voting in United States Regions

REGION*	FREQUENCY OF RANK							RANK-INDEX SCORE†
	1st	*2nd*	*3rd*	*4th*	*5th*	*6th*	*7th*	
West Central	5	1	1					10
Mountain	1	3	1	1			1	14
New England	1	1	3		1‡		1‡	24
East Central	1‡	1‡	1	1	2	1		26
Pacific		1		4	2			28
Mid-Atlantic					2	5		40
South		1‡			1	2	3	40

* See Appendix D for the composition of the regions based on the various
definitions.
† Ties were counted twice; then the next rank was skipped. The maximum
possible index score is +49; the minimum, +7.
‡ The deviations from the usual rank order found in two 1960 surveys.
Source: Derived from Table 2.

[28] These inferences are advanced with caution. The definitions of regions are
not consistent for every survey, and in the single 1948 survey available, the
rise of the over-all level of class voting found in the Michigan survey does not
appear. Even so, the regional pattern which it portrays may be found in other
1948 surveys.

region. It is noteworthy that most of the sharpest deviations from the usual pattern were found in 1960 surveys, particularly in regions where a pro-Catholic or anti-Catholic effect might have been expected: New England and the South. Class voting in New England was actually —1 in one survey. Further analysis by religion showed that this effect was indeed due to the Catholic vote, since class voting among Protestants was +22. Class voting in the South was higher in this election than in any since 1948, and the South ranked second in level of 1960 class voting in at least one survey.

No dwindling of the political diversity of America's regions appears from these data, therefore, and no apparent trend toward the reintegration of the South is found. There is also little evidence that the more urbanized regions such as New England or the Middle Atlantic states have high levels of class voting. . . . It seemed plausible to predict that class voting would be higher rather than lower in the regions both older and more urbanized in the United States, unlike Great Britain, because of the disappearance in urban and long-settled areas of various parochial political loyalties interfering with the emergence of class-based politics. No pattern of that kind seems to exist in the United States as yet.[29]

No detailed exploration of the regional regularities can be un-

---

[29] New England and the Middle Atlantic states have denser populations, a greater proportion of their populations employed in manufacturing, and more manufacturing establishments per 1,000 population than other regions, but not any higher proportion of "urban" population. (See *The World Almanac and Book of Facts* [New York, 1962], pp. 255, 280–96, 693. The original data are from the Census). The East North Central states did not differ much from New England on any measure. Urbanization may be an excessively crude measure for our purposes, and there are too few regions to be able to determine a meaningful rank order.

An ecological study of a smaller unit—congressional districts—in four election years (1944 to 1950) found that the correlation between the percentage of laborers in a district and the percentage of the Democratic vote was greater in urban than in rural areas. (Duncan Macrae, Jr., "Occupations and the Congressional Vote, 1940–1950," *American Sociological Review*, XX [June, 1955], 333). The author suggests that there is a stronger spirit of community and of cohesion that cuts across class lines in rural areas and small towns. The regional data available to the present author are apparently too "coarse" to exhibit the same result.

dertaken. It seems probable, however, that they are not accidental, and that certain historical and structural features of these regions could be found to account for the differences. The consistently low level of class voting in the South is no surprise and easily explained. But why does the West North Central region exhibit almost the highest consistent pattern of class voting? These are the midwest agrarian states, which are largely Republican: Minnesota, Iowa, Missouri, North and South Dakota, Nebraska, and Kansas. Clearly this is not a "regionalism" like that of the South, because both strata are not pulled over to a single party. On the contrary, as Table 2 indicates, the Democratic vote of manual workers is usually above the average; that of non-manuals, usually below. For some of these states, the high level of class voting may reflect the historical patterns of agrarian revolts, expressed through the Nonpartisan League in North Dakota and the socialist traditions of Minnesota.[30] But, whatever the cause, class voting in this midwest region is usually as high as in the London metropolitan area of Great Britain or in urban Australia.

The vacillations of the mountain region (the strip along the Rocky Mountains from Montana to New Mexico) are not so easily laid to a particular historical tradition and may merely reflect the small numbers of cases (the fewest in any region) or the heterogeneity of the region. But, as will be noted in the case of the Prairie provinces in Canada, part of this vacillation may be due to the frontier character of the region. Further research might be able to pin down some of the reasons for this and other regional regularities of political behavior.[31]

Although national surveys offer no evidence that the South, at least, is becoming more like other regions in its level of class voting —and is therefore losing its special regional allegiance to the Demo-

[30] It must be noted that these data do not include farmers, but only manual and non-manual occupations.

[31] The Mountain and West Central or North Central states not only have either high or vacillating levels of class voting, but also have had greater swings back and forth between the major parties than the other regions. See Harold F. Gosnell, *Grass Roots Politics* (Washington, D.C.: American Council on Public Affairs, 1942), pp. 13–17.

cratic party—other studies indicate that such a change may be immi-
nent. The Republican vote has steadily climbed in the South and
may be derived from middle-class more than from working-class
persons.[32]

Also, to some extent southern political distinctiveness may be
due to its character as a "backward" area and not to true differences
in the allegiances of similar kinds of voters. Evidence to this effect is
that urban Republicanism in the South has become quite similar to
urban Republicanism elsewhere.[33] The higher Democratic percentages in the South may increasingly come from rural Democratic
loyalties (which are Republican elsewhere) and which will be as
hard to change as any rural traditionalisms.

The authors of *The American Voter* note that "generally speaking, [status] polarization is lower in the South than in other regions
of the nation," but their data show that "Between 1952 and 1956 . . .
when levels [of status polarization] were declining elsewhere, there
was an actual increase of polarization in the South, from a coeffi-
cient not much above zero to a point of clear significance in
1956."[34] In a footnote, they suggest that "this trend may reflect
growing industrialization and urbanization in the South, processes
that are likely in the long run to blur traditional differences in
political behavior generally." This suggestion reflects a hypothesis
which the present author shares: Class voting should increase if
and when the influence of the traditional regional, ethnic, and religious loyalties to party dwindles.

Also, "status voting [was] more prevalent among *weak* party
identifiers than among strong in the South in 1952," with a smaller

[32] A gradual equalization of the contribution of different regions to the vote
of the major parties from 1896 to 1952 is shown in Paul T. David, "The
Changing Party Pattern," *Antioch Review,* XVI (Fall, 1956), 338–41.

[33] See Donald S. Strong, *Urban Republicanism in the South* (Birmingham:
University of Alabama, Bureau of Public Administration, 1960), for an ecological study of several southern cities. The author concluded that "Prosperous
southerners are now showing the same political preferences as their economic
counterparts outside the South. Here one may see the abandonment of ancient
loyalties forged a century ago and their replacement by voting based on
calculations of class advantage" (p. 57).

[34] Campbell *et al., The American Voter, op. cit.,* pp. 367–68.

but consistent such relationship in 1956.[35] This might indicate that persons who are breaking away from their Democratic identifications are predominantly middle-class and are the voters who are both least strongly identified with the Democrats and those whose shift to the Republicans accounts for the increasing class voting (or status polarization) in the South in 1952 and 1956 shown by *The American Voter* data.

Some evidence that the South may yet split along national lines when two parties develop there is given in recent unpublished studies by Herbert McClosky. He found that the Republicans in the South were even more conservative on a number of issues (and even more authoritarian) than the southern Democrats. The southern Republicans have therefore not been the natural home of liberals hoping to express their disagreement with the control of the Democratic party in the South by conservatives. The national two-party split between Left and Right is repeated in the South, the main difference being that *both* party elites are further to the Right than their northern counterparts. This indicates that changes tending to bring the South into two-party competition will not result in a liberal Republican party and a conservative Democratic party, but rather the same alignment as the rest of the nation.

In 1962, the congressional elections afforded further evidence of the dwindling importance of the traditional regional strongholds of both parties. The Republicans gained four more House seats in the South, won the governorship in Oklahoma for the first time in history, and nearly won a number of formerly safe Democratic seats. The Democrats in turn penetrated into hitherto safe Republican strongholds in New England, and Wisconsin possessed two Democratic senators for the first time.[36]

Religion and Class Voting

The continuing diversity of American politics is also shown by

[35] *Ibid.*, p. 368. Italics in original.
[36] See the *New York Times,* November 8, 1962, for a summary of the election results.

religious differences in class voting. As before, the main questions here are: Has class voting dropped among either Protestants or Catholics, and what possible significance do shifts by either grouping have for a future trend in class voting?

Evidence from six surveys in five different presidential elections indicates that class voting may be declining slightly among Protes-

Table 4. Democratic Preference, by Religion and Occupation Type, United States, 1944–1960

OCCUPATION TYPE	PER CENT PREFERRING DEMOCRATS			INDEX OF RELIGIOUS VOTING
	CATHOLIC	PROTESTANT	TOTAL	
		1944		
Manual	78 (245)*	60 (530)	66 (1104)	+18
Non-Manual	59 (165)	37 (537)	46 (949)	+22
Total	70 (410)	48 (1067)		+22
Index of Class Voting	+19	+23	+20	
		1948		
Manual	58 (316)	49 (674)	52 (1032)	+9
Non-Manual	50 (215)	24 (643)	32 (936)	+26
Total	54 (531)	37 (1317)		+17
Index of Class Voting	+8	+25	+20	
		1952, Sample No. 1		
Manual	52 (540)	44 (1598)	47 (2224)	+8
Non-Manual	34 (347)	25 (1168)	30 (1681)	+9
Total	45 (887)	36 (2766)		+9
Index of Class Voting	+18	+19	+17	
		1952, Sample No. 2		
Manual	64 (196)	52 (461)	56 (697)	+12
Non-Manual	38 (101)	23 (344)	34 (502)	+10
Total	55 (297)	42 (805)		+13
Index of Class Voting	+26	+24	+22	

* Total number of respondents is in parentheses.

OCCUPATION TYPE	PER CENT PREFERRING DEMOCRATS			INDEX OF RELIGIOUS VOTING
	CATHOLIC	PROTESTANT	TOTAL	
		1956		
Manual	59 (118)	49 (300)	52 (422)	+10
Non-Manual	48 (67)	29 (170)	36 (256)	+19
Total	55 (185)	41 (470)		+14
Index of Class Voting	+11	+20	+16	
		1960, Sample No. 1		
Manual	79 (214)	51 (444)	60 (711)	+28
Non-Manual	73 (233)	32 (600)	46 (936)	+41
Total	76 (447)	40 (1044)		+36
Index of Class Voting	+6	+19	+14	
		1960, Sample No. 2		
Manual	85 (385)	47 (869)	60 (1356)	+38
Non-Manual	75 (282)	29 (741)	45 (1128)	+46
Total	81 (667)	38 (1610)		+43
Index of Class Voting	+10	+18	+15	

Sources: 1944: AIPO Survey Nos. 323, 423; 1952: Sample No. 1, Past vote, asked in the "Stouffer Study" in 1954, Sample No. 2, recomputed from the Michigan study of the 1952 election, reported in A. Campbell, G. Gurin, and W. Miller, *The Voter Decides* (Evanston: Row, Peterson, 1954); 1956: AIPO Survey No. 573; 1960: AIPO Survey No. 636K and Roper Survey No. 7S (Sample Nos. 1 and 2). Discrepancies of totals are due to inclusion of Jews and persons in other religions or with no religion in the totals. The designation "index of religious voting" assumes that the percentage-point difference between the voting preferences of Protestants and Catholics, holding social class constant, reflects the degree to which religious affiliation affects political behavior. The Michigan voting studies found a level of religious voting (as measured by this indicator) of 14 in 1956 and 44 in 1960, identical or very close to the Gallup figures. See Philip E. Converse, "Religion and Politics: The 1960 Elections" (Ann Arbor: Survey Research Center, University of Michigan, dittoed, August, 1961).

tants, but that non-class factors affect the voting behavior of Catholics so much that no clear trend exists. Table 4 and Figure 3 show the vacillations of class voting among Catholics and an apparent slight decline among Protestants.[37]

The decline found among Protestants is not sharp, and the margin for error is such that we must conclude that for Protestants as well as for the total electorate in the United States, there is no evidence of any change in class voting. As a matter of fact, the level of Protestant class voting is more consistent than the Catholic and implies that much of the vacillation of class voting, possibly even in earlier years, has been due to the greater shifting of Catholics than Protestants.

Protestants have exhibited a higher level of class voting than Catholics in each election except in 1952. The general pattern is consistent with the presumed ethnic and minority sentiments among Catholics which override class sentiments as bases for political loyalties. If only the 1944, 1948, and 1952 data were available, it would appear that Protestants and Catholics were becoming just alike in their levels of class voting, since a pattern of convergence culminated in actually higher class voting among Catholics than among Protestants in 1952.[38] This change was due to a rise of Catholic class voting—not to a drop of Protestant class voting. More specifically, it was due to a pull of the Catholic middle class to the Republican nominee.

The 1952 election was the only one in which the religious deviation of both manual and non-manual Catholics was about equal. In all of the other surveys, Catholic non-manuals were much farther from Protestant non-manuals than Catholic manuals were from

---

[37] Here, as with the data on regionalism, the lack of more than one survey for each election makes the evidence on trends rather speculative. Since the more complete evidence from fifteen surveys shows no consistent decline of class-voting over-all, and the Protestant trend parallels the slight decline over-all found in these selected surveys—except for the 1960 estimate—it is possible that the Protestant decline of class voting is merely a function of the slight over-all decline found in these particular surveys.

[38] This is shown by both of the two surveys available which asked about the 1952 vote of respondents.

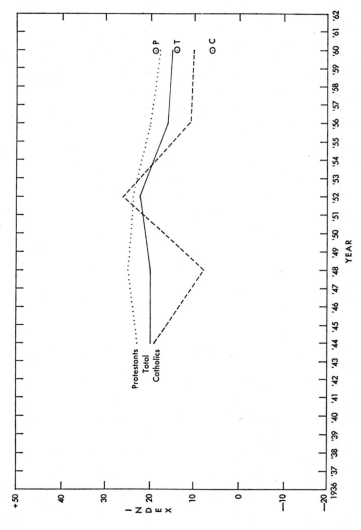

Figure 3. Class Voting among Catholics and Protestants, United States, 1944–1960

Protestant manuals. Catholicism seems in the United States to have more political consequences for persons in non-manual occupations than for manual workers. Because non-manual occupations are less identified as a particular social class (they are less homogeneous than working-class occupations), non-class loyalties and identifications affect the political behavior of persons in non-manual occupations more easily. But in 1952, this possible process affecting religious voting failed to operate. Non-manual persons in different religions were, for the only time, more alike than manual persons in different religions. In 1956 and 1960, they returned to the usual

Table 5. *Democratic Preference, by Religion, Occupation Type, and Subjective Class Identification, United States, 1952*

OCCUPATION TYPE	SUBJECTIVE CLASS IDENTIFICATION			INDEX OF SUBJECTIVE CLASS VOTING
	WORKING	MIDDLE	TOTAL	
	Protestants			
Manual	54 (314)*	39 (88)	52 (422)	+15
Non-Manual	45 (126)	23 (185)	29 (330)	+22
Total	52 (440)	25 (273)		+27
Index of Objective Class Voting	+9	+16	+23	
	Catholics			
Manual	68 (144)	47 (34)	65 (184)	+21
Non-Manual	52 (46)	22 (50)	38 (98)	+30
Total	64 (190)	32 (84)		+32
Index of Objective Class Voting	+16	+25	+27	

Source: Michigan 1952 Survey. Persons declaring that there were no classes in the United States are not included in the totals. Further analysis of the same survey which considers the effect of class identification upon political behavior appears in Heinz Eulau, *Class and Party in the Eisenhower Years* (New York: The Free Press of Glencoe, 1962). Eulau uses a different index of class, so that his results are not precisely comparable.

* Total number of respondents is in parentheses.

pattern. This 1952 deviation may have been due to the "strong foreign policy appeal to the ethnic groups, especially the Catholics and Germans." [39] The 1952 data indicate that such an appeal, if it was the cause of this Republican shift among the middle-class Catholics, did not affect Catholic workers, who were tied to the Democrats by both class and religious loyalties; thus class voting among Catholics increased to a point above that of the Protestants for the only time in sixteen years.

Whether class is defined objectively or subjectively, class voting was higher in 1952 among Catholics than among Protestants, as Table 5 shows. Although the Democratic vote within similar strata, defined *both* by subjective and objective class, was higher for Catholics than for Protestants (except among non-manual middle-class identifiers, among whom the Democratic vote was uniformly low), both objective or subjective class made more difference for the politics of the Catholics than of the Protestants. Holding occupation constant, the association of subjective class identification with voting was higher among Catholics than among Protestants. Holding subjective class identification constant, the association of occupation and voting was higher among Catholics than among Protestants. This is additional evidence that the lack of difference between Catholics and Protestants in 1952 was not spurious, and that class overrode the religious factor more in that year than in others before or since.[40]

In 1960, class voting among Catholics did not change appreciably from the 1956 level, but the association of religion and voting

[39] Lipset, *op. cit.*, p. 297.

[40] However, Oscar Glantz found sharp differences between Protestants and Catholics in a Philadelphia study shortly after the 1952 election, even when subjective social class and social status were controlled. Differences in political preferences were considerably less among persons in the two religions sharing a pro-business or pro-labor ideology, and, among persons with both high-status and a pro-business orientation, the religious difference in political preferences disappeared. This finding parallels that in Table 5, showing that middle-class Catholics (both objectively and subjectively) were no more Democratic than middle-class Protestants. These data were recomputed from Oscar Glantz, "Protestant and Catholic Voting Behavior in a Metropolitan Area," *Public Opinion Quarterly*, XXIII (Spring, 1959), 73–82.

went up sharply, undoubtedly because of the candidacy of a Catholic for President. Whether this swing was enough to offset anti-Catholic shifts is a moot point.[41] Even manual Protestants did not give the Democratic candidate a majority. Whether the victory of a Catholic candidate will finally end Catholic minority consciousness is an open question. American political scientist Peter H. Odegard suggests that "minority" consciousness may be the chief cause of the Catholic deviation:

As consciousness of "minority" status declines for any religious group, one may assume that other factors than religion will play a larger and larger role in determining voting behavior. That is to say, as intensity of religious identity or distinction declines, economic and social status may be expected to increase in importance in explaining voting behavior. As this occurs among American Catholics and Jews, their party preferences will be less and less influenced by religion and more by other factors. They should then become indistinguishable from the preferences of others of the same or similar economic and social status, regardless of religious affiliation.[42]

Although certainly this argument is plausible and should hold for the regional as well as the religious deviations from class voting in the United States, no evidence of a consistent increase of class voting or a decline of the religious deviation is as yet manifest. It might be noted that only among non-manual persons identifying themselves as middle-class did the religious difference in voting behavior disappear, as is indicated by Table 5. Not only objectively

[41] See Philip E. Converse, "Religion and Politics: The 1960 Elections" (Survey Research Center, University of Michigan, August, 1961), and P. E. Converse, A. Campbell, W. E. Miller, and D. E. Stokes, "Stability and Change in 1960: A Reinstating Election," *American Political Science Review,* LV (June, 1961), 269–80. These authors conclude from their careful analysis of a 1960 national survey that Kennedy suffered a net loss of slightly more than 2 per cent of the national vote, with a 4 per cent gain from Catholics and a 6 per cent loss from Protestants (p. 278).
[42] Peter H. Odegard, "Catholicism and Elections in the United States," in P. H. Odegard, ed., *Religion and Politics* (Published for the Eagleton Institute of Politics at Rutgers, the State University, by Oceana Publications, Inc., 1960), pp. 120–21.

higher status but a subjective sense of being part of the "great middle class" is required to rid Catholics of their sense of minority consciousness and, as a consequence, of their Democratic loyalties.

Obviously much more could be said about various political cleavages in the American electorate, but this chapter has focused on whether any consistent pattern of decline or increase of class voting was evident in general, within various regions, or within the two major religious divisions.[43]

Conclusion

No evidence of either a decline of class voting or any substantial change in the pattern of class voting among major United States religions or religious groups has been found. The diversity of American politics, remarked on by most political observers, remains as great as ever. Some signs of regional economic and political integration have been cited which may mean the pulling of the South into line with other parts of the country, but the outcome is not yet visible in any increase of class voting in that region. The 1960 election marked the greatest difference of Protestant and Catholic voting behavior since 1944, even when similar occupational groups were compared; therefore there is no sign yet of any decline of this source of non-class voting.

But despite this continuing diversity, data from a number of surveys from 1936 to 1960 have shown no unmistakable decline of class voting in the United States since 1936, despite the move to the Right in the Eisenhower period. As S. M. Lipset has said, "such factors as occupational status, income and the class character of the district in which people live probably distinguish the support of the two major parties more clearly now than at any other period in

[43] It should be emphasized, however, that there is more variation politically within Protestantism than between Protestants in general and Catholics. See Wesley and Beverly Allinsmith, "Religious Affiliation and Politico-Economic Attitude: A Study of Eight Major U. S. Religious Groups," *Public Opinion Quarterly*, XII (Fall, 1948), 377–89.

American history since the Civil War."[44] The data [presented here] reinforce the conclusion that there has not yet been, in V. O. Key's phrase, a "secular realignment" of the class bases of the political parties in the United States.[45]

Another incidental conclusion of the attempt to investigate changes of patterns of voting over time is that as wide a time-span as possible must be taken into account when attempting to assess not only political change but also the particular political behavior of a social group. The exceptional behavior of middle-class Catholics in 1952 is a case in point. If the only evidence for their political behavior were taken from that election, many false generalizations concerning the decline of religious deviations could be erected. Especially when the political realignment of entire social groups (rather than of individuals) is the research focus, as many surveys as possible over a broad range of time are necessary.

The lack of any consistent decline of class voting since 1936 does not necessarily mean that class loyalties and consciousness have remained strong. Workers might continue to vote Democratic and businessmen, Republican, but the sense of identification of this behavior with class interests might be becoming obscure and weak. Such a change could occur within both parties and social classes: the parties themselves could be moving ever closer together in their platforms and appeals, and/or occupational groups could be moving closer together in their values, styles of life, and political perspectives. An important line of research is implied by these possible changes: to determine what changes of political values and attitudes can take place *without* any substantial shift in the actual political alignment of a social group. The data on class voting give no direct clue to these changes, but they do give pause to the easy conclusion that the Eisenhower swing and postwar prosperity of the United States greatly modified the class differential in voting behavior.

[44] Lipset, *op. cit.*, p. 304.
[45] Key, "Secular Realignment and the Party System," *Journal of Politics*, XXI (May, 1959), 198–210.

Suggestions for Further Reading

GABRIEL A. ALMOND and SIDNEY VERBA, *The Civic Culture* (Princeton, N.J.: Princeton University Press, 1965). An excellent comparative study of the political culture of democracy in five nations: Great Britain, the United States, Germany, Italy, and Mexico.

ANGUS CAMPBELL, PHILIP CONVERSE, WARREN MILLER, and DONALD STOKES, *The American Voter* (New York: Wiley, 1960). This study deals with some of the determinants of voting behavior in the United States.

SEYMOUR M. LIPSET, *Political Man* (New York: Doubleday, 1960). A good study of the relationship between stratification and politics, showing the correlation between "modernization" and stable democratization.

LESTER W. MILBRATH, *Political Participation* (Chicago: Rand McNally, 1965). Milbrath presents a useful inventory of propositions concerning political participation. The propositions are arrived at from examination of previously published literature and data from the 1956 Presidential election study conducted by the Survey Research Center, University of Michigan.

✎Men Who Manage*

MELVILLE DALTON

The great German scholar Max Weber was the first sociologist to attempt a systematic theory of bureaucratic organization.[1] Weber noted several characteristics of the fully developed bureaucracy, among them: division of work and authority into a hierarchy of distinct "offices"; appointment of officials according to technical qualifications; remuneration through fixed salaries and pension arrangements; promotion according to seniority or achievement, or both; and separation of an official's organizational duties and privileges from his interests as a private person. Weber's theoretical approach was essentially formal in its emphasis on the structure and rules of bureaucracy, and the influence of his formal categories is evident in studies of bureaucratic organizations and behavior undertaken since his time.[2] Yet, as Melville Dalton points out in his Men Who Manage, *to understand the workings of a bureaucratic*

* The material reprinted here is from Chapter 6 of *Men Who Manage* by Melville Dalton. Copyright © 1959 by John Wiley & Sons, Inc. Reprinted by permission.

[1] H. H. Gerth and C. Wright Mills, eds., *From Max Weber: Essays in Sociology* (New York: Oxford University Press, 1946); Max Weber, *The Theory of Social and Economic Organization,* trans. by A. M. Henderson and Talcott Parsons, ed. Talcott Parsons (New York: Oxford University Press, 1947).

[2] See, for example, Chester Bernard, *The Functions of the Executive* (Cambridge: Harvard University Press, 1938); Peter Drucker, *Concept of the Corporation* (New York: Day, 1946); James G. March and Herbert A. Simon, *Organization* (New York: Wiley, 1958).

organization, it is necessary to examine the organization's informal structure as well—to study the unplanned interaction of individuals and groups within the planned bureaucratic arrangement. In Men Who Manage, *Dalton deals at some length with formal expectations and rule-oriented behavior, but he is mainly interested in "process"—behavior as it actually occurs within the preordained structure. His focus is on "power struggles" as they affect staff-line relations, managerial careers, and many other aspects of organizational life.*

The findings reported in Men Who Manage *are based on Dalton's many years of participant-observer research in several business firms. The scene of the study is four firms (three factories and a department store) ranging from 400 to 20,000 in number of employees. The company described in most detail is the "Milo Fractionating Center," a manufacturing plant with 8,000 employees, over 200 of whom comprised the executive force. Dalton was employed at Milo when he conceived the idea of studying the firm, and he collected data both during and after his employment there. The portion of his study presented here is concerned with the process of entry into and advance through Milo's organizational hierarchy. In gathering data at Milo and the other firms, Dalton sought the aid of experienced, reliable, and representative "intimates" who were to be aware only of Dalton's general research interest. The greatest number of these were located at Milo, where Dalton had 85 such informants: 11 workmen, 24 first-line foremen, 14 general foremen, 6 line superintendents, 8 staff heads or assistants, 18 staff supervisors or specialists, and 4 secretaries.*

Dalton notes the following steps for collecting information: "first, to interview formally several high officers with whom I was not intimate, with Milo presumably only one of several local firms to which the best informed managers would be asked the same question: 'What are the things that enable men to rise here in the plant?' Next, I explored official statements in the supervisory manuals and handbooks. Only then did I turn to intimates for unofficial

*statements and seek to check accumulated data against those in the
company files which a group of intimates were working to open for
my study."* [3] *Dalton also kept work diaries, in which he recorded
events, biographical information, gossip, and unusual practices or
"critical incidents" occurring in the plant. And much information
he, of course, gathered through informal observation as a Milo
employee.*

*As with all data-gathering techniques, participant observation
has both strengths and weaknesses. Certainly, it provides for breadth
and depth of detail; indeed, many latent or obscure patterns of
behavior could well go unnoticed except for the observer's participation. Moreover, since the observer is present during much of the
interaction under study, he is in a position to grasp the processes
and patterns of a behavior as a whole. On the negative side, the
presence of the participant-observer may bring about changes in
the action he wishes to study, and that he is playing a role in the
behavioral situation poses the hazard of limiting or distorting the
perspective of his observations. Dalton of course recognizes these
pitfalls; he argues persuasively that they are more than balanced
by the strengths of his methodology.*

The Managerial Career Ladder

Career Studies

Like other aspects of executive behavior, the subject of careers
in management is discussed with voluminous disagreement. Students of various backgrounds and interests have (1) made ques-
tionnaire surveys of high-level executives; (2) explored biographical
dictionaries as far back as the 1870's in search of data to reveal
career patterns; (3) recorded the anonymous remarks of executives
called to research conferences for group discussion of their world

[3] Melville Dalton, "Preconceptions and Methods in *Men Who Manage*," in
Phillips E. Hammond, ed., *Sociologists At Work* (New York: Basic Books,
1964), p. 70.

44

and its activities, with psychologists and psychiatrists present to put questions and to assess exchanges made around the circle; (4) built on other studies and brought them up-to-date in the search for backgrounds as career-shaping forces.[1] These reports variously suggest that industrial leaders are more likely to spring from some social groups than others; that opportunity for certain types of individuals to achieve success in business and industry is greater or less at one time than another; that individual success in some respects means probable losses in others; that formal or informal selection of executives is more effective; that one kind of executive training is superior to another; that selection and promotion should be from within or from without; that leaders should or should not be "bureaucratic-minded," etc.

Most of the studies have focused on the origins and traits of individuals as related to their social and occupational rank at the time of study. The correlation among these variables is often made a conclusion. This slights the functioning of executives in their various positions, their struggles for success, their gains and losses from moving in and out of cliques and other informal groups, their explanations and feelings about success, and the attendant complications of their progression through formal offices. Treated as the controlled digestion of information fitted to specific job categories, their formal education is overstressed, while the meaning of what is often simultaneously acquired—an unwitting but pertinent education in social skills—is not recognized. The search for quantitative bulwarks often leads students to treat their admittedly indispensable factual data as terminal answers, rather than as starting points for questions.

The Focus on Milo

It is easy to attack and hard to conclude, but in this chapter the stress will be on some of the "related factors" and "attendant complications." This will limit the report to Milo and comments on the findings of others, for Fruhling files were closed and those at Attica were undeveloped and inadequate for study of training,* and steps in careers. Our aim is to look at factors affecting the success of Milo officers in winning high place. Who was recruited and advanced? What were the bases on which people were chosen for preferment? What did "ability" mean, and how weighty was it in success as over against seniority, etc.? How did people go about climbing in the ranks?. . . . As a participant observer, with all the implied evils of self-deception, I of course asked questions on the basis of what I thought I already knew. But logical procedure demanded the corrective of checking my warped vision against other sources of information before returning for systematic soundings of several dozen intimates among the managers. The official sources of information also serve as a background for presenting the other data. In order, therefore, the research steps were to (1) formally interview several high officers with whom I was not intimate, (2) explore official statements in various supervisory

---

* "Misleading" would be a more correct term. As the Attica Central Office extended its rational controls, it requested copies of the personnel records of department heads and other high officers. These records were to go in the Office payroll files so that the local managers could be paid directly from the Office. Reynolds and the others of the pioneer group believed that "it would not look good" for their favored group to have a background of, say, ten years as a laborer, eighth grade schooling, and a commonplace title throughout the period. So with the understanding and cooperation of the plant chief, they "doctored" the personnel records of the fifty-eight men who would be known in the Office chiefly by these documents. This was, of course, meeting rationalization with rationalization. Those who had a labor record were given a respectable clerical title for that period. All members were reported as having at least a high school education, and one or two years of college was preferable and commonly reported, though many of them apparently had no high school training at all. Some of the drab current titles, such as "department foreman," were changed to "Master Mechanic," "Director of," "Administrative Head," "Plant Accountant," "Works Paymaster." The extent to which these records had been altered could not be determined.

These practices were of course not confined to Attica, nor are they unique to business and industry. For some comment on background enlargements by individual job-hunting executives, see Perrin Stryker, et al., *A Guide to Modern Management Methods,* McGraw-Hill Book Co., New York, 1954, p. 259.

manuals and handbooks, (3) get unofficial statements from intimates by systematically posing the same questions to all, and finally to (4) check these accumulated data against those found in plant files which a group of intimates were working to open for my study.

The answers of one high line and one high staff officer to a question indicate the typical official statements that were made on qualities essential for success. The comments of these men, both Roman Catholics, on the topics of religion and secret societies were not provoked by me. Although ages and years of service, etc., will be presented later for all the managers, some of these items are usually given with each person's comments for whatever additional relevance such information may have for more specialized students. The question asked was, "What are the things that enable men to rise here in the plant?"

L. Bierner, an inactive divisional superintendent suffering from heart trouble, aged fifty-seven, and employed by Milo for thirty-eight years, answered:

Integrity, loyalty, and honesty! Nobody can keep an honest man down! If you deliver the goods, you'll be pushed. If you help your superiors they'll help you—they'd be fools not to! I've heard a lot of stuff in the plant about Catholics and Masons and how you have to be one or the other. There's nothing to that! It's just in men's heads and has no basis in fact! If you're loyal, your boss doesn't give a damn what your religion is—he'll probably be glad you've got some and that's all. Men come in and raise hell because somebody got to be a foreman and they didn't. They bring up all this stuff about being a Mason or a Catholic or something else. There's nothing to it! The men who say this sort of thing are merely trying to find excuses for their failing—because they don't have anything on the ball. All you've got to do is to show people you're a right guy. All you've got to do is get on the ball and hit it, and nobody will raise any questions as to what your religion is or what you belong to. Any unbiassed objective person can see this. The guy who's always making charges of this kind has nobody to blame but himself— he won't take the necessary steps to improve himself. When men complain about not being foremen, I tell them the truth. I tell them so they can improve themselves or go somewhere else, but I never want to ruin or discourage them. I've often turned men down who later improved themselves and were given foremen jobs. There's no substitute for honesty and fair-dealing among men in industry.

You talk about people getting up in industry. Do you know that seventy-five per cent of supervisors don't want to advance if it means more work and responsibility? They want money but not what goes with it!

The staff officer, T. Cowper, was forty and had been with Milo nine years. His formula was simple.

I think there are three important things necessary to success in industry: First, ability. There's nothing that can replace ability. Second, freshness and flexibility of viewpoint. A manager must be able to meet changing situations. If he can't do this he won't be a successful supervisor or manager. Finally, a man must have willingness to work. It takes no end of hard work to be a manager. You've probably heard talk here in the plant about the company requiring you to be a Mason or a K. of C. to be a member of management. That's a lot of bunk. Nobody ever told me that I have to belong to anything. Sometimes management names certain people to be members of the Chamber of Commerce. But that's not forcing them into anything. Membership in that is not a social affair but a business relationship. It's part of the job. It's just helping to look after the company's interests. There's a lot of people in management who are Masons, and who belong to the Country Club, but they aren't required by management to join. We had a man who was chairman of the Ration Board and quite a number of the boys were on draft boards during the War, but nobody required them to be. People in management can belong to anything they wish. I'd say the organization is fairly democratic. It was once said that the Masons were prominent. Now the Masons don't show their rings and buttons as they used to.

Where Bierner stresses character attributes and implies the need of an unspecified kind of ability, Cowper is saying that dynamic plant conditions demand originality, flexibility, and hard work. They both say in effect that the essential qualities are obscured by the excuses and lamentations of those lacking the qualities.

These were little more instructive than Bierner and Cowper. They spoke of "ability," "honesty," "cooperation," and "industry" as qualities important for advancement. "Merit-rating" plans were referred to as a means for appraising fitness, but no sample plans or enumeration of important characteristics were cited in these booklets. Nor were leads given concerning the steps for the managers to follow in getting a rating, etc. The term "ability" was not defined anywhere in the manuals or interviews. Still it was obvious that, though unarticulated, many of the managers could agree on what they meant by the term. They used the term to mean capacity (1) to maintain high production, but low operating costs and a low rate of grievances (without illegal strikes) and of accidents; (2) to make "good contributions" toward the solution of critical issues, (3) to preserve "good relations" in the department and between departments, and (4) to subordinate personal to organizational aims. Some of these tacitly acknowledged factors could have been measured roughly, but no record of such indexes in relation to a promotional scheme existed. Some of the staff groups did, however, make periodic though conflicting appraisals of their members with possible promotions in mind.

UNOFFICIAL STATEMENTS

Most intimates, from the work level to near the divisional level, strongly denied that promotions were subject to any formal system, or that such a plan would be followed if it did exist. The following ten partial statements are selected as representing those who in theory would be most eager for promotion—skilled workers, first-line foremen, and staff personnel. Their responses are to the same question asked of Bierner and Cowper.

J. Bennett, a skilled worker of forty-seven with thirty-one years in the plant, gave this explanation:

Promotion comes about by being a Mason. Twenty-five years ago Henry Blair brought in the Masons when he was made division boss. Now ability or nothing counts so much as being a Mason. Look at Hall and Diller—[his foreman and general foreman] they're both Masons, but Rolland [another foreman of Diller's] ain't, and he's got a college education. And that's why he don't have to Diller's job. Rolland knows more about mechanics than anybody in the shop. You need to get wise. Look around. Hell, all the bosses are Masons. You can get by with murder if you're a Mason. Take Diller. He'll "yes" a man to shut him up, but if it goes higher, he'll "yes" whoever's above him. Hell, you don't have to be a Mason just to get a promotion, you have to be a Mason to keep your job.

The first-line foreman, Hall, to whom Bennett referred, was content to remain where he was in the ranks. At fifty-three, Hall had eight years of schooling and had been with the company thirteen years. He had been a machinist four years before being promoted. His answer:

By hard work. I got where I am by hard work. I always done what I was told and was willing to do more. I never asked for any favors, but was willing to help others.

With the corporation for twenty-two years, Sam Perry had been a first-line foreman for nine years. He was forty-five and had attended school eight years. His comment:

Well, I think a lot of things help a man get ahead. I think a lot of the old-timers around here got in by having friends. Some of them got up by ability. But it beats hell out of me how some of them got their jobs and how they keep them. I got my own job by helping people and doing things I wasn't expected to do. When Taylor was assistant superintendent over here I always helped him out every time I saw a chance. He asked me one time how I'd like to come up and see them install officers in the Masons. I knew damn well that was an invitation and that I couldn't lose. I went up and applied to get in. When he got to be soop, [superintendent] he asked me to take a foreman's job. Well, here I am. I wouldn't want to get any higher though—you catch too much hell. I always dread vacations. I have to take Hampton's [general foreman] place for a week every year. The least little thing you do you'll find you've stuck somebody's neck out. When I used to just work in here I couldn't hardly wait for vacations, but now I hate 'em.

H. Trimble, a sixty-three-year-old first-line foreman with eight years of schooling and thirty-seven years' service with the corporation, answered:

Mostly their own ambition. If they do their work well and anything else that comes along, they'll do all right. A man has to do more than what's expected. First you'll be trusted with a few small jobs to see how you handle them. If you do well—you're on the way up.

I used to be ambitious when I was a young fellow, but I never knowed how to keep my damn big mouth shut. I'd just as soon tell my bosses to go to hell as to look at them. If I'd used my head I could have been someplace. Two different times, after I got to be a foreman, my bosses got big jobs in some of the other plants and wrote to me asking me to come and be a superintendent for them. I had five kids in school and owned my home and just didn't want to tear up and move to a strange place. Besides, back in 1929 when I got the first offer, I was making pretty good money then—about $360 a month. I thought I had the world by the tail and a down-hill haul. When the depression come I lost all my savings and wished I'd taken the job. It pays to have friends but it's my own fault it didn't pay me.

J. Evans, aged fifty-three, was an outspoken foreman who had been with Milo for thirty years. A high school graduate, he boasted that he had "read more" than his college trained children. He laughed at my question:

I'm surprised that anybody who's been around here as long as you have would ask that question. You know as well as I do that getting in and running around with certain crowds is the way to get up. Nearly all the big boys are in the Yacht Club, and damn near all of 'em are Masons. You can't get a good job without being a Mason [Evans was a Mason]. Hell, these guys all play poker together. Their wives run around together, and they all have their families out to the Yacht Club hob-nobbing together. That's no mystery. Everybody knows it. It's the friendships and connections you make running around in these crowds that makes or breaks you in the plant.

Look at Rupert [the assistant superintendent]. He's the misfit suck-ass in his department. By his toadying in the Yacht Club—making boats, repairing them, making models, giving parties, and so on, he's been able to keep in their good graces. That's why he can fall down on job after job they've given him. He gets by with murder.

Rutherford [predecessor of Stevens] got up by family connections. His father owned a plant in the East. It finally became a part of our corporation. Rutherford was manager of a plant six years after getting out of college. Now by God that's not working your way up from the bottom. You're a college man, too, but by God you couldn't do that—you've got nobody pushing you. Take Geiger. I don't want to take any credit away from him. He's a damn good man. There's no doubt of it. But he was a good friend of Berelson [predecessor of Rutherford] who used to be the big shot. Berelson was thick with Rutherford. Geiger was Berelson's private chauffeur and took over the same job for Rutherford when Berelson retired and moved South. That's how Geiger got up.

There's no promotion system whatever. Seniority, knowledge, or ability don't count. You've got to be a suckass and a joiner. You've got to polish the old apple and have a lot of "personality." I was once asked to join the Masons, and it was hinted that there'd be a good job in it for me. I told them it was against my religion. They said, "Why Jim! You're not a Catholic. What do you mean, it's against your religion?" "I mean that if I can't have a job on my own ability I don't want it!" Well, I cut my legs off by talking like that. I didn't realize it at the time, but when I was passed up three times in favor of somebody else, I caught on, but I raised hell anyway. They told me I "wasn't a good salesman," that I wasn't "known—nobody knows you!" Since then there's been two more promoted past me. There's fifty men right here in the plant who could tell you a story just like mine. That's why over a dozen of us ignored the invitation to the big dinner and a medal for twenty-five years' service. Some of them went, but half of them didn't.

Bridges [president of the corporation] sent out a letter a couple of years ago to every member of supervision. In this he requested that any foreman or supervisor having a grievance should carry it up step by step through his superiors until he received satisfaction. If he's turned down at one level go to the next, and so on, even if it comes to Bridges himself.

That's a lot of bull! There's not a man in the plant that would do it. They're all afraid to go above whoever made the decision on it. They know damn well how they can be made to suffer without being able to prove that everything's not on the up-and-up. They'll all accept whatever decision is made about their beef and do nothing about it.

A night supervisor, aged sixty, J. Cunningham had two years of college and had been with the firm seventeen years. His views were similar to those of Evans:

Well, by God, it's not by ability! I can tell you that! It's who you know that counts, not what you know. Take Dick Pugh. He knows nothing about accounting but he has a man under him who's a trained accountant. Hell, that's not right. Anybody can see it's not. The accountant gets a little over $400 a month while Dick pulls down better than $600. Do you see any justice in that? Look here [showing a list of supervisors], there's one, two, three, four—nine men who are drawing the pay of foremen and carrying the title. Yet none of 'em have over five men under them. One man could easy boss the whole damn bunch. Why do you think they get away with it? Because they're Masons? Not by a long shot! That's part of it, but there's other reasons. Fisher's uncle is one of the directors. He thinks we don't know that, but that's how he gets by. Jones is a son-in-law of the assistant superintendent. Brown is always flunkeying out at the Yacht Club. And the soop [Cunningham's superintendent] gets a hell of a kick out of dancing with Davis' good-looking wife. If she's going to dress well and keep on looking good, Bill's got to make his $515 a month and feel like staying up nights—and a lot of these nights he spends home with the kids. His kids are damn nice. Two little girls. But Bill wants a boy, and Liz [the wife] says there'll be no more kids.

Look at my own job! On nights I'm responsible for the same thing that it takes Blaine, Taylor, Hampton, Vick, and Streeter to do on days. They average about $850 a month while I get only $575. Figure it out— five hundred seventy-five bucks compared with forty-two hundred and fifty. [Total monthly salaries of Blaine, Taylor, Hampton, Vick, and Streeter.] Now you tell me. How do you think men get up in industry? [All salaries mentioned have been increased considerably since the interviews.]

L. Wilkins, forty-eight, assistant staff head with twenty-two years' service, answered by comment on his own lack of success in the organization.

I've quit raising hell, but I don't let it get me down. I go ahead and do a good job because I know there are a lot of innocent people dependent on my doing a good job. They [his superiors] know I've got three kids and that I'm not as young as I used to be and that I probably couldn't get as much money starting anywhere else. I don't think [the Office] would tolerate the things going on here in the plant if they knew about them. There's some people around here that think they're little tin gods and they want to draw a group around them that'll treat 'em that way. And if you treat them that way you won't have any honesty or principles left. That's the part I can't take and that I've never been able to swallow. I've got to live with myself, and I regard my own self-respect more than I do dollars, when I've got enough to live on. Most of these fellows are boot-lickers with a set of principles made of rubber. If you study the matter closely you'll find that to succeed here in the plant you've got to be unfair—favor some and mistreat others. That's why Phillips [his former superior] left. He couldn't be unfair with people—it just wasn't in him. If you get ahead around here it won't be on ability but on agreeing with everything you're told whether you think it's fair or not—and keeping your thoughts to yourself. When election time comes around and you think the Democrats have a good man, keep it to yourself and pretend you're a Republican. Now I never do that. Sometimes I vote one way, sometimes another way—and I never hide who I think is a good man. [Wilkins was recently demoted to a low rank in a different staff and put on hourly pay. His associates say "the reason was, he talked too much."]

A college graduate, aged thirty-nine, E. Stein was a staff officer who had spent much time in the Central Office. His response was:

The company naturally talks of having a promotion system. But this thing of "ability" is damned hard to pin down. It's easier to get at when you've got something concrete to work on. For example, when you're down on the lower levels in industry—say a machinist or a time-study man—you can always be checked on your worth to the company. Your superiors can see that you're doing something. If you were suddenly asked at the end of a month or a year just what you'd contributed to the company's cause you could point to some statistics. It's not that way when you get up higher. The higher you get, the more your advancement depends on impressions that your superiors have of you. And these impressions are based on almost no real evidence. If a high staff officer or a division superintendent were asked what he'd done for the company during the last year he'd have a hell of a time pulling up anything concrete. When you're in a position like that you know all the time that other people want your job and are trying to get it—and you know that impressions are constantly being formed of you. I know it goes on. I see my supervisors here. I find that people up in the front office have impressions of them. They're typed. And the whole damn thing is usually wrong and always unfair. Vaughn or McNair will see my supervisors for maybe twenty minutes once or twice a month and will form impressions of their merit on such evidence as that. Hell, you can't judge a man's capabilities from no more knowledge of him than that!* Yet these guys insist on getting first-hand impressions. They know damn well they don't have any foolproof means of rating men so they're conceited enough to think they can look at a man and size him up—find out how he stacks up alongside others and how much he's worth to the

---

* Based on wide experience in both large and small firms, T. K. Quinn supports Stein's observations. See *Giant Business: Threat to Democracy*, Exposition Press, New York, 1953, p. 139. Stein's observations on "ability" have been echoed elsewhere and from much higher vantage points than his. See Eli Ginzberg, ed., *What Makes an Executive?* Columbia University Press, New York, 1953, pp. 67–68, 71, 73–74 and 79, in which various top level executives (1) deny the existence in their firms of any "list of qualifications . . . for promotions," and admit that they promote on the basis of their liking the person and his success on the previous job; (2) confess they do not know what leadership qualities they are looking for and doubt the validity of much of the writing on leadership; (3) reject all formal promotion schemes and instead judge the merit of a man for promotion by "how loud an outfit screams when you want to take a man away," a device recommended by the late sociologist, Louis Wirth, for discovering the operations and effectiveness of an institution. The existence of an abstract, transferrable ability is scouted by some. See C. Wright Mills, *The Power Elite*, Oxford University Press, New York, 1956, pp. 140–141.

Stein's concern for "some statistics" supports W. H. Whyte, Jr.'s (*The Organization Man*, Simon and Schuster, New York, 1956, p. 167) observation on the search for "some index of achievement that no one can dispute."

company. And their impressions just boil down to whether they like a man or don't like him. When you walk into a room with them you can see that they're intent on getting every impression of you that they can. You've got to always be on guard about your dress, speech, manners, and general conduct. All that has nothing to do with brains or ability. Look at Edison, or Lincoln, or Henry Ford—they were too busy doing things to be fussy about how they looked. Yet even if I'm an hour late of a morning, I'll shave. Some people will skip their shave if they were up late the night before. But it doesn't pay. I first noticed this when I was in [the Office.] There, the higher you went the more you got involved in politics. Everybody was uneasy and trying to beat everybody else in making a favorable impression. [Stein was recently promoted to the top post in his staff.]

C. Gregg, a low-ranking staff supervisor, aged twenty-eight, had been with Milo for four years. He responded with rambling attacks on the "front," the "sham" and the "insincerity" of Milo managers as a group. He noted that ten years earlier, Milo had

. . . decided to do away with the hard-nosed boys of the old school. They want men that can pat you on the back and hand you a smooth line without meaning it. They want guys who can put on a front. Men here in the plant get their jobs by connections, not by ability.*

In most cases the heads get a good man under them and let him make the decisions. They bear down on the assistants because the assistants are afraid of their jobs and have to carry the major part of the responsibility for their decisions, as well as the few the head himself may make. Take [a reorganized and newly tooled department]. Word comes down that being more modern they shouldn't have to use as many men as before. That's a damn lie—it nearly always takes as many workers as before, but skip that. The point is that everybody gets the shivers. They're all afraid of their jobs, and rumor increases the fear. And ability plays only a small part in their getting or holding their jobs.

* Production workers, elsewhere, have observed that after meeting all formal qualifications, "pull" and "connections" were still needed to become a foreman or advance from that position. See Eli Chinoy, *Automobile Workers and the American Dream*, Doubleday and Company, Garden City, N.Y., 1955, pp. 52–60.

Among line personnel, only Hall, Perry, and Trimble suggest that "work" and "ability" are factors in advancement. Evans admits that Geiger has ability but does not see this as the major factor in his success. Evans, Cunningham, and Wilkins clearly think ability is lost in the shuffle of personal relations and the requirement that candidates know the right people.

As staff men, both Stein and Gregg suspect ability is a minor item. But Stein more perceptively does not deny that ability is sought and considered so much as he laments the absence of techniques for uncovering it, and the association of inappropriate earmarks with it.

These contradictory statements mean little without the more objective evidence that comes from study of ages, job experience, years of service and time spent in each level, amount and kind of education, etc.

Occupational Data

If a firm selects and advances its supervisors on the basis of skills and experience that fit them for more important and difficult work, we can assume that some detectable relation exists between job rank and the factors we have just mentioned. Certainly we could expect some fairly clear age limits for people entering at the bottom and at each successive level if there were to be regular advances. For responsible administration of others we might also expect a minimum term of service as a measure of fitness before appointment to higher levels, not that age and experience guarantee wisdom. Then too, in a firm with great specialization and division of labor, such as Milo, we would expect a close tie between job and type of training. Let us see how the Milo data fit into some of these categories; for example, age at time of appointment, years of service at appointment, and education in terms of amount and subject matter. This last, as the assumed open-sesame to all rewards, deserves close attention.

Table 1 includes current ages and all but one of the above items for the three line groups and the staff. The "superintendents" include all levels and categories—full, assistant, and assistant-to. . . . The first entry for each management group shows the age at appointment to that group expressed as the average, the median, and the range for all. The age range of 42 years for foremen, 33 for superintendents, and 30 for staff people shows only—excepting the one adolescent first-line foreman—that entrants must be adults, young or old.

Table 1. Occupational Data on Milo Managers

MANAGERIAL GROUP	DATA CATEGORIES	MEAN	MEDIAN	RANGE
First-line foremen	Age at appointment	36	37	16–58
	Years service at appointment	12	11	0–38
	Years education	11	11	6–20
	Current age	48.5	48	31–65
General foremen	Age at appointment	44.4	44.5	26–62
	Years service at appointment	16.2	17	1–31
	Years education	11.8	12	8–16
	Current age	50	50	35–65
Superin- tendents	Age at appointment	41.4	41.5	25–58
	Years service at appointment	19.8	19	3–35
	Years education	13.8	14	9–19
	Current age	48.7	49	35–65
Staff group	Age at appointment	36.6	33	24–54
	Years service at appointment	13	10	3–35
	Years education	15.2	16	9–19
	Current age	42.9	41	29–61

YEARS OF SERVICE AT APPOINTMENT

Here, too, we see that some members of all levels were with the corporation as little as three years before achieving their present rank. In the two lower line levels some members entered as supervisors without previous experience in that role, at Milo or else-where. The narrowest range of service was 30 years for the general foremen. With their average of 16 years, this suggests no clear service prerequisite for entry. Six general foremen had less than 5 years' service, whereas 11 had 25 or more years as they came to the job.

The relation between years of service and entry for the staffs and superintendents defies classification. Sixteen superintendents starting as production workers required 8 to 30 years (M. 19.3, Md. 20.5) to make the grade. Six of the 16 by-passed the level of general foreman. The other 10 were caught as general foremen for 1 to 8 years. Nine superintendents came from staff organizations where they had been employed 3 to 35 years (Md. 14).* Six super-intendents entered Milo as first-line foremen and spent 3 to 12 years there before taking superintendencies. The remaining 5 su-perintendents took the office after 14 to 33 years (Md. 21) in the line as clerks or secretaries.

The absence of regularity is clear. Seventeen superintendents served in some line supervisory role, but never as general foremen. Only 16 of the 36 superintendents started as workers and became first-line foremen, and 6 of these got double promotions in skipping the rank of general foreman. Five members became superintendents with no previous administrative experience. However, we must note for its later relevance that, apart from systematic promotion, these five, with their average of 21.8 years of handling confidential records and observing events, undoubtedly had immense knowledge of internal affairs, both economic and political, and used it.

In terms of their job histories, education, and ages, the staff force fell into two clusters. One group of 23 with an average of 16.5 years of schooling entered Milo as staff employees and rose to current positions in from 3 to 11 years (Md. 7), at which time they averaged 31 years of age. The other group of 13 entered the

* Dispersion of the data was so great in some cases that the mean values, having coefficients of variation in excess of 50 per cent, were deficient as meas-ures of central tendency. See T. C. McCormick, *Elementary Social Statistics,* McGraw-Hill Book Co., New York, 1941, p. 130.

line organization with 12.8 years of formal training. In various clerical and minor supervisory roles they remained there for 17 to 35 years (Md. 22), where apparently they were tolerated as near failures for various reasons. They were gradually moved over to less rigorous staff positions at 39 to 53 years (M. 48) of age.

Looking at the median years of service at time of appointment for the 190 line officers we may fancy we see a pattern of promotion: personnel became first-line foremen after 11 years, general foremen after 17, and superintendents after 19 years. But this is misleading. First, the obviously disproportionate numbers would bar most foremen from rising to the top. Ignoring this limitation, the foreman's case was still hopeless, for fewer superintendents were being drawn from the bottom and the rate of progression for foremen was falling sharply. We saw above that over half of the superintendents did not start at the bottom, and that six of those who did skipped a step. Study of current ages shows that foremen were moving up more slowly. For example current foremen had already held their positions 12.5 years,* which was 5.2 years longer than current general foremen had served as first-line foremen. Also the foreman's remaining years before retirement were little more than those of his superiors: he was only 1.5 years younger than the general foremen and only 0.2 years younger than the superintendents. If the first-line foremen had immediately become general foremen and held that office for only the time that the general foremen had served (M. 5.6 years), and had then become superintendents, they would have been 54.1 years old and would have been employed 30.1 years, as compared with the superintendents who served 19.8 years to reach that office, but after being there 7.3 years† were still less than three months older than the foremen.

Despite the weakness of this kind of statistical discussion, it is clear that movement through the hierarchy varied greatly and that age and years of experience were not important for appointment and promotion at Milo.

---

* Current mean age minus mean age at appointment.
† See preceding note.

EDUCATION

Years of schooling expressed as an *average* for each group was related to rank in management. Education included time of attendance in grade school, high school, college, trade schools, night schools, and years of study by correspondence. As seen in the table, each ascending level in the line had more education than the one below it.* These differences were not due to exaggerations of time spent in night school or correspondence study. For even when averages of only the grade, high-school, and college totals were considered, the difference persisted: first-line foremen, 10.5 years; general foremen, 11.2 years; superintendents, 13.1 years. And though only trifling, differences in the same direction persisted when night, trade, and correspondence schooling were totaled and averaged separately for each level: first-line foremen, 0.5 years; general foremen, 0.6 years; superintendents, 0.7 years. The tie between education (grade, high school, and college only) and rank was also found when the 36 superintendents were broken down into their formal levels: departmental chiefs, 12.5 years; divisional chiefs, 13.7 years; plant head and assistants, 15.3 years.

This bond between rank and schooling suggests several things. First, that those with the greatest amount of relevant subject matter and formal skill logically earned higher rank. However, this was not true at Milo. Only a minority of the managers were in positions associated with their college training. Lumping the 226 managers together, the formal duties of at least 62 per cent of them did not relate to their specialized education. Considered by rank, the percentages whose duties did not match their training were: first-line foremen, 61 per cent; general foremen, 81 per cent; superintendents, 61 per cent; staff, 50 per cent.

As examples of training among first-line foremen not directly applied, one man had two years of schooling in traffic; another, three years in physical education; a third, two years in advertising; a fourth, two years in journalism.

* Differences between educational means of the line strata, as well as between the latter and the staff group, were statistically significant at better than the one per cent level in all but one case, which barely missed that level.

Among general foremen, one had three years in chemistry; another, two years in pre-medicine; a third, trained in engineering, was in charge of a warehouse.

Among the superintendents, one trained in medicine; a second in law, and so on.

In the staffs, an M.A. in engineering was an auditor of non-engineering matters. Another, with the same degree and subject, was a cost accountant. The head of industrial relations had a degree in chemical engineering; his assistant, aeronautical engineering. These gaps were also common at Fruhling, and are probably widespread* for reasons discussed below. Thus the subject matter of education was not a magic key to success.

A second theory might be that amount of education was important as a test for elevation. Certainly this is often used as a rough screening device. Some executives see it as a measure of ambition, reliability, persistence, and character.† Volume of edu-

* The Wharton School of Finance reports a low relation between the training and later work of some of its alumni. Cited by W. H. Whyte, Jr., *The Organization Man,* Simon and Schuster, New York, 1956, p. 88. See also W. Lloyd Warner and J. C. Abegglen, *Occupational Mobility in American Business and Industry,* University of Minnesota Press, Minneapolis, Minn., 1955, p. 29, who note that only one-third of the business leaders in their sample had commercial training in college.

Comparing the vocations and inventions of inventors, David Cort points to a frequent gap between formal training and the products of creative output. See "World's Most Valuable Men," *The Nation,* December 8, 1956, pp. 497–500.

† Ginzberg, *op. cit.,* pp. 50–51. Strong criticisms of currently fashionable criteria for recognition of executives are offered by the English writer, Aubrey Silberston, in *Education and Training for Industrial Management,* Management Publications Limited, The Millbrook Press, Ltd., London, 1955. He holds (pp. 15–16) that "systematic selection methods, however carefully devised, are no substitute for long acquaintance with a person." He doubts (p. 6) the "universal validity" of any of our pet traits and categories, such as "high standards of integrity and loyalty, courage, imagination, initiative, acceptability to others, intelligence, pertinacity, and optimism in the face of adversity." He quotes an "experienced manager" who suggests that "the quality which matters most of all is resilience under adversity." In other terms this quality is examined below in chap. 9. He admits that (p. 12) "some technical understanding is required in nearly all managerial jobs," but ranks personal qualities as probably more important in most cases.

cation was not ignored at Milo, because some reference was almost invariably made to education when promotion was discussed. But specific merits of education were not stressed, and the fact that some men rose to high levels without college training[2] while others with it remained near the bottom speaks for itself.

Another common explanation points to family origin as the source of both education and aid to success, so that the father's occupation and background become the clue. Students disagree on this[3] and the incomplete data on Milo managers gives little support to the view. Data on father's occupation were available for only 31 of the 72 superintendents and staff officers, and these show little that could be regarded as a definite pattern of impetus accounting for placement of the sons. For example, the fathers were: 4 small farmers, 2 grocers, 9 skilled workers, 2 school-teachers, 1 telegrapher, 1 police officer, 1 barber, 2 sales clerks, 1 insurance agent, 4 industrial foremen, 1 consulting engineer, 1 realtor, 1 streetcar motorman, and 1 locomotive engineer. The sons had a median education of 14 years, and 18 were on jobs not related to their training.

The most workable theory in the present case is that increased years of schooling at the college level are directly, but complexly, related to managerial skill in carrying on the endless round of unavoidable compromises. This is to say that the total experience of going to college may be more important for the executive than the technical courses he takes. In the last decade or so, executives themselves, with various educators and students,[4] have questioned the adequacy of some subject matters and have proposed curricular changes, but they have given little if any attention to the career consequences of the student's campus life, drives, and competition as an *experience*. It is much too simple to say that candidates are selected because of their education. Doubtless they are to a degree, depending on how status-givers interpret education. But in view of the controversies over subject matter and the evidence that years of schooling relate to rank, there is merit in thinking that educated candidates select certain ranks. Education in this sense means the student's total growth during his tenure on campus; the formal doses, yes, *and* the inseparable unintended acquisitions.

Before we can talk of the transfer of college experiences to executive tasks, we must compare the unofficial executive and student roles. . . . Here in a paragraph we must note salient features of the executive's environment. He deals with ambiguity. Though he has defined goals and understood ways of reaching them, he functions only as he fashions new routes that are always out-of-date. Yesterday's guide often fails him in today's contradictions. His indispensable ability is not to act out cut-and-dried precepts, but to carry on where there are no precepts. If he is to escape "ulcer gulch," survive as a leader, and protect himself without permanently alienating associates, he must precipitate but channelize crisis, and aptly compromise to preserve the uncompromisable.

The student's career on campus is trivial as compared with future rewards and responsibilities, but given certain common conditions, his experiences are an unwitting preparation for the executive role. Years of "education" have many implications for the type of student (*a*) who attends school with more vocational than intellectual purpose; (*b*) who wishes to participate widely on campus and yet craves good marks; and (*c*) who for these and other reasons is forced to budget his time. Such a student may have both vocational aims and intellectual fire, but the first is essential and seems typically dominant. He may have received a financial and psychological boost from his family, or his campus cronies may have awakened his career consciousness. Knowledge of employers' expectations may give him the "A-fever" if campus honors do not. Long before he completes high school, the student has learned that in our society he must participate or be a "grind" in danger of becoming "introverted" or "maladjusted" or even "antisocial." Social activities take time but may pay unexpected returns. These activities would of course include the efforts to enter and climb in fraternities, most recreation, and dating.

Taking a part in campus politics gives the student an experience he may not get outside of college, at his age, short of entering professional politics. He tries his hand at helping select and elect officers, and may himself serve. His part in the intra- and inter-organizational struggles is educational. He learns to move in and out of cliques and organizations with minimum friction. He mixes with the mentally elect and competes with those who also have pangs of status- and career-hunger. Success as a campus "wheel" is instructive and good for his record.

If with all these activities, and the helpful obstacle of part-time work, he is still able to make good marks, he has learned how to function inside limitations. Probably he has become adept at analyzing his professors and utilizing his social contacts whether he is consciously calculating or not.* If his limited time demands more short cuts to maintain his grade points, he studies his professors to (*a*) isolate their pet theories; (*b*) outguess them in preparing for examinations; and (*c*) to please them. Although apple-polishing may not always pay off as expected, the exercise in grappling with the unknown still enlarges his executive potential. He compares notes and impressions with other students. This requires cooperative exchanges and sharpens skill in cracking cliques that have a corner on past examinations. Some of his circle of friends may be part-time library personnel and help him to monopolize hard-to-get books, and/or to keep them out overtime, as well as escape fines or have them reduced.†

However, competition for grades and contacts, the deadlines for delivery of term papers and reports, and the occasional baffling professor, may defeat all these maneuvers. This is good, too, for developing possible administrative talent. For in addition to the skill of easy cooperation with others, the student now has to gamble on his own and determine the unascertainable. He becomes

---

* Those who cringe at the activities of this alert student were obviously never campus "wheels" and will not be executives.

† Some of my successful intimates (in terms of their high marks in college and quick rise in industry) at Milo and Fruhling and acquaintances in other firms have boasted of these practices. Also see Ginzberg, *op. cit.*, p. 175, on executive performance in relation to overcoming obstacles in getting a degree.

sensitive to intangibles, and learns to live with the elusive and ambiguous. This unofficial training teaches him to get in his own claims and gracefully escape those of others that he must. He learns to appear sophisticated and to adjust quickly to endless new situations and personalities.

Despite what we have said against subject matter, some of the student's courses may contribute to his developing social skills. The first two years of college are usually designed to "broaden" and "give perspective." His travel through time and space on the wings of biology, history, anthropology, politics, sociology, philosophy, psychology, may bring him home with a new view of family and neighborhood precepts. He may lose some dogmas about what is worthwhile, what is good and bad, and about the virtue of fixed ways of doing things. Even if he doesn't change deeply, some desperate situation may provoke him to activate his inert knowledge of successful means used by dead heroes. At least he may avoid the error of thinking that "politics" and "rat races" are peculiar to our time or to a particular kind of organization. Thus subject matter of this kind may combine with the unofficial education acquired under various stresses to produce a type of person with hidden executive possibilities.* Such students receive much more "vocational education" than they bargain for or pay for.

This is not to say that all college graduates are executives in the rough. Obviously not all fit the type we have posed, which was based on rather narrow but close study of such people as Hardy, Springer, and Rees at Milo and others at Fruhling. For instance, a kindergarten teacher might fit our type, though there is a ques-

---

* Some top managers argue in favor of recruiting campus "big shots" as potential executives, while others say such persons are "spoiled" and can function happily only as "adulation" is heaped on them. This second group would focus on candidates who make high marks without concern for their popularity. But a third group, supported by some evidence at Milo, reports most satisfaction from hiring those students who were both big men on the campus and high scholastically. See Ginzberg, *op. cit.,* pp. 45–47. For executive impressions of formal knowledge versus judgment as factors in success, see The Editors of *Fortune, The Executive Life,* Doubleday, Garden City, N.Y., 1956, pp. 213–214, 216–217.

tion about the force of her status aspirations, and never show the qualities we attribute to the successful executive because her role is very different from that of executives—however much she might protest to the contrary!

Whether experience in college gives the urges or merely stirs latent qualities born elsewhere, or whether earlier conditioning and college are necessary, at Milo the drive for personal* success as the major end of life was the goal of the college-bred oftener than the noncollege.

Evans, as we saw, was widely read and verbal but was not "college-processed," and was most critical of the behavior he saw as essential for success. Also noncollege, Trimble admitted the "error" of his earlier views. Perry, with eight years of schooling, frowns on what is needed for success. Gregg, a high school graduate, is of the same view, and Wilkins, with two years of high school, thinks the formula is to "be a bootlicker with a set of principles made of rubber."

On the other hand, Cowper, with a degree, emphasized the value of "flexibility" in success. In another connection he remarked, "I'm always willing to deviate in clearing up problems. By that I mean to ignore principle for the moment in order to follow it in the long run."

Haupt, a college graduate, usually successful in compromising on unessentials to preserve the sinew of policy, made a maxim in Milo by his repeated defense, "I always try to make two and two equal four. Sometimes I wind up with three-point-nine or four-point-one, but that's close enough."

Cunningham was an exception. With two years of college, he denounced the behavior associated with success.

---

* D. Starch, "An Analysis of the Careers of 150 Executives," *Psychological Bulletin,* 39:435 (1942); A. W. Kornhauser, in *Industrial Conflict,* First Yearbook of the Society for the Psychological Study of Social Issues, The Cordon Company, 1939, XI, pp. 210–211; Warner and Abegglen, *op. cit.,* p. 132, show that, in their sample of around 8000 executives, college graduates required 20 years to reach their positions, as compared with an average of 31 years for those with little or no formal schooling.

The few cases of noncollege men who practiced and approved the compromises essential for success were atypical. Successful practices are of course contagious and can be variously imitated by some, but many of this group were barred by moral feelings from adopting the more rewarding conduct. Implicitly preaching the morality of fixity, they demanded simple and unvarying practices in their daily relations. . . . Their potential for accommodation, or ability to adjust to change, was low. Rank seems to relate directly with this potential. That is, success as an executive requires aptness in fitting means to ends inside the limitation of preserving the organization, which includes its indispensable personnel. The intruding moral issues are part of our problem of explaining how the managers rose in the structure, but we too must compromise and ignore them for the present.[5]

Thus age, work background and service, and formal education as training adapted to positions, all showed such variations at Milo that none of them could regularly be formal tests for recruitment and promotion.[6] Scattered cases indicated the same was true for Fruhling's 940 managers.

Case materials are a threat to the researcher. His loving care to turn his matchless insights on every crumb of his findings easily trips him into platitudes. With this threat as a monitor, I should like to comment quickly on typical unofficial events attending (1) the choice of candidates for open positions, (2) demotions, (3) sinecures and competence for office, and (4) salary variations.

Careers in Process

VACANT POSITION AND PROMOTION

Inconsistencies about the official route upward naturally provoked fears, speculation, and search for unofficial routes. Vacation of an office by the advancement, death, or transfer of its occupant was followed by a period of silence and suspense as to who the successor would be. Except in case of sudden death, there had usually been some planning for the vacancy, but this was often vague even to those who counted themselves as likely candidates.

At Milo a small group of superiors, which included Hardy, conferred and prolonged the suspense by delays of one to three weeks in naming a successor. Importance of the office was naturally a factor. Sometimes it was allowed to die, but no notice would be given of this intent. Assuming the office would continue, the field was left open for speculation on the criteria* that would be used.

The behavior of both those with and without hope of being chosen showed conviction that personal factors would decide, and that the choice would have personal consequences for subordinates. During this period, subordinates who professed to have excellent grapevines would slight their duties to impress others with their knowledge of what candidates were most in favor. Wagers were made with odds given and taken on two or more possible candidates. At the same time there was debate as to who *should* have the office with expressed fear and hope as to the consequences. While supporters of a candidate pointed to his favorable qualities such as age, experience, education, personality, influence, and family conduct, others noted cases where these factors meant nothing. Some of those fearing a certain appointment, assured the group they would transfer or quit "rather than work under him."

Unexpected appointments or promotions brought excited analyses of the selection. In some cases personal competence as a factor was never mentioned, though theorizing about the matter might recur for months.

The assumption that all members of a firm perpetually crave to move upward, and that only the aggressive can rise, has noteworthy exceptions. The case above of Perry could have been multiplied several times, even up to the divisional level. The mere wish not to go higher in the ranks, as in Perry's case, did not prevent

---

* On occasion some of the high managers implied a certain essential behavior in aspirants. Brady, the Milo griever, told me that at the time of Taylor's failure to get an expected post, he (Brady) asked Blanke why. Blanke replied: "Nobody knows him. It wasn't because he lacked ability but because he didn't use the plant politics the way he should have." As we have seen, this was *an ability* Taylor lacked.

the person from rising. Though some individuals successfully declined invitations to take higher office, others were coerced into entering management, or into taking higher supervisory posts.

The case of Evans illustrates successful rejection of higher rewards and the variations of upward drive in one individual. Despite the fact that he denounced the conduct associated with success, and that he "raised hell" with his superiors when he "was passed up three times in favor of somebody else," he recently declined the assistant superintendency when it was offered to him. His explanation to me:

Goddamn the job! When I was younger and needed the money, I couldn't have it. Now that my kids are all grown and nearly through college the old lady [his wife] and me can get by without it. It would have been damn good ten years ago to have a little extra cash. But I'm fifty-three now and I don't have the expense I used to have. There's a lot more hell goes with the job than used to. I don't mean to be catching hell the last twelve years I'm here. Some guys'd sell their souls to be a superintendent, but not me.

Some workmen of great skill and technical grasp were encouraged by Milo managers to enter the ranks, and in some cases were forced to.

L. Jackson was one of these. As a practicing Fundamentalist from a farm community he possessed certain presumed virtues for ascendancy. His habitual hard work, reliability, and often stated belief that "man was meant to earn his bread by the sweat of his brow," were not lost on H. Warren, general foreman of that area. Warren was convinced that "Jackson is a man you can trust when your back's turned." He asked him to accept a foremanship. Jackson declined. Warren offered uncommon privileges, including the right to select individual members for his work crew. Jackson still refused and explained that he was "not qualified to be a boss." Accustomed to bitter rivalries for foremanships, Warren was delighted and redoubled his efforts. Just before taking his vacation, Jackson again declined. Returning on Monday two weeks later, Jackson was approached by a work crew who asked for assignments. He responded with "Why ask me?" They quoted Warren as having ordered them the preceding Friday to report Monday to their new boss, Jackson, and they referred him to the bulletin board for proof. Jackson tore the notice from the board and went to Warren's office where he also found Warren's chief, O'Brien. They both apologized for their action, and explained that they were "on the spot. Please help us. There's not another man we value as much as you. We've got to get the work out and nobody else but you can do it." Jackson accepted, but rejected the position in less than three months. Division chief Springer had complained to Warren over some production detail in his province. When Warren conferred with his foremen and found that one of Jackson's men was responsible for the difficulty, he spoke sharply to Jackson. Jackson quit his job and went home. Warren and O'Brien drove over to see him that night and explained that they meant nothing "by bawling you out. That's part of the job. We have to do that to make things look right upstairs. You know there was nothing personal meant. Won't you reconsider?" Jackson refused to return except to his old job as workman.

When Warren was later made top manager of one of the corporation's smaller units he again turned to Jackson, and this time asked him to come and head a department. Jackson declined. His case shows that Milo directors were concerned to reward some kinds of ability.

The division chief, Revere, took that office under protest. Starting at the bottom at age twenty-two, he climbed to department head in twenty-two years. After ten years there he was asked to take his present position. He declined and gave bad health and diminished family responsibilities as reasons. However, his reluctance was based less on these considerations than on status and income factors. After having been department head for four years, Revere had seen Hardy take over this very division at the age of twenty-nine. Informants said Revere wanted the job at that time and was bitter over Hardy's getting it. And Hardy's moving into his present post six years later did not soften Revere's feelings. As division head Hardy had received $17,500 as compared to the $12,500 received by Revere when he took over the office. Although this was an increase for Revere of $3700 over his salary of $8800 as department head, it was still $5000 less than a rival had received. The gain of $3700 did not cover the injury to Revere's feelings and had to be supplemented by the command that he take the vacated position or retire.

The cases of Jackson and Revere point up both the complexities of career motivation and the play of personal relations in planned organizations.

DEMOTION

Little attention has been given to the fall of individuals in organizations.* Possibly as a status tragedy, the whole subject has been shunned, except for superficial post-mortems on "reasons for failure," which usually skirt the errors of status-givers, the validity of criteria used in selection, and the social factors in organizational defense tactics.

Demotion from failure is typically disguised to protect not only the individual ego and the organization's investment in him, but also his original sponsors. If the demotee has high status, a post is created for him, or he is made an "assistant-to," where "his skills will be most helpful to the company," or he is fitted into a staff "to round out his experience," etc. He retains his previous salary.

B. Schwann was Rees' second assistant. . . . Rees sought to hand down unofficially official decisions to strengthen first-line foremen. When Rees was visiting the Central Office or busy with other things, much of this work fell to Schwann. At other times Schwann was expected to "troubleshoot" and aid in nipping developing grievances by keeping Rees informed on shop affairs. At all times he was expected to have on tap a supply of effective suggestions. Because he was always available, hard-pressed executives called on him more and more for informal suggestions which were

---

* Demotion for failure is part of "social testing." See Pitirim Sorokin, *Social Mobility,* Harper and Brothers, New York, 1927, pp. 182–211. Where Sorokin's concern is the institutional testing of individuals for fitness to remain or be rejected, ours is how failure of the individual in a given position leads not to rejection but to his retention and reclassification in the organization.

treated as decisions by line chiefs—at their wit's end, or eager to involve the staff in trouble. Son of a school teacher, Schwann had little background for making potentially hazardous decisions. He took a degree in education, and in his own words, "led a soft life in college." He then taught in a small high school for several years, became "disgusted" with the work and pay, and took a job as timekeeper in industry. From there he entered Milo by personal connections. He moved to second assistant in five years and was transferred two years later to a newly created clerical office with routine functions in the same staff, "where we can make better use of his psychology." But according to superintendent Meier:

Schwann was eased out because he couldn't do the job. He'd complain of his stomach hurting him. Right in the middle of a meeting with a dozen people sitting around a table, he'd jump up in pain and run out into the hall to get a drink of water and come back with tears running down his cheeks. He knew of the relation between nervous strain and stomach ulcers so he'd pretend he had indigestion. Hell, we all knew he had ulcers. His nervous system just couldn't stand up under that sort of strain.

You'd go up to his office for an answer on some squabble you were in with the union. He'd listen and tighten up all over. Then he'd squirm and twist and strum his fingers on the table. Finally he'd give you an answer and say, "How's that? Is that about right? What do you think?" Well, hell! That's no answer! You go in to see him because you don't know what to do, and then a guy shows you *he* doesn't know what to do! You want a quick, decisive answer and no beating around the bush— something sharp and final, the way Rees hands it out. You're usually holding up things waiting for that answer.

Well, you know what happened. Schwann had to give up. He was too soft. He didn't have the nervous system to take it.

• • • • •

SINECURES AND COMPETENCE FOR OFFICE

Thinking of sinecures as flexible offices with pay but few if any fixed duties, we can see that the office of "assistant-to" was frequently a sinecure. In addition to the functions of "assistant-to," . . .

sinecures were used to accelerate and bolster careers. They could be created at nearly any level, be dropped arbitrarily, or they could be semipermanent and be succeeded to. But not all posts of "assistant-to" were sinecures, nor were sinecures confined to this office. Whether to reward those who were failing but had served well, or as a substitute for unavailable higher posts, to protect an overrated person from claims beyond his revealed strength . . . as an inducement, to cover errors in judgment of appointing officers, or when given in rare instances just as a favor, in all cases sinecures could have the dignity and façade of any office. For example, the formal organization chart shows that superintendent Ruf had a first-line foreman reporting directly to him. Informants said this foreman had no "real" responsibilities, but was only a "stooge." The same statement was made of the similarly-placed foreman in the charted department between Geiger and Meier. The chart also shows at least a dozen general foremen* without first-line foremen. Some of these offices were clearly more than sinecures, though several of them had few routine duties, and all the occupants received the pay of general foremen for no more than the duties, without the pressures, of first-line foremen. Confidential complaints by some foremen and "authentic" general foremen indicated that several of the offices were given as direct rewards for various reasons. And during reorganizations some had been preserved for morale purposes or to hold highly competent general foremen who might have quit if demoted. Like that of "assistant-to," use of these offices had followed expediency and social demands more than economic logic. However, it is likely that the long-run gains of Milo were greater than if rigid formal theory had been followed.

Never referred to as such, sinecures were common enough to be talked about a great deal at Milo. Informants estimated that the number of "good" sinecures, including those in the staffs, varied from fifteen to twenty-five, while those of less value might fluc-

---

* As bearers of the title, all but three of the most questionable cases of these general foremen were included with the sixty-one on whom occupational data were presented.

tuate to forty-five or more. The failures who held sinecures were spoken of as persons who had "fouled out" or who "couldn't cut the buck." Others were "just on the payroll" for unexplained reasons, or were "fair-haired boys," or possessed "flashy personalities," or had "a lot of get-up and go."

Attitudes toward sinecures were by no means always unfavorable. Much like our senators and their attitudes toward lobbying, few officers, including those at top levels, could be sure that changing conditions or ill-health would not at some time find them glad to be protected or rewarded by a similar post. However, there was resentment in some cases because the real nature and operation of sinecures could not be publicized. Hence some persons mistakenly regarded them as permanent positions and grew embittered after hungering for one specifically only to see it remain vacant for months, or even die. The unofficial existence of sinecures was obviously contrary to organizational theory as well as the ideal in American business and industry that measurable contributions and reward should clearly match in all cases.

VARIATIONS OF INCOME

Salary variations inside specific limits were officially thought to be natural if not inevitable because of tacitly recognized differences in seniority, experience, etc. However, as with other features of planned action, various conditions [7] intrude to produce unplanned results. Set up in part to protect morale, the limits for a given salary range are overstepped to (a) encourage the nearly indispensable person to whom material reward is uppermost; (b) correct negative errors in appraisal and protect the appointing officer by allowing the granted status to stand, but with reduced salary; (c) lift the spirit of certain persons during presumably temporary reorganization by lowering their rank without salary change, as with demotion of assistant superintendents to general foremen; (d) induce an officer to submit to being "loaned" to another department where his title will continue unchanged to conceal the salary increase and prevent disturbances.

We can get at these variations by comparing an official statement with the beliefs, actions, and analyses of those involved, and with some of the actual salaries.

Cowper (mentioned earlier) was very close to the administration of Milo's salary and wage rates. He spiritedly defended the ideal of a one-to-one relation between individual ability and pay. In his words:

Incomes are confidential. They're an outgrowth of an agreement between a man and his superiors. Each man is correctly merit-rated according to his ability. I'll admit there have been cases where some superintendents have wanted to promote a friend without inquiring whether there was somebody else in another department better qualified for the job.* But that stuff doesn't go around here. In a small loosely-knit plant [sic] people can get away with that. But in a large well-knit plant like ours [sic], you won't find that kind of thing. I think you'll find that's usually true of most big corporations. You wouldn't find it here anyhow, because Stevens doesn't stand for monkey business.

Our salaries are set up on a sliding scale. A man coming on a job is paid according to where he falls on that scale. There's no question of his being correctly placed on the scale, but *where* he's placed is nobody's concern but his own.

Contrary to Cowper's statement, there was widespread belief that amount of income was influenced as much by "connections" as by ability. The general eagerness to discover even approximate salaries revealed these suspicions. A piece of mail delivered to the wrong office was opened by an officer. When he discovered that it contained code numbers and related data that with other available information and long calculations would reveal the annual salaries of officers in another department to within fifty dollars, he called an assistant and began the computations. Foremen, general fore-

---

* Silberston, *op. cit.,* p. 14, reports this as common in England: "It seems inevitable in most firms that certain appointments should be made without consulting the appropriate official. This is particularly likely to happen when a suitable person is available within the department where the vacancy occurs." Neither he nor Cowper analyze the system of claims in the department that requires such action.

men, and finally the assistant superintendent stopped all work to await the results. The withdrawal of nine men from regular duties for over two hours reflected the disbelief that incomes measured only ability.

Superintendent Taylor professed a lack of interest in the income of others but revealed a knowledge of techniques for finding out:

Many people in management get a kick out of feeling that they know something other people don't—that they're on the inside. And sometimes they just pretend to know. There's a lot of ways used for finding out about other people's income. People are always alert around tax-paying time. If they can hear just a word out of a man about his taxes, it'll mean a lot. People here in the plant do a lot of figuring on their taxes right in their offices. If you come in suddenly on a man and he gets a phone call just then, you can always let your eyes wander around his desk [laughing]. If you know how many kids a man has and how much taxes he paid, you can come close enough to feel good. People are always straining for a glimpse of somebody's pay stub—that's all it takes—you know right where to look, and one quick look does it. If you know the charging rate * in small departments you can come awful close to figuring what the big wheels get. If you hear a man drop a word about how much company insurance he has, you can come within a hundred dollars or so of his yearly income. If you can learn what the general foreman gets, you can come close to the departmental superintendent. Or if you know a departmental superintendent's salary, you can hit close to the general foreman and the divisional superintendent. There's no doubt that you can learn a great deal about incomes if you compare points with others and give a lot of time to cultivating it.

Taylor also implies that there was always a fixed relation among the salaries of different levels throughout the firm. The evidence shows that, despite the official scales, the managers did not invariably stand in a fixed salary relation to each other. Excluded

---

* The "charging rate" was the total salaries of technical and administrative employees of a given department divided by the total hours of the year which that department operated, and expressed in dollars.

from the functional cliques, Taylor here again was apparently unaware of practices known to others.

Income data are deficient. At one point in the research at Milo, exact incomes were obtained for ninety-six officers. But while inflation progressed with the research, the timing, rapport, and hazards of my personal contacts lacked this regularity. And as the sources of my information closed, some salaries were increasing more sharply than others. For example, some of the divisional officers received as much as three $600 increases in one year, with two of the increases coming in the last three months of 1956. Some officers at other levels received only one increase for the year. Hence annual salaries for first-line foremen through department heads are $1200 to $2800 more than given, whereas divisional heads are $3000 to $8000 more. Estimates of varying reliability roughly double the salaries for the plant manager and assistant but "substantially increase" the distance between them. Since the increases were not to correct imbalances except in a small minority of cases, the original figures still serve our purpose.

The scale of first-line foremen ranged from $475 to $600 per month. Yet at least eight salaried foremen were below the minimum with salaries of $425 a month. Years of service were no key to where foremen were placed on the scale, for one foreman of seven years' service received $550 for the same job that a foreman of ten years' service received $475.

The scale for general foremen ranged from $575 to $675. Here at least one man was below at $550, and another was beyond the upper limit with $750.

The incomes of departmental and divisional heads were given as annual salaries. The actual departmental salaries, with no mention of a scale, ranged from $8500 to $14,500. Smith received $8500; Dicke, $9500; Taylor, $10,600; and Geiger, $14,500. The divisional heads ranged from $14,500 to $16,000 with Springer and Revere receiving $14,500 each,* and Blanke $16,000. P. Finch received the

---

* Revere had received increases totaling $2000 since taking the office, possibly in part to ease his feelings about discrepancies noted earlier.

highest staff salary in Milo, $15,000. Hardy received $20,500; and Stevens, $21,000, as against a salary of $27,000 paid to Rutherford, his predecessor, several years earlier.

Since need and informal compacts could force salaries below and above "fixed" ranges, they could obviously make changes inside the official ranges even more readily. An officer in the Auditing Department told me:

In the last three or four years certain jobs have jumped up to around $750 a month. A new man comes in and gets much less, maybe only $500. Yet inside of six months he'll be getting $750. There's a lot of politics in here somewhere. It looks to me like some of the flashy personalities * get themselves liked and get around the rules. Some guy that's not liked, or steps on somebody's toes, is held to the rules, or maybe he don't even get the advantages of the rules. It looks to me like Smith [the line superintendent] is one of these. He's a damn good man but he don't click.

Stein sought to justify income variations as largely the result of impersonal necessity:

Many appointments are made on the basis of expediency. Sometimes when things are all snarled up, management has to put in a much bigger man than will be needed later on. Since he's going to have to do something really tough he's going to be paid well. When he gets things going, he'll be taken off the job and the next man will get less for less, which is

* These are the "highly visible" people observed elsewhere—those, *e.g.,* in Evans' remarks (above) who were "known" (as against his not being known) and who in Stein's remarks (below) are "tops in pleasing." See Blanke's remarks in footnote on page 69. Also see P. F. Drucker, *The Practice of Management,* Harper and Brothers, New York, 1954, p. 155. Phrase-makers have only recently named the practice "high visibility," but the behavior has long been advocated for personal success. For example, a master of many roles in the Italian Renaissance privately counseled, "If you . . . are the follower of some great lord, and would be employed by him in his affairs, endeavour to keep yourself always in his sight. For every hour things will occur to be done which he will commit to him whom he sees, or who is at hand, and not to you if he has to seek or send for you. And whosoever misses an opening, however small, will often lose the introduction or approach to matters of greater moment." Francesco Guicciardini, *Ricordi,* trans. by N. H. Thomson, S. F. Vanni, New York, 1949, p. 85.

only natural. Then again once in a while you'll come across a man who's tops in pleasing. He makes the right impressions and pleases everybody concerned. Since everything high up is based more on impressions than on anything concrete, his real abilities may easily be overestimated and he'll get promoted to a job that his abilities don't justify. Before long this will show up. Well, you'll have to move him, but he stays right on at the same pay. If you were paying him what you thought he was worth, and now you had to move him to some little piddling job, why his pay'll sure as hell be out of line with other jobs of that kind.

Stein begs the question. Seeking to show that salary variations for a given position flowed naturally from the play of impersonal forces, his reference to people who are "tops in pleasing" suggests that personal action to protect failures also contributed to salary differentials. At another time Stein declared that "one big reason" why salaries could vary on the same level at any time, was that younger men were coming in and "finding things all set up for them." Hence they "could not be expected to get as much as the men who had worked long and hard to get things organized." Unless one assumes some unrevealed differences in abilities or initial problems to be overcome, this explanation hardly covers the case of Springer's receiving $12,500 on taking office at the age of thirty-five, whereas Hardy, taking an office on the same level, several years earlier when inflation was less, received a salary of $17,500 at the age of twenty-nine. The same holds for the salary of $27,500 that Rutherford commanded at the age of twenty-nine as compared with $21,000 given Stevens several years later at the age of sixty-one and after thirty-five years of service with the corporation.

Thus the character of demotions, the use of sinecures and the office of assistant-to, the events attending promotions, the unofficial variations in salary and the multiple contradictions prompting them all complement the conclusions drawn about the data on personnel histories. These findings are of course not breath-taking but are a prerequisite to examining the recurrent charges that a set of unofficial standards was used for regulating careers.

Many profess to know that ability is only one factor in success, but scorn attempts to explore other influences as time wasted on the "obvious." Yet it is equally obvious that when speaking for the record, these same persons deny concern for any individual quality but "ability." Barnard [8] is a sophisticated exception. And another top executive ironically observes: "I really don't know how we find the natural leaders. I suppose mostly by smell. However I would not want to deny that there is an element of patronage and pull there [utility field] as everywhere else." [9] Stryker [10] sees executive criteria as "strictly nebulous," and "based 20 per cent on the record and 80 per cent on the personality." These figures are admirably neat. However even in organizations requiring a high degree of formal education and originality for entrance, as in academic and other institutions, personality can outweigh scholastic fitness in the eyes of both recommenders and selectors of candidates. Aspirants in some cases have stood in the top one per cent of their classes but have been damned as in only the top fifteen per cent because of attitudes and interests dissonant to "sponsors." Unacceptable attitudes can, of course, also lead "recommenders" to overrate the person in helping him move elsewhere.

Unofficial Requirements for Success

In the excerpts from interviews we saw spontaneous references by Bierner, Cowper, Bennett, Perry, Evans, and Cunningham to the Masonic Fraternity, with contradictory implications about membership as a factor in success. Their statements were cautious beside dozens of assertions from other people, non-Masonic Protestants and Catholics alike, that membership was essential. But other unofficial factors were also mentioned. In all we need to look at four alleged career aids: (a) membership in the Masons, which, as we shall see, had the negative aspect of *not* being a Roman Catholic; (b) having a predominantly Anglo-Saxon or Germanic ancestral, or ethnic, background; (c) membership in a local Yacht Club; and (d) being a Republican in politics.[11]

MASONIC MEMBERSHIP

Endless direct and allusive remarks about Masonry, and the fantasies among workmen about its importance, led me to question representative intimates about these charges.

C. Bicknell, an assistant superintendent who was a Thirty-second Degree Mason, held that:

Being a Mason doesn't help you get a better job, but it does make for better relations. The fact of being brothers in the lodge and being of service to each other is never mentioned, however. You always know that you can get service and help from each other because of that, but it has no direct bearing on you getting a better job. The Masonic Order demands that each man stand on his own feet. Being a Mason may help a man, but only in a general way. The Masons in a sense are a religious organization. If you know the Bible, you've got the principles of Free-masonry. We've nothing against the Catholics being Masons, but the Church don't like us.

Superintendent Ames, a Mason, avoided discussion of Masonry in connection with Milo but implied a great deal:

If you and I go into a strange town, and we're both broke and have no friends there, I'll have friends at once and you won't. That's what it means to be a Mason—you'll have friends among strangers and your friends who are Masons will do more for you than they would for people who're not Masons. Let me give you an example. I was down in St. Louis at the airport and wanted to get a plane for Chicago. I was in a long line. By the time I got up to fourth place, the three people ahead of me were all turned away—they wanted tickets to Chicago, too. I was about ready to leave when I noticed a ring on the finger of the ticket agent. I was smoking a cigar, so I casually put my elbow on the window and held my hand up where my ring could be seen. When the agent asked me what he could do for me, I told him I'd like two seats on a plane to Chicago. He looked me over and said, "Wait a minute, I think I can fix you up!" He stepped over and made a phone call and came back and said, "Yes, it's okay." What do you think of that?

C. Waring, a general foreman and a Mason, was noncommittal, but smiled and said, "I guess you know there's plenty of Masons around here. Well, that's not all. There's going to be a damn sight more of them!"

A staff supervisor who was not a Mason declared:

I think the Masons are a good organization, but not the bunch they've got around here. There's too many social climbers and ambitious people getting in. They're ruining the Masons. They don't want in to do the organization any good; they want it to help them get a better job. There's so many of the big wheels in the Masons now that they just about run the plant.

Younger Catholics regarded the Masons with rancor. But a fifty-four-year-old staff specialist of that group was more temperate:

I think the Masons are getting too strong in the plant, but a fellow has to be fair. You probably never heard of it since it was before your time, but we've had two managers here in the last twenty-five years that were Catholics. And one of them put in quite a few Catholics when it was convenient. Maybe not the way the Masons do now, but it was done. The big shots in [the Central Office] know that things work that way. I think they sort of alternate Catholics and Masons to keep the thing balanced up.

There was no evidence to refute or support this statement.

Another general foreman, J. Clancy, aged sixty-one, had received hints that his application for membership in the order would be welcomed, but he hesitated to apply:

I think the Masons are a fine organization. I've wanted to get in for years, but I'm afraid to. More than three-fourths of my men [workmen] are Masons. If I was a Mason they'd be on my tail all the time for special favors. That would worry the life out of me. Some bosses don't mind things like that—some of them might even want it like that. But I want to treat all my men just the same. I don't want to play favorites.

Blanke gave an indirect testimonial of Masonic strength among the managers. He advised the griever, Brady, who had applied and was acceptable to the Fraternity, "Don't join while you're a griever. You'll find too many of your boys (rank-and-file) yelling that you've sold out to management."

Catholics were acceptable to the Fraternity, but they considered themselves ineligible, they said, because of the Church's opposition to certain oaths required of Masons. Yet their conviction of the importance of being a Mason led several of them to drop out of the Church and join the Order. O'Brien was one of these. Appointed by an earlier Catholic plant head, O'Brien sat in one of the front pews with that manager during his tenure. But when this sponsor died and was succeeded by a Mason, and O'Brien saw various retiring Catholics replaced by Masons, he dropped out of the Church and joined the Fraternity. Most of the Milo Catholics were embittered toward him, but two Catholic general foremen and five first-line foremen followed him in a few months. Fraternity members admitted this. Several aspiring Catholics of Polish, Italian, and Lithuanian descent who made the change also changed their names. Younger Catholics were naturally uneasy about their future. They asserted that where the Catholics were only five per cent, or less, of management, they should be a majority as they were in Magnesia, where the current and preceding Mayors as well as the district national congressmen were all Catholics.*

Intimates were quizzed to establish who was Catholic and Mason and who was neither. The count and percentages of officers in these groups among the 226 managers are shown in Table 2.

Table 2. *Masons and Catholics in Management*

MANAGERIAL GROUP	MASONS		CATHOLICS		NEITHER		TOTAL OFFICERS
	NO.	%	NO.	%	NO.	%	
Staff	19	52.8	5	13.9	12	33.3	36
Superintendents	28	77.8	3	8.3	5	13.9	36
General foremen	39	64.0	12	19.7	10	16.4	61
First-line foremen	70	75.0	10	10.9	13	14.1	93
Total	156	69.0	30	13.3	40	17.7	226

* Their statements concerning the community and its public officials were correct. Senior priests in Magnesia observed that the number of Roman Catholic managers at Milo had been "declining for years," and they estimated Magnesia's Catholic population at 59 to 85 per cent of the total.

We see that the Masons, 69 per cent,* were considerably less than the 95 per cent alleged by the Catholics. But if we drop the Catholics from our calculation, because as a group they considered themselves ineligible, we see that nearly 80 per cent of the eligible managers were Masons. This is a highly significant difference and suggests, with the other data, that Masonic membership was usually an unofficial requirement for getting up—and for remaining there.

Assuming that Masonic membership, with the superintendents 78 per cent strong, was an unofficial test for success, we might expect the next highest concentration to be among the general, rather than first-level, foremen. Status uncertainty among the latter was probably a factor. In their confusion over whether they were in the fold of management or worker, they saw Masonic rings and buttons as symbols of being solidly in management. Also, 25 per cent of those foremen, more than any other level, were members of minority groups as foreign born or first generation Americans. Many had changed their heavily consonanted Central-European surnames to Anglo-Saxon names similar to those of top management. These first-line foremen also contributed most of those who dropped Catholicism to show another item of similarity to the status-givers, and to make a tacit plea for the opportunity to conform still further by becoming Masons.

The age, educational, and job differences we discussed in staff-line friction probably held the staff group to low Masonic membership. Most of the seventeen nonmembers aspired to be Masons, but feared that blackball by one of the lodges, any of which might contain line enemies, would jeopardize future entry at a more favorable time. Hence they waited. Also most of the staff Masons were older (only five under forty), former line men untrained in staff duties. Their ineptness, lack of contributions, and use of the staff as a refuge with known line sponsors protecting them, all generated internal frictions disposing these older officers not to vote the younger "pure-bred" staff people into the Fraternity.

* The difference between the 69 per cent who were Masons and the 31 per cent combined Catholics and "neutrals," would, by Chi-square, occur by chance about 7.5 times in 100.

Cowper, as a staff non-Mason, was the highest placed Catholic in Milo. He was secure because of his contributions and personal charm, because he showed loyalty in crises,[12] and because he had been around long enough to destroy doubts and to win the esteem of all groups. In the staffs he was a sustaining nucleus for the non-Masons.

The informal power chart also shows the importance of Masonic membership: of the twenty-one officers, only Stevens and Knight were not Masons.

ANCESTRY, OR ETHNIC COMPOSITION

In Mobile Acres, as elsewhere,[13] there were feelings of varying intensity about differences in national origin. Talk of this was of course more open and crude on lower levels than on the higher,[14] but some feeling was common on all levels. Those in the groups least acceptable to the majority naturally missed nothing of the animus against them. Especially, low-level minority staff employees made the common lament of minority groups, "You've got to be twice as smart to get half as far." Obstructors were identified by the repeated charge that "there are too many Johnny Bulls and Kraut-eaters around here." At the work level one might find brunette Scottish, Welsh, Irish, Scandinavian, and German extractees referring to those (sometimes blond) of Italian, Polish, Slovak, and Lithuanian descent as "dagoes," "hunkies," and "wops." Thus both majority and minority members identified each other more, or as much, by personal knowledge sharpened by rivalry than by physical traits.

We have already referred to name changing. Workers and first-line foremen of Slavic origin were especially sensitive about their polysyllabic names and the related problem of spelling and pronunciation that brought ridicule on them. Several minority families developed permanent rifts over name changing by the children.

Resentment over failure to rise sometimes led minority persons openly to charge discrimination. Paul Sarto, a first-line foreman of Italian descent, despaired of becoming a general foreman and resented the fact that two German-born associates had reached that level. His resentment exploded during one of the weekly cost meetings held in his department after regular quitting time. Some thirty minutes into these meetings, he typically arose, announced he was going home, and left. On one occasion his chief, Ames, objected. Sarto answered:

I've told you what I had to say and I've listened to you guys beat around the bush for half an hour after quitting time. I've got nothing to stick around here for. I'm not going any higher. I've got the wrong complexion to get any place. I'm going to stay right where I am regardless of how much I do. I don't want any hard feelings about it, but facts are facts. See you tomorrow.

The meaning of other cases was similar.

The alleged exclusive selection by ethnic stock was checked by studying the national origins, surnames, and birthplaces of the managers. This was done in part by personal knowledge, by check-

Table 3. The Ethnic Character of Management

ETHNICITY	STAFF		SUPTS.		GEN. FORE.		FOREMEN		TOTAL % IN SAMPLE
	NO.	%	NO.	%	NO.	%	NO.	%	
Anglo-Saxon	18	50	26	72.2	41	67.2	47	50.5	58.4
German	12	33.4	10	27.8	16	26.3	22	23.6	26.5
Scandinavian	5	13.9					10	10.8	6.6
Italian	1	2.7			2	3.3	3	3.2	2.6
Polish							4	4.3	1.8
French					1	1.6	3	3.2	1.8
Croat-Serb					1	1.6	2	2.2	1.3
Spanish							1	1.1	0.5
Negro							1	1.1	0.5
Total	36	100.0	36	100.0	61	100.0	93	100.0	100.0

ing with intimates to uncover name changes and get the family name, by use of personnel records, by free interviewing with doubtful persons, etc. The total members of each ethnic group and their percentages in each class of managers are shown in Table 3.

We see that Sarto was both wrong and right—2 Italians did make the grade of general foreman, but 16 German ethnics did also. The important thing for the minorities though, is that the Anglo-Saxons constituted at least half of each group of managers, that the German ethnics were next in number, and the two together made up all the superintendents. And the Anglo-German combination increased directly from bottom to top. In percentage the Anglo-Saxons were lower and the Germans higher in the staffs than elsewhere. Together they made up 83 per cent of that body, their lowest combined proportions in any group but the first-line foremen.

Differences* in the various levels leave little doubt that one's ethnic make-up was a factor in his success. But the differences take on still greater meaning when, as the Milo Catholics did, we look at Magnesia's ethnic pattern. Using a new city directory and making surnames† the gauge of national origin, a random sample showed the Anglo-Saxons to make up only 26 per cent, and the Germans 12 per cent, of Magnesia's population. And though only a minority of Milo's dominant ethnics were foreign born, the census data showed that this reservoir in Magnesia was also limited: those born in Germany and the British Isles together constituting less than 15 per cent of the city's population. Thus ethnics

---

* Differences in percentages of Anglo-Saxons between first- and second-level foremen and between superintendents and first-line foremen were significant at the 5 per cent level. But between general foremen and superintendents the difference could have been due to chance nearly three times in ten.

† This device of course overlooked the extent to which names may have been changed and the fact that migration weakens the criterion. Since nearly all of Magnesia's Negro population had Anglo-Saxon names, all such names from the area in which Negroes resided were counted with the non-Anglo-Saxon and non-Germanic ethnics.

composing probably less than 38 per cent of the community filled 85 per cent of Milo's advisory and directive forces.*

MEMBERSHIP IN A YACHT CLUB

Discussions of outings, week-ends, the "blowouts" of past seasons, party planning at the Yacht Club, and plant gossip about the meaning of social activities there—all indicated that the Club was indeed a place where careers might be influenced. . . . Here we need to view the Club (*a*) as the less successful supervisors saw it, and (*b*) as it related to the managerial group in terms of the alleged bearing of membership in it on rank in Milo. Milo managers had no exclusive control of the Club. The managers of Fruhling, Attica,

* Ethnic stratification has long been documented by students. See, among many others, P. Sorokin, *op. cit.,* pp. 11–128, 280–312; W. L. Warner and L. Srole, *The Social Systems of American Ethnic Groups,* Yale University Press, New Haven, 1947; R. M. MacIver and C. H. Page, *Society: An Introductory Analysis,* Rinehart and Co., New York, 1949, pp. 349–416; J. O. Hertzler, *Society in Action,* The Dryden Press, New York, 1954, pp. 232–234. Selection by ethnic affinity, other things equal, is not of course confined to industry or to the present. My colleagues have pointed out to me cases in the academic world. Barnard (*Functions of the Executive,* p. 224) notes the need, in order that men may function together, of using many social characteristics and personal traits as tests of fitness in selection. Specific situations may stress some and exclude others. But these criteria, including "race, nationality, faith, politics, sectional antecedents," etc., represent "in [the] best sense the political aspects of personal relationships in formal organizations." He believes these informal tests to be "most highly developed in political, labor, church, and university organizations," because "the intangible types of personal services are relatively more important in them than in . . . industrial organizations."

History is replete with cases of ethnic selection, even where there is zeal for reform as in the Emperor Diocletian's administrative reorganization in the third and fourth centuries. With ability scattered through dozens of provinces, he, an Illyrian peasant, chose Maximian, of similar origin, for his co-Augustus. For their subordinate *Caesars* they selected Constantius, of Illyrian origin; and Galerius, born in adjoining Thrace but tested in the service of Aurelian and Probus, two earlier Illyrian peasant emperors. Whether or not Diocletian chose these associates explicitly because of the ethnic tie, there seems little doubt that their common backgrounds were assumed in some sense to give a common outlook, as well as the promise of deference to his judgment on doubtful questions. See the *Cambridge Ancient History,* Cambridge University Press, 1939, Vol. 12, pp. 200, 325–330.

and other firms, and high civic figures of Magnesia shared its social activities. The Club in effect was (*a*) an outpost of Milo social life (managers and aspirants), (*b*) a center for the city's unofficial inter-industrial communication, and (*c*) a major bond between all the industries and the community.

Evans and Cunningham referred above to the Club, but others attacked it as the center for self-advancement for those who lacked "ability." The implication was that in the softening atmosphere of beach picnics, group swimming and water games, dancing in the pavilion with each other's wives and daughters; and in the small intimate gatherings for cruising and fishing, many ideal situations arose for making personal contacts and demands that extended to the plant.[15] These claims allegedly would be applied directly by climbers and reinforced by community figures intimate with both the aspirants and various high managers. The community career brokers included two former mayors, the leading bank 'president and several of his officials, lawyers, physicians, and various business leaders.

Activity in the Club was statistically less of a test for entry in management than was ethnic background and Masonic membership. Club activity aided the candidate who had other things in his favor. Hence we find that Milo members of the Club were less neatly ordered by rank than they were with respect to national origin and membership in the secret society.

One hundred fourteen Milo employees were members. This included 14 superintendents of whom Geiger was one and president of the Club, 24 general foremen, 29 first-line foremen, and 47 staff personnel. The latter group contained 14 officers in the sample, and 33 lower supervisory and nonsupervisory personnel outside the sample. With what we have seen of staff ambition and insecurity, the total of 47 suggests that staff people saw life in the Club as solid preparation for the future, but their greater preference for parties and clubbing must also be considered as a factor in their membership. Observation in the Club, and many casual but re-vealing remarks showed that freely·given efforts to increase and maintain the Club's physical plant were not forgotten by higher officers pondering the future of this candidate as against that one.

POLITICAL AFFILIATION

. . . All the managers were Republican in politics, or feigned to be as an essential for their success. Three conditions showed this: (1) With newspapers at hand representing the usual range of political views, the managers almost to a man carried a famous "isolationist" paper into the plant. (2) Discussions among managers favorable to Democratic ideologies were covert and occurred chiefly among first-line foremen. (3) All managers who at some time had served in public office did so as Republicans.

• • • • •

However, there were Democrats among the managers, including at least twenty-nine of the first-line foremen. Cunningham was exceptional in being a Democrat in middle management. When questioned as to how this squared with the typical feelings about the need of being a Republican, he replied:

I *am* supposed to be a Republican. Don't get the idea I pop off to other people on politics the way I do to you. I'm just trying to help you with what you're doing. And don't think that they [top management] don't know you before you get to be a general supervisor! You've got to be a damn good actor or you don't get that far!

Bearing the stamp of an authentic Republican was in some cases an open-sesame to placement at high levels. Superintendent J. Lambert had held a political office for the Republican Party in Magnesia, and he had been state auditor for several years on the same ticket. On losing the auditorship to a Democrat he entered Milo, without industrial experience, as "chief" [16] of a department. The title was changed to superintendent two years later, though informants say he started with the salary of superintendent. Lambert's political experience and party loyalty filled his conversation. Many of his employees, known by their friends to be Democrats, felt coerced to echo his political sentiments to escape suspicion of holding contrary views. Their friends ridiculed them for having "no guts."

Milo also employed the county auditor following his defeat after five successive terms on the Republican ticket. He too lacked industrial experience and specific training for his Milo post, but was made assistant staff supervisor at once and general supervisor six years later. Without supporting evidence, informants made much of the probable ties between the earlier political roles of these officers and tax assessments on Milo properties, with the implication that Milo was indebted to them. Since these were the only cases of this kind, it is not known whether persons of similar experience but other political leanings would have been chosen in this way or not.

Assuming that Republican dogma reflected the convictions of Republican managers, one can see how a theory of private enterprise would operate in career activities to resist or evade formal step-by-step procedures for advancement.

Discussion and Conclusions

Use of unofficial tests of fitness for entry and rise through the levels should not imply that appointing officers are interested only, or even primarily, in the aspirants meeting these tacit standards. The problem is more complex. The replacement of Lane by Rees, the choice of Blanke over Taylor, the movement of Schwann, the manipulation of Jackson, the use of sinecures, etc., all indicate concern with ability in the sense of getting the job done with minimum disturbance for the organization. Talent to carry on in this vaguely pragmatic way was understood to be a requirement in all selections. Certainly no superior at Milo or elsewhere would want a subordinate in a responsible position who could not passably meet both stated and tacit expectations. This basic competence was understood, despite occasional errors in the judging and selecting of candidates.

Why, then, the use of informal standards of fitness? Milo chiefs were like Reynolds of Attica, Jessup of Fruhling, and several executives cited by Ginzberg in having little interest or belief in the merit of formal selection. Even where there is interest, the means usually proposed do not measure what is essential.[17] Dimock's [18] contention that the executive must be a "tactitian and a philosopher," a "statesman," and a "responsible manipulator," is relevant for our data, but these concepts have not been formalized into schemes for appraisal of executives. These labels refer to varieties of leadership the meaning of which often varies with the speaker.[19]

Barnard's [20] discussion of leadership continues to be one of the most penetrating. He is concerned with the executive's problem in making personnel changes. Any change is likely to bring demand for more change when individuals and groups are competing for advantage and reward on the assumption that all are equally able and deserving. Dealing with the democratic situation, in which subordinates have the right to talk back and to do something about their dissatisfactions, requires political skills in addition to formal competence. However, open discussion of differences in this respect is taboo because of potential discord, loss of confidence among members, etc.

Nevertheless higher officers must consider the capacity of competing candidates to utilize and aid necessary cliques, control dangerous ones, etc. Too often the search for men who combine formal competence with this unspecified skill throws a top officer into despair. He is likely to put a premium on "loyalty" in terms of the candidate's seeing the job as he does. Wittingly or not, he begins to look for attitudes like his own as assuring a basis for understanding and cooperation. But he knows the difficulty of getting at the disposition and probable behavior of untried and artful people, however overwhelming their credentials. Hence at varying levels of conscious purpose, the appointing chief gropes for more valid marks of loyalty. This does not of course mean that he does not value subordinates who on occasion differ with him.

With considerable scientific support, his search moves on the assumption that those with qualities and interests like his own will think as he does. Hence in his quandary he finds it good that the prospective candidate is also Irish, went to such-and-such a school, came from a "good" family (socioeconomically like his own),[21] and has civic activities and recreational tastes similar to his own. These likenesses would naturally not be advanced as proofs of fitness in general discussion, but tacitly or unconsciously they predispose judges to see the prospect as one with a "good job outlook" and readiness to act jointly on critical issues.* Moved by these pleasing characteristics, the desperate personnel assessor may easily overlook other qualities. He receives every encouragement from the ambitious and "highly visible" subordinate who is probing for ways to please, and for marks he can copy to show the chief how much they have in common.† This aggressive self-advertisement and social mimicry may quite naturally be interpreted as a sign of the desired political skill. Certainly it indicates strong desire and a will to succeed which can push the inert excellence of other candidates out of the picture. But such behavior is not a guarantee of executive finesse, and may well indeed conceal the lack of it as well as other necessary qualities. It is thus quite possible for the highly visible appointee to be attitudinally out of step with his

---

* See Bicknell's remarks above on Masonry.

† Stein frankly stated that he became a member of Hardy's church because he "thought it would help." He pointed to others who variously followed the practice. Currying of favor by simulated likenesses is immemorial. In his *Letters* to his son (especially the letters of May 11, June 26, November 11 and 16, 1752—in Dobrée ed.) Chesterfield confidentially recommended it, and he successfully practiced it. Machiavelli openly advocated it (*Discourses,* Bk. 2, D. 2), but was much less successful in practicing it than his contemporary Guicciardini, the historian, who publicly denounced it but privately advised it (H. Butterfield, *The Statecraft of Machiavelli,* Macmillan, New York, 1956, p. 115). Hazlitt attacked it (*e.g.,* the essay, "On Patronage and Puffing"), and suffered from his refusal to practice it. Writing on industrial organization, as an active executive, Willkie (*A Rebel Yells,* D. Van Nostrand Co., New York, 1946, p. 191) declares that "all men tend to ape those above them in the hope of becoming socially and professionally acceptable." Also see the systematic comments of Samuel Haig Jameson, "Principles of Social Interaction," *American Sociological Review,* 10: 6–10, February, 1945.

sponsors, and yet misleadingly appear to have been lifted by favoritism based on his successful mimicry. He may of course fit both the formal and informal tests and still fail if the official criteria are not based on what is needed in the executive role.

Willkie,[22] however, fears that all such aping is likely to get out of control. The "powerful executive" surrounds himself with "a corps of hardened yes-men . . . who pick up ideas from their superior, amplify them, and parrot them impressively. . . ." In industry an "unconscious conspiracy" develops "a strong, secret, and tacit organization which maintains itself by accepting only those with similar ideas, or those friends, relatives, and class-conscious equals who can be counted on to support the hierarchy."[23]

Without being an apologist, one must note that this condition is the ultimate consequence of selection purely on the basis of social traits; it is not true of all industry,* nor confined to industry, nor inevitable. As a "rebel," Willkie is of course overstating what has always been present in varying degrees in most organizations in the more complex societies. It is pedantic even to mention that this can be documented voluminously by various students. Obviously an industrial firm is fossilizing when selective criteria—as any set of attitudes and characteristics—become ends in themselves. However when concern with social traits is limited to avoidance of what would be blatantly negative items to most members, the threat to the organization is much less than the other extreme of focus on purely formal qualifications. A fetish of formal tests can lead to their use as a blind to prevent charges of favoritism.[24] Employed with this intent, status-givers may still (*a*) select with attention to formal and social skills as without the test, and at the same time (*b*) adroitly inject various personal, cultural, and ethnic preferences to maintain a "balance of power" among two or more factions. Here, as elsewhere, men can decide what they want and then wilfully reason their way to a conclusion.

* Since about three-eighths of the Milo managers had relevant formal training, and most of them had years of industrial experience, this was not true there despite the weight of informal factors.

Those concerned to avoid this might first limit the pool of candidates to the technically fit,[25] so that the final focus can identify those most able to deal with internal tensions and the more subtle phases of group actions.

This dual focus promises (a) more judgment and less moral anguish in those who must communicate things forbidden to the dignity of formal channels,[26] and gives (b) some assurance of the approximate homogeneity basic to ready cooperation.[27]

Despite mountains of print on the subject, there are still no generally accepted indexes of competence in office. We cannot say how much of what develops after a decision is the result of the decision maker's insights, and how much arises from unassessed factors in the ongoing complex. Some executives [28] see the situation as so ambiguous that "most people don't live long enough to get blame or credit" for their decisions, and that one's decisions may never be proved wrong.[29] Drucker [30] expects a steady increase in the time-span for testing a decision, and even stronger, Urwick [31] feels that an indefinite future is required to tell the effects of a decision.

Our showing the minor role of formal as compared with informal factors does not mean that no effective managers * made the grade at Milo, or that if they did, it was by chance. Certainly not. For if we see the able executive as one who inspires confidence, who finds a way where apparently none existed and adapts rules without destroying their intent, who balances official and unofficial claims with minimum damage to himself and the organization, then Hardy, Ames, Dicke, Boesel, Meier, Geiger, Blanke, Springer, and others were competent leaders who met the informal tests as well as the few explicit formal requirements. On the other hand, Stevens, Taylor, Smith, Revere, Ruf, and O'Brien were lesser

---

* In terms of profits and dividends paid, Milo was definitely successful and presumably well-managed. However, one former "insider" in another industry declares that if capital and market are large enough, a firm may be a "huge financial success" and hide the fact that it is poorly managed. See T. K. Quinn, "Sovereign State of G.M.," *The Nation,* May 26, 1956, pp. 447–448.

leaders—by this standard—who met the ethnic and Masonic test (excepting Stevens), but did not meet the subtler requirements of sharing off-the-job activities that interlocked with those of the community. Certainly they did not meet the expectation that they effectively move in and out of clique activities as necessary, and compromise readily on smaller things to preserve greater ones. To push the theory, their high visibility and smiling haste to meet the more obvious informal requirements led to overevaluation of their fitness, relative to the other group.

Since higher officers eventually move, die, or retire, obviously no specific social earmarks can be fixed, however much a given set may be the focus of imitation today. Given the internal struggles that play around every important replacement, there is each time some unavoidable departure from the current balance of formal and informal factors. As at Milo, gradual changes over thirty years converted the item of a Catholic majority to a minority and a Masonic minority to a majority.

In terms of democratic theory, any set of informal requirements may become discriminatory. And when they are made ends in themselves, they certainly become undemocratic. But when controlled, they are likely to form a basis for cooperative effort. Men need not like each other to cooperate, and people with similar characteristics may dislike each other. But mutual liking—which is more probable when key characteristics and viewpoints are similar—assures a cooperative tie that formal selection and guidance, with all its merits, cannot guarantee.

Movement up any organizational ladder is subject to many influences outside individual and official control. Among these are (a) the effects of rivalries for personal success; (b) the limited number of positions; (c) the loose and shifting nature of our society, which weakens existing formal means of ascent and biases personnel against new ones; (d) the unavoidable influence of personal feelings in any interacting group; and (e) the clash of individual and organizational interests, which minimizes the official ways of getting up and encourages the unofficial.

Documentary Notes

1. See for example, such reports as "The Nine Hundred," *Fortune,* 42 (5) 132–135, November, 1952; William Miller, ed., *Men in Business: Essays in the History of Entrepreneurship,* Harvard University Press, Cambridge, 1952; F. W. Taussig and C. S. Joslyn, *American Business Leaders: A Study in Social Origins and Social Stratification,* Macmillan, New York, 1932; Suzanne I. Keller, "Social Origins and Career Lines of Three Generations of American Business Leaders," Columbia University Ph.D. Thesis, New York, 1954; C. Wright Mills, "The American Business Elite: A Collective Portrait," *The Tasks of Economic History,* Supplement V to *The Journal of Economic History,* December, 1945; Eli Ginzberg, ed., *What Makes an Executive?,* Columbia University Press, New York, 1955; Mabel Newcomer, *The Big Business Executive,* Columbia University Press, New York, 1955; W. Lloyd Warner and J. C. Abegglen, *Occupational Mobility in American Business and Industry,* University of Minnesota Press, Minneapolis, Minn., 1955, and the same data prepared for the nonprofessional reader, *Big Business Leaders in America,* Harper and Brothers, New York, 1955.

2. See also "The Nine Hundred," *loc. cit.;* Delbert C. Miller, "The Seattle Business Leader," *Pacific Northwest Business,* College of Business Administration, University of Washington, 15: 5–12, 1956; Gordon F. Lewis and C. Arnold Anderson, "Social Origins and Social Mobility of Businessmen in an American City," reprinted from *Transactions of the Third World Congress of Sociology,* 3: 253–266, 1956.

3. Delbert C. Miller and William H. Form, *Industrial Sociology,* Harper and Brothers, New York, 1951, pp. 717–774; C. Wright Mills, *The Power Elite,* Oxford University Press, New York, 1945, chap. 6, p. 386.

4. Wallace B. Donham, *Education for Responsible Living,* Harvard University Press, Cambridge, 1944; Chester Barnard, "Education for Executives," *The Journal of Business of the University of Chicago,* 18: 175–182, 1945; H. Frederick Willkie, *A Rebel Yells,* D. Van Nostrand Co., New York, chaps. 12, 14–24, 1946; W. H. Whyte, Jr., *The Organization Man,* Simon and Schuster, Inc., New York, 1956, p. 79.

5. See T. V. Smith, "In Accentuation of the Negative," *The Scientific Monthly,* 63: 463–469, December, 1946, and his scintillating little book, *The Ethics of Compromise,* Starr King Press, Boston, 1956. Also

pertinent here is chap. 12 in Ralph Barton Perry, *Realms of Value,* Harvard University Press, Cambridge, 1954.

6. P. F. Drucker, *The Practice of Management,* Harper and Brothers, New York, 1954, pp. 154–155, admits this condition is widespread in industry. C. Wright Mills, *The Power Elite,* Oxford University Press, New York, 1956, pp. 133–134, 386, contends that corporate careers in America are not "bureaucratic" in the sense of regular upward movement by virtue of specific fitness and examination at each step. Studies touching this topic in government agencies include Peter Blau, *The Dynamics of Bureaucracy,* University of Chicago Press, 1954; R. G. Francis and R. C. Stone, *Service and Procedure in Bureaucracy,* University of Minnesota Press, Minneapolis, 1956.

7. Robert K. Merton, "The Unanticipated Consequences of Purposive Social Action," *American Sociological Review,* 1: 894–904, December, 1936.

8. C. I. Barnard, *Functions of the Executive,* Harvard University Press, Cambridge, 1945, p. 224.

9. Ginzberg, *op. cit.,* p. 62.

10. Perrin Stryker et al., *A Guide to Modern Management Methods,* McGraw-Hill Book Co., New York, 1954, pp. 259–261.

11. See the comments of Donald E. Super, *The Psychology of Careers,* Harper and Brothers, New York, 1957, p. 134, on the use of informal criteria in research designs.

12. Everett C. Hughes, "Queries Concerning Industry and Society Growing Out of Study of Ethnic Relations in Industry," *American Sociological Review,* 14: 218–220, 1949.

13. Orvis Collins, "Ethnic Behavior in Industry: Sponsorship and Rejection in a New England Factory," *American Journal of Sociology,* 51: 293–298, 1946; Everett C. Hughes and Helen M. Hughes, *Where Peoples Meet,* The Free Press, Glencoe, Ill., 1952.

14. See comment on the effects of "spurious tolerance" and "human-relations mindedness" in the organizations of today. Charles H. Coates and Roland J. Pellegrin, "Executives and Supervisors: Informal Factors in Differential Bureaucratic Promotion," *Administrative Science Quarterly,* 2, No. 2, September, 1957, pp. 212 ff.

15. For discussion of the weight of informal situations in decision-

making, see Floyd Hunter, *Community Power Structure,* University of North Carolina Press, Chapel Hill, 1953, and "The Decision-Makers," *The Nation,* August 21, 1954, pp. 148–150.

16. *Chief* was his title. The term was rare at Milo, though I have used it loosely throughout the book as synonymous with *department head* and *superintendent.*

17. Aubrey Silberston, *Education and Training for Industrial Management,* Management Publications, Ltd. The Millbrook Press, Ltd., London, 1955, p. 6 ff.; Ginzberg, *op. cit.,* pp. 164–165.

18. M. E. Dimock, *The Executive in Action,* Harper and Brothers, New York, 1945, pp. 4–5, 8, 65–66.

19. See the introduction in Alvin Gouldner, ed., *Studies in Leadership,* Harper and Brothers, New York, 1950; P. Selznick, "An Approach to a Theory of Bureaucracy," *American Sociological Review,* 8: 51–54, February, 1943; R. Tannenbaum, V. Kallejian, I. R. Weschler, "Training Managers for Leadership," *Personnel,* 30 (no. 4), 2–8, January, 1954; L. Urwick, *The Pattern for Management,* University of Minnesota Press, Minneapolis, 1956, pp. 56–73; Dimock, *op. cit.,* pp. 195–205.

20. C. I. Barnard, *Organization and Management,* Harvard University Press, Cambridge, 1948, pp. 24–47.

21. See the provocative, humorous, and over-neat book of W. H. Whyte, Jr., *Is Anybody Listening?,* Simon and Schuster, New York, 1952. And on the influence of family at the start of industrial careers in a southern metropolitan area, see Coates and Pellegrin, *op. cit.,* pp. 200–215.

22. Willkie, *op. cit.,* p. 186.

23. *Ibid.,* p. 188.

24. Ginzberg, *op. cit.,* pp. 74–75.

25. Drucker, *op. cit.,* pp. 154–155.

26. Barnard, *Functions of the Executive,* Harvard University Press, Cambridge, 1938, p. 225.

27. *Ibid.,* pp. 147, 224; E. Dale in Kruisinga, *op. cit.,* p. 33; Stryker, *op. cit.,* p. 259.

28. Ginzberg, *op cit.,* p. 126.

29. *Ibid.,* pp. 128–129.

30. Drucker, *op. cit.,* p. 15.

31. Urwick, *op. cit.,* p. 31.

Suggestions for Further Reading

CHESTER I. BERNARD, *Functions of the Executive* (Cambridge: Harvard University Press, 1938). One of the earliest studies of the executive. Bernard's work has served as a stimulus for several more empirical examinations of executive life.

ALVIN W. GOULDNER, *Patterns of Industrial Bureaucracy* (New York: Free Press, 1954). An interesting work about the consequences of bureaucratic rules for the maintenance of organizational structure.

JAMES G. MARCH and HERBERT A. SIMON, *Organizations* (New York: Wiley, 1958). A penetrating analysis of the extent to which the organization arises from the limitations of human rational capacities. The book also presents an excellent discussion of the works of several organizational theorists.

MAX WEBER, *The Theory of Social and Economic Organization*, trans. A. M. Henderson and Talcott Parsons, ed., Talcott Parsons (New York: Oxford, 1947). The first, and a still important, theoretical analysis of formal organizations and their bureaucratic characteristics.

ᐤStrangers Next Door:
Ethnic Relations in
American Communities*

ROBIN M. WILLIAMS, JR.

American sociologists use the term "minority groups" to refer to those groups in the United States who face certain handicaps, who are subject to discrimination, and who are objects of prejudice from most other people.[1] These minority groups can be objectively distinguished by one or more of four different characteristics: race, nationality, religion, and language. A concern with relations between majority and minority groups has become prominent in social science research only within the last generation.

Although several studies of majority-minority relations have been made,[2] Strangers Next Door is probably the most compre-

---

* The material reprinted here is from Chapter 6 of Robin M. Williams, Jr., *Strangers Next Door: Ethnic Relations in American Communities,* © 1964. Reprinted by permission of Prentice-Hall, Inc., Englewood Cliffs, New Jersey. (The book was written with the collaboration of John P. Dean and Edward A. Suchman.)

[1] Arnold M. Rose, "Race and Ethnic Relations," in Robert K. Merton and Robert A. Nisbet, eds., *Contemporary Social Problems* (New York: Harcourt, 1966).

[2] For example, Bruno Bettelheim and Morris Janowitz, *Social Change and Prejudice* (New York: Free Press, 1964); John Dollard, *Caste and Class in a Southern Town* (New Haven: Yale University Press, 1937); Gunnar Myrdal, with the assistance of Richard Sterner and Arnold M. Rose, *An American Dilemma* (New York: Harper, 1944).

hensive empirical study of intergroup relations that has thus far been conducted in the United States. The purpose of the research program evolved into Strangers Next Door, *as Williams states in his preface to the book, was "to lay a basis for a better understanding of attitudes and behavior involved in relations among racial, ethnic, and religious groupings in the United States." Originally, Williams and his associates had planned a three-year study of Elmira, a middle-sized industrialized community in upstate New York. As they began to collect data, however, it became clear that attitudes and behavior in Elmira might be less universal than they had first thought, that the attitudes and behavior of the white majority of gentiles toward minority groups in Elmira might not fully indicate those of majority group members elsewhere in the country. Additional information was obtained from an elaborate mail survey of almost 250 cities with populations of 10,000 or more. Special attention was given to four cities in the study: Hometown (Elmira, New York), Steelville (Steubenville, Ohio), Valley City (Bakersfield, California), and Southport (Savannah, Georgia). At the time of the survey, all of these communities were industrial areas with populations ranging from 40,000 to 120,000. Each had a predominantly working-class population, and each had at least two ethnic minorities—one of which was Negro. Although the research staff collected much of their data through interviews, they also employed a wide variety of other techniques, including direct observation, participant observation, and analysis of documents.*

Williams and his associates devoted considerable attention to examining intergroup attitudes and experiences in American society. Among their goals in this broad and ambitious undertaking were attempts to determine the extent that Negroes and whites accepted various stereotypes of one another, whether minorities were seen by majority-group Americans as demanding too much, and the level of the Negroes' feelings of social distance toward white people. In this book, Williams discusses the significance of the findings for the way complex societies function and change. He emphasizes the urgency of determining what specific societal conditions produce cooperation rather than conflict, and he notes the importance of discovering how conflict can be used to enhance understanding and social growth. The potential significance of a study such as this one is suggested by the words with which Williams closes his book: "There may be strangers next door, but we too are visitors in a world we did not make. Enrichment of our understanding of the others possibly will enrich our understanding of ourselves. It may even help us to make the most of our stay on this small planet."

In the section of Strangers Next Door presented here, the main concern is with patterns of segregation, discrimination, and conflict. The authors describe these patterns in a highly sophisticated way, taking the data collected from the nationwide survey of 248 cities and systematically analyzing the elements of size, location, and ethnic makeup as these relate to segregation and discrimination in a particular community. Most of the data, of course, were collected in the period 1948-1952, and care must be exercised in judging the applicability of some of the study's facts and interpretations to current conditions. In the main, however, the report of this research project's method and findings stand firmly as an excellent guide and standard of comparison for future research efforts, as well as a valuable source of enlightening data and interpretation.

Patterns of Segregation, Discrimination, and Conflict

In the following [pages] . . . we will attempt to discover whether there is a national pattern of intergroup relations, how practices of segregation and discrimination vary among regions and types of communities, and what social conditions are associated with intergroup conflict. Variations in five major factors insure that patterns of intergroup behavior will differ from one community to another. These factors are:

1. *Size of community and size of minority population in the community.*

2. *Official segregation.* Segregated schools, restrictive covenants,

separate Negro and white chapters of organizations, etc., erect highly effective barriers to interaction.

3. *Discrimination.* In all communities in the United States, although in varying degrees, discriminatory practices exist that serve to limit the number of opportunities for intergroup contact. Usually such discriminatory practices exclude minority-group members from certain activities and places and produce effective unofficial segregation.

4. *Customary community practices.* Less obvious than segregation and discrimination are the many operating practices for intergroup behavior that arise in all communities. These are community patterns that define whether or not intergroup situations are appropriate and acceptable.

5. *Intergroup positive action programs.* Active promotional efforts to increase intergroup interaction affect the opportunities available to individuals for intergroup contacts.

Size of Total Community and Minority Population

Our data show that some demographic variables are highly related to a wide range of patterns of segregation, discrimination, and intergroup conflict. Group relations are markedly different not only in the North and South, but also in big cities and small towns, and in cities with a high proportion and those with a low proportion of members of particular minorities. Demographic conditions make some patterns of intergroup relations more probable than others; they circumscribe the forms these relations take. No single demographic variable, however, is consistently related to all patterns of Negro-white or other intergroup relations.

Data from our national sample of 248 cities show significant differences in intergroup practices between large cities and small towns. Obviously, the mere fact that one city has 100,000 residents and another has 50,000 does not account for these differences. Instead, the size of the city indexes other factors that are related to intergroup practices. Some of these may be:

1. *Patterns of interaction between Negroes and whites.* In the smaller towns, Negroes and whites come into contact with each other because of the limited number of employment opportunities or recreation facilities and the proximity of their homes. Isolation depends upon a large city area and a Negro population of sufficient size to be in some respects self-supporting.

2. *The tradition of the large American city.* With the exception of a few agrarian protest movements, the smaller towns in the United States have been traditionally more conservative than the larger cities. Changes, even in intergroup relations, seem more readily proposed and accepted in the larger cities than in the smaller towns. On the other hand, our data show that overt interracial conflict tends to be a big-city phenomenon.

3. *Differences in residents of big cities and small towns.* Although the migration of rural people to the urban centers continues, not everyone migrates. Those who derive satisfactions from living in the larger cities possibly may be psychologically different from those who prefer to live in the small towns. These hypothetical differences might account in part for different outcomes of interracial contact.

4. *Regulation of personal behavior.* In the smaller towns, an individual is likely to be known to a large proportion of the residents; in the larger cities, this is impossible. The effects of being known or being somewhat anonymous may influence behavior in interracial situations.

A crucial aspect of Negro-white relations affecting the basic meaning of population size is residential segregation. A rigid pattern of residential segregation has its sources in many of the same social conditions that give rise to other forms of discrimination against Negroes. However, once established, residential segregation becomes crucial in determining other kinds of segregation and discrimination. Concentration of Negro housing can be expected to frustrate attempts to integrate the schools for years to come in many communities, even if only because of such factors as the preference of parents for sending their children to schools within walking distance of their homes.

. . . One part of the Cornell Studies consisted of a nationwide survey of intergroup practices in a stratified sample of 250 cities in all parts of mainland United States. The data provide a broad outline of segregation and discrimination in urban centers. The relevance of most of the data reviewed to the questions of main concern in our total program of analysis will be evident. Thus, we shall review the distribution of Negroes and other minorities in cities of the North and South, both large and small. The sheer

Table 1. Distribution of Minority-Group Populations in the Cities of the Nationwide Sample

	REGION					
	NORTH			SOUTH*		
	CITY SIZE			CITY SIZE		
	OVER 100,000	25,000- 100,000	UNDER 25,000	OVER 100,000	25,000- 100,000	UNDER 25,000
	(71)†	(82)	(36)	(28)	(21)	(10)
Proportion foreign born in the population						
under 1%	1%	4%	6%	53%	75%	80%
1–4.9%	13	25	14	21	10	10
5–9.9%	30	23	30	14	10	0
10–14.9%	28	16	28	4	0	0
15–17.9%	17	16	8	4	0	0
18% or more	11	11	6	0	0	0
no information	0	5	8	4	5	10
Negro population						
under 100	0%	16%	45%	0%	5%	0%
100–499	4	16	25	0	0	0
500–1,499	6	29	11	0	5	30
1,500–4,999	15	26	11	4	24	50
5,000–14,999	34	6	0	0	42	10
15,000 and more	41	2	0	92	24	0
no information	0	5	8	4	0	10

	RELIGION					
	NORTH CITY SIZE			SOUTH* CITY SIZE		
	OVER 100,000	25,000-100,000	UNDER 25,000	OVER 100,000	25,000-100,000	UNDER 25,000
	(71)†	(82)	(36)	(28)	(21)	(10)
Proportion Negroes in the population						
less than 1%	13%	35%	44%	0%	5%	0%
1–4%	35	33	31	4	10	10
5–9%	25	17	6	11	14	20
10–19%	24	6	11	21	14	20
20% or more	3	4	0	60	57	40
no information	0	5	8	4	0	10
Jewish population						
under 100	1%	17%	45%	0%	14%	80%
100–499	0	33	36	0	47	10
500–1,499	8	27	8	14	29	0
1,500–4,999	23	13	0	39	10	0
5,000–14,999	33	5	3	36	0	0
15,000 and more	31	0	0	11	0	0
no information	4	5	8	0	0	10
Proportion Jews in the population						
under 1%	10%	47	51	18	62	90
1–1.9%	15	24	22	39	28	0
2–4.9%	39	15	11	29	10	0
5% or more	34	9	8	14	0	0
no information	2	5	8	0	0	10

* The Southern cities are in these states: Alabama, Delaware, Florida, Georgia, Kentucky, Louisiana, Maryland, Mississippi, North Carolina, Oklahoma, South Carolina, Tennessee, Texas, Virginia, West Virginia and the District of Columbia. "North" includes all other cities.
† Number of cities. The total percentage for each column of each of the five items equals 100 per cent.

population distributions affect a great many aspects of intergroup relations. For example, intergroup contact opportunities are limited by both the physical size of the minority groups and the limited number of activities in which most individuals have the time and capacity to take part. In a community with only small percentages of minority groups, majority-group members are very unlikely to have many random opportunities for contact with minority-group members. This situation, of course, does not hold for minority-group members, although such opportunities often will be of a restricted type.

In both absolute numbers and relative proportions, Negroes are concentrated in the larger cities of both the North and the South. (See Table 1) However, Southern cities in each size class have larger Negro communities and a higher ratio of Negroes to whites than do Northern cities. In twenty-four cities in this sample, usually either small Northern towns or suburban areas, there are no Negroes. Jews are absolutely and relatively more important in the larger cities; they are entirely absent from only six cities. There is a higher proportion of foreign-born in the Northern cities. The foreign-born of the South are concentrated in the larger cities; in the North they are fairly evenly distributed in cities of all sizes.

PROPORTION OF MINORITY GROUP IN THE POPULATION

Many social scientists have thought the proportion of a minority to a majority in a population important in influencing intergroup relations. In our nationwide sample, half of the Southern cities had over 20 per cent Negro populations. Half of the Northern cities had less than 5 per cent Negro populations. Of the Northern cities, only Chester, Pennsylvania; Gary, Indiana; and East St. Louis, Illinois, had as high as 20 per cent. How does the proportion of Negroes relate to discrimination, segregation, and conflict?

The likelihood that Negroes will be segregated is greater in those cities where the proportion of Negroes is higher: in schools, playgrounds, hospitals, and public clinics. (See Table 2) This is true for cities of all sizes of both the North and the South.

Cities with a high proportion of Negroes are more likely to have discrimination in the use of barbershops, hotels, restaurants, movies, and buses. Also, occupational discrimination against both Negroes and Jews appears to be positively related to the proportion of the respective minority groups in the population.

Some kinds of overt conflict between Negroes and whites are characteristically reported by the cities, North and South and large

Table 2. *Relationship of Segregation of Northern Playgrounds and Proportion of Negro Population**

	PROPORTION NEGRO	
	LESS THAN 5 PER CENT	5 PER CENT OR MORE
	(PER CENT OF CITIES WITH SEGREGATED INSTITUTIONS)	
Grade schools	3% (106)	18% (65)
High schools	2% (106)	8% (65)
Playgrounds	5% (106)	25% (65)

* This relationship is unchanged when the size of the city is controlled. All Southern schools were at this time segregated by law.

or small, with a high proportion of Negroes: street fights between Negro and white youths and instances of police brutality toward Negroes. The relation does not hold, or is present only in modified form in the instances of burnings of crosses, vandalism, and objectionable newspaper reporting concerning Negroes.

Official Segregation

Segregation involves a process of differentiation and distinction. As a result of natural and social selection operating through free competition and conflict an individual or group in time acquires a habitat, a function in the division of labor, and a position in the social order. By such characteristics individuals or groups are distinguished and set apart. Physical separation of groups with different characteristics—whether accomplished by force, or through sanctions imposed by another group, or by the formation of a self-contained defensive aggregation for protection against unfamiliar ideas and customs, or from escape from ostracism and persecution—achieves the same purpose, that of isolation of one group from the other.[1]

When the Supreme Court ruled in 1896 in *Plessy vs. Ferguson* that provision of separate but equal facilities for Negroes in public transportation vehicles did not violate the "equal rights" amendment of the Constitution, the way was clear for segregating Negroes on playgrounds, in schools, and in hospitals.[2] Although city ordinances restricting Negroes' area of residence have been declared unconstitutional, group pressure by whites upon members of their own race, including restrictive covenants, have also limited Negroes' choice of residence. Segregation in many communities in the early 1950's extended from the hospital nursery to the cemetery.

PLAYGROUNDS AND SCHOOLS

As of 1954, all of the Southern states had laws requiring separate schools for Negroes and for whites; and many Northern cities had segregated schools. The Negro schools seldom had equal building and teaching facilities, budgets, or staff, and, consequently, the education was frequently inferior. Somewhat fewer than one-third of all the elementary schools, secondary schools, and playgrounds in cities in the nation-wide sample were both segregated and judged inferior to those provided for white children, according to the standards of well-informed local people.

Approximately 5 per cent of the educational and recreational facilities were segregated but locally judged to be as good as those available for white children. Sixty-six per cent of the cities permitted

[1] Charles S. Johnson, *Patterns of Negro Segregation* (New York: Harper & Row, Publishers, 1943), p. xvii.
[2] Mangum, C. S., *The Legal Status of the Negro* (Chapel Hill: The University of North Carolina Press, 1940). For a discussion of race distinctions with reference to education just prior to the Supreme Court decision in the *Brown* case see R. A. Leflar and W. H. Davis, "Segregation in the Public Schools—," *Harvard Law Review,* LXVII, No. 3 (January, 1954), esp. 420.

some Negro and white children to use the same playgrounds; in 67 per cent of the cities, some children of both races attended at least some of the same grade schools; and in 72 per cent of the cities, there was some integration of high schools. In most instances, only some of the schools represented any substantial intermingling of white and Negro pupils.

About one-fifth of the cities in the nation-wide sample mentioned education as their most controversial intergroup relations problem. In only 1 per cent of the Northern cities, but in 48 per cent of the Southern cities education was reported as an intergroup relations issue. (The size of the city does not alter this relationship.)

The size of a city was not significantly related to the presence or absence of segregated school buildings or recreational facilities. In the Northern states there was a slight tendency for the larger cities to maintain segregated school systems—a consequence, in large part, of residential concentration of Negroes. In general, though, all schools and playgrounds in the Southern states were segregated, and there was much community concern about the problem. In the Northern states, schools and playgrounds were less often segregated, and concern among white people was low, as of the early 1950's.

HOSPITALS

In a great many cities, hospitals either were segregated or hospitals for Negroes were completely lacking. Like the schools, many hospitals were supported by taxes, wholly or in part, and were considered to be public service institutions. The medical profession officially espouses a code of ethics that does not seem to support racial discrimination. Yet, 28 per cent of the cities' hospitals were segregated; in 19 per cent, the segregated facilities for Negroes were judged inferior to the hospital facilities provided for whites.

Southern cities more often maintained separate medical facilities for Negroes than Northern cities: 93 per cent of the large Southern cities report segregated hospitals and clinics, whereas 13 per cent of the larger Northern cities had segregated medical facilities. Seventy-five per cent of the smaller Southern towns had segregated hospitals compared to 14 per cent in the smaller Northern towns. Undoubtedly, smaller towns have greater difficulty in bearing the costs of separate medical installations for Negroes. Without the sanctions of state legislation that enforce segregation in the schools, and without the direct "transfer" of behavior as from the schools to the playgrounds, some small Southern towns did have common hospital facilities. Almost all of the large Southern cities had segregated medical facilities. In the North, where it is the usual practice to have integrated rather than segregated hospitals, economic resources are not so important in determining the pattern of segregation.[3]

FORMAL ORGANIZATIONS

Social scientists have often noted the remarkable proliferation of formal organizations in American communities. There are civic, social, business and professional clubs attracting different kinds of people in support of a wide range of goals. Our data from the nationwide sample support the observation that communities in the United States are indeed "organized." Almost every city has local chapters of all the national organizations for which we sought information. Only the YWCA is absent from as many as 10 per cent of the communities. Table 3 shows that some national organizations accept Negroes as members, some make no provisions for Negroes to belong, and others segregate them.

Like segregation in hospitals or schools, the pattern of segregation in formal organizations differed in cities of different size and in the North and South. These differences are of interest.

[3] Of course, in many of the officially nonsegregated Northern hospitals the actual day-to-day activities are substantially affected by ethnic factors. See for example: David N. Solomon, "Ethnic and Class Differences among Hospitals as Contingencies in Medical Careers," *American Journal of Sociology,* LXVI, No. 5 (March, 1961), 463–71. This study's main conclusion, on p. 469, is that: "The social system of medicine in Chicago—and, no doubt, in other large urban areas—is not a unified homogeneous whole but, rather, one which reflects the ethnic and class segmentation and stratification of the city. The medical community, like the community as a whole, consists of a set of social worlds which are to a degree separate and discrete."

Table 3. Integration and Segregation in National Organizations

ORGANIZATIONS	INTE-GRATED	NO PRO-VISIONS FOR NEGROES	SEGRE-GATED	NO ORGANI-ZATION	NO ANSWER/DON'T KNOW
Masons	2%	12	79	0	7
Rotary	4	80	1	2	13
American Legion	19	8	64	1	8
Chamber of Commerce	27	46	9	1	17
YMCA	42	13	28	9	8
YWCA	48	10	24	10	8
Community Chest	64	18	6	4	8
Local Council of Churches	73	10	7	2	8

Separate Organizations. In 79 per cent of the cities, Negroes belonged to segregated Masonic lodges. In almost all the larger Northern cities, separate Masonic lodges had been established for Negroes. The smaller the city in the North, the less tendency to make provision for Negroes in the Masons. In the South, both the large cities and small towns reported separate Negro Masonic lodges.

The American Legion was second only to the Masons in having segregated organizations for Negroes. Seventy-eight per cent of the posts in Northern cities over 100,000 were segregated but about 20 per cent were integrated. The smaller the towns in the North, the fewer reported segregated posts. Instead, either Negroes were accepted into existing posts or no provisions were made for them. But again the Southern cities of all sizes usually maintained separate posts for Negroes. All Legion posts in the larger Southern cities were segregated. Eighty-two per cent of the Southern cities under 100,000 had separate posts. One Southern city under 100,000 reported no provisions for Negroes, and two had integrated posts.

No Provisions for Negroes. In 82 per cent of all Northern cities and 75 per cent of all Southern cities, the Rotary clubs neither permitted Negroes nor had established segregated clubs. There was little difference between the practices of Rotary clubs in the larger cities and small towns of either region.

The Chambers of Commerce also tended to exclude Negroes and to make no separate provision for them. Forty-two per cent of the Northern cities over 100,000 made no provisions for Negroes to belong to the Chamber of Commerce. A slightly higher percentage of smaller Northern towns excluded Negroes or failed to set up separate organizations for them. However, those Northern cities in which Negroes are permitted in the Chamber of Commerce tend to have common organizations for Negroes and whites. In the South, the pattern was somewhat different. There, too, many cities reported no provision for Negroes to belong to the Chamber of Commerce, and a few reported integrated organizations. But most Southern cities either made no provision for Negroes or reported separate Chambers of Commerce for Negro businessmen.

Integrated Organizations. Most of the local Councils of Churches were made up of both Negro and white ministers. But again regional differences were important. Most Northern cities, especially the larger ones, reported integrated Councils of Churches. But less than 4 out of 10 of the Southern councils were integrated. The larger Southern cities were more likely than the smaller towns to establish separate councils for Negro ministers; the smaller places more often reported no provisions for Negroes.

The YMCA and the YWCA represented hybrid forms of segregation, tending to be integrated in the North and to have separate organizations for Negroes in the South. The YWCA's were more often integrated than the YMCA's in both regions.

A similar pattern appears again in the case of the Community Chest or United Fund. Most Northern cities have integrated Community Chest directorates, but some smaller Northern towns have no provisions for taking Negroes into the drives to collect funds. About half of the Southern cities report integrated organizations, but 29 per cent of the Southern cities with populations over 100,000 established separate organizations and 21 per cent of the Southern towns under 100,000 made no provisions for Negro participation.

Let us summarize this picture, as of the early 1950's, of segregation in formal organizations. First, those organizations that appear to have a nationwide practice of segregation (Masons, American Legion) provide segregated chapters for Negroes in the larger cities of the North and South. The smaller towns of the South follow the regional folkway of separate but equal and provide Masonic lodges and Legion posts for Negroes. Lacking this tradition, the smaller towns of the North, with their smaller Negro communities, make no provisions for Negroes to belong to these organizations.

Second, if an organization maintains a practice of excluding Negroes and not encouraging the establishment of separate clubs, there simply is no provision for Negroes in any city of either region. If this practice is less rigidly enforced, as by the Chamber of Commerce, Negroes in the North tend to be taken into integrated organizations, and Negroes in the South establish separate chapters.

Finally, those religious and civic organizations that make a universal appeal to common motives of all people in all communities present a dilemma for some Southern cities. Northern cities report that Community Chest drives and ministerial groups are integrated, but in the South joint participation is not accepted in about half the cities. The larger Southern cities report the presence of separate organizations for Negroes, but in the smaller Southern towns no provisions are made for Negroes to participate. Except for these philanthropic organizations, there are usually separate organizations for Negroes in clubs or lodges in small Southern towns.

Discrimination

Segregation is one kind of discrimination. There are many other kinds that do not necessarily involve the provision of separate facilities. These are acts of selective and differential behavior which violate important institutional standards that usually are obligatory in certain areas of conduct.

Although discrimination against a minority group is more often the overt expression of prejudice, discrimination can exist without prejudice. Some discriminatory practices reflect a policy decision protecting the interests of the majority group. Some represent adherence, through the forces of group conformity, to fragments of the cultural heritage. A hotel manager may turn away Negro customers because other hotel managers turn them away. As we have said before, he may feel that his white customers would object, although they have no strong feelings one way or the other.

DISCRIMINATION IN EMPLOYMENT [4]

Eighty-one per cent of the cities report that there is discrimination against qualified Negroes in the form of failure to promote them to more skilled industrial jobs. Of these cities, 67 per cent report instances within the last year. This particular kind of discrimination in employment occurred much more frequently in the larger cities than in the smaller towns. While discrimination was reported more often in all Southern cities than in Northern cities, the differences were small. In about 20 per cent of the cities it is reported that Jewish doctors are denied full privileges at the local hospitals. More of these cities are in the North than in the South. They are also the larger cities of both regions. Both Jewish doctors and qualified Negro industrial workers are more often discriminated against in the larger cities. Jews, however, are singled out for discriminatory treatment in the Northern cities, whereas Negroes are penalized in the Southern cities.

Employment is considered to be the most controversial intergroup relations problem in 45 per cent of the communities, and is so ranked more often in larger cities than in the smaller towns.

[4] We are not here concerned with defining or analyzing the economic aspects of discrimination. For an impression of the complexity of these problems see Gary S. Becker, *The Economics of Discrimination* (Chicago: The University of Chicago Press, 1957).

Concern about employing Negroes is greatest in the largest Northern cities and least in the smallest Southern towns.

DISCRIMINATION IN USE OF PUBLIC FACILITIES

Discrimination against Negroes varies from community to community, from institution to institution within the same community and from individual to individual in the same institutional setting. In one West Virginia city, Negroes' use of the same public rest-rooms as whites is a controversial issue. Across the river in an Ohio city, Negroes' use of public rest-rooms is accepted. But in this

Table 4. Acceptability of Negroes' Using Public Facilities

CAN NEGROES:	TAKEN FOR GRANTED AS NOT ACCEPTABLE	CONTRO-VERSIAL	TAKEN FOR GRANTED AS ACCEPTABLE	NO ANSWER/ DON'T KNOW
Try on dresses in white department store?	2%	9%	88%	1%
Sit in the same part of buses as whites?	16	4	79	1
Use the same public rest-rooms as whites?	17	6	76	1
Sit among whites in movies?	26	6	67	1
Have beds in hospitals side by side with whites?	29	18	52	1
Use same swimming pools with whites?	30	22	45	3
Be served in white restaurants?	30	30	39	1
Belong to white Protestant churches?	38	31	30	1
Stay in white hotels?	39	34	25	2
Use white barbershops?	68	22	8	2

Ohio city Negroes cannot generally stay in white hotels. Marian Anderson was not permitted to stay at one of the better hotels there. (Yet, when a Negro social scientist from Cornell asked for a room in this same hotel, it was given to him without question.)

Table 4 shows the variability that exists in what is considered to be appropriate behavior for Negroes in different localities, from the high percentage of cities where it is acceptable for Negro women to try on dresses in white department stores to the low percentage of cities where Negro men can get haircuts in white barbershops. There is a remarkably orderly ranking of discrimination. Some behaviors are more often tabooed for Negroes than other. There is a single rank-order of acceptability of practices.

In some cases, Negroes' freedom of action is well defined. For instance, in 79 per cent of the cities Negroes can sit in the same part of buses as whites, and in 16 per cent this is not acceptable. Only in 4 per cent of the cities is this controversial. In other cases the situation is poorly defined. Twenty-five per cent of the cities report that Negroes can stay in white hotels; in 38 per cent of the cities this is not acceptable; and in 34 per cent this is a controversial issue. This means that Negroes are likely to encounter conflict; they cannot generalize from one hotel to another.

Despite this tremendous variability, discrimination definitely is patterned. Both Myrdal and Johnson earlier spoke of a "rank-order of discrimination." [5] This means that different kinds of behaviors by Negroes can be arranged along a continuum of more acceptable and less acceptable. Table 4 shows this. It also shows that cities can be ranked in a clear unidimensional order of their acceptance of Negroes' use of public facilities and institutions.

However, the activities included in this list do not appear to be ordered on the "personal intimacy" continuum that Myrdal and many others have suggested. It is difficult to see why Negroes' being served in a white restaurant should be more intimate than their

[5] Gunnar Myrdal, *An American Dilemma* (New York: Harper & Row, Publishers, 1944), pp. 60–67, 587–88; Charles S. Johnson, *op. cit.*, pp. 3–155, 173–85.

using the same rest-room as whites. No single one of several possible factors—intimacy, public character, potential economic gain to whites, recency of the institutions' establishment, importance of the service or facility (barbershops and churches) and so on—seems to explain the order of the items.

Thus we have several important and puzzling facts: there is great variability in the acceptability of the practices and in the consensus upon acceptability; there is a strikingly clear unidimensional order among the practices; but, there is no obviously plausible basis for the ordering. Could the clue lie either in size of the city or region of the country?

While acceptance of Negroes in public facilities is definitely patterned for the sample of the cities as a whole, Northern cities differ from Southern cities and large cities differ from small towns in the areas of freedom extended to Negroes.

With very few exceptions, Negroes in Northern cities of all sizes can try on dresses in department stores, sit in the same part of buses as whites, use the same public rest-rooms as whites, and sit among whites in movie houses. They are often excluded from swimming pools, restaurants, churches, hotels, and barbershops. In the smaller towns more often than in the larger cities, they are forbidden use of public facilities and institutions. However, more large Northern cities consider Negroes' use of these facilities to be controversial than do the smaller towns. Therefore, with the exception of Negroes' staying in white hotels, unqualified acceptance of Negroes is greater in the small towns of the North than the larger cities.

In the South, Negroes' use of most public facilities is clearly unacceptable, and in many cases their use of the facilities is not even controversial.[6] It is difficult to say in most cases whether

---

[6] It must be remembered again that these data antedated the controversies over public transportation in the South that have followed the Supreme Court decisions of 1954 and 1955. It has not been very long since "Freedom Riders" was an unknown expression. But the stirrings of change were there long before the incidents in Montgomery, Little Rock, Jackson, or New Orleans.

Negroes are given more freedom to use public facilities in the larger cities of the South or in the small towns. More small towns report that Negroes can sit among whites on the buses and can use the same rest-room facilities. While Negroes' use of white barber-shops, white hotels, and swimming pools is forbidden in almost all Southern towns, these were at least controversial issues, rather than unthinkable innovations, in the smaller towns.

The detailed breakdown of the data by region and size of city does not destroy the rank-ordering: on the whole, the same general ranking prevails in both North and South, and in both small and large cities within each region. The regional difference is overwhelmingly important, far outweighing city size.

We might suspect that the ordering of practices could merely reflect the sheer availability of facilities and service within a highly segregated residential pattern. That is, if a city contains a Negro ghetto that is large enough to have many of the facilities in question, those that are available to both groups on a neighborhood basis would be most likely to rank as "not acceptable" to the whites. This possibility, however, does not seem to constitute a good explanation. In the highly segregated large Northern cities, there are only a few cases of cities having general exclusion of Negroes from restaurants and hotels, both of which are available on a neighborhood basis. It is true, however, that the facilities and services that are most likely to be available on a desegregated basis are those likely to be found in central districts of cities and to involve relatively transitory and impersonal situations—department stores, buses, rest-rooms, movies. General location and casual, transitory character, however, are rather weak factors in comparison with regional culture and city size.

The particular character of the facility or service is possibly significant in two cases. The first is that of the white Protestant church, which in the South clearly is a deviant in the rank-order. The anomaly of segregation in a religious institution having certain traditions and beliefs concerning brotherhood and the spiritual worth of individuals undoubtedly is partly responsible for the frequency of controversial situations. The other somewhat special case concerns barbershops, in which there appears to be a most complicated set of special factors including technical skills, the peculiar characteristics of proprietorship and unionization, the historical background (the processes by which Negro barbers were forced out in the South), and the quasi-recreational or social-club qualities of some neighborhood establishments.

In sum, it appears that the ordering of discriminatory and segregative practices derives to a large extent from functionally arbitrary historical circumstances. The practices are not sheerly whimsical or without cause; but the position of any one practice seems to be a function of many particular causes set in the context of a pervasive institutional pattern. In the South, for example, there is a generalized inclination to segregate and discriminate in nearly all areas of life. This institutionalized commitment tends to spread to a great variety of practices and settings—Oklahoma at one time had a state law requiring separate telephone booths for use of whites and Negroes. A variety of factors, suggested in our own discussion here, come to bear in different combinations upon various situations at different times. Variations in segregation and discrimination have not been neatly laid out on the basis of a single set of clear principles.

Although we can do no more than suggest a range of factors that help us to understand the "Negro Acceptability Scale," the fact that some discriminatory behaviors are so definitely ordered, without any obvious single base (intimacy, threat, competition, etc.), may have rather far-reaching implications. Persons who assume that discriminatory behaviors are random or capricious, all equally amenable to change if only the proper strategy is found, may find resistance to change especially great in some areas of Negro-white relations. On the other hand, the lack of any clear indication that the ordering of the discriminatory practices rests on a single set of strong interests (economic gain, or power, or status, etc.) suggests that item-by-item change may be possible without the necessity for a major transformation of all prejudices simultaneously or of the total distribution of power, wealth, and prestige.

The validity of the latter point is indicated by our data concerning many discriminatory behaviors and types of segregation in which neither a generalized culture pattern nor generalized prejudices seem to be as important in determining behavior as arbitrary circumstances such as an organization's policies regulating the admission of Negroes or the personal wishes of some strategic gatekeeper. In some cities the Chambers of Commerce were segregated whereas American Legion posts were integrated; in other cities the pattern was reversed. Where the norms of interracial behavior in some segmental environment were either unclearly stated or explicity in conflict with prevailing community sentiments regarding appropriate interracial behavior, patterns of Negro-white relations tended to vary from community practices.

The data concern specific cities. It is evident from the North-South differences, however, that cities are part of larger systems and that states as legislative units are most important in the field of race relations. Indeed, there is a wealth of evidence, available to any alert newspaper reader, of the decisive importance of political policies, legal actions, and political and administrative leadership at the state level. All subordinate political subdivisions such as counties and cities may be affected by a statewide policy or movement. This conclusion has been verified by the experience of investigators who have sought to establish predictive correlations between demographic factors, on the one hand, and the rate of public school desegregation on the other. As Pettigrew and Cramer have summarized this experience:

> One of the first findings was that each state had to be analyzed separately. Apparently, the political leadership of the various states differs so widely in respect to race relations that county-by-county predictions across states is impossible. Further, the demographic characteristics of the southern states vary sharply.[7]

[7] Thomas F. Pettigrew and M. Richard Cramer, "The Demography of Desegregation,"*Journal of Social Issues,* XV, No. 4 (1959), 65. This study found, nevertheless, that ". . . it is the poor, traditional, rural areas with large percentages of uneducated Negroes that form the core of racial conflict [concerning school desegregation]" (p. 70).

RESIDENTIAL SEGREGATION

The most ubiquitous condition reported in the national survey is that discrimination resulting in residential segregation of Negroes is typical of most American cities. The pattern of residential segregation tends to produce or perpetuate segregation in other areas of community life and sets the prevailing tone of Negro-white relations.

In over half of the cities (56 per cent), Negroes are living in either one or a few residential areas.

Table 5. Residential Segregation of Negroes*

NEGROES ARE NOW ALLOWED TO ESTABLISH RESIDENCE IN:	
Only one area of the city	5%
Only a few areas	51%
Most areas	30%
All areas	11%
No answer/don't know	3%
Total number of cities	(221)

* This sample was stratified in such a way that the larger cities are over-represented. The sample is somewhat biased in favor of the large Northern cities.

In only 11 per cent of the cities are they living in all possible areas of residence. Even in these latter cities Negroes usually are not free to live where they choose. Pockets of Negro dwellings can be scattered throughout a city, yet any expansion into new residential areas might be resisted. Of the 93 cities stating that Negroes live in all or most areas, 55 reported that within the last year an attempt had been made to prevent a Negro from moving into a predominantly white district. In private housing, then, Negroes are rather rigidly segregated.[8]

[8] It is enough for present purposes to use these carefully checked estimates of residential segregation. The actual measurement of areal segregation in American cities (from published Census data and other official sources) is a large and difficult task in itself. For some of the difficulties, see Otis Dudley Duncan and Beverly Duncan, "A Methodological Analysis of Segregation Indexes," *American Sociological Review*, XX, No. 2 (April, 1955), 210–17.

The situation is similar in public housing. Negroes are completely excluded from public housing in 15 per cent of the 170 cities having projects. In nearly half (47 per cent) of those 145 cities that permit them to live in public-housing facilities, Negroes live in separate projects. Seventy-seven cities have mixed projects, but in 38 per cent of these, Negroes live in separate buildings. Thus, Negroes are given the same opportunities as whites in only 33 per cent of the cities permitting Negroes in public-housing projects or 27 per cent of all those having projects.

There is evidence that residential segregation has increased in recent years in many cities. By 1950, 90 per cent of Chicago's 337,000 Negroes lived in a predominantly Negro area. This had not always been the case.

In 1910 there were no communities in which Negroes were over 61 percent of the population. More than two-thirds of the Negroes lived in areas less than 50 percent Negro, and a third lived in areas less than 10 percent Negro. By 1920, 87 percent of the Negroes lived in areas over half Negro in composition. A decade later 90 percent were in districts of 50 percent or more Negro concentration. Almost two-thirds (63.0 percent) lived where the concentration was from 90 to 99 percent Negro.[9]

Now in about half (45 per cent) of the cities in the nationwide sample, housing is considered to be the community's most controversial intergroup relations problem. Sixty-one per cent of the cities reported that an attempt had been made to bar a Negro from a white residential area within the last year. This had occurred in an additional 22 per cent of the cities in the last ten years. Less than one-fifth of the cities (17 per cent) had avoided an interracial housing incident.

Thus, we know that segregation in private and public housing is the rule in American cities, and that housing is an explosive intergroup relations issue.

Actual *de facto* segregation of Negroes into highly constricted areas is a characteristic of the larger Northern cities, often to a degree greater than in Southern cities. Although there is no South-

[9] St. Clair Drake and Horace R. Cayton, *Black Metropolis* (New York: Harcourt, Brace & World, Inc., 1945), p. 176.

ern city as large as Chicago, it is nevertheless impressive to note that Chicago may well be the most highly segregated city in the United States. In 1950, 84.1 per cent of the white population of the city lived in census tracts containing less than one per cent Negroes, and 52.9 per cent of the Negroes lived in census tracts in which 97.5 per cent or more of the population were Negro.[10]

Size of the Negro Community. Residential segregation might be expected to increase directly with the absolute number of Negroes in a city. However, the relationship between the size of the Negro community and the extent of residential segregation is not simple. In the North, Negroes are more likely to be living in most areas of a city in those cities where they are either few or great in numbers. This may also be true for the Southern cities; however, there are too few cases to state this conclusively. Perhaps the presence of a few Negroes is not perceived by whites as a threat; thus, initially, residential segregation is not rigidly enforced. With an increase in numbers, Negroes' residences are more likely to be concentrated. Beyond a certain point, however, Negroes cannot be contained. Their numbers alone make it necessary to spread out into other areas of residence.

In summary, residential segregation of Negroes within a city is related to its size, the region in which it is located, the proportion of Negroes in its population, and their absolute numbers. Although the associations are not highly predictive, the data do give some important clues as to the kinds of cities that are most likely to be segregated. There is a greater likelihood that Negroes living in large Southern cities having a low proportion of Negroes and a Negro population of from 500 to 5,000 will live in a restricted residential area. Negroes living in small, Northern towns with a low proportion of Negroes and a small Negro population would more often be scattered throughout the residential areas.

Detailed cross tabulations show that residential segregation is closely associated with segregation in all other areas of community

[10] See: Otis Dudley Duncan and Beverly Duncan, *The Negro Population of Chicago: A Study of Residential Succession* (Chicago: The University of Chicago Press, 1957).

life.[11] Where Negroes are concentrated in a few residential areas, one is more likely to find segregated schools, public-housing projects, hospitals, and social organizations. There, also, Negroes' use of public accommodations is a more controversial intergroup relations issue. Residential segregation obviously reduces the neighbor-to-neighbor contacts between Negroes and whites, and participation of Negroes and whites in the many activities dependent upon proximity is rendered impossible. Concentration of Negroes in a few areas makes it possible to construct schools or hospitals for Negroes only. In time, whites come to expect that Negroes should have a separate community life of their own. Integration ceases to be thought of as a real possibility.

In cities with a long tradition of segregation, Negroes sometimes had come to resign themselves to segregation and tended to work to get the best segregated facilities possible for their own use. Thus, the presence of a segregated YMCA building may also index the Negroes' attempt to provide some recreational outlet for their youth.

Each race develops its own closed system of interaction, and frequently feelings of hostility develop toward the outgroup. Thus, residential segregation goes along with a high incidence of interracial conflict—contrary to what many people have argued. Although this association partly reflects the fact that segregation is greatest in the South, where conflict is also most likely for other reasons, even in the North incidents of Negro-white conflict [12] are

[11] Cf. Don J. Hager, "Housing Discrimination, Social Conflict, and the Law," *Social Problem,* VIII, No. 1 (Summer, 1960), 80–87.

[12] For example, police brutality, vandalism, anti-Negro newspaper reporting, burning-cross incidents. We may note in this connection Grimshaw's observation in "Urban Racial Violence in the United States: Changing Ecological Considerations," *American Journal of Sociology,* LXVI, No. 2 (September, 1960), 112. "Violence in time of major race riots has been concentrated in Negro slums, which in many cities were served largely by white businesses. Casualties and fatalities occurred most often in slums or along their fringes, and destruction of property, particularly looting, was greatest there." And again: "In the riot in East St. Louis in 1917, the Negro section was invaded, Negro residences and businesses were set on fire, and Negroes were shot down in large numbers as they attempted to flee from the burning buildings."

most likely in the cities with the tighter patterns of residential segregation.

Conflict and Protest

Within each region, Negro-white relations are more often tense in larger cities than in the smaller towns. In larger cities, too, intergroup relations organizations are more active. Especially in larger Northern cities, protest organizations seem better able to achieve their goals. Although these generalizations stand as statistical tendencies, there are exceptions. Some kinds of conflict and discrimination are reported more often in Northern than in Southern cities or in small towns than in big cities. There are differences between cities of the same region and size. And there are marked internal variations within each city of any considerable size. The variations form regularized patterns—even in the disorder of violent intergroup conflict. For example, the incidence and type of violence varies with the characteristics of the ecological areas of the city. Little violence occurs in the Negro residential areas without business establishments. These are the middle- and upper-class residential areas, which do not offer extensive opportunity for looting and which typically have the better police protection. These areas also are far removed from those in which violence typically starts. The middle- and upper-class white residential areas also are relatively free from violence, except for raids by automobile on Negro domestics going to and from work.[13]

In the cities surveyed, although segregation, discrimination, and

[13] *Ibid.,* 109–19. This study notes on p. 109: "Urban racial social violence has occurred in every geographic region of the United States. It has not occurred in every city in every area. Certain similarities in its background and social context are found in the cities which have had major race riots. East St. Louis, Washington, Chicago, Tulsa, and Detroit all had sharp increases in Negro population in the years immediately prior to major interracial disturbance, and there were accompanying strains in the accommodative structure, generated in part by the Negroes' assaults on it and in part by the sheer pressure of population on facilities."

conflict were quite common, there were signs of change. The more violent forms of conflict were less prevalent, and the more obvious forms of segregation in public facilities have largely disappeared from many Northern cities. But other forms of social and economic discrimination are still common. The data suggest strongly that Negroes react most militantly to segregation and discrimination in

Table 6. Per Cent of Cities with Organizations Fighting Local Discrimination Cases Within Last Ten Years

	REGION			
	CITY SIZE		CITY SIZE	
	NORTH		SOUTH	
ORGANIZATIONS	100,000 AND OVER	UNDER 100,000	100,000 AND OVER	UNDER 100,000
NAACP	93%	51%	100%	65%
Urban League	56	9	57	3
B'nai B'rith or Anti-Defamation League	86	43	68	19
A State Commission Against Discrimination	54	18	0	3
Federal Fair Employment Practices Commission	56	21	25	3
Congress of Industrial Organizations (CIO)	72	23	68	23
American Federation of Labor (AFL)	43	5	36	6
Other	79	41	54	23
None or none listed	1	27	0	29
Total number of cities	(71)	(118)	(28)	(31)

cities where some gains have been made in abolishing discrimination. A Negro community sensitive to discrimination, led by an aspiring Negro middle class, and realistically hopeful for more equal treatment tends to support militant organizations. Without presenting the large amount of evidence for this conclusion, we may illustrate the point by noting the large amount of protest activity in the larger Northern cities, at the time of our survey. See Table 6, which shows that the various organizations that fight discrimination are most often found in the large cities, especially in the North.

The distribution of incidents of overt conflict of whites and Negroes is somewhat different from the distribution of active organizational efforts to fight discrimination. Such evidences of conflict as vandalism against Negro property, anti-Negro newspaper reporting, and police brutality toward Negroes [14] occur more frequently in the South and in the larger cities of both regions. Vandalism against Jewish property and derogatory statements against the group are also more likely to be big city phenomena, but it is the Northern cities more often than the Southern cities that report conflict incidents involving Jews. Street fights between Negroes and whites and conflict over housing also occur more often in the North, most frequently in the larger cities. Burning-cross incidents are more often reported in Southern cities and especially in large Southern cities. The fact that interracial conflict is more likely to occur in the larger cities than in the smaller towns may reflect, among other things, the greater anonymity, the weaker personalized social control, and the stronger feeling of whites that Negroes are getting "out of their place."

There is a particular historical pattern of violence in the South,[15] and there is still a marked tendency for violence of all kinds to be more prevalent in Southern states than in the Northern states. Sixty per cent of the Southern cities in our sample had a per capita aggravated assault rate of over one-tenth, whereas only 12 per cent of the Northern cities had a rate this high.[16]

[14] Seventy-one per cent of the large Southern cities reported publicly known instances of police brutality toward Negroes in the year preceding the survey inquiry.

[15] W. J. Cash, *The Mind of the South* (Garden City, N.Y.: Doubleday & Company, Inc., 1954), pp. 42–70.

[16] *Uniform Crime Reports for the United States and Its Possessions* (Washington, D.C.: Federal Bureau of Investigation, United States Department of Justice), XXIII, No. 2 (1952), Table 38, pp. 98–105.

We have seen that the region in which a city is located, the city's size, and the proportion of Negroes or other minorities are fairly good predictors of patterns of intergroup behavior. Other demographic variables, such as income level, mobility rate, population growth, or unemployment rate have predictive value only in rather special circumstances. Specific examples follow.

Population Growth. Cities having rapid increases in population in the preceding decade were more likely than other cities to report (1) the use of public accommodations as a controversial problem of intergroup relations (North only); (2) discrimination against Negro workers in promotion practices (North only); (3) recent attempts to prevent Negroes from moving into predominantly white residential areas; (4) discrimination in restaurants, hospitals, department stores, and other semipublic facilities; and (5) police brutality toward Negroes.

However, the following are no more likely to occur in cities that have grown rapidly than in those with relatively stable populations.

1. High rating of general level of conflict and tension.

2. Negro-white relations considered to be a crucial problem.

3. Housing and education considered to be crucial problems.

4. Some kinds of conflict: anti-Negro newspaper reporting, street fights between Negro and white youths, vandalism against Negro property, burning crosses to intimidate Negroes.

5. Some kinds of discrimination: Negroes' use of barbershops patronized by whites or of the same sections of movies as whites.

Mobility of Population. Cities with a large proportion of their population made up of people who have recently arrived have been thought to be more susceptible to intergroup conflict. New arrivals have not established community moorings and, therefore, are exempt in part from the informal sanctions that regulate the behavior of those with longer residence. Cities with a highly mobile population are usually either in agricultural areas requiring seasonal workers, or they are manufacturing cities with fluctuating demands for workers. For instance, over 9 per cent of the populations of Bakersfield, California; Spokane, Washington; and Battle Creek, Michigan, in 1950 lived in a different county the year before.[17] These could be characterized as "boom cities." The migrant workers attracted to them are often the less well educated drawn from the lower-class groups of the rural areas, especially of the South. Many of the rioters of Detroit and some in Los Angeles during World War II belonged to this type of migrant population.

Employment, housing, and the use of public accommodations are more often considered to be controversial intergroup relations problems in Northern cities with larger proportions of mobile people in their populations. For example, 61 per cent of the cities with less mobile populations reported an instance of a qualified Negro industrial worker being denied promotion because of his race within the preceding year, as compared to 76 per cent of the cities with more mobile populations. Negroes' use of semi-public and public facilities was also a more controversial issue or not acceptable in the highly mobile cities.

While a city's proportion of mobile residents is positively related to a wide range of discriminatory practices, it is unrelated to the incidence of overt conflict. Police brutality toward Negroes, interracial street fights, vandalism against Negro property, burning-cross incidents and attempts to bar Negroes from some residential area are as likely to occur in high-mobility as in the low-mobility cities. Negro-white relations were considered no more controversial in one kind of city than the other. There is even a suggestion that Jewish-gentile and Protestant-Catholic relations are more strained in the low-mobility cities. It cannot be assumed that cities having a highly mobile population necessarily have more intergroup conflict in all of its manifold forms.

[17] Compare these cities to those with a small proportion of mobile residents. The latter includes: Bridgeport, Conn., Campbell, O., and Union City, N. J. In 1950 less than 2 per cent of their populations lived in other counties in 1949. No Southern cities had mobility rates this low.

Proportion of Unemployed and Level of Income.[18] In periods of mass unemployment, such as the depression years of the 1930's, Negroes typically suffer more than white workers. The services they perform are often expendable. Given the widely shared prejudices against Negroes, white employers facing economic crises usually fire Negroes first and hire them last.

An increase in unemployment perhaps might be especially likely to increase discrimination and/or conflict if the general level of income were low relative to previous levels or to that of other areas. Then Negroes and whites of similar socioeconomic classes would be thrown into direct competition for the few jobs that were available. Employers have been known to capitalize on this racial competition, further increasing the antagonism between the races.

Contrary to expectations based on these considerations, in the nationwide sample a city's level of unemployment or the median income of its population tells us little about its pattern of intergroup relations. (The tables on which these conclusions are based were controlled on the region in which the city is located.) Negro workers are no more likely to be discriminated against in regard to job promotions in cities with a high level of unemployment than in those with a low level. Job discrimination is no more likely in the poor towns than the rich towns. Neither income level nor level of unemployment was related to the incidence of conflict. Like the other demographic variables that have been mentioned, a city's rate of employment or income level is inadequate when used alone as an index of its intergroup relations pattern.

Negro Protest in Tightly Segregated Cities. Another reaction to segregation is to fight to overcome it. Typically, within a given

[18] Of the cities in the nationwide sample, those with the highest proportions of unemployed workers were generally located either in the Northeastern states or in California. National City, Cal., and Providence, R. I., are two cities with 7 per cent or more of their populations unemployed in 1950. Cities bordering the Great Lakes had the lowest level of unemployment. South Bend, Ind., and Wooster, O., had less than one per cent of their populations unemployed. Southern cities generally fell somewhere between these two extremes. However, cities with low income levels are almost always found in the South.

region and city-size class, there are proportionally more organizations working to improve conditions for Negroes in the rigidly segregated cities. These include labor unions and civic improvement associations as well as organizations interested primarily in intergroup relations.

The National Association for the Advancement of Colored People usually has a larger membership in the highly segregated cities. However, white members are no more likely to join the NAACP in one type of city than the other. Nor are the NAACP's in the segregated cities reported to be any more active than those in the less segregated cities.

Summary. We have found that when Negroes are confined to living in one or a few areas of a city, civic and social organizations are more likely to be segregated, and discrimination and interracial conflict are more serious problems. Denied access to the facilities of the white community, Negroes develop their own professional class and community services. Also, in the rigidly segregated city Negroes are more likely to join protest organizations, and to move toward more militant action.

The more determined efforts on the part of Negroes to reduce discrimination and segregation through organized action tend to occur in the larger cities (but not always—witness Montgomery, Alabama), in the North (again, not always or at all times), and where both the proportion and the absolute size of the Negro population is large. Also, organized protest and defense is more likely in cities characterized by improving conditions, by the presence of a relatively large Negro middle class, and by recent instances of successful group action against discrimination.

The total pattern of the data suggests that militant response to segregation and discrimination are in large part dependent upon a community of Negroes who can realistically hope for better conditions, the leadership of an active Negro middle class, and the widespread conviction that conditions are not as they should be. There is a final factor that is important in determining whether

Negroes react militantly to discrimination. To be an instigation for militant minority group activity, discrimination must be perceived by Negroes and resented by them. This may help to explain the lack of concern about discrimination in some cities where it might appear to an outsider as intolerable, and the high degree of concern with this problem in some cities where conditions are relatively favorable for Negroes.

Summary and Implications

ARE SOUTHERNERS MORE PREJUDICED THAN NORTHERNERS?

• • • • •

It is often claimed, in effect, that schools in the South are segregated because Southerners are prejudiced against Negroes and that schools in the North are generally integrated because Northerners are less prejudiced. But Floridians who move to New York may send their children to integrated public schools whereas the children of New Yorkers wintering in Florida often attend segregated schools. Their prejudices do not determine their behavior, since the former may favor and the latter object to segregated schools. What seems to be essential in accounting for discriminatory practices is the individual's acceptance or nonacceptance of the prevailing patterns of behavior toward minority group members.

But let us suppose that Southerners are more prejudiced toward Negroes than Northerners are. Would this, by itself, account for the regional differences in the extent of discrimination? The nationwide data raise serious questions. In many respects large Southern cities resemble large Northern cities more than they do small Southern towns. Almost all of the large cities of both the North and the South reported a recent instance of job discrimination, whereas this occurred in less than half of the smaller towns of the two regions. Furthermore, there are unaccountable local variations in discriminatory practices. In one small town, Negroes cannot participate in high school athletics; seven miles away in another small town, they may do so. Or, one restaurant serves

Negroes, whereas across the street another restaurant excludes them. Are we to assume that these variations reflect only individual prejudices?

INDIVIDUAL PREJUDICES ARE NOT THE EXPLANATION

The nature of change in the patterns of intergroup behavior also conflicts with the notion that individual prejudices completely account for discriminatory practices. If discriminatory behavior is based on personal prejudices, then the only way to change behavior is to eliminate prejudice. This is a slow process. Yet some forms of discrimination are abolished in a relatively short time. In May, 1954 the schools of Washington, D. C., were segregated; in September they were desegregated. The prejudices of Washingtonians were *not* so malleable, but the institutional pattern did change.

The inadequacies of individual prejudices as a means of predicting discriminatory behavior and accounting for changes in practices call for a reorientation in our thinking about these problems. A frame of reference is needed to explain the *variations* in discriminatory behavior as well as the *patterns* and to account for the persistence of some practices as well as the instability of others.

CHANGING AND RESISTANT PATTERNS OF DISCRIMINATION

The kinds of discrimination that occur in American cities are not merely random or capricious. Although an integrated YMCA is sometimes found in a city where social mingling of the races is not considered to be appropriate, in more crucial areas of intergroup contacts the patterned nature of discrimination persists. There is a cultural component in the patterns of discrimination that resists change. The etiquette of race relations in some rural areas of the Deep South has changed little in the last fifty years.

The forms of prejudice and the patterns of discrimination are part of the cultural heritage. A generation ago, Bogardus found that white Americans objected to some nationality groups more than others.[19] Then, more recently he readministered the test and found

[19] Summarized in G. E. Simpson, and J. M. Yinger, *Racial and Cultural Minorities* (New York: Harper & Row, Publishers, 1958).

that, in general, the order of rejection of the various minority groups remained the same. There are parallels in Negro-white relations. Whites often report that they would find it more objectionable to eat with a Negro than to work with a Negro, and more objectionable to live next door to a Negro than to eat with him. The degree of personal intimacy has been suggested as the underlying dimension that explains the order of these items; however, this seems inadequate, since Negroes often live with whites as maids or nurses. Although the acceptance of Negroes in some situations and their rejection from others is difficult to explain, the effects are real. For instance, only 19 cities of the 248 in the nationwide sample permitted Negroes to get haircuts in white barbershops.

Cultural Heritage Prevails. Earlier it was suggested that individual prejudices do not solely determine whether or not a white person will participate in integrated activities with Negroes. Instead he tends to accept the prevailing practices of the situation in which he finds himself. The accepted policy regulating relations between the races in particular settings, then, becomes crucial. This policy can often be at variance with the local climate of opinion about race relations. For example, Southern ministers of both races may meet for lunch. Some institutional settings, such as a church or a union hall, regulated by policies of a strategic gate-keeper may be called segmental environments; these can either conform with or deviate from local opinion.

Deviations. Deviations from local patterns of discriminations are more likely to occur in some situations than in others. If the norms regulating interracial behavior are poorly defined in some situations, behavior in those situations is likely to be at variance with community sentiment. Where, for instance, do Negroes park their cars in drive-in theaters? The norms of some segmental environments may expressly forbid integration or insist upon it regardless of the prevailing community practices. The Masons, for instance, have a separate order for Negroes. On the other hand, Community Chest drives usually include both Negro and white workers. Finally, if there are competing sets of norms within any one organization, it may even happen that the tolerant set may prevail in intolerant communities, and the intolerant set may prevail in tolerant communities. There are integrated ministerial alliances in the Southern cities and segregated ones in the North.

THE VICIOUS CIRCLE OF SEGREGATION

Without opportunities for getting to know Negroes, whites use the prevailing patterns of segregation and discrimination as a guide or model for their behavior in the few contacts they have with Negroes. Defensively, Negroes develop their own community life, which further reduces their contacts with whites, which in turn increases the possibility of misunderstanding and conflict, and so on in a familiar vicious circle.

Thus, we come full circle to the point at which we began this chapter. Restrictions and freedoms for intergroup contact and communication depend upon prevailing community definitions of what is appropriate and acceptable. These definitions emerge from shared social experience. Once interlocked into common expectations and interests, they set the boundaries for any given time, place, and situation for intergroup contact. But the experience of interaction, when it does occur, may in turn reinforce or modify the beliefs and norms that guide intergroup relations at the level where one man speaks to another.

From the national scene we focus upon our four communities. Limited in number as they are, they provide for much variation—as in the clear and striking contrast in the pattern of segregation in Southport as over against the more open situation in Valley City.[20] In a comparison of 15 community facilities, from churches to bowling alleys, Southport displayed the characteristic Southern pattern of complete segregation. On the other hand, in Valley City Negroes and whites shared access to many of the facilities that were regarded as public, for example, department stores, playgrounds, churches, schools, and movie theaters, although other

---

[20] Cf. Lionel S. Lewis, "Discrimination and Insulation: An Inter-Community Comparison" (M. A. Thesis, Cornell University, Ithaca, N. Y., 1959), Chapters I and VI.

facilities (which seem to be more personal or social) were generally segregated in actual practice, for example, restaurants, some recreational facilities, hotels, and barbershops. On the whole, however, there was an enormous difference between the partial and informal segregation in Valley City and the pervasive, tightly controlled segregation in Southport.

But even in New York State, where law and public policy are firmly set against public segregation and discrimination, our peaceful city of Hometown showed us one great initial fact: the marked isolation and separateness of racial and ethnic segments of the community. Communitywide sample surveys showed that members of various ethnic categories in Hometown tended to follow beaten social paths that did not often intersect with paths of other groups. These observations were confirmed by project observers. Research observers in Hometown noted that most people seemed to develop an "Indian path"—a well-beaten, often trod, social trail from home to work, back to home, to lodge meeting, back to home, on Sundays to church and back, and then perhaps to visit relatives and friends. Once the pathways had developed, persons tended to stay on them; only once in a long while did they go into parts of the forest frequented by other tribes. For most persons, such paths were narrow walks of life that exposed them to only a few limited social environments. These environments bore down powerfully with their social pressures, their group processes, their standards of attitudes and behavior.

We see, then, that these routine patterns of daily activity have great significance for intergroup relations—that more than almost anything else they determine whom a person will get to know.

Suggestions for Further Reading

BRUNO BETTELHEIM and MORRIS JANOWITZ, *Social Change and Prejudice* (New York: Free Press, 1964). One of the better studies of prejudice against Jews in the United States.

NATHAN GLAZER and DANIEL PATRICK MOYNIHAN. *Beyond the Melting*

Pot (Cambridge: M.I.T. Press, 1963). Glazer and Moynihan say that American ethnic groups maintain significant aspects of their own cultural identity, even after many have achieved middle-class status.

GUNNAR MYRDAL, with the assistance of Richard Sterner and Arnold M. Rose, *An American Dilemma* (New York: Harper, 1944). A major work in the field of race relations, financed by a grant from the Carnegie Corporation. The central thesis of the study is that, despite economic, social, and political factors, the race issue in the United States is at bottom an ideological one.

THOMAS F. PETTIGREW, *A Profile of the Negro American* (Princeton, N.J.: Van Nostrand, 1964). A detailed report on the Negro American at mid-century: his personality, genetic composition, mental and physical health, intelligence, and his current protests.

~Group Process and Gang Delinquency*

JAMES F. SHORT, JR.,
and FRED L. STRODTBECK

Although sociologists have been studying adolescent gangs and juvenile delinquency for more than thirty years, only since World War II has gang delinquency been generally recognized as a problem of major proportions. The problem has been especially marked in the larger American cities: New York, Philadelphia, Los Angeles, and Chicago. In 1958 the YMCA of Metropolitan Chicago designed an action program to combat gang delinquency through the use of "detached workers." The detached worker "movement" had begun in Chicago during the late 1920's, following the recommendations of Frederick M. Thrasher, who originated the concept. The period following the Second World War saw the movement spread to Los Angeles, Washington, D.C., Philadelphia, Boston, and New York City.

A detached worker is usually associated with an established social agency, but he is "detached" from regular programs to operate outside the agency's walls. His job is to search out and work with those delinquent groups, consisting frequently of both adolescents and preadolescents, that make little use of available or-

* Reprinted from *Group Process and Gang Delinquency* by James F. Short and Fred L. Strodtbeck by permission of The University of Chicago Press. Copyright © 1965 by the University of Chicago. All rights reserved.

ganized leisure-time programs. The worker has the considerable task of hanging around with the gangs, winning the respect and confidence of their leaders, and persuading the gangs to adopt peaceful pursuits. Detached-worker programs aim to leave the gangs intact while attempting to re-channel their energies and activities.

In the Chicago YMCA program discussed by Short and Strodtbeck in Group Process and Gang Delinquency, *a research project was included to evaluate the success of the detached-worker program, and to accumulate new knowledge that might prove of use in improving the action program's effectiveness. Several persons collaborated in planning the research project, but James F. Short and Fred L. Strodtbeck assumed major responsibility for its formulation and execution. Short and Strodtbeck had originally intended to obtain data to apply to the gang theories of Albert K. Cohen, Richard A. Cloward and Lloyd E. Ohlin, and Walter B. Miller; but as the project proceeded, they saw the possibility for their own unique contribution, that of "the group process level of explanation, which complements and in some instances calls for modification of the other theories."*

The theories that began their project may be described briefly. Cohen [1] *contends that the delinquent subculture emerges as a response to status problems experienced by working-class boys. Unable to succeed in terms of the criteria of the dominant middle-class, these boys suffer loss of status and self-respect. Similarly disadvantaged youngsters join together to reject middle-class standards and values and to establish their own criteria of success. Cloward and Ohlin,* [2] *on the other hand, suggest that restricted access to legitimate opportunities is the crucial determinant of gang delinquency. Lower class boys have less access than middle-class boys to legitimate means for achieving the economic success so extolled in our society. Moreover, boys with no access even to illegitimate*

[1] Albert K. Cohen, *Delinquent Boys* (New York: Free Press, 1955).
[2] Richard A. Cloward and Lloyd E. Ohlin, *Delinquency and Opportunity* (New York: Free Press, 1960).

means for economic success are most likely to resort to gang delinquency and to the use of drugs. Walter Miller [3] argues that gang delinquency is a direct expression of distinctive patterns of the lower-class not shared by the middle-classes. He sees the lower-class community as possessing a long-established, distinctively patterned tradition with an integrity of its own, rather than viewing it as a so-called delinquent sub-culture that has arisen through conflict with middle-class culture.

What Short and Strodtbeck have added to these concepts is an emphasis on the "exchange" of "nurturant sociability" in the group process. Failing to obtain basic emotional gratifications elsewhere, gang boys obtain them from an exchange process within the group. For the loyalty a boy gives to his fellow members of the gang, he receives in exchange their approval and attention. Short and Strodtbeck also argue that because these lower-class gang boys are deprived of opportunities to learn how people act in the world outside, they simply do not know how to participate in the larger society. To test these ideas, the YMCA program studied both the gang boys and boys who did not constitute "gangs" in the formal sense. The researchers included in the study non-gang lower-class boys from boys' clubs, settlement houses, and other youth-serving agencies in the area where the gangs under study were located. They also included groups of white and Negro boys not from lower-class backgrounds, these groups having been selected from YMCA Hi-Y Clubs in middle-class areas. Although a vast number of boys were studied, the investigation focused on six groups: a lower-class Negro gang, a lower-class white gang, a lower-class Negro non-gang, a lower-class white non-gang, a middle-class Negro group, and a middle-class white group.

The section of Short and Strodtbeck's account of the project presented here explores "social disabilities" among the gang boys, disabilities thought to help account for the specifically delinquent aspects of their behavior. The reported findings, based primarily

[3] Walter B. Miller, "Lower Class Culture as a Generating Milieu of Gang Delinquency," *Journal of Social Issues,* XIV (Summer, 1958), pp. 5–19.

on field observations by the research team and the detached workers, make a significant contribution to the literature on gang delinquency and gang leadership. One must be careful of course in generalizing these interpretations to delinquent gangs in other cities and other parts of the country, but the method and results of the Chicago YMCA's project do suggest a pattern very much worth emulating and testing in other communities.

Explorations of Social Disability, Class, and Gang Status

In his classic analysis of street-corner society, Whyte quotes Doc as follows:

Fellows around here don't know what to do except within a radius of about three hundred yards. That's the truth, Bill. They come home from work, hang on the corner, go up to eat, back on the corner, up a show, and they come back to hang on the corner. If they're not on the corner, it's likely the boys there will know where you can find them. Most of them stick to one corner. It's only rarely that a fellow will change his corner.[1]

Whyte's comment is that, "The stable composition of the group and the lack of social assurance on the part of its members contribute toward producing a very high rate of social interaction within the group. The group structure is a product of this interaction." He continues, "Out of such interaction there arises a system of mutual obligations which is fundamental to group cohesion."

Whyte attributes corner boys' lack of social assurance to the limited range of social experiences of corner boys, with attendant rigidity in behavior patterning.

Each individual has his own characteristic way of interacting with other individuals. This is probably fixed within wide limits by his native endowment, but it develops and takes its individual form through the experiences of the individual in interacting with others throughout the course of his life. Twentieth-century American life demands a high de-

[1] William Foote Whyte, *Street Corner Society* (2nd ed., 1955; Chicago: University of Chicago Press), p. 256.

gree of flexibility of action from the individual, and the normal person learns to adjust within certain limits to changes in the frequency and type of his interactions with others. This flexibility can be developed only through experiencing a wide variety of situations which require adjustment to different patterns of interaction. *The more limited the individual's experience, the more rigid his manner of interacting, and the more difficult his adjustment when changes are forced upon him.* [Italics added.] . . . gang activities proceed from day to day in a remarkably fixed pattern. The members come together every day and interact with a very high frequency. Whether he is at the top and originates action for the group in set events, is in the middle and follows the origination of the leader and originates for those below him, or is at the bottom of the group and always follows in set events, the individual member has a way of interaction which remains stable and fixed through continual group activity over a long period of time. His mental well-being requires continuance of his way of interacting. He needs the customary channels for his activity, and, when they are lacking, he is disturbed.[2]

While the nature of the disability (lack of social assurance) is similar among gang youngsters in the present study, its etiology appears to be different. Certainly the lack cannot be attributed to intensity and rigidity of interaction patterns with the same group. For the gang boys these patterns are not stable enough to produce such rigidity. There can be little doubt, however, that the gang boys also lack the variety of experience which increases role playing ability.

Doc's first point, at the beginning of this [section], is apposite. The range of gang boys' physical movements is severely restricted. They are ill at ease when outside their "area," in part because of fear that they may infringe on a rival gang's territory, but in part due also to a more general lack of social assurance such as that to which Whyte refers. Without the base of stable composition of the group, the rate of social interaction within our gangs is lower than was the case with Whyte's corner groups. Mutual obligations, therefore, are tenuous among most gang members and, hence, according to the argument, group cohesion is low.

Excerpts from a detached worker's interview illustrate both

[2] *Ibid.*, pp. 263–64.

the low degree of mutual obligation among gang members outside the arena of immediate interaction, and the sensitivity of one gang leader to the lack of social assurance of fellow gang members and of his girl friend. This leader clearly was more in command of the social graces than were the others, and he realized this fact, but the worker suggests that the leader, too, needed bolstering in this regard. In the following excerpt the worker is discussing his negotiations with Duke, leader of the King Rattlers, concerning the disposition of tickets for the annual banquet of the YMCA of Metropolitan Chicago.

A: When I first started thinking about the annual YMCA banquet, I knew I'd be able to get about five tickets, and I had planned on taking three boys and using the other two myself. I talked it over with Duke. First thing Duke suggested, he wanted me to get him a date with one of the YMCA girls from the downtown office. . . . I told him I thought maybe he'd be better anyway to take Elaine because. . . "You've never actually taken Elaine anywhere of importance. You've taken her to the show, but she's never been to a downtown affair."

Q: Is Elaine the girl who has Duke's two children?

A: She has a baby girl who is a year old and one that's three. Duke's never taken her to a real nice place, and I thought it would be nice if he asked her to go. He was real excited. "Okay, I'll ask her." So that was closed.

Then I had one extra ticket. I said, "Well, Duke, seeing that you and Butch get along real well, maybe Butch would go."

The first thing Duke said was, "No, no, we don't want to take Butch because he doesn't know how to eat out in company."

So naturally I smiled and said, "Crisake, he knows just as much as you do."

"No, he just don't know how to eat out in company."

Then he went all the way back to the time I took them to the Prudential Building. I suggested that we go in and get a cup of coffee, but Butch said, "No, we'd better go back to the area [home territory] and get a hot dog or Polish [sausage]." And Duke was all for it, too, because he didn't want to go in there either. On the "Top of the Rock" they did their sight seeing, but they didn't want to go into the little restaurant and get coffee. They didn't feel they were dressed, or something. They're real shy about going into a strange place that's real nice.

Earlier in the summer I took Duke, Butch, and Harry out to Lake Meadows, and they were real shy. They didn't want to go in because they felt they weren't dressed good enough. But I made them go in and at least have a cup of coffee. We went early. They had a little combo and I figured a guy could sit and listen to them play for maybe half an hour and drink coffee. 'Course, they went in the restaurant part. They didn't go in the other side where you can really hear the combo. They all felt the same way—they weren't dressed good enough.

Anyway, Duke didn't feel Butch was qualified. So I smiled and said, "Okay, how about Harry?"

"Hell no. Harry hasn't got enough clothes to go."

Harry only has one suit. I had mentioned the banquet to him earlier in the week, but he didn't know whether or not he could go—meaning that he didn't know whether he could get his suit out [of hock or the cleaners]. He didn't know whether he'd have any money. But Duke felt so strong about Butch's not going that I didn't push Harry. So I dropped it, and that was it.

On the way over there I did as much talking as I could about the meeting. I told them approximately what was going to go on, about the main speaker being President Eisenhower's doctor, and that there would be a lot of skits from the different YMCA's in the Metropolitan area. When we got to the amphitheater, I dropped Elaine, Alice [Duke's aunt and the worker's date for the evening], and Duke and I went to park the car. Duke asked me if I would pick him up a pack of cigarettes, so I told him I would. I told him to go in and check the coats. He looked around and finally came back because he didn't know where they were supposed to go. Then I found the tables and I put Duke and Elaine together.

Q: Did Duke comment at all about anybody else at the table or about the dinner?

A: Over-all, he had a real good time. He told his aunt and grand-mother that he met Mrs. Hoot, or something like that. Really it was Mrs. Shoup. She's chairman of the Women's Auxiliary Board. I told Duke after we had left the amphitheater coming home that Mrs. Shoup has got enough money to bury you. What I meant was she is a good woman to know.

Also, I pointed out Mr. Grammercy. He was up on the stage and I wanted him to meet Duke real bad, because I told Duke quite a bit about Mr. Grammercy before—about his apartment on the north shore where I think he pays something like $1,700 a month. I wanted him to meet Mr. Grammercy real bad, but we couldn't meet him. I told him later on maybe I'd be able to introduce him.

Elaine complained because Duke insulted her and she couldn't eat her meat. Duke was trying to show her how to cut the meat. He said Elaine didn't know which hand to hold the knife in. She was real hungry and she ate everything but the meat, because Duke was rapping on her so much.

Q: I wondered why she kept looking around the table. She was very self-conscious.

A: Right. She felt real bad for not having eaten the meat. She didn't know whether it would have been appropriate to have Duke cut her meat or not. Duke said the meat was so tender he could cut it with his fork.

Duke and his girl friend were noticeably silent throughout the YMCA banquet. The accident of seating arrangements found them sitting at a table adjacent to the one where the worker sat. They never initiated conversation with the half dozen other guests at their table, and their responses to others' conversational efforts were brief and subdued. Throughout, Elaine seemed cowed by the experience, Duke less so, but obviously at some pains not to make a behavioral miscue. The two exchanged meaningful glances with one another during the course of the meal and the entertainment which followed. Their behavior was stiff and uncertain, quite in contrast to the generally relaxed and friendly atmosphere of the crowd.

Social Disability, Values, and That Old Gang of Mine

The lack of social assurance of gang boys was apparent from our very first contact with them and with the YMCA Program for Detached Workers. Workers reported frequently that their boys did not feel comfortable outside "the area" and that they were ill at ease in most social situations outside the gang context. . . . The analysis of semantic differential data * . . . and an interpretation of data from a motivation opinionaire . . . directed our attention to an apparent lack of gratification even of gang membership and interaction, and hence to a hypothesis concerning a fundamental lack of social skills on the part of gang boys which seems even more crucial to an understanding of their behavior than does lack of social assurance. . . . Negro gang boys evaluated "someone who is a member of your GANG" lower than did other boys, and also showed a greater tendency to evaluate themselves (SELF) higher than GANG. Even more revealing of gang boys' ambivalence concerning their peers, however, was a tendency, relative to the other boys, to endorse such apparently conflicting statements as: "Friends are generally more trouble than they are worth" *and* "You can only be really alive when you are with friends." In the treatment which follows we will attribute this apparent ambivalence to mutually reinforcing characteristics of gang boys, individually and collectively, which may be summarized in the term "social disability."

The coping ability of gang boys and their confidence in themselves—significant "social abilities"—may well be reflected in the disparity of private vs. gang values and behavior. The disparity concerning the boys' individual and collective *family* attitudes, and their individual attitudes and subsequent behavior is paralleled by similar observations concerning the world of *work*. On two widely separated occasions the following observations were made:

1. Fred commented on the similarity of his experience while conducting the family interviews with the Chiefs and a recent incident in the same area. Fuzzhead, a regular but low-status member of the Chiefs, approached Fred in a pool hall hangout and began to talk very seriously about his plans to get and keep a job so that he could provide for the

* [These evaluations were based on the "semantic differential," a method for measuring the meaning of an object to an individual. Boys were asked to rate a given concept or descriptive image (e.g., "someone who saves his money," "someone who sticks by his friends in a fight") on a number of seven-point bipolar rating scales. These seven-point scales include such bipolar scales as the following: (1) good-bad, (2) kind-cruel, (3) strong-weak.]

girl he wanted to marry. Fred probed Fuzzhead and, finding him deadly in earnest, encouraged the boy in these ambitions and indicated his willingness to help him secure a steady job. In the midst of the conversation other Chiefs entered the pool hall and came over to where Fred and Fuzzhead were conversing. Upon discovering the topic of conversation they began ridiculing Fuzzhead's ambitions. Fuzzhead abruptly discontinued this discussion and despite Fred's encouraging words withdrew from the conversation.

2. This was my last field trip into the gang areas. Fred and I went first through the Chiefs' area where we found Billy sitting on a chair on the sidewalk in front of a pool hall, with one of his (illegitimate) children on his lap. I recalled his prophecy more than three years earlier that such a fate might come to pass. Fred joshed with Billy about his failure to hold a job, and Billy, in turn, tried without success to borrow money from Fred. He allowed as how his "old lady" would give him some money.

While we were chatting with Billy, others in the old Chiefs gang came on the scene. One of the boys pulled Fred off to one side and began telling him that he planned to get married but that he wanted to have a steady job first. Fred was skeptical but encouraging. When the other boys caught the drift of the conversation they began immediately to "razz" the boy concerning his ability to attract and support a wife. The boy dropped the subject completely.

These boys' prospects for steady jobs were poor, despite their sincere desires and intentions. In addition to the instability of that segment of the labor market for which they were qualified, their associations on the street, even though the gang hardly existed any longer (as was the case with the Chiefs in the summer of 1962), was a deterring and disruptive influence. The influence of the gang clearly cannot be explained as a reaction formation against middle class values, nor can it, we believe, in terms of "delinquent norms." Boys in our gangs often were actively discouraged from the expression of conventional values in the gang context, chiefly by derision of individual ambitions and abilities, and espousal of group goals which were alternative but not necessarily anticonventional. Boys "rapped" with girls, and their choice of mates might be derided, but if a boy persisted in his choice and was successful, other members of the gang accepted the situation. Marriage was not tabu, as witness the marriages (common-law and conventional) of many active gang boys, but "making out with the broads" was a greater value on the street.

So, too, with employment. Detached workers were barraged by requests for jobs, but "hustles" of great variety were bragged about on the streets. Boys who had jobs were not derided for this fact— the Y program practice of giving favored treatment to gang leaders in securing jobs may have been a factor here—but life on the street was far removed from life on the job, and boys who were working knew full well that street life continued, whether or not they were there. One of the problems for these boys is the fact that the job as such is not an acceptable status alternative to the gang. For these boys the job situation is likely to be alien to those experiences he finds most rewarding. An example is the suspicion (in many cases justified) which gang boys experience on the part of plant security personnel:[3]

Ringo: Them plant policemen—you go down the hall, they ask you, "You got identification?" and "You work here?" and all that . . . well, I mean, they see you come into the building every morning and leave.

Jones: Like you're convicts, man.

Ringo: I told him, look here man, I ain't never been in no trouble.

Cooper: That's worse than being in the place [jail], isn't it?

Ringo: Yeah.

Cooper: At least in the place they don't ask you for no I.D.

Ringo: They know you're going to have your identification card.

[3] "Youth Consultant Symposium on Jobs," YMCA of Metropolitan Chicago, mimeographed (spring, 1962). In the interview Ringo and Jones are gang boys, eighteen and nineteen years old, both with job experience through the Program for Detached Workers, both with unstable job histories. Both are core gang members, having occupied positions of considerable influence and leadership. Ringo, the younger of the two, is married. Jones is single. Charles N. Cooper is Assistant Director of the Program for Detached Workers, and Benjamin Ross has at various times been a detached worker, Field Supervisor, and Employment Coordinator with the program.

Ross: Don't you think this is part of his job?

Jones: What, to be bugging people all the time?

Ross: What would you do if you had the gig [job], would you sit up there and cool it?

Jones: Man, if you know I'm working here . . .

Ross: I mean, how many people they got working there?

Jones: Man, I don't know.

Ringo: Well, I know they've got lots of workers there . . .

Jones: The man, he knows who he wants to pick on. Now like I see you, Benny, if you don't look right, you look like you're going to do something wrong, well lookit, I'm not going to forget you, Jack. I guess that's the way we look to him.

Jobs for these boys tend to be neither challenging nor very well paid. When one of these conditions is improved, the other may cause trouble:

Ross: Have we ever gotten you a job that you think you might have stayed on for the rest of your life?

Jones: Yeah, this job at the laboratory, I was working at, was a nice job. I was learning how to do most of the things, and as I worked I was gradually catching onto everything and I took interest in it, but it was a small company. Well, it wasn't paying much from the start. Vallis explained that to me, and when I went for an interview with the owner of the company, he told me that it was a small company but that I would be starting with the company and I could grow with the company, and he said that in the first three months I would get a raise, and then after the first six months I'd get a raise. I think I worked about four and a half months and I was looking for my raise . . .

Ross: What happened?

Jones: The cat, he says, "All right, all right, tomorrow." Two weeks later he gave me a nickel raise. About then it was time for me to get the second raise, my six-month raise. And he fired me.

Ross: Why did he fire you?

Jones: I was getting on the cat's back.

Cooper: You got your first raise.

Jones: About thirty-eight dollars. I was making about $1.20. I was making thirty-six at first, my take home pay. And he gave me a nickel raise.[4]

Even in the rare cases when pay is adequate, job challenging, and with a good future, the lure of the gang may spell disaster. In the spring of 1962 the director of the Program for Detached Workers reflected that after three years not one of the Chiefs was employed, despite the fact that every one of them had been employed at one time or another, some two or three times through efforts of the employment coordinator. This was sheer frustration for the director, who had worked hard and well with these boys when he was their worker, later as field supervisor, and now as director of the Program. He was especially disappointed with Walter, one of two high school graduates among the Chiefs. Walter was a likeable boy, not given to aggression or excess as were many of his fellow Chiefs. The Program had secured for him a good paying job at a large cosmetics firm, and he had impressed his employer and other workers with his industry. After awhile, however, he began to be tardy and he missed work a few days. As a consequence, he was fired. Said the director, "Walter was always one of the boys. It's hard for such a guy to make it. Only the guys who stay on the fringe of the gang, or leave it altogether, have much of a chance to make it."

Gang boys do not reject the validity of job responsibilities, but life on the streets is not conducive to meeting these responsibilities:

> Ross: Suppose you had a factory gig for yourself and you say I'm going to hire me some studs, give them a break because I know how it was when I was coming up, and you hire these cats. What would you expect of them?
>
> Jones: I'd expect them to get there on time and do their work.
>
> Ross: And if they didn't, what would you do?

[4] The notion that one should "live fast, die young, and leave a beautiful corpse" might be romantically attractive to a few gang boys, but it would also be regarded as the height of folly. The very few boys who persist in extreme aggression or other dangerous exploits are regarded generally as "crazy" by the other boys.

Jones: Fire them.

Ross: Would you give them a break, would you talk to them or what?

Jones: That's understood—I'd talk to them.

Ross: For how long? Or would you walk in and tell the cat, "Look baby, if you're late one more day, you going to be in the wind; I ain't paying you for coming in late."

Jones: If a person is a nice worker, even if he does come in late, if he can get his work out and not slacking on the job, I don't give a damn what time he got there.

Here Jones clearly indicates his lack of awareness or appreciation of the interdependence of tasks in modern industry—a not too abstract idea, but one very little understood by these boys.

Ross: What would you do in the case of Smith? This joker went down to the gig and the first night he stood around and he looked, 'cause you figure he's learning. And the second night he went down and looked, and you figure he's still learning. And the third night, and he stood in the same spot, and he looked . . . would you fire him?

Jones: I'd give that cat a week's pay and tell him to leave town.

Ross: So what you're trying to tell me is that the cats do not miss the gigs on Monday morning because they tore up [got drunk].

Jones: Aw, maybe on a Monday.

Ross: But not during the rest of the week.

Jones: There you go. Once you get past Monday, Benny . . .

Cooper: You're just liable to make it.

Ross: What did Billy tell me the other night? "I know damn well I'm going to make it tomorrow because it's Friday and Friday is pay day." But you will miss a Monday morning or be late on Monday morning?

Jones: Well, you're trying to get over a weekend, drunk or whatever you've been doing. Especially, Jack, if those broads have been keeping you up all night.

Ross: It ain't always the Thunderbird, sometimes it's them broads.

A dependable supply of money is seductive, however, and even the gang *may* exert a favorable influence on job *getting,* if not on job stability:

Ross: This is what I wanted to ask you . . . Do you get some group pressure, you know, like Billy. I'd have swore up and down that Billy would never get a job. Do you think that Billy got a job because the rest of the fellas were working around there and he sort of got bugged or something?

Jones: They are riding Billy too hard, you see; Billy is a person that loves money. He'll do anything, even work.

Ross: That's what I was trying to find out, you know, if with the majority of the cats working, do you feel like maybe this makes the rest of them want to work. If there ain't nobody working, then the rest of the cats want to quit their jobs.

Ringo: If everybody's working, then they'll try to get a job. If you're out loafing, they're with you; if they've got somebody to drink with, they're with you.

• • • • •

Jones: Once you get used to that money coming in once a week, Jack, it's hard to get over.

Ringo: If you think that you are going to work next week or something, you ain't worried. But when you get fired and ain't got nothing coming in, that's the time to worry.

Jones: Boy, that money is habit-forming, Jack.

Finally, family responsibilities, when they are taken seriously, influence employment attitudes of gang boys just as anyone else:

Ross: Do you have any kids?

Ringo: One.

Ross: Is your wife working?

Ringo: Nope.

Ross: How long you been out of work—three days?

Ringo: Three days. I went out to Mailway, Carson Pirie and Scott. I'm in the habit of working now—I don't feel right just free-loading no more.

Ross: Did you talk to Vallis (employment coordinator) yet?

Ringo: No, Al (detached worker) has been talking to Vallis. He's been down two days straight, you know. Vallis sent word he's going to try to do something for me. I was thinking about going to the relief board for a couple of days, you know. Around about

Christmas time, too, you know. My old lady she just got out of the hospital; she wants this, she wants that . . .

Ross: How old is the baby?

Ringo: About five weeks.

But, the "glamour" of family responsibilities is short-lived. The harsh realities of "making both ends meet" with low wages and minimal skills soon assert themselves. A young husband and father, even with the best intentions, is likely to chafe under restrictions imposed by wife and family. The lure of the street is not easily forgotten, and it is culturally supported.

There is no reason to believe that gang boys' performance on the semantic differential and their behavior in conversation with detached workers is any less real than are gang norms and behavior. Indeed it is quite possible that the boys' abstract evaluations of conventional and deviant images and their earnest discussions of the future with detached workers are in a sense "more real" than is the culture of the gang. With very rare exceptions, even the most ardent gang boys do not conceive of the gang as "forever." Much of gang behavior represents a striving toward *adult* status, and older gang boys soon come to put down gang fighting as "kid stuff." Other forms of delinquency which may be more integral to their particular form of lower class culture are not so easily put down, as we have seen. Harsh reality intervenes, also, to make conventional adjustments difficult to achieve. It is easier as well as more status-giving to continue the gang ways and the ways of lower class culture, particularly for boys who possess few of the skills which equip them for achievement outside of these systems and for boys caught up in the status system of the gang.

The apparent paradox of gang boys' allegiance to competing value systems really is not a paradox at all. Their coping ethic simply confirms that value systems do not apply consistently to all situations, or to all roles. Different situations and different roles require different values and different behavior patterns. The reality of contradictory value systems, so endemic to modern society, is especially acute for adolescents who must learn abruptly that they are no longer children and that they are supposed to behave as young men and women while foregoing many of the privileges of adulthood. The ambivalence of adolescents generally, and of gang boys in particular, with respect to parental values, for example, is attested to by a host of studies, past and present. Like Shaw's "jack roller," many adolescents long both for nurturance and security, and for freedom and adventure.[5]

The relation between values and behavior is further complicated by a time perspective. It may be useful if we conceptualize gang life as a *career phase,* much as did Shaw earlier and in the terms of reference of the literature on professions.[6] Thus, for example, Becker *et al.*[7] report that medical students talked idealistically of the medical profession when they were alone with the investigators but they never did so when other medical students were around. Idealism was an important factor in their choice of medicine as a career and in terms of their hopes and aspirations for the future. Some problems of student life and their later decisions concerning the choice of general practice or medical specialty would call forth other, sometimes quite different, values. In all of this the candor of the medical students seemed unquestionable.

A basic difference between gang boys and medical students is

[5] See Clifford R. Shaw, *The Jack-Roller: A Delinquent Boy's Own Story* (Chicago: University of Chicago Press, 1930). Cf. Erik H. Erikson, *Childhood and Society* (New York: W. W. Norton Co., 1950); Frederick Elkin and William Westley, "The Myth of Adolescent Culture," *American Sociological Review,* XX (1955), 680–84; S. B. Withey and E. Douvan, *A Study of Adolescent Boys* (Ann Arbor: University of Michigan, Survey Research Center, 1955); E. Douvan and C. Kaye, *Adolescent Girls* (Ann Arbor: University of Michigan, Survey Research Center, 1957); and James Coleman, *The Adolescent Society* (New York: Free Press of Glencoe, Ill., 1961).
[6] See Clifford R. Shaw, *The Natural History of a Delinquent Career* (Chicago: University of Chicago Press, 1931); cf. Sutherland and Cressey's discussion of "Behavior Systems in Crime," in Edwin H. Sutherland, *Principles of Criminology,* rev. by Donald R. Cressey (6th ed.; New York: J. B. Lippincott Co., 1960).
[7] See Howard S. Becker, Blanche Geer, Everett C. Hughes, and Anselm Strauss, *Boys in White: Student Culture in Medical School* (Chicago: University of Chicago Press, 1961).

that for gang boys career phases are less clearly demarcated, and commitment to or involvement in gang life hampers achievement of values held with respect to future phases. For medical students each phase equips for the next—they "grow into" successive stages. Gang boys are expected to "grow out of" gang life and into adaptations for which the gang in many respects has been poor preparation. This is not to deny Miller's contention that certain aspects of gang life are functional to subsequent lower class adult life:

Some school-connected experiences such as football—with its long, tedious practice periods and drills, interspersed with a weekly battle that calls for a sharp focus of all physical skills and strength in concentrated measure and for a short duration—find analogies in lower class life and in certain kinds of lower-class occupational roles. A dull, slow, and typical week in this subculture frequently culminates in a "night out on the town" and by "hanging one on." It should also be noted that a substantial portion of the labor force today (about 50 per cent) still consists of laborers, unskilled workers, and routine factory operatives. Most of these jobs are filled by lower-class individuals. Graduates of the street corner, as they grow and assume their roles in the world of work, have been prepared to operate within these interactional milieus, for their street-corner and occupational groups share similar sets of ideas, principles, and values. The job routines of the fireman, trucker, soldier, sailor, logger, and policeman reflect the occupational rhythmic pattern characteristic of lower-class community living, street-corner activity, and football—long periods of routine activity broken by intense action and excitement. As one views occupational needs of the future and, at the same time, analyzes the prevailing features of street-corner society, the following conclusion emerges: *The essential outlines, values, and language patterns; the emphasis on "smartness"; the regard for strength and physical prowess, all appear to remain functional, adjustive, and adaptive for these youngsters.*[8]

Gang life is not conducive to punctuality, dependability on the job every day, discipline, and consistency in job performance, however—all basic requirements of modern industry and of the jobs

[8] William C. Kvaraceus, Walter B. Miller, *et al., Delinquent Behavior: Culture and the Individual* (New York: National Education Association of the United States, 1959).

to which Miller refers. To the extent that the gang is delinquent, or defined as such by the larger community, its "rep" may damage the prospects for conventional job and other types of adjustments. Thus, a gang leader complained to the Program for Detached Workers that he had been picked up by the police and held in jail for several days "on suspicion" of a crime for which he was in no way responsible. The young man admitted that his *past* behavior may have warranted the suspicion, but this did not alter the fact that the police action placed his current job in jeopardy.

The failure of individuals to make satisfactory adjustments in any institutional sphere inevitably handicaps their ability to achieve future goals. Our gang boys fail often in school, on the job, in conventional youth-serving agencies, and in the eyes of law enforcement officials (and therefore in the public eye). They fail more often in each of these respects than do the non-gang boys we have studied, both middle and lower class. These failures, combined with limited social and technical skills, and blocked legitimate opportunities, constitute an overwhelming handicap for the achievement of the goals they endorse.

It is possible at this time to add to the social disability hypothesis preliminary observations from the personality assessment and one general observation of gang boys compared with other boys studied. From the former, data suggest that gang boys are less self-assertive (in this conventional test-like situation), they are more reactive to false signals than are the other boys, they tend to be slightly more neurotic and anxious, less gregarious, and more narcistic.[9] The possible cumulative effect of these differences is more impressive than are the individual findings, for they add up to boys who have less self-assurance and fewer of the qualities which engender confidence and nurturant relations with others. It seems likely that these characteristics heighten status insecurities of gang boys in many contexts. For example, our psychological testing team observed that gang boys were much more sensitive to how others

[9] From a report by Desmond S. Cartwright, "Psychological Test Differences Between Gang Boys and Others: Summary Prepared for Advisory Group Meeting" (August, 1962, dittoed).

were answering questions, completing instruments, and performing various tasks than were the other boys, and they appeared to be more anxious concerning their own performance relative to others. When we talked to gang boys about the research program, they indicated a special sensitivity to why *they* were being studied. We had to take special precautions in these respects, both to protect the anonymity and the integrity of responses and to assure gang boys that they were not being singled out for any peculiar and derogatory reason. Their public image is of concern to them and, like so many things, is a source of ambivalent feeling. Newspaper headlines and other mass-media references to the gang often are a source of prestige among and within gangs, but they are the *raison d'être* also for changes in gang names, e.g., from Vice Kings to Conservative Vice Kings, from Cobras to Executives.

It is unlikely that gang experience, with its constant challenge to boys to prove themselves tough, adept with the girls, "smart," etc., in any substantial way alleviates status insecurities or their related social disabilities except insofar as gang experience better equips boys to respond successfully to gang challenges. These skills are not calculated to enhance gang boys' status prospects outside the gang, however. And so the cycle is perpetuated.

The carefree image of "that old gang of mine" as a solidary group—all for one and one for all—and the notion that the gang prepares a youngster for adult roles, are tarnished, to say the least, by this interpretation. One suspects that this image derives from nostalgia concerning their own childhood of former members of gangs or of middle class individuals (including sociologists) whose interpersonal skills are more highly developed than are those of our gang boys. Careful observation of lower class gangs has been extremely limited and in most cases superficial. It is unlikely, for example, that Thrasher was able to receive more than a casual impression of the nature of interpersonal relations among the 1,313 Chicago gangs which he surveyed.[10] The romantic note sounded in discussions of the wanderings of gang boys away from home

[10] Frederic M. Thrasher, *The Gang* (Chicago: University of Chicago Press, 1936; abridged, with a new introduction by James F. Short, Jr., 1963).

and school, and references to the hangout as the gang boy's castle may reflect the vicarious gratifications of adult investigators and their own childhood fantasies to a greater extent than they do the perspectives of gang members. To be sure, it is a mistake to read into the behavior of youngsters the motivations of adults, and elements of fantasy are involved in the behavior of gang boys today, as they were at the time of Thrasher's classic study. But the behavior and the fantasies of gang members today are less like Sir Galahad and King Arthur and more like the power plays of syndicate hoodlums and racial bigots among their adult contemporaries.[11]

Thrasher was acutely sensitive to the necessity for accurate communication between adults and adolescents, and he urged that "to understand the gang boy one must enter into his world with a comprehension, on the one hand, of this seriousness behind his mask of flippancy or bravado, and on the other, of the role of the romantic in his activities and in his interpretation of the larger world of reality" (p. 96). Our quarrel with this interpretation is not that fantasy plays no role in the world view of gang youngsters, but that even these fantasies are sharply restricted by harsh realities of life and by the spectacular successes achieved by a very few,[12] rather than by fairy tales of an earlier and middle class generation. Hero worship, yes, but romantic fantasy, no.

Our argument, further, is that the "seriousness behind his mask of flippancy or bravado" reflects fundamental lacks in social skills and other socially rewarded abilities which are characteristic of the majority of gang boys. Far from being "blythe of heart for any adventure" (Thrasher, p. 86), there is among these boys a deadly serious character in their fantasies and even in their horseplay. And while their fantasies concerning gang membership and prowess may be adventurous, their fear of the world outside "the area" and of association with persons beyond the rather narrow circle of their acquaintance suggests the need for security as a motivation rather than new experiences.

While this argument varies considerably from Thrasher's *inter-*

[11] Cf. Lewis Yablonsky, *The Violent Gang* (New York: Macmillan Co., 1962).
[12] Such as popular entertainers and sports figures, politicians, and hoodlums.

pretations, it is consistent with much of his data. Thrasher noted the generally unstable character of gang membership and structure, and the short-lived nature of many gangs. These facts, and the ability of gang boys to survive and find food and shelter by various means while wandering the city streets or otherwise away from home impressed Thrasher as evidence of their *independence.* It may be questioned, however, whether this type of existence was adequate preparation either for psychological maturity and general well-being, or for social and other skills. It should be emphasized that we are not arguing that the gang is devoid of play and interpersonal gratifications. Quite the contrary, it is likely that gang membership offers these youngsters a larger measure of these types of rewards than does any alternative form of association of which they are aware and which is available to them by virtue of preparation and other reality considerations. Many gangs have a history of long association, some extending over periods of more than a generation. Further, close and systematic observation of our most highly delinquent gangs reveals much camaraderie and genuine friendship. These are often very unstable, however, for a variety of reasons. There is, for example, the underlying tone of aggression which characterizes so much of the interaction within the gang. There is a threat which hangs over even the closest of friendships that one may have to prove oneself against one's friend, perhaps as a result of forces within the gang but extraneous to the friendship. Status within the gang is subject to challenge from many quarters, and status threat may disrupt even close friends. There is, over all, the atmosphere of mutual distrust of "insiders" as well as "outsiders" which pervades much of lower class culture. The gang boy is likely to come to the gang suspicious of the motives and the dependability of human relationships generally—a suspicion that carries over to the gang itself, and to which the gang contributes in terms both of interpersonal relations within the gang and external to it.

Yet the gang is not characterized by *desperation* in search of stable human relationships, nurturance, and security. It seems, rather, to have worked out a reasonably realistic solution to problems. The gang boy in many respects is a pragmatist, not "driven" to accept personal relationships which are less than satisfactory, but accepting them, nonetheless, with the expectation that while they may fail him, he will share in-process rewards which offer a considerable measure of gratification.

Similarly, with few exceptions, gang boys do not appear to be "driven" to the excesses involved in their delinquencies, e.g., aggression, alcohol, and sex. These, too, may be seen in part as situationally determined, arising in the course of interaction on the street. Once experienced, inherent gratifications may be pushed to extremes in part because other types of gratifications are so elusive and undependable. Only in our retreatist group did the boys seem "driven" to excess, in the sense that they were obsessed with the search for "kicks," through drugs in great variety and through personal experiences which carried a strong element of self-destruction. . . . For the most part, however, the behavior of these boys appeared less determined by personal idiosyncrasies than by the demands of status and role within the context of the immediate situation. Their social abilities, or the lack of them, determine in important ways the nature of the problems to which they respond and the coping mechanisms at their disposal.

The Roots of Social Disability

The importance to personality development of relations with other persons is a much honored theme in the behavior sciences. From the perspective of role theory, however, interpersonal relations are involved not only in development of personality; in important ways, they come to *constitute* personality. Thus, Brim has noted, "that what is learned in socialization, is interpersonal relationships. To express it slightly differently, much of personality is learned interpersonal relations. . . ." [13]

[13] Orville J. Brim, "Socialization Through the Life Cycle," revision of a paper prepared for a conference on this topic, sponsored by the Social Science Research Council, May, 1963 (mimeographed).

Observations from an experimental nursery school for lower class Negro children at the University of Chicago suggest that at the age of four and one-half these children are less able to maintain nonaggressive close physical bodily contact with their age mates than are children from middle class homes. The early development of these children appears to be a product of a combination of harsh socialization practices, frequent cautions about a threatening environment, and little cognitive development or verbal skill.[14]

Variations in the socialization practices of these A.D.C. mothers were related to the popularity of the children among their peers and to I.Q. changes registered over the thirteen-week nursery school experience. The finding of most general interest from this study is that these two independent variables were very differently related to the character of the mothers' relations with their children.[15] Specifically, use of *verbal* (vs. physical) means of discipline was positively related to I.Q. gain, but unrelated to sociometric popularity; while children with strict (vs. lax) mothers were popular but undifferentiated with respect to I.Q. gain. The irony in these relationships is that the rationale for strictness most often employed by these mothers is that they wish to help their children to do well in school. A factor described as maternal warmth and acceptance of dependency was negatively related to I.Q. gain, but positively associated with popularity. Aggressive children tended to be less well liked.

While it would be unwise to bridge so large a gap on the basis of such limited evidence, the similarity of observations concerning popularity among peers of lower class nursery school and gang youngsters is suggestive. Nurturant non-aggressive boys are rewarded with popularity. The fact that these characteristics are

---

[14] For preliminary documentation of this program, see Fred L. Strodtbeck, "The Reading Readiness Nursery: Short-Term Social Intervention Technique," Progress Report to the Social Security Administration (Project 124), the Social Psychology Laboratory, University of Chicago, August, 1963.

[15] *Ibid.* (1964).

negatively related to I.Q. gain in the nursery school situation suggests still another reason for gang boys' poor performance in school. Caught between the need for friendship and for long-range gains in the form of institutionalized learning, the very young child is likely to choose the former. The aggressive child, on the other hand, is not likely to meet with favor on the part of harried teachers in overcrowded schools, and so does not achieve the gain made possible in the experimental nursery school situation.

Thus, while it cannot be doubted that later experiences in adolescent and adult groups give specific content and order to the display of aggression, and condition its provocation, this early linking of child socialization and aggressive posture suggests that aggressive behavior is not a simple function of later experiences. The early development of aggression as a characteristic means of interpersonal interaction, with its sociometric consequences, should they be confirmed by more systematic research, would add to observations of social disability which flow more directly from gang participation, whether of stable corner boys, à la Whyte, or of our more delinquent and less stable gangs.

The gang presents a boy with a dilemma similar to the school: group norms place a high value on toughness and the ability to fight, yet aggressive behavior waged injudiciously makes one unpopular with peers. To succeed within such narrow boundary conditions requires great skill indeed, skill which most of these boys lack. The "status game" tends not to be played well by these boys, but it *is played*, with gusto, most often in the form of body-punching, signifying, and other forms of pseudo-aggressive behavior— pseudo-aggressive because few boys are hurt in such encounters, despite their intensity. The game takes such a form, we argue, because the boys' social disabilities, compounded by status uncertainties, preclude other games requiring higher order skills.

A further hypothesis to account for the limited social skills of gang boys concerns the narrow range of their social experience within as well as outside the family. The two areas of experience are mutually reinforcing in this respect. The family does not equip the child with role-playing facility adequate to the demands of such institutions as the school, and unsatisfactory experiences in school further narrow the range of role-playing opportunities which later facilitate job success—"getting along" with employers and fellow workers, and more than this, "getting along" in new and strange situations generally. The ability to move easily from one role to another and to adjust rapidly to new situations is a much cultivated art in modern urban society, particularly among upwardly mobile persons. This ability is inculcated in their children by middle class parents at an early age, and this may prove to be one of the major differentiating areas of early family experience between gang and non-gang boys within the lower class. Certainly the range of favorable role-playing opportunities in school has proven to be greater among non-gang than gang boys. 15.3 per cent and 20.5 per cent of Negro and white lower class, non-gang boys, respectively, were found to have achieved successful school adjustment, compared to 9.9 per cent of the Negro and 9.5 per cent of the white gang boys. The contrast is even more striking with respect to *un*successful school adjustment: NCL = 22.5 per cent, WCL = 24.0 per cent, NG = 46.8 per cent, WG = 42.7 per cent.[16] The negative opportunities through unfavorable contacts with police, courts, and correctional institutions, and association with delinquent peers also have been greater for the gang boys.

Middle class parents teach their children to be sensitive to behavioral requirements of a variety of situations—to role play in an appropriate manner even though the situation may be new to them. They are taught by example and by direction to be sensitive to the nuances of behavior expectations, to look for cues as to what is appropriate behavior and what is not. "Company" is different from "family," entertaining "the boss" is an important educational ex-

[16] The data are reported in Jonathan A. Freedman and Ramon J. Rivera, "Education, Social Class, and Patterns of Delinquency," paper read at the annual meetings of the American Sociological Association, 1962; and in James F. Short, Jr., "Gang Delinquency and Anomie," in *Deviant Behavior and Anomie,* Marshall B. Clinard, ed. (New York: The Free Press of Glencoe, Inc., 1964).

perience for it teaches socially approved means of relating to authority as well as something about situationally shifting requirements
of dress and manners.

We cannot document systematic differentiation of gang from
non-gang family experiences of this nature. In addition to the
balance of favorable and unfavorable experience in other institutional contexts which was referred to above, however, we know also
that more non-gang than gang boys of both races report having
contact with high-status adults and they less often choose local (and
therefore lower class) occupational role models than do the gang
boys.[17] These are further indications of the broader range of social
experiences shared by non-gang boys.

Intelligence. We may speak directly to the question of the
intelligence of gang and non-gang boys. Whether or not differential
experiences of this nature are responsible, it is the case that gang
boys had lower scores on measured intelligence than did non-gang
boys studied in the Chicago project. Intelligence was measured by
a "culture free" method, a standardized arithmetic test, and by
vocabulary, memory, and information tests designed especially so
as not to bias the tests against lower class and gang subjects.[18] A
general intelligence factor was extracted from intercorrelations of
other tests. On all six intelligence measures available from these

[17] "High-status adults" were defined as those having occupations above the
mean national socioeconomic (or occupational-prestige) level as determined by
the Duncan index. See Ramon Rivera and James F. Short, Jr., "Occupational
Goals: A Comparative Analysis," in *Juvenile Gangs in Context: Theory, Research, and Action,* Malcolm W. Klein and Barbara G. Myerhoff, eds. (Youth
Studies Center, University of Southern California, Conference Report, 1964).
[18] Standard tests from the Institute for Personality and Ability Testing were
employed. See R. B. Cattell and A. K. S. Cattell, *Handbook for the Culture
Free Test of Intelligence,* Vol. II (Champaign, Ill.: University of Illinois Press,
1958); and R. B. Cattell *et al., Handbook for the Objective-Analytic Personality
Batteries* (Champaign, Ill.: University of Illinois Press, 1955). Specially de-
signed tests were prepared by Desmond S. Cartwright and Kenneth I. Howard.
Findings are presented in greater detail in Kenneth I. Howard, Alan E.
Hendrickson, and Desmond S. Cartwright, "Psychological Assessment of Street
Corner Youth: Intelligence," unpublished manuscript, Youth Studies Program,
University of Chicago, 1962.

procedures, *gang boys scored lowest,* followed by lower class non-gang, and then by middle class boys. I.Q. estimates, based upon transformation of culture-free test scores for the six population groups are presented in Table 1.

These findings are impressive because of their consistency and the care with which the test program was developed and administered. They offer convincing evidence that the gang boys were disadvantaged with respect to intellectual ability of the sort which is rewarded by the institutions of conventional society. We need not enter into the nature-nurture controversy concerning measured intelligence. The point is that the school in particular, but other institutions as well, reward the "bright" child and that with respect to this variable, the gang boys are handicapped. Measured intelligence clearly cannot explain all of the variation in behavior among these boys, but it is an important component of the social

Table 1. I.Q. Estimates for Lower Class Gang and Non-Gang Boys, and for Middle Class Boys, by Race*

SOCIAL CLASS AND GANG STATUS	NEGRO	WHITE
Lower class gang	69.0	85.0
Lower class non-gang	74.0	91.5
Middle class	96.5	111.0

* Adapted from Kenneth I. Howard, Alan E. Hendrickson, and Desmond S. Cartwright, "Psychological Assessment of Street Corner Youth: Intelligence," unpublished manuscript, Youth Studies Program, University of Chicago, 1962.

disability of these boys.[19] That other factors influence selection for gang membership and behavior is equally clear from the very low I.Q. measure obtained for lower class, Negro non-gang boys.

Leaders, Girls, and Gangs. Whyte observed that among his street-corner boys, "The members do not feel that the gang is really

[19] Reiss and Rhodes also report that delinquents are less intelligent than non-delinquents when social class is held constant. See Albert J. Reiss, Jr., and Albert Lewis Rhodes, "Delinquency and Social Class Structure," *American Sociological Review,* XXVI (October, 1961), 720–32.

gathered until the leader appears." This does not appear to be the case among the gangs we have studied; yet, leaders perform in ways which are very important to the other boys, individually and collectively. Some leaders are so powerful that they are referred to by the boys as leaders even during prolonged absence from the gang, e.g., a stretch in the service or in jail. Even among gangs with such powerful leaders, it is the case that boys in any segment of a gang, when gathered together, are likely to identify themselves as members of a gang, and, more importantly, to be identified by others as members of the gang. The gang, *in toto,* does not often gather. Hence, the gang has in fact gathered when any number of members are gathered.

Field observation suggests that there is a tendency for smaller group segments to come together around those in leadership positions, but even in these cases it is likely that there will be a number of separate interactions, e.g., around a playground or restaurant hangout, in and outside an apartment, etc. One of the reasons for this is the presence among many gangs of girls on the occasion of most evening gatherings. This, in turn, relates to a difference in function of the adolescent gang as compared with the adult groups Whyte studied. . . . The adolescent gang is an arena for heterosexual activity, in many cases exploitative and in many cases for courtship purposes. Here is where the boys first "try their wings" in relations with girls. Whyte's young men apparently were less involved in these processes, though they were hardly lacking in heterosexual interest, as Whyte eloquently demonstrated in his description of "A Slum Sex Code." [20]

The point is that, despite the availability of willing females, these boys tend not to be sophisticated in relations with girls. They are largely ignorant of the biology of sex, and though they may "make out" with what many middle class boys might regard as enviable frequency, sex is a matter of much concern and some anxiety to them. The pressure of the gang compounds the matter,

[20] William F. Whyte, "A Slum Sex Code," *American Journal of Sociology,* XLIX (July, 1943), 24–31.

for it is less easy for gang than for non-gang boys to withdraw from sexual competition, by excelling in some other endeavor, for example.

The evidence on this point, while somewhat sketchy, is convincing. Baittle reports that among the gang boys he studied intensively, sexual matters were a source of much anxiety to all the boys regardless of the nature of their sexual experience.[21] Miller and his associates describe the physically aggressive interaction of boys and girls as being "aggressive in form only" in the sense that the *object* of such aggression is quite the opposite of aggression, namely to encourage friendly relations. The rough and tumble of "accidental" bumpings, wrestling, and body punching between boys and girls is a means of establishing liaisons for many youngsters who are embarrassed at their own ineptness in relations with the opposite sex.[22] A detached worker with the "female auxiliary" of a gang of Negro boys refers to this "mock fighting" as "one of the most frequently pursued activities between the boys and girls while on the corner. This play appears to be a form of sexual excitation, invitation, or, at times, prologue. I have rarely witnessed a girl flirt with a boy or be seductive in any other way." [23]

Some gangs contribute to the dilemma of the boys by sanctioning exploitative sexual behavior, while at the same time regarding with cynicism and disdain nurturant relations between boys and girls in the courtship process. Hence, on the corner, at least, the boy has little alternative but to behave aggressively toward girls. This doubtless is related in part to age. Among some older gangs,

---

[21] Reported to a Ford Foundation sponsored Faculty-Agency Seminar on Juvenile Delinquency at the University of Chicago, 1960. See also Brahm Baittle, "Psychiatric Aspects of the Development of a Street Corner Group: An Exploratory Study," *American Journal of Orthopsychiatry* (October, 1961), pp. 703–12.

[22] Walter B. Miller, Hildred S. Geertz, and Henry S. G. Cutter, "Aggression in a Boys' Street-Corner Group," *Psychiatry,* XXIV (November, 1961), 283–98.

[23] We are grateful to Robin Sheerer, detached worker, for these and other observations as a participant in seminar work at the University of Chicago during the summer of 1962.

the "lover" is given great prestige, and "technique" with girls becomes less physically aggressive and more verbal—one's "rap" with the girls is a criterion of status within the gang.

Among the gangs we studied [there was a] relatively high incidence of sexual intercourse, particularly among Negro boys. . . . Detached workers' reports suggest that "making out with the girls" was highly valued among all the gangs studied and received much attention in the endless conversations on the corner. Yet, a field observer from our research team reported the following incident among members of the King Rattlers, a gang noted for their sexual exploits:

About a half an hour later Roy was talking with Billy over on a couch which was placed under the bay windows in the front parlor. I could not hear what they were saying but after a few minutes they went over to the worker and Billy asked him a question, and the worker, after talking to them for a second, told them to "Call Larry (field observer) over to the side and tell him about it." Billy, the worker, George, and Roy then came over to me and Billy said after calling me into the dining room:

"Tell 'em something. Ain't it true that you can have intercourse with a woman during the time she's menstruating without her getting pregnant?"

Larry: "Yeah." (The worker is laughing and Roy is listening with great interest.)

Billy: "It might be a little messy—get a little blood on you, but she's wide open. One time Duke and I were screwing this girl and I couldn't get it in; I stood back and spit on it and it went in." (Billy gave this last part with animation.)

Though it was not specifically stated, the inference here clearly was that Roy did not understand the menstrual cycle.

Roy had fathered one illegitimate child and had a second child well on its way, yet he had little knowledge about the biology of reproduction.

Another research observer reported on a conversation with a young gang leader well known for his prowess as an auto thief.

Sometime later after we had returned to our seats, Sherman came back and sat with me. He said that he wanted to ask a question and he wanted an answer from "someone intelligent."

Sherman: "When you are trying to 'make' a girl, you don't tell her direct what you want but you hint around—What do you do—how do you say it?"

Answer: Well it depends on how well you know her and where you are—this is something you may want to avoid—but your approach is different depending upon the situation, your acquaintance with the girl, and the type of girl—."

The question was asked in a straight-forward manner and I tried to give him an answer in a similar fashion without the moral overtones, but pointing to the realistic problems encountered by youth as a result of such behavior.

Sherman showed considerable interest in the discussion. To show his understanding of the need for finesse in "making" a girl, he asked my opinion of some poetry he had composed while in jail. He recited a verse or two. The ideas and words used to express them revealed some thought on the matter.

Skill in "rapping to the girls" and in "making out" is highly valued among the gang boys and it often happens that boys with these skills are leaders. The relative ineptness of most boys in relations with girls stands in sharp contrast to the few who possess such skills.

Though systematic data are not available, detached workers and research observers agree that gang girls, especially those who hang with Negro gangs, also are considerably disadvantaged by social disabilities as well as objective opportunity. The girls are not, by and large, attractive by conventional standards either with respect to physical appearance or behavior. A research observer from the Youth Studies Program describes a group of thirteen- to sixteen-year-old Negro girls who hang with a gang of boys as "a loud, crude group of girls who not only curse and are sexually active, but who take no pride in the way they dress. They will come out on the streets or to the community center one day dressed fairly well . . . but on other days, they will turn out with their brother's pants on or jackets, and their hair will not be straightened nor combed and they will look one big mess." Like the boys, the girls are not articulate concerning their problems or possible ways of coping with them. Programs which seek to teach the girls how to dress, use cosmetics, and comport themselves find eager recruits, but sometimes with grotesque results which are comical despite their underlying pathos. Our observer reports a scene at a West Side community center:

. . . We walked up a long flight of drab stairs and entered a huge, almost barren, depressing looking room. At this time, there were about twenty girls prancing up and down the room, pretending to look and be like mannequins. But the sight of these girls was almost grotesque. They were dressed in a mannish manner; men's suit jackets, dirty sweaters and blouses, their hair was in disarray and their street-corner slouch was very much in evidence. Or I should say their toughness. Leading the prancing was a model-teacher who looked not like a model at all, although she was an attractive brown-skinned Negro woman who possessed some very unmodellish curves. The girls tried to imitate her, failed, and giggled. This seemed to me to be a very normal, girlish reaction.

Three weeks later, in an apartment hangout of the Vice Kings and their ladies, the observer reported:

. . . the model is still coming to give the girls modelling lessons. Both Alice and Lottie decided to show me how they had learned to walk and to sit. The boys started making jokes about their modelling lessons. But the girls proceeded to show me. They did the exact walking procedure that I saw the model teach them. They made no mistakes. However, their postures were as poor as ever and their heads still jutted forward, shoulders sloped and a gang girl "tough girl" lope. It was obvious to me that they did not realize that posture counts as well as learning this walking procedure.

Our observations in Chicago have been confirmed by Rice in New York.[24] His group, the Persian Queens, also slouched, looked at their sweater buttons as they talked, did their hair poorly, and

[24] Robert Rice, "The Persian Queens," *The New Yorker* (October 19, 1963), pp. 153 ff. See also Harrison E. Salisbury, *The Shook-Up Generation* (New York: Harper and Brothers, 1958). See especially Chapter 4.

suffered the concomitant decrease in self-esteem because of their ineptitude. On one occasion, when the Persian Queens tried to compose a three-line letter of gratitude to a beauty operator who had fixed their hair, they got out a "Dear Madame." The rest of the composition effort became hopelessly involved over their feeling that it was not proper to thank a benefactor directly, and, between them, they failed to find the appropriate circumlocution. Rice's impression was like that of our observer: it seemed as if nothing much ever happened at the meetings.

Thus, both boys and girls are caught in a cycle of limited social abilities and other skills, and experiences which further limit opportunities to acquire these skills or to exercise them if acquired. These disabilities, in turn, contribute to the status dilemmas of these youngsters and in this way contribute to involvement in delinquency. In the final section of this chapter a more direct relation between social disability, gang behavior, and some delinquent episodes is suggested.

Social Disability and Gang Behavior

Theoretically and empirically it appears plausible that gang boys are dependent upon each other for a large share of interpersonal gratification. Yet we have suggested that the gang is less than satisfactory as a source of nurturance and other gratifications. Other recent studies are consistent with this interpretation, though they do not bear specifically on the issue of gang membership as such. Thus Bandura and Walters report that their non-aggressive control boys were "warmer toward peers" than were the aggressive boys, and Rothstein finds that delinquent boys are less likely to regard loyalty and trustworthiness as attributes associated with high social status.[25] Even more revealing, perhaps, Bandura and

[25] See Albert Bandura and Richard H. Walters, *Adolescent Aggression* (New York: Ronald Press Co., 1959); and Edward Rothstein, "Attributes Related to High Social Status: A Comparison of the Perceptions of Delinquent and Non-Delinquent Boys," *Social Problems,* X (Summer, 1962), 75–83.

Walters also found aggressive boys more conflicted and anxious about manifesting dependency behavior than were the control boys.

Because adolescence is a period of emancipation from childhood dependency relations, dependency needs are difficult to express for most if not all adolescents. They are especially difficult for gang boys, however, for they are likely to be interpreted as an expression of personal weakness. The lower class focal concern of *toughness* pervades gang life, as evidenced by the highly aggressive nature of within-group interaction on the street and in many other social contexts such as at skating parties, quarter parties, and athletic contests.[26] The latter provide an instructive contrast between gang boys on the street, or even in a designated and equipped recreation area, and most non-gang boys. Athletic contests in a school setting or on a sandlot generate much camaraderie and feelings of loyalty to fellow teammates and to the student body, if such there be. The game is played hard by all, and, while there may be occasional charges and actual incidents of cheating or fighting, the game is likely to proceed according to the rules and to be carried to a conclusion according to these rules. Observation suggests that this is much less true of gang boys. Athletic contests are more frequently marred by conflict, among team members as well as between teams. Kobrin notes that adolescent gangs in an area very near one of our white gangs were "so completely committed . . . to the value of victory that the rules of the game seemed to have a tenuous hold on their loyalties. It was not unusual for them when stern adult supervision was absent to avoid impending defeat in a sports contest by precipitating a fight." [27] Among our gang boys the threat of violence during and after athletic contests was ever present, among participants and spectators alike. After one particularly

---

[26] See Walter B. Miller, "Lower Class Culture as a Generating Milieu of Gang Delinquency," *Journal of Social Issues,* XIV (1958), 5–19; and Miller, Geertz, and Cutter. *op. cit.*

[27] Solomon Kobrin, "Sociological Aspects of the Development of a Street Corner Group: An Exploratory Study," *American Journal of Orthopsychiatry,* XXXI (October, 1961), 688.

heated contest, twenty shots were fired by members of one gang at their rivals, as a result of an altercation over basketball officiating. No one was arrested for the incident, and fortunately, no one was hurt. We have noted, also, an exaggerated tendency by gang boys to *rationalize* failure by invoking by way of explanation factors beyond the boys' control, e.g., "We were so high we were almost blind when they beat us," or "They ran in a bunch of old guys—practically pros—or we'd 'a' beat 'em."

Importantly, for gang boys the *institutional* basis for bonds of loyalty among teammates and their supporters is lacking. The gang lacks the advantage of a major institutional function in which athletics and other activities are ancillary, albeit important. Even among high schools and colleges, athletic contests sometimes are marred by unruly crowd behavior, and followed by pitched battles between supporters of opposing teams, or riots of revenge or celebration. Institutional controls usually prevent such excesses, however, and supporters of both winning and losing teams customarily share rewards which make them unnecessary in any case. For the gang boy, athletic contests differ in this respect from gang fights. . . . In athletic contests there is likely to be no substitute for winning—no school fight song for expressing one's feelings, or sobering school hymn following the game, no homecoming parade, or dance afterward where old acquaintances are renewed and the pains of defeat can be salved by other bonds in common. A "moral victory" is not even in the vocabulary of most gang boys. The gang is neither cohesive nor dependable enough to provide solace in times of defeat. There is excitement galore, and identification with team members during athletic contests, but nowhere to go if the contest is not won.

Gang boys' problems in this regard, we suggest, are in part compensated for by involvement in delinquency. Reference to Thrasher again is appropriate. In discussing group control in the gang he observes that "A stable unity does not develop in the diffuse type of gang . . . until it becomes solidified through conflict." More recently Jansyn's study of a white gang with whom he worked as a detached worker is apposite. Jansyn found that group

activity, both delinquent and non-delinquent, and delinquent behavior by individual members occurred most frequently following
low points in a "solidarity" index which he constructed for the
group on the basis of independent observations. His interpretation
is that these activities represent responses to declines in group
solidarity. That they were successful in this respect is indicated by
the continued rise in solidarity which was observed following these
behaviors.[28]

It may prove to be the case that increased opportunity for
expression of dependency needs and their gratification is one of the
chief benefits derived from organized athletic activity such as that
which is sponsored by detached-worker programs. The YMCA
Program for Detached Workers in Chicago attempts to promote
team effort and loyalty by staging tournaments and leagues of
several types of athletic activity. A project newspaper publicizes the
results of such play and occasionally one or more of Chicago's
major dailies reports on them. Observation of basketball, pool, and
softball games indicates that for most groups a high degree of
enthusiasm is generated and the boys do generally receive interpersonal gratifications regardless of the outcome of the contests. It
should be noted, however, that some groups have proven very difficult to organize into stable teams. Detached workers with the
more delinquent gangs, especially, often have to forfeit games because team members fail to show up for games, or do so under the
influence of alcohol or in some cases of drugs. The retreatist boys
were never effectively organized into athletic teams, and much of
their conversation concerning their own involvement in athletics
related to how much better they played while "high." Finally, as
noted in the previous chapter, in order to compensate for status
threats involved in defeat in athletic contests, the YMCA finds it
necessary to provide numerous trophies so that all may share to

[28] See Leon Jansyn, "Solidarity and Delinquency in a Street Corner Group: A
Study of the Relationship between Changes in Specified Aspects of Group
Structure and Variations in the Frequency of Delinquent Activity," unpub-
lished Master's thesis, University of Chicago, 1960.

some degree in these glittering and tangible rewards of team play.

Field observation confirms, albeit unsystematically, that delinquency creates situations in which dependency needs among these boys may be met. This is apparent, for example, in the account of the boys' reactions to conflict behavior. It is even more clearly evident among the retreatists, who protect and care for members who are helpless under the influence of drugs or who have suffered debilitating injury. Boys who are in danger of wandering into traffic patterns will be restrained. When police arrive on the scene the other boys will attempt to shield from view a boy who is obviously under the influence. . . . Concern for the boys who were beaten by adults, and the righteous indignation of the gang over this assault molded that amorphous group, including the criminal clique, into a unit bent on retaliation. The fact that the worker was able to prevent the boys from carrying out their planned assault of the responsible adults suggests that the chief (latent) purpose of their wrath may have been interpersonal gratifications experienced by the boys in the course of the incident. A new bond of loyalty existed among the boys as never before. The fact that it was short-lived underlines the unstable basis of such gratifications among these boys and the necessity for contriving repeated instances in which dependency needs may be satisfied.

The tentative nature of the social disability argument should be clear. Should the hypothesis prove correct, it will provide an important and previously missing linkage between broad categories of individual pathology and group process in the causation of behavior. Family data from our project to this point unfortunately are inadequate to elucidate hypothesized differences between gang and non-gang boys in social disabilities such as those on which we have focused. Later research hopefully will contribute such information.

Suggestions for Further Reading

RICHARD A. CLOWARD and LLOYD E. OHLIN, *Delinquency and Opportunity* (New York: Free Press, 1960). Cloward and Ohlin argue that

American culture makes the seeking of success goals morally mandatory, but differentially distributes the morally acceptable means to these success goals.

ALBERT K. COHEN, *Delinquent Boys* (New York: Free Press, 1955). A study that views working-class boys as being driven to develop a delinquent subculture by the need to recoup the self-esteem destroyed by middle-class-dominated institutions.

ROBERT K. MERTON, *Social Theory and Social Structure* (rev. ed. New York: Free Press, 1957), especially Chaps. 4 and 5. The original version of the formulation adapted by Cloward and Ohlin in their work *Delinquency and Opportunity.*

WALTER B. MILLER, "Lower Class Culture as a Generating Milieu of Gang Delinquency," *Journal of Social Issues,* XIV (Summer, 1958), pp. 5–19. Suggests that there is emerging a relatively homogeneous and stabilized native-American lower-class culture, the focal concerns of which are trouble, toughness, smartness, excitement, fate, and autonomy.

℘The Urban Villagers *

HERBERT J. GANS

In 1956 the Boston Housing Authority received local and federal approval of a plan to redevelop the "West End" of Boston. In 1957 the project was transferred from the Housing Authority to a newly created Redevelopment Authority. During the last week of April, 1958, the city took official title to the area's land under the power of eminent domain. By November of 1958, almost half of the 2700 households had departed. And by the summer of 1960, the vast majority of the area's 7000 residents had departed.

A myriad of reasons were involved in the city's decision to redevelop the West End. One of the reasons frequently cited was that most Bostonians were convinced the area was a slum, and that for the good of its residents it should be torn down. Although the West End was a "slum" from the standpoint of middle-class values, it was, at the same time, the home of 7000 people with a distinct sub-culture of their own. Herbert Gans, a sociologist and urban planner, was interested in learning more about an area characterized as a slum, and about the way of life of a low-income population. In 1957, under a grant from the National Institute of Mental Health, United States Public Health Service, Gans embarked upon a study of the West End. His study, resulting in The Urban Vil-

* Reprinted with permission of The Free Press from *The Urban Villagers* by Herbert J. Gans. Copyright © 1962 by The Free Press of Glencoe, a Division of The Macmillan Company.

lagers, *was one element of a larger research project on "Relocation and Mental Health: Adaptation under Stress," conducted by the Center for Community Studies in Boston.*

As with Dalton's Men Who Manage, *the method of Gans's study is mainly that of participant-observation. Gans and his wife moved to the West End in October, 1957 and lived there until May, 1958. Gans employed six major approaches in his field work: (1) as a resident, he used as many of the West End's facilities as possible (for example, stores and services); (2) he attended formal meetings and observed informal social gatherings; (3) he and his wife visited informally with friends and neighbors in the area; (4) he conducted formal and informal interviews with religious and civic leaders, as well as with other community functionaries; (5) he used informants—individuals who trusted Gans and freely gave information about the West End; and finally, (6) he relied on his own general observations of life in the community and the community's relations with the world outside the West End. Altogether, he talked with between 100 and 150 residents of Boston's West End and had intensive contact with about twenty.*

At the time of Gans's study, the West End was populated by a great variety of ethnic groups, mainly Italians, Jews, Poles, and Irish. But the Italians formed the largest group—about 42 per cent of the whole—and they and their culture dominated life in the "urban village." Gans distinguishes such a community from what he calls an "urban jungle." The latter he defines as an area "populated largely by single men, pathological families, people in hiding from themselves or society, and individuals who provide the more disreputable of illegal-but-demanded services to the rest of the community." An urban village, on the other hand, he describes as an area "in which European immigrants—and more recently Negro and Puerto Rican ones—try to adapt their non-urban institutions and cultures to the urban milieu." In his view, an urban village like the West End is not really a slum.

Gans's analysis of the West End's social structure—family, peer groups, community, and relationship of the community to the out-

side world—yields conclusions contrary to preconceived middle-class ideas of the needs of an urban village. He defines the difference between what urban planners want and what this kind of neighborhood really needs. The portion of the study presented here describes the West Enders' way of life within their community and the nature of their experience of the world outside. Gans discusses the individual's participation in the community: for example, his relationship to the church, his affiliation with formal organizations, and his association with commercial establishments. Gans shows how the West Ender's relationship to the "outside world" is reflected in his view of his work, his educational background and his opinions of education for his children, and his approach to health and medical care.

Although Gans's study is based on participant-observation and lacks quantitative data, his observations and analysis of life in Boston's West End provide a great number of interesting hypotheses about working-class life in an American city midway in the twentieth century. He leaves to future investigators the testing of these hypotheses against the results of more systematic social science research.

The Community

The Nature of Community

Sociologists generally use the term "community" in a combined social and spatial sense, referring to an aggregate of people who occupy a common and bounded territory within which they establish and participate in common institutions. I shall employ the term in a purely social sense, however, to describe the set of institutions and organizations used by the West Enders to perform functions that cannot be taken care of within the peer group society. While these institutions are located in the neighborhood, this only puts them within reach of their users. Their functions otherwise have little to do with the area or neighborhood. For this reason the role of the institutions in the lives of the West Enders can be described almost without reference to the spatial community or neighborhood.[1]

In fact, the West End as a neighborhood was not important to West Enders until the advent of redevelopment. Early in my study, for example, when asking people why they liked the West End, I expected emotional statements about their attachment to the area. I was always surprised when they talked merely about its convenience to work and to downtown shopping. Then, after I had lived in the area a few weeks, one of my neighbors remarked that I knew a lot more about the West End than they did. This led me to realize that there was relatively little interest in the West End as a physical or social unit. West Enders were concerned with some of the people who lived in the area, but not with the entire population. Their interest in the physical features of the area was limited generally to the street on which they lived, and the stores which they frequented. This fact was illustrated by the fact that during past election campaigns, politicians made a somewhat different speech on each street, filled with promises of what they would do for the street if elected.

Indeed, only when the outside world discovered the West End and made plans to tear it down did its inhabitants begin to talk about the West End as a neighborhood, although, of course, they never used this term. And yet some felt sure until the end that while the West End as a whole was coming down, *their* street would not be taken, which helps to explain the lack of protest about clearance until it was too late. Only after it was too late did people begin to realize that they did have some feelings about the entire area.[2] Even then, however, they talked mostly about losing their

[1] I shall use the present tense to describe patterns that are associated with the way West Enders live wherever they reside, but I shall use the past tense to describe institutions that no longer exist.

[2] This has been reported about the entire West End population by Marc Fried, "Developments in the West End Research," Boston: Center for Community Studies Research Memorandum A3, October 1960, mimeographed, p. 7. For a more detailed analysis of how this population felt about the West End, see Marc Fried and Peggy Gleicher, "Some Sources of Residential Satisfaction in an Urban 'Slum,'" *Journal of the American Institute of Planners,* vol. 27 (1961), pp. 305–315.

apartment, and being torn from the people with whom they had been close so long. It is for these reasons that I use the term "community" in a more limited, nonspatial sense.

The specific institutions that constitute the community are the church; the parochial school; formal social, civic, and political organizations, some of them church-related; and some commercial establishments. These institutions—predominantly Italian—exist outside the peer group society, but are linked with it if and when they can be used to meet group and individual needs. The peer group society so dominates West End life, however, that the community is relatively unimportant. Excepting the church, the success of the remaining institutions therefore depends on the extent to which they are allied and subservient to peer group needs.

The community must be distinguished from still another set of functions and institutions which may be of more importance to the West Ender, but which he views either as necessary evils required by the larger, non-Italian society, or as services offered him by that society which he uses selectively and with little enthusiasm. These include work, education, health services, welfare agencies, government, and the mass media of communications. Because these institutions are, in differing degrees, imposed upon the members of the peer group society, I have described them as the outside world.

Patterns of Community Participation and Leadership

In the middle class, people are viewed as participating in community activities. That is, they enter organizations becuase they share the values and aims fostered by them; or because they find organizational activities—such as the acquisition of prestige, leadership experience, or social and business contacts—useful for their own purposes. Since for the West Ender, parallel functions can be satisfied within the peer group, participation in the community is ancillary. Sometimes, however, a single peer group does become active in an organization to help out a friend who has become an officer. But most of the more active individuals are either socially marginal or mobile.

West Enders usually will belong only to those organizations which offer opportunities for peer group activity that are not available elsewhere. For example, the Holy Name Society of the parish church gave the men an opportunity to take communion as a group, and to bowl together. When one of the members decided to run for office—undoubtedly at the urgings of his friends—and was elected, he brought in family members and friends to help run the organization. Peer group ties obligated people to help the officer; and the group, in effect, ran the organization. Politicians followed somewhat the same procedure. In the West End, they called on relatives and close friends to form a campaign staff, who, if their man was elected, became an informal kitchen cabinet that advised him. Since a peer group's competence to counsel on citywide affairs was limited, the politician used the group to unburden himself, and to test the advice he got from experts.

Most of the remaining participation was handled by the socially marginal and a few community-minded West Enders who are middle-class mobiles. For example, Italian participation in the Save the West End Committee—the group organized to protest the area redevelopment—was limited to a handful of intellectuals and artists. Although they were active within their own peer groups, their career and creative interests separated them from these groups psychologically, and also caused them to be treated with some suspicion. As a result, they developed a strong symbolic identification with the West End, which provided a feeling of belongingness, and, at the same time, allowed them to express feelings of protest about the redevelopment which could not be expressed as easily by their neighbors. Partially because of their skills and their marginality, they were able to develop a holistic concept of the West End as a neighborhood.

Community participation also provided an entree into the peer group society. For example, one of the most active participants turned out to be a man of Baltic descent whose activity helped him become part of the Italian group. Most people were unaware that he was not of Italian origin, and those who did know believed him to be French. His entry into the peer group society was aided by the fact that he had no brothers or sisters in the West End, and that he had married an Italian girl. His skill in carrying out activities in which other West Enders had no interest or ability helped him in becoming part of a male peer group. Another active West Ender used participation to remain in the peer group. He explained that his activity was motivated by his desire to be a model of respectability for his children. Since he was also an inveterate gambler, I suspect he used his organizational activity to counteract this failing, and to maintain his standing in the routine-seeking peer group to which he belonged.

Most of the other active people—and they were few—were mobile, some with white-collar jobs, and all of whom were seriously thinking about sending their children to college. Several had been asked to participate in the community by the church, or by settlement houses which typically attracted such people.

As already noted, many West End women belonged to informal and nameless clubs that were actually peer groups. Adolescents and young adult peer groups were organized as clubs for a variety of reasons. Adolescents formed them so as to be admitted into the settlement houses for "club night." Young unmarried men, scattered geographically and few in number, needed clubs in order to come together. Within the clubs, however, activities differed little from informal peer group pursuits. Thus, such groups were not really part of the community.

The remaining West Enders, that is, the large majority, did not participate in the community at all. The reasons for non-participation are to be found in the peer group society. . . . West Enders are not adept at cooperative group activity. The peer group must, above all, give life to the individual, and cooperative action directed toward a common end detracts too much from this central purpose. Moreover, West Enders are reluctant to place themselves in a leader-follower, officer-member relationship, which would detract from the individuating function of the group and would also require members to assume a subordinate, if not dependent, role toward the leader. Consequently, only a highly charismatic leader seems to be able to attract followers and retain their loyalty for any length of time.

Leadership itself is sought, however, because it provides considerable opportunity for individual expression. In fact, one of the reasons for the inability of the Save the West End Committee to function was the desire of most of the participants to be leaders and their unwillingness to carry out the routine tasks required. The familiar complaint of community organizations everywhere— "too many chiefs and no Indians"—is perhaps nowhere more true than among people like the West Enders.

Now, leadership requires some detachment from the group. But any such act of detachment from the group immediately lays the leader open to suspicion that he is out for personal gain. This suspicion dogs every political leader, particularly since his activities take him into the outside world where he is free from peer group control. Consequently, he is expected to participate in the exploitative relationships thought to be dominant there. Milder forms of this suspicion also greet the leader of local organizations. In fact, the only people who seem to escape it are religious figures. Even then, this is true only as long as they are concerned with purely religious activities. The moment a priest involves himself in worldly affairs, such as city politics or even church building plans, the halo is removed, worldly motives are imputed, and suspicion reigns. Thus, even in the absence of any real evidence, West Enders were sure that the leadership of the Boston archdiocese had a set of venal motives for the destruction of the West End.

The suspicion of leadership can frustrate community participation only because the majority of the people see no need for such participation. As West Enders see it, problems are solved either by the individual, the peer group, or by going to the politician to ask for a favor. Should these methods fail, they resign themselves to the problem's insolubility, and attribute the lack of action to the immorality of those in control. For example, West Enders were quite upset about poor municipal services and the disrepair of local streets, but aside from complaints to the politicians, no further action was taken. During the late 1930's and early 1940's the West

End did have a Citizen's Planning Board that took such complaints to City Hall and that was fairly successful in having them corrected. This Board, however, had no citizen members, and was run by three Jewish settlement house workers, only one of whom lived in the West End.

Because of the absence of citizen participation, leaders do not even think in terms of citizen activities. Nor are organization programs designed to involve them as participants. For example, the Save the West End Committee, after endless meetings to discuss ways of meeting the redevelopment threat, acted mainly by publishing leaflets which documented the immorality of the city. These offered no opportunity for citizen action, and the anger that they expressed was ony repeated—and dissipated—in peer group discussions. One West Ender who shared fully the beliefs of the Committee argued that it should not "get people all stirred up, because they do not unstir easily." He felt that this would only incite useless riot, and did not even consider the possibility of group action. In fact, among the West Enders of Italian background who participated in the Committee, violence against the mayor, or burning him in effigy was the mode of action most often and most enthusiastically proposed. The only group action scheme to get beyond the talking stage was a mothers' march on City Hall, planned in the belief that even the immoral men who had decreed the destruction of the West End could not remain deaf to the plaints of mothers, especially old ones. But although such a march was actually scheduled, only its planners showed up, and it had to be cancelled.

The behavior of West End leaders appears irrational—and threatening—to outsiders. Thus, settlement house people viewed the protests against redevelopment as rabble-rousing, and local politicians as demagogues. The leaders—especially the politicians—are caught in a difficult dilemma. Even when they do not share the West Enders' personalized view of events—and quite often they do—they know that West Enders will become interested only when their anger is aroused. Moreover, West Enders expect their leaders to arouse them, and to express for them their own anger at the outside world. Should a politician fail to do so, he is suspected of having sold out. Thus, he must often function in ways that the outside world interprets as rabble-rousing, even though his inflammatory appeals are not likely to produce much citizen action.

Leaders of all kinds always labor under some suspicion. They are expected to produce results, and, if they do not, someone is sure to suggest that they have been paid off. If they do succeed, they may be suspected of having profited handsomely in the process. Even if a leader does remain above suspicion, he receives little reward for his efforts, for West Enders are fundamentally uninvolved in community activities.

The Church

The most important formal institution in the West End was St. Joseph's Roman Catholic Church, which provided West Enders with a facility for religious worship and for the parochial education of their children. Its Holy Name and Catholic Women's Societies accounted for most of what little "rank-and-file" community participation did occur.[3]

Even so, West Enders were not closely identified with the church. There are a number of reasons for this. Southern Italians, and especially Sicilians, have been traditionally anticlerical because the church, in the past, had sided with the large landowners against the peasants and farm laborers. And although events in the Sicilian past are of little interest to the American-born West Ender, they have created a tradition of nonidentification which the American church has had to overcome. This, it has failed to do, at least in the West End.

Yet, West Enders are a religious people, and accept most of the moral norms and sacred symbols of the Catholic religion. They believe that the church ought to be the source and the defender of these norms, and expect it to practice what it preaches. At the same time, they observe that it is in reality a human institution

---

[3] I use the past tense here because although the present church has survived the redevelopment, most of the parishioners were West Enders, and have been dispersed.

that often fails to practice what it preaches. Thus, they identify with the religion, but not with the church, except when it functions as a moral agency. For example, most West Enders attend Sunday Mass because it is a religious duty—and absence a sin—rather than because of any identification with the local parish.[4] Men see the conflict between religion and church more sharply than women; and the action-seeking group, more than the routine-seeking one. It is reflected in lower male and action-seekers' church attendance. Men also are more impatient than women with religious ritual. A small Italian-Protestant church on the edge of the West End was scorned because its members took too great an interest in religion. One West Ender described them as "holy jumpers," not because they acted out their religious feelings physically, but because of the emotional intensity of Protestant congregational participation.

The male attitude toward the church is based in large part on lack of respect for the priesthood. For while priests are expected to be morally superhuman, they also are suspect for being not quite human enough, because they have chosen a way of life that requires celibacy. They are criticized for playing parish, diocesan, or city politics, for having favorites among parish members and choosing them so often among the more well-to-do, and for personal "vices" such as drinking. Thus, they are scorned for acting like normal men, even while they cannot perform the one act that would prove their masculinity. The priesthood is felt to be a suitable role for those uninterested in sex and unwilling to marry. This was underscored by a rumor that one of the few priests who had gained the affection of the West Enders some years back was said to be keeping a mistress. This rumor was told me with relish and pretended disapproval that reflected respect for the priest's manliness. Conversely, West End men have considerable regard for the nuns who teach in the parochial school, because the nun's virginity and her total dedication to whatever duty she is assigned

---

[4] Attending Mass also provides an opportunity to dress up, to see people and be seen, to promenade after church, and to socialize with friends and neighbors.

by the male leadership of the diocese implement to perfection the male idea of the good woman.

In his moral role, the priest is respected. He functions as judge and jury on all religious matters and on moral transgressions. The police in the West End, for example, took juvenile delinquents not to the station house but to the priest in order to mete out punishment for initial offenses; only when a boy became a habitual delinquent was he booked and judged by secular law. When a priest did cross over what West Enders defined as the line between sacred and secular concerns, however, legitimate authority ended, and he was either openly chastised by the parishioners or his transgression was reported to the pastor. Similarly, the Archbishop was severely criticized for taking a stand on the clearance of the West End—he was for it—and for permitting the destruction of the area's Polish church.[5]

Part of the lack of identification with the local church must be ascribed to an ethnic conflict. The parish had been founded at the time when the West End had been predominantly Irish. And, although the Irish had long ago moved out and the congregation was now overwhelmingly Italian, the pastor, many of his priests, and most of the lay leaders still were Irish. West Enders referred to the parish church as "the American church." Even so, they were not visibly bothered by the dominance of the Irish, if only because the church did not really engage them strongly. Perhaps they were also resigned to the inevitable, for the church has always been under Irish control in Boston. As the Catholic church does permit its adherents to attend mass outside the parish, some West Enders went to the Polish church because its schedule of masses suited them better. They also could have gone to one of the Italian churches in the North End, but only some of the old people did so, mainly for language reasons.

[5] West Enders were upset because the Polish church building was only fourteen years old, while the parish church, which was spared from destruction, was over a hundred years old, and considered by its congregants to be an ugly and drafty old barn. Built in 1844 as a Congregational church, it was preserved for its architectural value.

The West Enders' detachment from the church may also be a result of the differences between the Irish and the Italian concept of the Catholic religion. Italian Catholicism emphasizes the worship of the Virgin Mary; the source of authority is matriarchal. Indeed, West Enders displayed pictures and statues of the Madonna and Child in almost every room of their apartments. Irish Catholicism stresses, among other things, the Trinity, which is male, and its source of authority is patriarchal. But as Italians are notably resistant to patriarchal authority, those who did give any thought to the matter had little sympathy for the stern and less permissive Irish Catholicism being taught to their children at church and in the parochial school.

A factor distinctive to the West End was the pastor's policy that the church should minimize church-related social and neighborhood activities. The pastor himself had little contact with his parishioners, leaving this function to the other priests. The ones who were assigned to the West End parish during the time of my study had little interest in, and sympathy for, the neighborhood. In fact, the two members of the church staff whom I interviewed described the area as a slum in which it was not safe to walk at night and viewed its residents as mostly transient and socially undesirable people. They looked forward to the redevelopment of the West End, and hoped for a more middle-class group of parishioners.[6] Their attitudes resembled those of the church's Irish lay leaders. Most of these, living on the Back of Beacon Hill, felt that the West End had deteriorated significantly when it had become predominantly Italian.

Although the pastor did permit the Holy Name Society and the Catholic Women's group to function, these and the St. Vincent de Paul—a group of laymen who administered charity to a small

---

[6] Some time ago, the church carried on its staff a priest who was deeply involved in the community, and who ran athletic programs for the adolescents. He was evidently much liked in the community, and the fact that he was Irish did not detract from his influence. The central character in Joseph Caruso's novel, *The Priest,* New York: Popular Library, 1958, bears some resemblance to this man.

number of parishioners—were the only groups attached to the church. By contrast, the Polish church, which served a smaller congregation, had ten such satellite organizations.

The Catholic Women's Society, dominated by Irish parishioners until the area was torn down, functioned as the main social circle for the Irish women of the church, and enrolled few Italian parishioners. The Holy Name Society leadership, however, had been taken over by Italians during the 1950's. The Society's program was a fairly representative one: the group took communion together once a month, and held meetings afterwards at which films or speakers on male topics were presented. There was also a weekly bowling league. In 1958, 30 per cent of the male parishioners were said to belong to the Society, although most of them were inactive.

The parochial school was run in conjunction with the church. Having once had sixteen grades, it had since been cut to eight grades, and, in its last few years of existence, only first graders were accepted as new students. Thus, it was difficult to estimate how many West Enders sent their children to the parochial school. There was general agreement that the parochial school was better than the public ones, mainly because it expelled students with discipline problems, who then wound up in the public schools. I believe that most West Enders who could afford the tuition fee sent their children to the parochial school.

This choice was based neither on identification with the church, nor on a belief in the school's Catholic curriculum, but on the ability of the nuns to obtain and maintain discipline. Indeed, West Enders often suggested that the main purpose of school was to train the children in self-control, obedience to female and religious authority, and submission to discipline generally. As one mother explained, "Education teaches [my son] to keep away from bad boys." Parents respected the nuns for their dedication and sternness, and hoped that their methods would help keep the children out of trouble as they became adolescents. The students were exposed to a classical academic curriculum, but little rubbed off on them beyond the fundamentals. Dutifully learned by rote methods, it was all forgotten when the examinations were over. Conversely, some West Enders who were dedicated to Italian Catholicism complained that the school was indoctrinating their children in Irish Catholicism, but whether this indoctrination takes hold cannot be judged fully until the children reach adulthood. Observations of Italian families in the suburbs, however, would suggest that third-generation adults have continued to keep themselves aloof from church activities other than attendance at mass.[7]

Formal Organizations and Associations

By 1958, the only West End organizations with members of Italian origin were the American Legion post and the Augusta Society. The Legion post, located just outside the West End, had been founded when the community was predominantly Irish, but was now largely composed of Italians.[8] It was, however, almost defunct, and was run by a West End barber who assailed his customers with complaints about the lack of cooperation he was getting to his appeals for help in reviving the post. In 1958, the post came alive only before St. Patrick's Day and Christmas, when about two hundred women attended the "penny sales"—lotteries in which nearly a hundred prizes were raffled off at the cost of one cent a ticket.[9] These sales, like the church bazaars and card parties, provided a religiously legitimated opportunity for the gambling that the men—and some women—pursue day in and day out by betting on the numbers and on sporting events.

The Augusta Society, open only to Sicilians who have come

[7] This impression is based on comments by Michael Parenti, of the State University of New York at Oyster Bay, and on my own observations in suburban communities. This problem is also discussed by Nathan Glazer, *Peoples of New York,* forthcoming.

[8] Another post, located within the West End, was frequented by Polish legionnaires.

[9] Just before the 1958 St. Patrick's Day penny sale, the Legion commander decided that it should be associated with Easter rather than with the Irish holiday. Since the post had been predominantly Italian for many years, he confessed sheepishly that the change should have taken place at least ten years earlier.

from the village of Augusta in eastern Sicily, attracted mostly immigrants. I was told that less than half of its members still lived in
the West End, and that most of these came from a three-block area
of the West End that had not been included in the slum clearance
project.[10]

Another organization based on residential origin is the Old-
Time West Enders club, which meets in a downtown hotel once a
year. It was started about 1950 by some Irish and Jewish men who
had grown up in the West End between 1900 and 1915. Limited to
men who were born and raised in the area, the organization attracts
about three hundred men to its annual gatherings. The main event
of the annual meeting is a speech by a prominent person who grew
up in the West End. The meeting which I attended was addressed
by a railroad president, who attributed his occupational mobility
and worldly success to lessons learned "at the university of hard
knocks" in the West End of his childhood. He also contrasted the
heavy responsibility of his current social status with the simpler,
if more poverty-stricken, way of life of a slum child. I was told that
other speakers stressed similar themes, and that there was much
nostalgia about the good old days and the joy of life in the West
End. Most of the members are middle-class men who now live in
the suburbs of Boston. Although the West Enders who I have been
describing . . .were eligible to belong to the group, only a few ever
came. The handful who did attend the meeting at which I was
present had little sympathy for the speaker's feeling about the West
End, and pointed out acidly that the group had not opposed the
redevelopment of the area.

Just after World War II, the West End also boasted a number
of young men's social clubs, which were formal organizations only
to the extent that they had names and constitutions. This enabled
them to hire meeting rooms, and to extract tribute from politicians
at election time in exchange for an endorsement. Although the
clubs took little or no part in the campaigning, I was told that if
the candidates had not contributed funds, club members would

[10] This area has since been scheduled for clearance as part of the Scollay Square
redevelopment project.

have entered the campaign by maligning them.[11] Members met nightly for card games, and held informal parties on weekends. The club rooms also provided an opportunity for peer group sociability, inexpensive entertainment, and privacy for dancing and drinking, as well as for after-hours sexual activities with whatever girls could be persuaded to stay after the dance was over. The clubs seemed to have divided on somewhat the same college-boy—corner-boy basis that Whyte had observed in the North End.[12] By 1958, only one such club still survived, consisting primarily of young men who had attended college or who held white-collar jobs. Most of its members no longer lived in the West End, but returned to the area to meet childhood friends, or because they could not find compatible associates in their new neighborhoods.

Commercial Establishments

The West End's taverns, stores, and restaurants were part of the community because, like most of the previously discussed organizations, they served the peer group society in a variety of special functions. Some provided meeting places for groups that had no other home, and others served as ganglia in the area's extensive communication network.

The West End was also dotted with lunch counters and "variety stores," the latter selling newspapers, magazines, candy, school supplies, a small stock of groceries, soft drinks, and sandwiches. These places too—as well as the tavern and barber shops—provided hangouts for men who were not visibly employed, and for others who stopped by after work. Since Italians drink less liquor than other working-class populations, the taverns tended to attract few

[11] The West End clubs seem to have been less important politically than those which Whyte described as operating in the North End. In the 1940's and 1950's, the candidates of Italian background came primarily from the North End, and evidently felt that the West End was less important to their political fortunes. For an analysis of the political club in the North End, see William F. Whyte, Jr., *Street Corner Society,* Chicago: University of Chicago Press, 1943, 2nd ed., 1955, Chaps. 2 and 5.

[12] Whyte, *op. cit.,* Part I.

of the West Enders. Several of the smaller ones, however, were taken over entirely by young men who spent their afternoons and evenings there, and who drank enough beer to pay the rent. They so dominated these taverns, in fact, that other West Enders rarely entered. In the tavern which I visited occasionally, the bartender was part of the peer group, and participated in the card games and conversational competition as an equal. Much of the time he did not even function as bartender; the regular customers came behind the bar to serve themselves, and put their own money in the cash register. Similarly, in one of the luncheonettes where I sometimes drank coffee, the regular customers did not give orders to the owner, for he knew exactly what they wanted. Women did not "hang out," of course, but they did combine shopping with socializing, mostly in the small groceries.

Teenagers also frequented some of the stores, but most of them congregated on corners near one of the variety stores or small groceries, where their presence was met with mixed feelings. For although they did buy ice cream, candy, and cigarettes from the stores, they also expressed their hostility toward the adult world to the adult customers. The owners occasionally would try half-heartedly to chase the teenagers away. But they had little success, for, in most cases, the same corners had been used for "hanging out" for two generations.

The owners and managers of the bars and luncheonettes were kept busy also in taking and passing along messages for their regular customers. The latter, who frequented the stores at regular and unchanging times during the day, often received phone calls there. Moreover, as many of them did not seem to have telephones at their own homes, they could best be reached at their regular hangout. In addition, the establishments served as centers for the exchange of news and gossip. Since the West End did not have its own newspaper, and since West Enders placed little trust in the city press, the commercial establishments thus played an important communication function in the area.

Some of the commercial establishments also served as hangouts and communication centers for *sub-rosa* activities. A number of the men who could be seen in the area during the day made their living as petty gamblers, or by working for more organized gambling endeavors. Some of the luncheonettes and variety stores had installed special pinball machines equipped for gambling, with payoffs increasing with the amount of money put into the machine. With the right combination of skill and luck, investments of several dollars in nickels could pay a 50 to 200 per cent return to the player. I use business concepts to describe the play, because the men who played these machines regularly approached them with the same amount of deliberation and care that a middle-class person would use in playing the stock market. Less dedicated gamblers generally stayed away from the machines.

Most of the extrabusiness activities that I have described took place in establishments owned or managed by people who lived in the West End, and who were socially and culturally like their customers. Indeed, they were able to compete against the more modern stores outside the West End only because they could attract regular customers whom they treated as peer group members rather than as customers.[13] Many of them probably earned little more from their establishments than the employed West Enders. Some of the luncheonettes were perhaps able to stay in business only because of income derived from the ancillary gambling activities. Maybe this is why they had been opened in the first place.

The Outside World: Work, Education, and Medical Care

The Structure of the Outside World

To the West Ender, the organizations and institutions that constitute the community are an accepted part of life, since their functions are frequently auxiliary to those of the peer group society.

Other organizations and institutions, however, which play an

[13] In addition, the food stores retained their customers by giving credit and by being near at hand to West Enders who were restricted in their movements, especially the elderly and the people without cars.

equally if not more necessary role in the life of the West Ender, are less freely accepted. Added together, these make up what I have called the *outside world*. Although the term is mine, it reflects what West Enders describe as "they" or "them." This is the world beyond the peer group society and the community: the world of employers, professionals, the middle class, city government, and—with some exceptions—the national society. Although the outside world is almost entirely non-Italian, it is not defined by its ethnic characteristics. Thus, even Italians who adopt its values are scorned by the West Enders. In short, then, it consists of those agencies and individuals who interfere with the life of the peer group society.

The agencies which I have grouped under this rubric differ widely, both in function and the way in which West Enders relate to them. At one extreme, for example, are the worlds of work and health care, which are so vital to the individual and the peer group society that they have little choice but to accept them. Then, there are the services that social agencies from outside the West End offer to West Enders, notably the settlement houses. These are treated with a mixture of curiosity and suspicion. But, since they are not necessary for peer group life, they are essentially ignored—at least by adults. In between is education, especially at the high school level, which most West Enders now accept as being necessary, although they are still ambivalent as to its usefulness. At the other extreme are the law, the police, and the government. Conceived as agencies that exist to exploit West Enders, they are thus viewed with considerable hostility. If possible, contact with them is minimized, and relegated to the politician. Off to one corner is the world of consumer goods and the mass media of entertainment, whose products are welcomed into every West End home, albeit with considerable selectivity. Even so, the mass media do constitute one of the major ties to the outside world.

These diverse agencies can be discussed together because they are external to the peer group society. Since they are manned by nonmembers, who are expected to treat West Enders in object-oriented ways, the rules of behavior that govern the peer group society are not applicable to them. The services of the outside world are to be used if they are desirable and to be ignored or fought if they seek to change or injure the individual or the peer group. . . . The West Ender always expects to be exploited in his contact with the outside world, and is ready to exploit it in return. If he is treated in a person-oriented fashion, he is pleasantly surprised and ready to do likewise. But he still remains on guard, and the burden of proof rests with the outside world.

Attitudes toward the outside world are not homogeneous. Action-seeking people, for example, are much more suspicious and hostile than the routine-seeking. Likewise, men are more hostile than women, mainly because they have frequent contact with the outside world, and more often need to defend themselves against it. Even so, everyone shares the basic gulf that exists between the peer group society and the outside world—a gulf that must be crossed by one or the other before the West Ender will become a part of the larger American society.

The World of Work

The parents of the West Enders were farm laborers in Italy, and were employed as unskilled factory or construction laborers in America. While the second generation's fortunes have improved considerably, most West Enders still are employed in unskilled and semiskilled blue-collar jobs. Although the bureaucratization and unionization of employment have vastly increased job security, the West Ender continues to think of employment as insecure and expects layoffs—temporary or permanent—to come at any time. There are good reasons for his suspicion. Since Boston has not experienced the large immigration of Negroes that has taken place elsewhere, Italians occupy a "lower" position in the Boston labor market—and in the city's division of labor—than they do in New York, Chicago, and other large cities.[14] Moreover, they work in

[14] See, for example, Irvin L. Child, *Italian or American? The Second Generation in Conflict,* New Haven: Yale University Press, 1943; and Nathan Glazer, *Peoples of New York,* forthcoming.

more marginal industries, where layoffs, the disappearance of jobs, and the closing down of firms are not unusual. West Enders also told me that discrimination against Italians still occurs occasionally.

These conditions help to define the West Ender's attitude toward work. Work is thought of as a necessary expenditure of time and energy for the purpose of making a living, and, if possible, for increasing the pleasure of life outside the job. Thus, West Enders work to make money, and they want to make money to spend on themselves, the family, and the peer group. Since most of them must work for other people, their jobs often take them outside the peer group society and the community. It is for this reason that I have classified work as part of the outside world.

For the West Ender, work means manual labor, and the expenditure of physical energy under frequently unpleasant working conditions. Nonmanual jobs are not considered to require work. Thus, white-collar people are described as not really working, but as being able "to sit on their can." Similarly, executive and supervisory work is seen as consisting of giving orders and talking, neither of which is considered work by voluble West Enders.

The ideal job is thought of as one that pays the most money for the least physical discomfort, avoids strenuous or "dirty" physical labor, demands no emotional involvement, such as "taking the job home with you," requires no submission to arbitrary authority, and provides compatible companions at work. Taxing and dirty jobs are associated with the parental generation. West Enders today feel that such jobs should go to Negroes, Puerto Ricans, and immigrants who have recently arrived from Italy. They do not, however, reject physical labor as such, especially if other working conditions are pleasant. Some of the young West Enders, for example, who work in the food markets of the North End spoke with satisfaction of the unregimented nature of their work, and of the ability to see friends and continue the peer group conversations during working hours.

Indeed, West Enders expect to work hard, and they derive satisfaction from doing a good job. Although they may talk freely about the pleasures of loafing, a few days' illness or a vacation spent at home quickly convinces them that life without work would be unbearable. Because most West Enders work in small firms, and because they do not find it easy to accept authority of any kind, one of the most important criteria for job satisfaction is having a good boss. The good boss treats his employees as close to equals as possible, works hard himself, and does not unduly exert his authority, especially in matters unrelated to work. As the West Ender's most intimate contact with the outside world is with the boss, his behavior is thus watched closely. Should he act unreasonably, he will quickly lose his employee's respect and good will. Further, should the West Ender feel that he is being exploited, he will exploit his employer in turn wherever and whenever he can —short of losing his job.

The expectation of exploitation comes most often from those working in large firms, and, when it does occur, considerable satisfaction is derived from fighting back. One West Ender, who had once worked as a sweeper in a company that cleaned office buildings, spent considerable time in "goofing off," and methodically violating the rules set by management, because the wages were low, and the union was in a strong position. He intimated that the pleasure of his revenge reimbursed him for the poor wages. During the war, he also had worked in a government-owned defense installation, and described the ways in which his colleagues stole time or materials from the government. Mainly because the federal government had done nothing to exploit him, he had not participated in this activity. He was highly critical, however, of the hasty cleanups that took place when visiting dignitaries came to the plant, and tried his best to minimize his share of what he considered to be fraudulent activity. A younger West Ender, who had recently been mustered out of the Army, took great pride in the wholesale evasion of work and rejection of authority he practiced against the Army to get even for being separated from his friends in the West End.

Even when work is well paid and satisfying, the West Ender will try to minimize any involvement in it beyond that required of him. Work is a means to an end, never an end in itself. At best, single-minded dedication to work is thought to be strange, and, at worst, likely to produce ulcers, heart trouble, and the possibility of an early death.

Thus while the West Ender has developed skills which he seeks to practice, and in which he takes some pride, notions of a career are still rare. Indeed, the difference between the West Ender and the middle-class person is perhaps nowhere greater than in this attitude toward the career. The idea that work can be a central purpose in life, and that it should be organized into the series of related jobs that make a career is virtually nonexistent among the second generation.

This is best illustrated with respect to professionalism. Middle-class professionals see themselves as striving to bring their own activity into line with an idealized conception of their calling and to refine their work method so as to be professionals in the best sense of the word. Although a few West Enders have moved into professional occupations—especially in law and accountancy—their work is devoted less to the achievement of professional perfection and recognition from fellow professionals than to the application of skills—and contacts—in behalf of the peer group society. Thus, lawyers become politicians and agents of the Italian community in the outside world. Consequently, their legal practice consists primarily of cases to help Italian clients get what is theirs from the outside world. They also use their legal skills and contacts for business dealings. But while these lawyers do want to maximize both income and status, their primary reference group is still the peer group society. As a result, they are person-oriented service agents, and have no desire to be object-oriented practitioners of "the law." It should be noted, of course, that as "the law" is largely in the hands of high-status individuals of Yankee Protestant origin, lawyers of Italian or other ethnic origin have little access to the more prestigeful types of legal practice, even should they want these.

Similar orientations can be found among other Italian professionals. The singer, for example, aims to achieve a personal style of delivery, rather than technical virtuosity. The artist and writer want to portray their society to the outside world, and to come to terms with both of them personally. Thus, most of the novels written about Italian-American life are at least partly autobiographical. The photographer works for "effects" that will please the client. In short, all of them give lower priority to the formal esthetic and technical concepts of their craft.

The attitudes that stand out most clearly among the first Italians to enter the professions are present among other workers as well. For example, as most of the semiprofessional people came to their work without the educational background usually associated with it, they have a less secure foothold in their occupation than middle-class colleagues. As a result, they are less embued with the beliefs and goals of their craft. The only West Enders who could be said to think in terms of a career were lawyer-politicians. Yet, even they were quite ambivalent about pursuing politics as a career and were not sure that they wanted to advance on the rungs of the political ladder. It should be noted, however, that the insecurity of political life does not encourage career aspirations.

People who work in low-skill white collar jobs, or in blue-collar ones, cannot really begin to think in career terms. Such thinking assumes the existence of broad opportunities and a moderate assurance of job security. I have already noted that West Enders believe, with some justification, that jobs are scarce and that job security is nonexistent. With luck an individual may get one job that he can define as good, but this is not likely to happen twice in a row. Even workers with specific skills do not expect that they will always be able to find jobs in which they can practice them.

The lack of identification with work is hardly surprising. Second-generation Italians, it must be remembered, were raised by parents whose occupational skills and choices were few, and for whom work usually mean backbreaking labor at subsistence wages. But although the immigrants encouraged their children to escape this kind of work—if they needed any encouragement—they had no reason or precedent to urge them toward any identification with work, or to expect any satisfactions from it. Unlike the Jews who came to America with something approaching middle-class occupational aspirations and who passed them on to their children, the Italians had only a tradition of farm labor with no hope for anything else. And given the conditions they encountered in America, it would have been foolhardy for the immigrants to encourage their children to seek emotional involvement in work. Instead, they prepared them to work hard, and to accept job loss and temporary unemployment as inevitable.

The second generation, in turn, encourages its children to equip themselves for better jobs, and urges them to get as much education as they can for this purpose. Although West Enders are interested in job mobility for their children, they have not yet begun to encourage career thinking, for they have not had the job security that would enable them to do so. The children listen to the parental urgings about education, but they also observe the attitudes toward work that are expressed all around them day after day, and they share the group's lack of interest in thinking about the future. Parents are disappointed if their children announce that they will not continue their education beyond the legal minimum, and that they have no interest in better jobs than their parents', but this disappointment is not intense. After all, work is not a fundamental purpose in life, and if they have gotten along, so will their children.

West Enders are employees more from necessity than choice. Indeed, the peer group society, by developing people who compete with each other for emotional satisfaction within the group, tends to encourage what Miller and Swanson have called "entrepreneurial personalities." [15] Because of this, many West Enders are predisposed to self-employment—an attitude they share with many other ethnic and working-class groups.

[15] Daniel B. Miller and Guy E. Swanson, *The Changing American Parent,* New York: Wiley and Sons, 1958, Chap. 2.

The desire for self-employment is also closely related to the West Ender's conception of work. As already noted, work means manual labor, and self-employment may permit him to make more money without such labor. Also, the self-employed person does not have to take orders; he is independent and free from authority. Moreover, he may even be able to limit his contact with the outside world, and, if he cannot do so, he has considerable opportunity to exploit it, and to get even for the actual or imagined exploitation to which the peer group society is exposed. One self-employed West Ender described with glee the satisfaction he derives from creating "short cuts" in his work that are not visible to his customers, but that give him the feeling that he is putting something over on them.

The hostility toward the outside world also allows the West Ender to condone illegal work activities. Consequently, little disapproval is expressed toward gamblers, and even racketeers, as long as their activities do not hurt the peer group society. Thus, West Enders usually had only words of praise for a well-known gambler —one of the wealthiest men in the West End—because he gave lavishly to local organizations and to charities. And while the bootleggers and racketeers who had lived in the area during the days of prohibition were not praised, even they were thought to have done no harm, because their illegal activities had been aimed at the outside world, and their violence had been restricted to their own associates and competitors. Since the parents of West Enders made their own wine for family use—in the bathrooms and cellars of their tenements—they also had little sympathy for the prohibition laws that forbade this activity.

The preference for self-employment, however, still stops far short of entrepreneurial ambition. West Enders have little capital, and not much interest in risk-taking. They say that when a Jew goes out of business, he will open another place and try again, but that an Italian, in the same circumstances, will go to work for someone else. Entrepreneurial activity, unless it is a group venture, invites failure or success, both of which are likely to separate the individual from the peer group. Also, whereas the immigrant generation saved its money to buy land or an apartment building, their children, who have embraced American standards of living, find it difficult to save. Moreover, as they are not imbued with peasant values, the ownership of land as an end in itself has less meaning to them. Apartment buildings can no longer be bought cheaply, and West Enders have no desire to become landlords or their own janitors, a kind of work that is considered to be undesirable.

Consequently, self-employment opportunities that require little capital and allow the owner to use family members are preferred, and the West Enders naturally gravitate toward service functions. Opening a garage is sometimes mentioned, as are services that involve display or the management of display of others—being a barber, for example, or a tailor, or owning a clothing store. Running a luncheonette or a restaurant is still liked, partly because the owner can have peer group company on the job. Contracting, on the other hand, once a popular avenue for self-employment among Italians, now requires too much capital; and grocery store ownership lost its attractiveness with the coming of the supermarkets.

Most of the talk about escaping employee status, however, is at the level of dreams rather than goals. Few West Enders are either able or willing to think about such a change in status. In effect, work is simply not that important. And as the small owner becomes more and more marginal, even the dreams about self-employment become more infrequent, and are not passed on to the next generation.

Work, of course, is entirely a male pursuit. Husbands do not want their wives to work after marriage, nor do the women themselves. They are expected to be ready to work if the husband is laid off, or if the family budget requires their help. I encountered no women who worked because they wanted to, however, or because they wished to obtain money for individual and family luxuries, or for that matter, because they wanted to compete with their husbands for economic mastery of the household. Even childless wives preferred to be housewives and aunts. For the women, then, work itself holds even fewer attractions than it does for the men.

Education

West End children can go either to the parochial or public elementary schools, but most of them must go to the public ones for their high-school education. Although their parents prefer parochial to public institutions, the distinction that is of most significance to them and that creates uncertainty about schooling is between person-oriented and object-oriented education. Person-oriented education teaches children rules of behavior appropriate to the adult peer group society, and stresses discipline. This is identified with the parochial school. Object-oriented education teaches them aspirations and skills for work, play, family life, and community participation.[16] Rightly or wrongly, this type of education is identified with the public school. It is also the source of West End ambivalence, and accounts for the placement of education in the outside world.

On the one hand, West Enders do recognize that education is needed to obtain employment, and urge the children to get as much schooling as is required for a secure skilled blue-collar or white-collar job. On the other hand, parents are suspicious that education will estrange the children from them, and from the peer group society as well. Consequently, they are somewhat fearful about the public education to which the children are exposed in high school.

These fears are best illustrated by the West Enders' conception of the public-school teacher. They see her as a woman who has little interest in teaching, and who is more concerned with making money, chasing men, or "boozing" after hours. As one West Ender pointed out, the nun who teaches in the parochial school is unpaid, and her work is motivated solely by religious dedication. Consequently, her life is limited to teaching and prayer, and she is likely

---

[16] In some ways, this is the traditional Southern Italian peasant distinction between "buon educato," being well-mannered or well brought-up, and "buono istruito," being well-instructed in book learning, which was considered of little importance. R. A. Schermerhorn, *These Our People,* Boston: D. C. Heath and Co., 1949, p. 242.

to be in bed by 9 P.M. The public-school teacher, however, is either working at an extra job, or drinking in a tavern during the evening hours when she should be resting or preparing herself for the next day's teaching. Therefore, she is not fit to teach self-control to the children, and is thought to be too tired even to keep order.

This fantastic conception stems partly from the public-school's reputation as a haven for incorrigibles who cannot accept parochial discipline.[17] It also reflects the considerable social distance between the West Ender and the school. Public-school officials claimed that parents took little interest in their children and even less in the school. Over the years, several attempts to develop Home and School associations in the West End failed because only a few parents showed up. As might be expected, the parents of children with scholastic or behavioral difficulties were least likely to come to school, whereas those whose children were doing well did take an interest.

Parental lack of interest in the school is a function of the segregation between adults and children in the adult-centered family, a process that begins just about the time that the child starts attending school, and that increases with age. The public school is keyed, of course, to the child-centered family in which parents do involve themselves in their children's lives; the parochial school accepts the adult-centered family, and does not expect or encourage parental participation, except when the child gets into trouble.

From the parents' perspective, then, education is useful only for behavior training and for obtaining a job. They see no need for subject matter that does not contribute directly to this aim. As one skilled worker told me: "What good is archeology in a mechanical arts high school? You want to learn it if you're a teacher, but not for other things. I am a working man." Some West Enders are not yet convinced that additional schooling will be useful even occupationally. For example, they point out that depressions and layoffs take no notice of education, and that whom you know rather than

[17] This is ironic, because I noted earlier that public-school principals found their students to be surprisingly quiet and well-behaved.

what you know is still the key to occupational success in many places. This attitude is voiced mainly by those who are satisfied with their own occupational achievements. Other West Enders, especially those who are not satisfied with their jobs, and those in white-collar positions, realize only too clearly that they would have done better had they been able to stay in school beyond the elementary grades or the first years of high school. Most West Enders of the present generation, however, had little choice in the matter, for they were expected to go to work as early as possible. It is these people who urge their children to finish high school.

By and large, full-blown skepticism as to the value of education now centers on college attendance, especially at a private liberal arts school, which West Enders consider to be playgrounds for the idle rich. They delight in telling stories of college-educated people who hold jobs no better than their own, or who are total failures. One story, for example, concerns a West End "character" with several university degrees who now makes a living by scavenging through area garbage. The implications of the story are clear: college education does not assure occupational success, and over-education may lead to mental illness. Yet the same people who tell such stories will also speak of their hopes that their boys will continue their education after high school so as to get a better job. At the same time, they sense that college attendance can estrange parents and children. Consequently, they question the desirability of a liberal arts or academic education, explaining that "college is only for the very brightest boy." Indeed, academic skill is viewed as a kind of virtuosity, much like musical ability and is thought to be desirable—and attainable—only for the rare youngster who is intellectually gifted. Lower-class West Enders, on the other hand, retain some of the traditional hostility toward the high school and consider it as keeping the child from going to work at the earliest opportunity.

Attitude differences also exist between mothers and fathers, and between their aspirations for boys and for girls. Generally, mothers are more favorably inclined toward the school, partly because of their concern that the child learn behavior control. Fathers, however, are less interested in behavior control, and are more fearful that boys will become "sissies or girl scouts" if they become too identified with the ways of the school. Moreover, since most of the teachers are women, fathers see education as a feminine undertaking that might endanger their boys' maleness.

Girls are thought to need less education than boys, since they will get married soon after leaving school. Responsibility for the girl's educational decision is therefore left up to the mother. If the girl does well in school, she has her mother's approval to continue as long as she wishes; and, if family finances permit it, her father's silent acquiescence. But the father is primarily interested in the boy's education. If a boy does not do well in school, and wants to drop out, he is likely to get support from his father, especially should the latter be satisfied with his own occupational fortunes. His mother may object, but will probably resign herself to the alliance of father and son. Whenever possible, West End parents will express their doubts and negative feelings about education only in adult company. As they have enough respect for the value of schooling as a means to occupational success, they try to speak only favorably of it to the children.

Despite these parental efforts, many of the children do not take to education. Even though family finances permit them to stay, they often drop out of school at the earliest opportunity. The general picture drawn by the school officials with whom I spoke was that the majority of children displayed little interest in learning, that many had learning difficulties, and that even more were waiting only to reach the legal school-leaving age. The West End principals estimated that about half of the students—from all ethnic groups and class levels in the area—completed senior high school. During the 1950's, 3 to 5 per cent of the junior high-school graduates had been sent to Boston Latin, the city's college preparatory senior high school, but only some of these eventually got to college. The junior-high-school principal's main problem was truancy, and the parental acquiescence concerning this. Boys were more likely to be truant than girls, and to be poorer students as well.

The reasons for the failure to respond to education—especially on the part of boys—can be found in the influence of the peer group society. Success in school depends to some extent on student motivation, and this is largely absent. In part, this lack can be traced to the parental ambivalence about the usefulness of education, and to the absence of books and other intellectual stimuli in the home. Class differences between student and teacher are also crucial. But other factors come into play even before the child is old enough to develop motivation for school learning. For one thing, educational achievement depends largely on the ability to absorb and manipulate concepts, to handle the reasoning processes embedded in the lesson and the text, and to concentrate on these methods to the exclusion of other concerns. West End children are adept at none of them.

The peer group society trains its members to be sensitive to people, rather than to ideas. Words are used, not as concepts, but to impress people, and argument proceeds by the use of anecdotes rather than by the common sense forms of logic. The rhythm of peer group life, the impulsive approach to child-rearing, the stress on the episodic—whether in the form of action or anecdote—and the competitive nature of peer group conversation—all encourage a short attention span. It is this very shortness of attention and the inability to concentrate that seem to accompany, if not cause, many of the learning difficulties. Certainly it is not a lack of native or acquired intelligence. For even in their early years, West End children—like children everywhere—are sensitive to the ins and outs of interaction with parents, and they quickly learn how to use words and acts to bend people to their wishes.

The school also conflicts with the many and opposing attractions of the children's peer groups. In fact, it tries to break up these groups, although not always consciously, and expects the children to act as independent individuals. But as many are either unable or unwilling to act in this way, they respond with passivity. The moment they leave the school building and the teacher's control, they coalesce quickly into peer groups to spend the afternoon learning the lore of the streets.

Neither children nor teachers get much help from parents. Most of them, having left school before the tenth grade, find the material strange. Although parents tell their children to learn, and to do homework, there are still people like one West Ender who castigated his eight-year-old daughter for wanting to go to the library again after just having been there the previous day. Bright children are encouraged by their teachers, but have peer group difficulties, unless they can find like-minded colleagues. I was told that this had been much easier before the Jews moved out of the West End, since the occasional Italian who was interested in learning then could have attached himself to a Jewish group, at least through elementary school age.

For the child with learning difficulties, school is probably a real torture. By the time this child has reached adolescence, he usually has accepted his handicap with sullen passivity. But as soon as the activities of the peer group are stepped up, and require more pocket money, there is little incentive to stay in school. Thus, if the parents permit it—and even if they do not—the teenager may become a habitual truant until he reaches the school-leaving age. His departure from school is experienced as a release from prison. Later on, when these boys become aware of the limited choice of jobs to which their decision to leave school has sentenced them, they wish they had remained to graduate. But then it is too late.[18] Actually, the drop-outs that occur at the legal school-leaving age are only a formality, the outcome of factors that have estranged such boys from school for many years prior to their physical departure.

The people who staffed the West End schools seemed to be resigned to the students' lack of interest in education. I should explain here that I spoke only to principals, but not to any teachers, and that my observations are limited by this gap in my research. Nor was I able to evaluate the quality of the teachers, although I was told by people inside and outside of the West End that most

[18] It would be highly desirable if a far-sighted government allowed these youngsters to leave school when they wanted to and provided them with scholarships and subsistence for their families so that they could return to school when they became so motivated in their mid-twenties.

of them were older women who were serving out their years in the system without much enthusiasm for or understanding of their students. Whether or not this judgment is accurate, it is true that there was little incentive for a bright young teacher to work in the West End, since it was known as a slum area by the average Bostonian.

I was able to interview two of the three public school principals in the area. One, who had been in the West End school only a few years, liked his students and accepted their lack of interest in learning with stoic resignation. He prided himself on being one of the first Irish Catholics to become a principal—the Boston public school system is still largely under Yankee Protestant control—and looked back nostalgically on the intellectual rewards of teaching in a predominantly Jewish school before becoming a principal. He also looked forward to the redevelopment of the West End, with the expectation that the new student body would be more interested in education.

The other principal, with a similar social and ethnic background, had been in the West End for many years, and had adapted himself to the values of his students. He argued that occupational success was to be ranked above learning, for, as he put it, "dollars are more important than IQ's." He also noted that some of his poorest students had gone on to well-paying jobs, or now owned profitable enterprises. Both principals, aware of the cultural differences between school and students, viewed these as problems residing in the latter, and in the economic position of the students' parents. Both were also surprised but grateful that their charges provided no serious discipline problems.

Yet the picture is not as black as I have painted it here. The third generation does stay in school much longer than the second generation, if only because students do not have to leave to support their families, and because child-labor laws, as well as changes in the labor market entrance age, have encouraged their staying in school. This is especially true of the girls, who not only remain in school longer, but seem to absorb more of its offerings. The girls find it easier to identify with the female teacher than the boys, and, as noted earlier, receive more encouragement from their mothers to stay in school. In addition, the school culture is more congruent with the routine-seeking working-class culture norms that mothers defend and pass on to their daughters, and with the functions girls perform at home. They are expected to learn to sew, cook, and help in child-care—duties that are more akin to school requirements than are the peer group activities of boys as they roam the streets. The girls may not go on to college after they graduate, but they are more likely to work in a store or office until marriage, while their brothers will probably gravitate to blue-collar jobs. The girls who do go to college often find husbands there and leave areas like the West End. Since the number of mobile girls exceeds that of boys, I suspect that some of the girls have trouble finding a husband in the Italian group and will intermarry or stay single as a result. Neither is considered desirable by the peer group society. Boys who go to college also may fail to return to the West End, but they are much less likely to shed West End associates and ways of behaving. Even if they work in the middle-class world, they often revert to the style of the peer group society when they come home at night—to the chagrin of their wives.

Early marriage may abort college even when the desire and the financial resources are present. This was illustrated dramatically by the son of a well-to-do West Ender who had made plans to attend law school at one of the better universities in the Northeast. His plans were interrupted by marriage, however, and he decided instead to go to a local night law school. The middle-class practice of being supported by his family or his wife while in school was out of the question. After marriage, he went to work as a law clerk and his wife stayed home; occupational aspirations were quickly relegated to a lower priority, and seemingly without regrets.

Medical Care and Health

Medical care is another necessary function for which the West Ender must go into the outside world, at least in cases of serious illness. Minor ailments are treated by patent medicines and home remedies. These represent a modern folk medicine that has largely replaced the Italian equivalent brought over by the immigrants.[19]

The care of more serious illness has been classified as part of the outside world for two reasons. First, since there are no doctors in the peer group society, West Enders must use outsiders. Second, their conceptions of illness and care differ from those of the doctors. Consequently, the West Enders have not embraced the latter's medical care wholeheartedly. Rather, they have resigned themselves to it because they have none of their own. They accept it with some hesitation and suspicion, and this in turn affects their attitude toward doctors, as well as the nature and efficiency of the care process.

Medical care in the West End was provided by two sets of outsiders, the local practitioners and the Massachusetts General Hospital. While the hospital was held in affectionate regard by many West Enders, it was nevertheless viewed as part of the outside world, mainly because of its affiliation with Harvard University, and the absence of Italian doctors on the staff. West Enders used the hospital freely, especially its out-patient clinics, but they perceived the hospital as an organization of extremely high status, endowed with economic and political influence of gargantuan proportions. Its high status image stemmed from its association with Harvard, which is regarded as a university for the upper class. Since few West Enders have attended Harvard, or know anyone who has, they consider it as totally inaccessible, and regard it with a mixture of respect and suspicion. The hospital's power was ascribed to the presence of many of Boston's social and power elite on the board of trustees and administrative staff, and to its success in obtaining West End land and other privileges from the city. For example, West Enders noted wryly that whereas they were ticketed frequently for parking violations, hospital staff members had only to go down to the police station to register their license

---

[19] I did not collect any data on the number of Italian home remedies still being used by the West Enders, or on the proportion of illnesses which are treated without the aid of a doctor.

plate numbers in order to avoid this. The hospital also was thought to have had considerable influence in the decision to redevelop the West End, and some people were sure that the area was really being cleared for hospital expansion and parking lots. Although their view of the hospital's status and influence was somewhat exaggerated, it was essentially accurate.

Most of the time, West Enders turned to the local practitioners for their medical care. These were older men, most of them Jewish —and none Italian—who had been born in the West End or had come to it when it was predominantly Jewish. Although they had taken part in the Jewish residential exodus, they had also kept their practices in the area. One of the few who had not moved his home lived in a huge townhouse on the best street in the West End and was probably the area's last owner-occupant of a free-standing house.

The local doctors continued to practice in the West End because they had become accustomed to their patients and were not highly motivated—or skilled enough in the latest techniques—to set up a new practice amidst younger and mobile people. They provided medical care in a fairly authoritarian manner, treating their patients almost as children who could not be expected to understand their own illness or the treatment for it. This approach is in sharp contrast to a middle-class practice, where the patient is treated as a more active participant in the care process, is informed about the diagnosis and the methods of care, and may even be told when the doctor is uncertain as to either the diagnosis or the efficacy of the treatment.

The West End doctor derived much economic and emotional security from his authoritarian role, but it was not entirely a matter of his own choosing. The West Enders came to the office with their own beliefs about illness and medical care and with a considerable lack of confidence in the medical profession. Their suspicions in turn led the doctor to command in an omniscient and dogmatic style, hoping thereby to persuade his patients to follow his recommendations for treatment.

The West Enders view illness as resulting either from a breakdown in self-control, or from conditions beyond the individual's control. The first type is thought to require self- or group-inflicted punishment as part of the treatment. In the second type of illness, the doctor's services may be used, but the possibility of a cure rests to a considerable extent on the workings of fate.

Psychosomatic and mental illness are attributed to lack of self-control. Ailments such as ulcers and high blood pressure, which seem to occur frequently, are ascribed to "hot-bloodedness." Hot blood is conceived as a physiological characteristic of Italians, which is not easily amenable to self-control. Heart attacks, however, are thought to be the result of overwork that is brought on by the inability to control ambition. Mental illness, whether expressed by deviant behavior or depression, is thought to stem from the individual's unwillingness to control his impulses, and is described in moral, rather than pathological, language.

As the lack of self-control is considered a personal failing, treatment thus must be punishing as well as therapeutic. For example, an ulcer patient with whom I talked refused to follow the diet prescribed by his doctor. He felt it would do no good, and that a more painful treatment—he did not specify what—would be needed. Although deviant behavior may be described as illness by West Enders, they reject any treatment of it that does not include strict punishment, especially if the act should be in any way antisocial. For example, depression is at first treated with sympathy, but should the individual fail to respond, he is then punished by social isolation.

Illnesses and disabilities such as respiratory diseases, cancer, arthritis, or broken bones are not thought to result from lack of self-control. Some illnesses are ascribed to the negative effects of the outside world. For example, many of the heart attacks and deaths among elderly people in the area were ascribed to the shock of redevelopment, thereby justifying West Enders to accuse the city administration of murder.

The cure of uncontrollable diseases is assigned to the removal of hostile forces in the outside world, to fate, and, last and least, to the doctor. West Enders will call the doctor, and expect him to deliver a cure, but they are skeptical that he can meet their expectations. If they do recover, the doctor's role is acknowledged grudgingly, but someone is sure to voice the suspicion that his treatment had nothing to do with it. Should the illness continue, people suspect that fate has willed it so, and that doctors are unable to provide proper treatment.

Such attitudes allow West Enders to postpone or even to avoid treatment of serious illness. Frightened of hospitals and even more so of operations, they will cite cases of people who have died on the operating table, usually because of medical incompetence. Fatalism reinforces their skepticism. One of my neighbors, for example, a factory worker, had suffered a head injury on the job. He had then gone to the hospital for an examination, was told that his injury might be serious enough to require an operation, and was given an appointment for further treatment. He failed to keep the appointment, however, and, although he suffered from recurring headaches, did not go back to the doctor. The fear of an operation and his fatalistic assumption that if his condition was serious, nothing could be done, prevailed over arguments—mine included—to get him to make another hospital visit.

Milder illnesses, especially those that are experienced by members of the peer group at the same time, such as viral infections, are not associated with fate. A doctor is called to treat influenza, for example, but once recovery is achieved, his role is minimized. People point out that he merely administers penicillin, and thus credit is given more to the magic of the wonder drug than to the doctor.

The West Ender's fatalism in the face of illness is due neither to superstition or helplessness. Indeed, the fabled belief in the evil eye that his parents brought over from Italy no longer exists. Fate is rather a reflection of a determined universe, the sacred portion of which is controlled by God, the secular portion by the powers-that-be of the outside world. It is this belief in fate that allows the West Ender to face illness and even death with resignation when there is little chance for recovery, and that softens the blow for his survivors, allowing them to continue to function. It is not an exclusively pessimistic belief, however, for the fatalistic attitude also permits the possibility of recovery, and explicitly recognizes the fact that sick people sometimes do get well without medical care. But although the West Ender is healthier than his parents or his Italian ancestors, physical or emotional breakdowns, serious injuries at work, and early deaths still do happen frequently and suddenly enough to justify the persistence of the traditional fatalism.

Thus the doctor plays a marginal role in medical care. West Enders do not like to consult him in the first place, and when they do, they have difficulty in describing their symptoms. Moreover, they may ignore his recommendations and fail to fill the prescriptions he gives them, especially when these are costly. Often he is described with considerable hostility as a man who takes poor people's money without exerting much physical effort or offering any sympathy. West Enders are not convinced that he is really working, for he does not like to make house calls, and even when he does come, he only prescribes rest, or gives shots. For this he collects fees that strike the West Ender—who has little contact with any other kind of fee-charging professional—as much too high. Actually, the fee for a house-call and a shot of penicillin was $4 in 1958. But since the doctor is extremely rich by area standards, West Enders still suspect that they are being exploited. Thus they love to tell scandalous stories about free-spending doctors, and about patients who were not helped by them, or who improved without ever calling one of them.

In many ways attitudes toward the doctor are similar to those toward the public-school teacher. The doctor is expected to be a selfless and monastically dedicated individual who should guarantee results but should not earn more money than the average West Ender. In short, he is expected to be a saint. Were he a member of the peer group society, these specifications would no doubt be reduced, but precisely because he is not, West Enders set an impossibly high moral standard by which to judge him, and thus to control his behavior. His inability to live up to sainthood creates and justifies their hostility and rejection.

The doctor-patient relationship therefore is incredibly difficult. Middle-class doctors who seek to incorporate the West Ender into the treatment process find that they cannot get a reliable account for their diagnosis, and that their recommendations are frequently ignored. For this reason, local doctors have resigned themselves to a detached role; they neither confide in the patient, nor expect him to obey their prescriptions. As class differences add to the conflict of expectations, there is little feedback between patient and doctor. This in turn only increases patient hostility and lack of confidence. Not only do few practitioners know how to overcome the obstacles to communication, but fewer still have any incentive to do so.

Suggestions for Further Reading

CONRAD M. ARENSBERG and SOLON T. KIMBALL, *Family and Community in Ireland* (Cambridge: Harvard University Press, 1940). A fascinating description and analysis of family patterns and social life among farm families in County Clare, Ireland, a quarter-century ago.

HERBERT H. HYMAN, "The Value System of Different Classes," in Reinhard Bendix and Seymour M. Lipset, eds., *Class, Status, and Power* (New York: Free Press, 1953), pp. 426–442. This important paper compares the various social classes with respect to different values. Especially important are the findings pertaining to class differences in the acceptance of success goals and in the belief in the accessibility of such goals in American society.

JANE JACOBS, *The Death and Life of Great American Cities* (New York: Vintage, 1961). While an attack on current city planning and rebuilding, it is at the same time a highly provocative analysis of city life in America.

WILLIAM F. WHYTE, JR., *Street Corner Society* (Chicago: University of Chicago Press, 1943, 2nd ed., 1955). One of the "classics" in the field of sociology. It is concerned with the Italian community in the North End of Boston, near the community of West Enders studied by Gans.

❧Blue-Collar Marriage*

MIRRA KOMAROVSKY

In 1960, according to the census of that year, middle-class families constituted about 27% of the population of the United States; working-class or "blue-collar" families—in which the breadwinners were skilled, semiskilled, or unskilled manual workers—made up approximately 54% of the population.[1] Most studies of marriage in American society have been concerned with the middle-class group, especially the college-educated segment of it. Investigations of working-class marriages have usually focused on families beset with serious problems, such as crime and delinquency. In the book Blue-Collar Marriage, *Mirra Komarovsky reports the results of her study of marriage in what might be considered "normal" working-class families. Using a "case-study" method of inquiry into 58 marriages, she sought to provide a basis for comparing working-class and middle-class marital patterns, and, ultimately, to discover those patterns that might be regarded as "universal" to family life in our society.*

Komarovsky selected her sample of blue-collar families from a community she calls "Glenton," situated about five miles from a city of some half-million persons, and about twenty miles from a large metropolis. Since Komarovsky wanted to isolate the influence upon

---

* From *Blue-Collar Marriage* by Mirra Komarovsky. Copyright © 1964 by Random House, Inc. Reprinted by permission.

[1] *Statistical Abstract of the United States,* 1963, p. 231.

222

marriage of social class, she tried to select a group comparable in race, religion, and nativity to groups studied by previous investigators, but differing in education, occupation, and income. Her sample was to be as homogeneous as possible: "All [respondents] were to be white, native born of native parents, Protestant, not over 40 years of age, and parents of at least one child. Only blue-collar workers were to be included. The highest level of education was set at four years of high school." [2]

The main source of respondents was the Glenton city directory, which gave the names, addresses, and occupations of all males heading a family, as well as the names of their wives. From the directory was drawn a list of all persons who appeared to qualify by virtue of occupation and of residence in a working-class neighborhood; Polish, Jewish, Irish, and Italian names were eliminated on the ground that they probably stood for non-Protestants. An interview with each family led to further elimination of subjects falling outside the age, ethnic, and other requirements of the desired sample. This procedure yielded 41 cases; an additional 17 were then obtained from the membership lists of five Protestant churches in the community. The final selection of 58 families corresponded closely to the initial specifications for the make-up of the sample.

The purpose of using the case-study method was to make the investigation as intensive and exhaustive as could be managed. Surveys using a fixed apparatus of identical questionnaires or identically patterned interviews for recording subjects' verbal responses are suitable for obtaining a necessarily limited amount of information from very large numbers of persons. But the case study is a method for collecting information in depth. Whatever the subject—person, group, community, situation, incident—the case-study worker, through both preplanned and impromptu techniques of inquiry and observation, tries to find out everything he can that will shed light on the question under study. The procedure of

[2] Komarovsky, p. 9.

Komarovsky and her associates was to conduct lengthy interviews with both husband and wife in each of the families selected. The interviews took place in the homes of the subjects, and the minimum time given to interviewing each family was six hours. Many significant aspects of marital attitude and behavior were explored in the time available, from relations between the marriage partners to the ways the couple related to friends and relatives outside the marriage.

The selection from Blue-Collar Marriage reprinted here deals with what Komarovsky found working-class husbands and wives expect from marriage. From each marriage partner were elicited reactions to two stories—one about a woman complaining that her husband refuses to talk to her when he comes home from work, the other about a man complaining that his wife "gabs" too much with her mother. In her analysis of their responses, Komarovsky is interested in determining the attitudes of working-class couples to friendship and companionship in marriage; using her knowledge of the respondents' educational, religious, and family backgrounds, she also tries to relate their responses to the middle-class "norm."

The major weakness of Komarovsky's work is in the selection of the study sample. Desiring a sample of families meeting several criteria, Komarovsky chose to eliminate persons with certain names, persons not living in working-class neighborhoods, and so forth. This makes it very difficult to ascertain exactly what universe her sample has been selected from. The problem is further magnified by her inclusion of persons from the membership lists of five Protestant churches. One must, therefore, be hesitant in "generalizing" from these results to blue-collar families in general.

While the study has this one important weakness, it also has several notable strengths. First, obtaining interviews from both husbands and wives is a procedure employed too infrequently in research on family life. Second, the employment of stories as semi-projective techniques allowed her to obtain more intimate information about working-class marriages than she could have gathered using only focused interview methods. Komarovsky's use *of these projective techniques—which allow the investigator to study people's motives, values, attitudes, and emotions by somehow getting them to "project" these internal states onto external objects (such as the individuals in the two stories)—adds considerable strength to her study. The richly detailed portrait of blue-collar marriage that Komarovsky's data enabled her to draw well illustrates the usefulness of the case-study technique in sociological research.*

The Marriage Dialogue: Expectations

"Among the many curious features of modern woman's life," states a recent book on women, "is one that would have thoroughly offended St. Paul, bewildered Tristan, and amused Don Juan—namely, the fact that she is her husband's best friend and he is hers." [1] To the traditional functions of marriage, such as sexual, reproductive, child-rearing and economic, modern society has added that of companionship. We expect that a married person will be his mate's closest confidant, with whom he will share his deepest feelings and thoughts. The romantic ideal calls for completeness of communication—no secrets from the mate. It implies also that the secrets of marriage must not be disclosed to outsiders.

These values of primacy and privacy of marital communications are illustrated in the words of a college senior, recently engaged. The young woman made a deliberate effort, after her engagement, to become more reserved with her mother. "I wanted," she explained, "to feel closer to John than to Mother, so that when we are all together I would exchange a look of understanding with him and not with her." The same values are reflected in a remark of a college-educated mother of a recently married daughter. "I wouldn't tell my daughter anything that had to be kept secret from her husband. It is important for a young couple to feel close and united."

[1] Morton M. Hunt, *Her Infinite Variety*, New York: Harper and Row, 1962, p. 199.

These values are often said to be characteristic of our society as a whole.[2] But such a generalization is based upon studies of middle-class couples. Much less is known of the working classes. The ideal of friendship in marriage presupposes a certain equality between the sexes, and is not likely to flourish in a strongly authoritarian family or in a culture that holds women in contempt. Neither will it emerge if the mode of life makes for sharp differences in the interests of men and women. There are other conditions that further and hinder it and we cannot therefore assume that the ideal itself, or its realization in life, is equally characteristic of all segments of our society. Several investigations of the English working classes report considerable psychological distance between husbands and wives. When one married woman in a London study used the word "we," she meant "my mother and I," not "my husband and I."[3]

[The following pages] will describe what 58 workingmen and their wives ideally expect, and subsequently, what they actually experience in the sphere of communication in marriage. We will study the sharing of deep emotional concerns with the mate, conversation about matters of mutual interest (which might be termed companionable talk), and finally the mate's role in providing emotional support. Although its primary purpose is to describe certain values held by the families, the discussion has a bearing upon the general problem of the acquisition of values. The "anticipatory socialization" of the upwardly mobile, the catalytic role played by personal misfortune, the socializing role of the mate and the influence of social institutions are some processes to be considered in the following pages.

It became apparent early in the interviewing that a sharp difference in ideals of marriage existed in this group of working-

[2] See, for example, Ernest W. Burgess and Harvey J. Locke, *The Family: From Institution to Companionship,* New York: American Book Co., 1953, p. 386.
[3] Michael Young and Peter Willmott, *Family and Kinship in East London,* Glencoe, Ill.: Free Press, 1957, p. 47.

class families. Some couples voiced what has come to be recognized as the dominant modern ideal of friendship. Thus a 27-year-old high school graduate, a truck driver, when asked whether women in his opinion had more need of heart-to-heart talk than men, said, "They both need each other. That's one of the purposes of marriage." To the question, "What helps you to overcome bad moods?" his answer was, "To talk about it with my wife." They made it a point, he said, when they were first married that if something was wrong, they would speak out. If her behavior puzzles him, "I make her clarify it . . . what goes on between my wife and I stays with us. I never talk to anyone about it. I am supposed to be adult; that is part of adult life." Again, a 33-year-old bottler in a beer company (with ten years of schooling) testified: "I can't think of anything my wife and I wouldn't tell each other that we'd tell someone else. I suppose there are some things one doesn't want to be thinking even, and so a husband wouldn't want to talk about it. But anything a husband can talk about, he can talk about to his wife, *at least I think he should* [italics ours]. If I don't get the drift of what she is saying, I'll ask her again, and perhaps over again, until I do understand." And a 27-year-old high school graduate, the wife of a machinist, commented: "If a wife can't talk to her husband [about very personal things], she can't talk to anyone."

Not only are such views not expressed in other interviews, but indeed different attitudes are explicitly stated. For example, asked whether she thought it was in general difficult for a husband to understand his wife, a 28-year-old woman with eight years of schooling, said, "Well, men and women are different. They each go their separate ways. A man does his work and a woman does her work and how can they know what it's all about?" When, after a long series of questions on communication, the interviewer remarked that the wife appeared to talk more easily to her girl friend and to her sister than to her husband, she exclaimed, "But they are girls!" A 21-year-old wife (with ten years of schooling) remarked, "Men are different, they don't feel the same as us. That's the reason men are friends with men, and women have women friends."

We attempted to tap conceptions of marriage by asking for comments on two stories. The first story deals with "companionship talk":

A couple has been married for seven years. The wife says that her husband is a good provider and a good man, but still she complains to her mother about her marriage. She says he comes home, reads the paper, watches T.V., but doesn't talk to her. He says he "doesn't like to gab just for the sake of talking." But she says he is not companionable and has nothing to say to her.—*What do you think of this couple?*

In commenting upon the story, some interviewees referred to their own marriages, identifying with the fictitious couple: "Say, you know, I feel like that guy"; "That's home plate, that's right on the button"; "Why, that's a typical marriage. My husband is a lot like that, so is my cousin's husband and my sister's husband." One man asserted: "If my wife acted like that, I would straighten her out in short order."

Apart from such incidental references to personal experiences, three themes are expressed in the responses to this story. The first theme reflects the view that *the lack of husband-wife conversation in the story presents a genuine problem.* Of the 99 men and women who commented upon this story only 37 per cent took this position. Not all of these blamed the husband—"Does *she* have anything interesting to say?" Some expressed resignation, while others proposed remedies. But whether pessimistic or "constructive" about the situation, these individuals share the view that it is deplorable:

A 27-year-old wife: "Maybe he is in a rut and needs her help. This girl would think up things to talk about if she had any sense."

A 40-year-old husband: "Looks like they are incompatible. If he never talks to her, they've got it bad, but if he's just that way once in a while, we all are that way sometimes."

A 31-year-old wife: "She should make it interesting enough around the house to get him away from the T.V. and the newspaper; invite people over or find some things like church work or hobbies that they can work at together."

A 31-year-old husband: "Maybe she should talk to him about subjects he knows about or things they have in common."

A 25-year-old husband: "He should listen to her and talk to her. He can't expect her to sit in the house all day and do her job and not have anyone to talk to at night."

A 31-year-old wife: "There is something wrong if he has nothing to talk about. If something is bothering him, he shouldn't hide behind a paper."

A 25-year-old wife: "If that's the way he is, you've got to live with it."

A 29-year-old wife: "That's something like him and me. There is nothing you can do about it except grin and bear it."

A 29-year-old wife: "He gets mad at me sometimes for wanting to talk. I learned to keep my mouth shut—you do that as you get older."

In contrast with these attitudes, another 37 per cent of the group *categorically denied that the wife in the story presents a legitimate grievance.* It is the wife who is criticized for her immaturity and selfishness—by women as well as their husbands, as illustrated below:

A 28-year-old wife: "Gee, can you tie that? He's generous, don't bother her, he just keeps out of the way, and she's fussing and wants him to sit there and entertain her."

A 40-year-old wife: "She isn't busy enough or she'd be glad to have him quiet. She is in clover and don't know it."

A 32-year-old wife: "That woman would have a lot more to complain about if her husband drank or beat her up. The husband is right."

A 38-year-old construction worker: "If you do right by the woman and your job, they owe you a little rest to yourself."

A 28-year-old butcher's assistant: "I don't know what is the matter with some women. Their husbands will come home and wish they could lie down and just forget everything and a woman will come yakity yak about nothing at all until a guy has to go out and get a drink. I don't know what they think their husbands are made of. They work their guts out making a living, trying to get along, and then they come home and their wives want them to be some kind of fancy pants, say silly things to them."

A 33-year-old metalworker: "Some women ain't satisfied no matter what you do. Ah, she makes me sick. A guy comes home, and wants a little bit of quiet and it's bad enough with the kids making a racket; his wife doesn't have to come and gab at him, too. How about her being companionable and not saying nothing? You should dance like a monkey on a string to keep them amused."

A 38-year-old pipefitter: "Oh, for Christ's sake! He ought to shut her up good and hard. Companionable! Let her work in a factory eight hours and be companionable."

A 25-year-old street cleaner: "That one needs the biggest spanking. Still complaining! What's he going to talk to her about, the price of beans?"

A 33-year-old truck driver: "That woman isn't grown up. Does she have to be entertained like a kid?"

A 20-year-old taxi driver: "Ah, that's a terrible thing. I know a whole lot of husbands who would just like to have a little peace and quiet when they get home, and their wives yammer and yammer."

The apparent assumption underlying these irritated outbursts is that the husband himself has little to gain from such evening talks. To talk is either to entertain the wife or to hear her "yammering." It is a concession to her—and one that no mature woman should demand.

Besides the two main types of responses, 11 per cent of the interviewees read into the story a particular situation that . . . is a source of great concern to women: "Maybe the husband's got something on his mind. She should leave him alone." When men appear worried, "poking at them only makes it worse. You let them alone and with time they'll come around."

The second story was intended to tap attitudes towards the primacy and privacy of marital communication:

Mrs. Fox is 26 years old. The Foxes live near Mrs. Fox's mother, and the wife sees her mother daily. Mr. Fox says he has nothing against his mother-in-law, but he doesn't see why his wife has to see her daily. He thinks they gab too much and he doesn't see why his mother-in-law should know what they have for dinner every day and everything else that happens to them. Mrs. Fox says it is natural for a woman to be close to her mother—that the husband is unreasonable.

The responses to this story fall into two types. About a third of the group disapproved of Mrs. Fox's daily talks with her mother on the ground that she *violates the privacy of marriage.*

Husband: "It is not natural to discuss intimate things with the mother. What goes on between husband and wife is nobody's business."
Wife: "You have to draw a line at what you are going to gab about to your mother. You're not going to tell her everything that happens in your married life."
Husband: "What a couple does is its own business."

In contrast to the above response, 63 per cent of the interviewees did not criticize the wife who talked a lot to her mother —at any rate, not for violating conjugal privacy. Unqualified approval is seen in such comments as these:

Husband: "Wife is right. She can always learn something about cooking and other things from an older person."
Husband: "Why shouldn't women talk to their mothers—it would probably do the women good."
Wife: "It's no skin off his nose, but kind of nice all around if they are friendly."

The qualifications cited by these respondents pertain not to violation of privacy, but, often, to interference with the wife's household responsibilities: "As long as she doesn't neglect her house or the kids, why not?" And husbands enter another qualification— that the mother-in-law not use the information to "tear the husband down" or to make trouble: "If mother-in-law doesn't bother husband, I see no reason why they shouldn't talk all they want to"; "Don't know why he raises Cain about a little thing like that unless his mother-in-law makes him trouble." Several husbands— far from expressing jealousy of the mother-in-law and a wish to share in confidences—want to be protected from them. Thus:

Husband: "As long as he don't have to listen to them, and she don't gossip, I don't see what difference it makes."
Husband: "As long as the man isn't around and doesn't hear them. Maybe the husband is mad at his wife for gossiping and telling him what she and her mother have talked about."

Attitudes of the Two Educational Groups

Responses to the two stories varied with the educational level of the respondents. The high school graduates tended to deplore the lack of conversation described in the first story—this might be termed the "companionable" or "middle-class" response.[4] Those with less than high school education were apt to feel that the wife has no legitimate grievance. Of 34 male and female high school graduates, 59 per cent believed that the lack of conversation is a genuine problem while only 26 per cent of the 65 less-educated respondents expressed a similar attitude. The level of education affects both men's and women's responses similarly.

The high school graduates criticized Mrs. Fox because she violates the privacy of marriage—the "middle-class" view. Fifty per cent of the 38 educated men and women voiced this criticism, as compared to only 16 per cent of the 67 less-educated persons. Again, the difference by education holds for both men and women.

Considering the fact that in the first story the plaintiff is the wife and in the second, the husband, the sexes are remarkably impartial in their judgments. Educational level clearly is more important than sex in influencing responses to these stories. The less-educated wives, however, differ from both their husbands and the high school men and women in one respect. They often remark: "She should leave him alone when he's like that." They obviously sympathize with the lonely wife in the first story and do not criticize her so often as their husbands do, but neither do they invoke the ideal of companionship in her defense. It is the

[4] We have no middle-class respondents. We assume on the basis of previous studies and common knowledge that responses to the stories expressing the values of companionship and of primacy of marital communication tend to be typical of middle-class persons. For example, Ernest W. Burgess and Harvey J. Locke claim that "when couples are asked what they have gained from marriage, one of the most frequent answers is companionship, intimate association, sympathetic understanding. . . ." The studies cited in their book involve predominantly middle-class respondents (*op. cit.,* p. 386). In any event, the comparison between the educational subgroups is not affected by the accuracy of this identification of the value of companionship with middle-class patterns.

educated men and women who condemn the withdrawal of the husband as a violation of an ideal.

But do the different responses to the two stories really indicate differences in ideas of marriage? The positive expression of a value is more conclusive than its absence. The expression means at the very least that the respondent knows this value and perceives its relevance to the situation. On the other hand, a person may fail to mention a value for a variety of reasons, not merely because he does not recognize it. For example, the wife who is herself a dependent daughter would have a strong motive for exonerating Mrs. Fox, whether or not she is aware of the norm of conjugal privacy. A husband who is especially fond of his mother-in-law can afford to be benevolent. And an unhappily married woman may consistently side with the wife and against the husband.

The responses to the Fox story were considered in relation to the personal situation of each respondent. Personal experiences do tend to color the responses but do not eliminate the differences between the two educational groups. Even in identical personal circumstances, the high school graduates voice middle-class values with greater frequency than the less-educated. For example, the male high school graduates tend to criticize Mrs. Fox even if they are happily married—of 8 happy husbands, 5 objected to Mrs. Fox's violation of marital privacy, but of 16 happy less-educated husbands, only 1 raised this issue. Moreover, the high school husbands prove more critical of Mrs. Fox although at the same time they report *fewer* mother-in-law problems than the less-educated men. The high school graduates, we conclude, disapprove of Mrs. Fox on normative grounds.

Linking the response to the story with the personal situation throws some light upon the acquisition of values. The "middle-class" response on the part of the less-educated husband tends to be associated with mother-in-law problems. The majority of them, as pointed out above, if they disapprove of Mrs. Fox at all, object to neglect of housework or possible interference on the part of the mother-in-law; but 7 less-educated husbands do invoke the norm of conjugal privacy. Of these 7 men, 5 have mother-in-law problems because of the excessive dependency of their wives upon the mothers. But of 28 less-educated men who gave the typical "working-class" responses, only 4 suffer from such mother-in-law problems. This may mean that personal difficulties sharpen the perception of congenial and supportive values present in the general culture although deviant for this educational level.

The different responses to the stories on the part of the two educational groups are not caused by their differences in age or in duration of marriage. Age for age and with the duration of marriage kept constant, the high school graduates still express the more "middle-class" attitudes. For example, only 7 of 13 less-educated men (married under seven years) reported that the lack of evening talk in the first story constitutes a genuine problem. The comparable figure for the high school graduates is 7 of 9. Of 9 less-educated women (married under seven years), only 6 said that the first story presents a real problem, but 9 out of 10 high school graduates (married under seven years) took this view.

In addition to the stories, another attempt was made to assess the importance attached to friendship in marriage. We asked 85 men and women to list the qualities of a good husband and a good wife.

The 563 qualities volunteered by our respondents are classified into three categories. Qualities pertaining to the major institutional roles of provider, homemaker, parent and in-law make up the first class. General human qualities, such as "kind," "doesn't nag," "loyal" or "honest," are in the second class. The third category is divided into sexual responsiveness or attractiveness and what is here termed "psychic compatibility," our principal interest in this chapter. "Psychic compatibility" implies some recognition of the uniqueness of each marriage and a concern with the interplay of personalities in it. Included in this subdivision are "companionship," "common interests," "emotional support," "love" and other expressions, however formulated, which seem to imply psychic compatibility—for example, "Gives husband peace of mind at home"; Is nice to wife"; "Likes the same T.V. programs"; "Partnership"; "Tries to fit in with husband and his wants." But even with such generous inclusion of items, psychic compatibility does not appear to loom large in the responses given by these couples. Of 563 qualities listed by men and women, only 95, or 17 per cent, are interpreted as belonging in the category of psychic compatibility; the proper performance of institutional roles ranks first and general human qualities, second.

The level of education affects the responses. Of the 361 qualities of a good mate listed by the less-educated, only 15 per cent refer to psychic congeniality, against 20 per cent of such traits of a total of 202 qualities volunteered by high school graduates. The low priority given by these working-class men and women to psychic congeniality (in contrast with general human virtues or effective performance of institutional roles) may not accurately portray their attitudes. The qualities mentioned or omitted in answer to such open questions partly depend upon the respondent's frame of reference at the moment. These questions came at the very end of the interview. On the one hand, the emphasis on communication with the mate should have brought this matter to the forefront of awareness; on the other hand, the section of the interview immediately preceding the questions about what is important in a good husband or a wife dealt with role performance. This may have slanted the answers towards the institutional roles of provider and homemaker. The fact nevertheless remains that in similar circumstances the high school graduates do place a somewhat greater accent upon compatibility.

"Middle-class" responses to the stories, in the case of the men, are associated with mobility aspirations and with marriages to high school graduates. All 5 of the less-educated husbands who are upwardly mobile and married to high school graduates gave middle-class answers to the stories, whereas of 31 less-educated men who lack one or both of these features, only 4 expressed such views. The reaching out for middle-class standards ("anticipatory socialization") on the part of the upwardly mobile husbands is manifested in a number of ways. One man confessed that he consented to the interview in order to hear the interviewer talk—he thought he might learn something from listening to her. Another man wanted to improve his English in order to associate with "people who have class." This orientation of the upwardly mobile men towards middle-class standards helps to explain their middle-class conceptions of marriage. The influence of the educated wives is apparent in two or three cases. Dissatisfied with the lack of companionship, one young high school wife repeatedly told her less-educated husband that that was "not the kind of marriage" she wanted; she felt she had finally succeeded in changing his behavior.

Church membership is also associated with "middle-class" responses. Church members tend to criticize the husband in the first story and the wife in the second. Not a single male grammar-school graduate unaffiliated with a church gave a middle-class answer to the first story, whereas one-third of the male church members with grammar-school education endorsed the value of companionship. Among high school graduates, both male and female, the church members expressed a higher proportion of middle-class views than the non-members. Among the less-educated women, however, the church members offered fewer middle-class answers than the unaffiliated—a finding seemingly inconsistent with the other replies and one which we will shortly consider.

Is the church a purveyor of middle-class values or do the more middle-class attitudes expressed by church members reflect some selective forces? The evidence mainly points to the latter explanation. Within our sample, the churches attracted the younger, better-educated and more upwardly mobile men, who regard church membership as an attribute of a "respectable" citizen. But the middle-class views of the male church members cannot be attributed wholly to this kind of selection. The church members tend to give a slightly higher proportion of middle-class responses even when we narrow the comparison to men of identical schooling, age and aspirations. Case records show that joining a church can increase the area of common interests and, perhaps, reinforce middle-class conceptions of marriage. For example, a young high school graduate, married to a man with nine years of schooling, had this to say about the first story: "Our marriage used to be that way. But we've been so close since we started church." The husband listed his attendance at church affairs as an activity he enjoys "very much." Since joining the church this couple have enjoyed reading and discussing devotional books in the evenings. The husband said: "That man is wrong. He should mix, and talk to his wife about her day and how the family is." Although this still is an unhappy marriage, the wife attributed to the church their newly found evening companionship. The minister had been consulted about their marital problems. The church has certainly given the couple a common interest, but whether it has also communicated new values to the husband remains uncertain though probable. Another couple also joined the church in a deliberate effort to improve their marriage. Such a move in itself reflects the middle-class view that marriage problems are soluble through increasing common interests and, in general, through some purposive action. Again, this fact does not rule out the possibility that once the husband becomes active in church his endorsement of middle-class values becomes more explicit.

The inconsistent finding noted above is that, among less-educated women, church members gave *fewer* middle-class responses than the unaffiliated. Why should church membership play a different role for men and women? In the first place, the selective forces differ: the older and the less-educated women are over-represented among church members. Among the less-educated respondents, relatively more women than men are affiliated with a church. The less-educated women, understandably, may attend church services and remain steeped in working-class values—some unhappy wives draw upon religion for psychological strength. The wife's grievance presented in the first story must have appeared trivial to one of these women, a mother of ten, with an alcoholic husband, who remarked (as cited earlier): "She isn't busy enough or she would be glad to have him quiet." In contrast with such church women who maintain their traditional values, upwardly mobile men and women may find in the "couples' club," and in their contacts with the minister, some reinforcement of middle-class conceptions of marriage. This illustrates again that individual responses to external influences are selective and depend upon pre-existing dispositions.[5]

The interview did not explore the influence of formal education per se or of family background upon responses to the stories. . . . The parents of the high school graduates had higher occupational status than those of the less-educated. The case studies provide many illustrations of other differences in parental attitudes linked with occupational and economic superiority. The current attitudes of the two educational groups in part reflect, no doubt, different family backgrounds.

A final question about the comments upon the two stories is: Have the stories actually elicited different norms of marriage or merely different attitudes toward verbal communication? When the high school graduate endorses the full sharing of concerns with one's mate, it is likely that he expresses a belief in the therapeutic value of "talk," not merely conviction about the importance of friendship in marriage. For the less-educated person, verbal communication may not constitute so significant a feature of any social relationship. The middle-class interviewer runs the danger of identifying friendship with some of its particular manifestations typical of his own social background. For the less complex personality, friendship is construed as being companionable, that is, having an evening snack together, going for a ride, exchanging gifts or giving each other sexual satisfaction.

[5] Rebellion against parents appears to explain the middle-class responses of two unaffiliated women. One grade school graduate, an impassioned union member, rejected the church as well as the traditional working-class values of her parents. "We ain't so hipped on church," she said. The couple never attends church. Another, rebelling strongly and resentfully against her religious mother, may have been thus led to acquire deviant values.

Different attitudes towards verbal communication are certainly an element in our findings. But more generally, the responses to the stories and fuller analysis of the cases strongly suggest that for some of Glenton's families—albeit a minority—marriage is "not for friendship." It is not merely the meagerness of verbal communication that characterizes these marriages, but the absence of certain norms, especially the norm that the spouse should be one's closest confidant. In interpreting specific cases, such norms were judged very weak or non-existent, not only because they were not voiced, but because emotionally significant experiences were regularly shared with others in preference to one's mate without any perceptible feeling that this reflected upon the quality of the marriage. Moreover, some persons acknowledged their ignorance of the thoughts and feelings of the mate without the apology or defensiveness usually accompanying violations of norms.

The following case will illustrate such a marriage. We have selected a "happy" couple whose meager verbal communication clearly does not result from marital conflict. The detailed summary is intended to illustrate concretely the interpretation offered above and to portray a style of marriage that excludes norms sometimes taken to be more or less universal in American family life.

Marriage Is Not for Friendship: The Case of Mr. and Mrs. Green

Mr. and Mrs. G. are a young couple, married for three years, with a 2-year-old son. The 23-year-old husband is a garbage collector, earning $2500 a year. He completed two years of high school; his 22-year-old wife is a high school graduate. But the interviewer commented: "It is hard to believe in view of her poor vocabulary and illiterate handwriting that she had completed high school." The husband said: "She was sort of a dumb-bell at school, but people liked her and she got through."

Mr. G. is a slim tall man, slow-moving and soft-spoken. Asked what makes him satisfied with himself, he replied, "People tell me

I'm easygoing but not a chump." The interviewer noted his deceptively lazy attitude as the manner of a man who thinks that most people, particularly women, become too excited about things and foolishly so. He "quit school at fourteen because I didn't like it." He has held a number of unskilled jobs, and concerning his present occupation as a garbage collector he stated: "People laugh at you for being in this line of work. I don't know what's so funny about it. It's got to be done. There is no future in it, though, and the pay is terrible. I'm going to make a break for it as soon as I can. Everybody's looking out for me now, and something is bound to turn up pretty soon."

Mr. G. appears to be quietly dominant in the marriage and both he and his wife express satisfaction with their sexual relations and with the marriage in general. A good deal of the communication between them is non-verbal. This had been anticipated during their courtship. When asked whether her husband when he proposed to her had said he loved her, Mrs. G. answered:

"He just got softer and softer on me and I could tell that he did and we got to necking more and more and he wanted to go all the way and I didn't want to unless we were going to get married. So finally we got engaged, so everybody knew about it, so we were going steady together." Prior to their marriage he had said a few times "when we were being mushy" that he loved her. "But we usually just started doing it without saying much." And now "when he'll come up and kiss me in the middle of a T.V. show or after he's going to the icebox for something, I know that he is going to want it later on." Has he ever said out and out that he could go for her or wanted her or anything like that? She said, "No, we don't go in for that kind of stuff." Did he say anything when she told him that she got pregnant? "He looked a little funny when I told him, but he didn't say much. You know that's what's going to happen. After a while, when I began to show a lot, he asked me sometimes how I felt."

Mrs. G. was asked to describe their quarrels. They quarrel little, but when they do, over such things as his failure to help move the furniture or her failure to do something he demands, she said, "We just get over it." He might "crab around and then he would know that he had been mean and make it up" to her. There is no conversation after such quarrels, but Mr. G. helps to dry the dishes or asks her if she likes a T.V. program or wants something else. Mrs. G. felt that it doesn't do any good to talk, it might make things worse.

When asked whether they like to talk about what makes people tick or to discuss the rights and wrongs of things, each said in separate interviews, "No, we don't hash things over." Mr. G.: "It's either right or wrong—what is there to discuss?" Mrs. G. said that they do not talk much about the future of their son: "No matter what plans we make, the times change and the children will have ideas of their own."

This "conversation of gestures" between Mrs. G. and her husband contrasts sharply with the full and open verbal communication characterizing her relationships with female relatives and friends. On many counts Mrs. G. reveals her emotional life more fully to the latter than to her husband. And this extends to spheres of experience beyond the "feminine world" of babies, housework or talk about people:

Mrs. G. sees her sister and her mother daily. "Oh yes," she said about her sister. "We tell each other everything, anything we have on our minds. We don't hold nothing back." But when asked whether she can talk to her husband, she answered: "Sure, I can talk to him about anything that has to be said." Her view is that "men and women do different things; he don't want to be bothered with my job and I don't want to be bothered with his. Sometimes we got to do the same things, something around the house and we have to tell each other."

When asked what helped her when she was "in the dumps," Mrs. G. replied, "Talking to my sister or my mother helps sometimes." She was then asked directly whether conversations with her husband ever have a similar effect. "No," she answered, "when I am in the dumps he can't help me feel any better."

Mrs. G.'s friends are also her neighbors whom she sees several times a day. One friend phoned her six times in one day, and that was unusual, but these women do often telephone one another. She was embarrassed to admit that she discusses her sex life with her friends. "You'd be surprised what they talk about, the things they do in bed. When somebody tells you something, you got to say something back or they think you are a wet fat dishrag and all washed out and they don't talk to you and you got no friends." Mrs. G.'s embarrassment in reference to sex appears to be caused more by the nature of the topic than by any violation of marital confidence. She is still under the domination of her religious and puritanical mother. Mrs. G. finds sexual fulfillment in marriage, but she shares her reflections about her own sexual responses and about the sexual behavior of men more fully with women than with her husband.

An incident reported by Mrs. G. illustrates her intimacy with her sister. During the first year of her marriage, Mrs. G. was troubled by her husband's habit of "walking around the house with his fly open." She remonstrated with him, but he persisted, saying that he can do what he wants in his own house. She then asked her sister's advice and was told to disregard the offensive habit. But her sister reported the conversation to their mother and Mrs. G. suspects that her mother in turn talked to Mr. G.'s mother. Mr. G. now "closes the zipper whenever a stranger comes into the room" and Mrs. G. is inclined to attribute the reform to the intervention of her mother-in-law. She added that she no longer minds this practice of his when they are alone.

Mr. G. enjoys an active social life with male friends and relatives, but it is doubtful whether he shares his emotional experiences with them to the extent that his wife does with her friends. Nevertheless, Mr. G. revealed to his father and his brother his fears that Mrs. G. was making a "sissy" out of their son, and he regularly consults them about his occupational plans. He does not discuss the latter topics with his wife because "there is no need of exciting her for nothing. Wait until it's sure. Women get all excited and talk too much."

Mr. G. "thinks the world" of the fellows in his clique whom he sees after supper several times a week and on Saturday afternoons. Mrs. G. does not always know where he meets his "friends" when he leaves in the evenings. Mr. and Mrs. G. testified independently that having a beer with the fellows is the best cure for Mr. G.'s depressions. When he cannot afford a beer, he can sometimes "sweat it out by working." Asked if his wife could help him when he felt in "the dumps," Mr. G. replied, "Yes, she can. I tell her, 'just keep out of my way,' and she does." Mr. G. appeared to know less about his wife's sources of emotional relief than she knew of his. Asked what helped his wife when she felt low, Mr. G. remarked "Oh, it wears off after a while. Sure I can tell [when she feels low] by the way her shoulders hang down and by her sour puss." He admitted that his wife sulks sometimes, and was asked whether they ever talk this over. "Nah, I don't pay no attention to it," was his reply.

Additional light is shed upon the couple's values by their responses to the projective stories and the schedules on "what makes a good mate." Both Mr. and Mrs. G. criticized the wife in the story who demanded more evening companionship with her husband. They moreover found nothing reprehensible in Mrs. Fox's daily conversations with her mother. "She don't have to aggravate her husband by gabbing about it to him, does she?" was Mrs. G.'s only comment. Presented with the case of a wife who complained about being lonely because her husband went out twice a week, Mrs. G. commented: "Why shouldn't he go out, she shouldn't nag him." And Mr. G. said: "If he can afford it, fine. She has the kids, she ain't alone."

The thesis that the lack of psychological intimacy in this marriage does not violate the ideal expectations of Mr. and Mrs. G. is supported by the satisfaction they express with their marriage.

With the exception of her lack of neatness ("But I guess I am fussier than most husbands," Mr. G. added) Mrs. G. is a good wife— "She suits me fine." Mr. G. described her qualities: she is good-natured ("I just tell her how it's going to be and she doesn't talk back. Of course, I'll ask her what she wants sometimes and we try to work it out. I'll try to satisfy her the best I can"); she never nags him about money and is economical; she doesn't "gripe" about his going out with the fellows, and she never denies him sex. He thinks, moreover, that she is very "cute." Her irritating tendency to gossip Mr. G. accepts as the natural failing of all women.

Mrs. G., on her part, is equally satisfied. She considers her husband a considerate sexual partner by comparison with the selfish men—often described by her friends—who "just take what they want and do nothing for their wives; we have a lot of fun sometimes." Her religious mother was critical of her; marriage brought emancipation from parental control. She hopes for an improvement in their financial status—to have the money for baby-sitters, a bigger television set, a better car and more housekeeping gadgets. But, rating her husband on the schedule of what makes a good mate, Mrs. G. gave him the highest of the three possible marks on the following qualities: "isn't afraid of hard work"; "is always on the lookout for an opportunity to better himself"; "is attractive to wife physically"; "is a considerate lover"; "has an attractive appearance"; "speaks his mind when something is worrying him"; "does the man's job around the house without nagging." And asked if she wished Mr. G. were more open with her, she said, "He crabs around if he wants to, and hollers if he feels like it." Sometimes, it is true, she starts talking to him when he watches T.V. and he tells her to "shut up" but "it usually isn't anything special and I can wait." Similarly, she may occasionally be too busy with the children to pay any attention to what he is saying, but that, again, is to be expected. In answering the interviewer's questions. Mrs. G. claimed that she understood her husband well and is, in turn, understood by him, and that she has "never given up talking to him about something because I felt it was no use."

Although generally happy in her marriage, Mrs. G. did reveal a few dissatisfactions with her husband: "He expects too much of our little boy, and treats him as if he was grown up." Moreover, she confessed that she would like to have her husband "around more" and sometimes when she feels warm towards him, "he brushes me off." Having previously rated these qualities "very important," Mrs. G. gave her husband only an "average" and not a high mark on the following: "is successful in his job so his wife can feel proud of him"; "doesn't chase after women" ("Hasn't yet, I don't think"); "easy to tell one's worries to"; and qualities pertaining to child rearing.

The case of Mr. and Mrs. G. illustrates a certain psychological distance in marriage tolerated because nothing more is expected. The fact that this distance was occasionally frustrating to Mrs. G. may appear to contradict our thesis. But human needs, though molded by culture, are not solely its creation. Needs may emerge in some situations regardless of social expectations. The right of the husband to go out evenings in search of male companionship may be accepted by his wife. But this acceptance does not rule out the possibility that when *she* feels warm towards *him,* he may not be around to satisfy her needs, whereas he can remain at home whenever his feelings dictate it. The significant fact is that these frustrations do not arouse any moral indignation in Mrs. G. She does not feel aggrieved.

A similar relationship is that of a couple, married eight years, who live in the same house with the wife's parents. The early years of marriage were troublesome, but now the wife claims: "We get along good." She appears to be quite satisfied with her economically successful and handsome husband. However, he is "not handy around the house" and is less interested than most Glenton husbands in the women's world of child rearing, interior decoration, housework and shopping. The wife shares such feminine interests with her mother and her girl friends. The impression of a certain distance in the marriage is conveyed by other facts:

Having checked "confiding worries" and "talking about what makes people tick" as activities she enjoys very much, she named her mother and her girl friends as preferred associates in such discussions. The standard question, "If there were two more hours every day, how would you like most to spend them?" was answered by this woman without hesitation: "Having a longer afternoon, visiting with my girl friends."

This woman, though apparently quite satisfied with her life, admitted feeling depressed periodically: "I feel out of sorts twice a year. It's kind of seasonal, spring and fall. I feel like a fat slob, the house is a mess; I feel depressed. I talk to Mother about it and she tells me she had the same thing." Has she ever talked to her husband about these moods? the interviewer asked her. She could recall no such conversation and she "couldn't really tell" whether he knew about her moods. Two incidents confirm the impression of meager communication between the spouses. The wife made arrangements for the interviewer's meeting with the husband's parents. A week later the husband was surprised to learn from the interviewer that she had met his parents; the wife never mentioned the incident to him. Moreover, during the first interview, the wife was enthusiastic about the T.V. play which she saw the preceding evening, on her husband's night out. She was subsequently asked whether she mentioned the play to him and the answer was negative.

Additional illustrations of the sharing of confidences with others than the spouse are provided by the women who, suspecting themselves to be pregnant, told their female relatives about it before informing their husbands. One woman first told her mother that she thought she was pregnant. Her mother advised her to wait a month before telling her husband, which the wife did. This procedure was repeated during her second pregnancy. Two other women reported similar incidents: "My sister told me to wait after I skipped my second period before telling him [respondent's husband]."

We estimate that, of 58 marriages, 7 are unmistakably of the type just described. A few others are similar, but do not exhibit so extreme a pattern. Of the 14 persons involved in the 7 marriages only 1 (Mrs. Green) is a high school graduate. This corroborates the evidence obtained by means of the two stories. The less-educated couples tend to be more traditional in their ideas about sex-linked interests and about "rights" of men to silence and protection from tiresome children and women's trivia. They tend to think that friendship is more likely to exist between members of the same sex, whereas they see the principal marital ties as sexual union, complementary tasks and mutual devotion.

Suggestions for Further Reading

NORMAN W. BELL and EZRA F. VOGEL, eds., *The Family* (New York: Free Press, 1960). An excellent collection of articles and essays setting forth problems of the family in terms of structure and function.

ROBERT O. BLOOD, JR., and DONALD M. WOLFE, *Husbands and Wives* (New York: Free Press, 1960). Focuses on decision-making, division of labor, children, companionship, emotional understanding, and love in the American family.

DAVID CAPLOVITZ, *The Poor Pay More: Consumer Practices of Low-Income Families* (New York: Free Press, 1963). A detailed description of the consumption practices of the poor, as well as of the functions and dysfunctions of the credit economy for these poor Americans.

LEE RAINWATER, RICHARD P. COLEMAN, and GERALD HANDEL, *Workingman's Wife* (New York: Oceana Publications, 1959). Presents the results of a national depth study of working-class housewives, with particular emphasis on their buying habits and preferences.

৯*The Authors*

ROBERT A. ALFORD is professor of sociology at the University of Wisconsin. He received his Ph.D. from the University of California (Berkeley) in 1961. From 1961 to 1963, he was Associate Director of the Survey Research Laboratory at the University of Wisconsin. His research is concerned with comparative urban politics, and he has published articles on this subject in the *Administrative Science Quarterly* and the *Municipal Year Book*.

MELVILLE DALTON received his Ph.D. from the University of Chicago in 1949, taught from 1950 to 1952 at the University of Kansas, and from 1952 to 1953 at Washington University, St. Louis. He has been at the University of California at Los Angeles since 1953 and is currently professor of sociology and research sociologist. Among his publications are articles in the *American Sociological Review, Applied Anthropology, Hospital Administration, Personnel Administration,* and *Social Forces.* He also has contributed a chapter to Arnold M. Rose (ed.), *Human Behavior and Social Processes.*

HERBERT J. GANS is senior research sociologist, Center for Urban Education, and adjunct professor of sociology and education, Teachers College, Columbia University. He received an M.A. in social science from the University of Chicago in 1950 and in 1957 earned a Ph.D. in city planning from the University of Pennsylvania. In addition to publishing in such scholarly journals as the *American Sociological Review,* the *Journal of the American Institute of Planners,* and *Social Problems,* he has written for *Commentary, Commonweal, Dissent,* and *The New Republic.*

MIRRA KOMAROVSKY, who is professor and chairman of sociology at Barnard College, Columbia University, received her Ph.D. from Columbia University in 1940. In addition to numerous articles in professional journals, she is author of *The Unemployed Man and His Family*, and *Women in the Modern World*. She also edited *Common Frontiers of the Social Sciences*. In 1965, Professor Komarovsky was Buel G. Gallagher Visiting Professor at City College of New York.

JAMES F. SHORT received his Ph.D. from the University of Chicago in 1951. Since that time, he has been at Washington State University, where he is now Director of the Sociological Research Laboratory and Dean of the Graduate School. He has published many articles on juvenile delinquency, measurement, and theory in such professional journals as the *American Journal of Sociology*, the *American Sociological Review, Crime and Delinquency, Journal of Social Issues,* and *Social Problems*. His publications also include co-authorship (with Andrew F. Henry) of *Suicide and Homicide*, several contributed chapters to books, and three encyclopedia articles.

FRED L. STRODTBECK received his Ph.D. from Harvard University in 1950, taught briefly at Yale University, 1950-53, and, since 1953, at the University of Chicago where he is Director of the Social Psychology Laboratory. In addition to being co-author of *Talent and Society* and *Variations in Value Orientations*, he has published in the *American Journal of Sociology*, the *American Sociological Review*, and *Social Problems*.

ROBIN M. WILLIAMS, JR., who received his Ph.D. from Harvard University in 1943, is professor of sociology at Cornell University. In 1943 he served as Statistician, Research Branch, Special Service Division, in the War Department; from 1943 until 1946 he was Senior Statistical Analyst in the War Department, attached to the European Theater of Operations. He has contributed numerous articles to scholarly journals, and is the author of *The Reduction of Intergroup Tensions* and *American Society*. He co-authored *The*